What Do We Need a Union For?

The Fred W. Morrison Series in Southern Studies

Timothy J. Minchin

What Do We Need a Union For?

The TWUA in the South, 1945–1955

The University of North Carolina Press

Chapel Hill and London

© 1997
The University
of North
Carolina Press
All rights reserved

Manufactured in
the United States
of America

The paper in this
book meets the
guidelines for
permanence and
durability of the
Committee on
Production
Guidelines for
Book Longevity
of the Council on
Library Resources.

Library of Congress Cataloging-in-Publication Data

Minchin, Timothy J.
    What do we need a union for? : the TWUA in the
South, 1945–1955 / by Timothy J. Minchin.
        p.   cm.—(The Fred W. Morrison series in
    Southern studies)
    Includes bibliographical references and index.
    ISBN 0-8078-2317-1 (cloth : alk. paper).—
    ISBN 0-8078-4625-2 (pbk. : alk. paper)
    1. Textile Workers Union of America—History.
2. Trade-unions—Textile workers—Southern States—
History—20th century.   3. Textile workers—
Southern States—History—20th century.
I. Title.   II. Series.
HD6515.T42T485   1997
331.88'177'00975—dc20   96-25419
                                                  CIP

01 00 99 98 97   5 4 3 2 1

contents

acknowledgments

During the research for this project, I have incurred many debts, especially to those who helped make my time in the United States productive and enjoyable. I wish to thank the staff of the personnel department of Dan River Mills in Danville, Virginia, for allowing me access to their private records and providing a place for me to look at them. My research was also made possible by the help of many archivists across the United States, particularly the staff of Perkins Library at Duke University. I am also greatly indebted to all the people who kindly agreed to oral interviews, for without oral history this book could not have been written. I especially wish to thank Mae Dawson in Tarboro, North Carolina, and Beatrice McCumbee in Rockingham, North Carolina, for their warm hospitality and help in locating other retired workers. Many others across the United States also made me feel welcome and helped me greatly in securing interviews and in many other ways. I especially wish to thank Joel Leighton, Junius Scales, and Norris Tibbetts, who provided accommodation as well as information while I was on my travels.

I wish to thank George Waldrep of Duke University for all his help in tackling this topic and for sharing long-distance research trips to Washington, D.C., and Wisconsin. John Salmond shared pizza and useful advice throughout and also kindly read an early draft; Bob Zieger also provided keen insight and support. I am particularly indebted to Jim Leloudis of the University of North Carolina in Chapel Hill who kindly agreed to supervise me while I was in North Carolina and encouraged my research. I owe other academic debts to Bob Korstad, Cliff Kuhn, John Thompson, Rick Halpern, Jim Hodges, Steve Spackman, and Howell Harris for helping me develop my project at various stages of its life. I would also like to thank Lewis Bateman of the University of North Carolina Press for his encouragement and support of my research. My supervisor, Tony Badger, has guided me throughout and has been a consistent source of encouragement and support.

The support and love of my wife, Olga, has helped me a great deal in completing this project, and it is to her that I dedicate it.

What Do We Need a Union For?

introduction

This study examines the experiences of the Textile Workers Union of America (TWUA-CIO) in the South in the decade immediately after World War II. It is concerned both with the intensive organizing efforts that the union made in the region in this period and with its activities to maintain a presence through the local unions that had already been established. The central question facing the TWUA between 1945 and 1955 was the need to organize the South. By the end of World War II, over 80 percent of the American textile industry was located in the South, but the TWUA was still weak in the region, with only 20 percent of workers under contract. By 1955, the TWUA had actually lost members in the South. The key question facing the historian, therefore, is to explain the reasons for the union's failure in these years.[1]

Although the focus of this work is on the TWUA, it is not intended to be an institutional history of the national union. While attempting to provide an overview of the union's activities in the South, this study will also give close attention to selected communities in order to provide a balanced picture that encompasses both the national and local level. It makes intensive use of oral evidence from workers and local union leaders in these communities so as to place the story in the context of worker experience and also to explore issues of race and gender.

In the last decade, southern textile workers have been the subject of a considerable body of sophisticated historical scholarship. The central question this scholarship has confronted, as historian Robert H. Zieger has written, has been "the distinctive character of the culture of the millworkers." Historians have concentrated on the effect of the company-owned mill village on worker culture. Various studies have emphasized the caution, insularity, and fear of southern textile workers, their inability to sustain organized protest because of the strict corporate control of southern textile communities. According to these studies, it was this distinctive worker culture that accounted for the failure of southern textile workers to unionize. Workers were unable to overcome what one study called an "oral tradition" of submission and defeat. This prevailing view has been challenged by a recent work emphasizing the way that workers used "a unique workers' culture" and other informal means to resist management domination.[2]

Since the focus has been on the company-owned mill village, the vast majority of this scholarship has been concerned with the period before World War II. These studies have explored in detail the origins and nature of the southern textile labor system. However, very little is known about the decline of this system in the crucial years immediately after World War II, or about the history of textile unionism in the 1940s and 1950s. In these years, indeed, houses were sold off to workers in large numbers, and workers achieved a large degree of independence from company control. At the same time, the TWUA, a strong CIO union that was only formed in 1939, made intensive efforts to organize the South. Although they were better financed and planned than previous organizing drives, these efforts were largely failures. If the company-owned mill village was responsible for preventing organization, why did these efforts also fail when the company-owned mill village had virtually disappeared?

Those accounts of southern textile workers that have looked forward to the postwar period have continued to stress the endurance of tradition in cotton-mill communities. Southern textile communities remained distinctive, isolated and unaffected by the forces transforming American society after 1945. One recent study of the 1930s, for example, has concluded that "there has been some remarkable continuity between the workers in the mills of the 1930s and those of the 1980s."[3]

In fact, the social and economic changes taking place in American society had a huge impact on southern textile communities. The war caused wages to rise for all American workers, and it was the platform for working-class affluence and consumerism in the 1940s and 1950s. Rising wages had a disproportionate impact on southern textile workers, however, because of the low standard of living prevailing before the war. In percentage and real terms, the wages of southern textile workers rose at a far higher rate than those of other industrial workers between 1941 and 1951. This rising standard of living was shared by both union and nonunion workers, moreover, as companies matched union pay and benefits in order to prevent unionization and secure labor in an era of labor shortage. It was this universal change in living standards that made it very difficult for the union to sell its message in the South, for workers perceived that their standard of living would continue to rise without their having to take the considerable risk of joining a union. This perception was the central problem facing the union in this period.

Indeed, the failure of the TWUA during the 1940s and 1950s had less to do with worker culture and employer hostility than with economic and social changes set in motion by World War II. The dramatic increase in southern textile wages altered the organizing climate in the South considerably and posed many new problems for the TWUA. It caused social and cultural change: in these years southern textile workers became home owners and, on the whole, car owners. These changes caused new problems in organizing and also made it more difficult for the union to win strikes, because workers had more to lose in a strike, especially given that many had begun to buy consumer items through installment plans. The fact that workers had disposable income transformed southern textile communities. Workers' lives changed dramatically through these economic and social changes, yet very little is known about their effect on southern textile communities.

TWUA national and southern leaders felt the 1945–55 period to be crucial, yet the key events that shaped the TWUA's fortunes in the South in these years have received little historical attention. For much of this period, the TWUA participated in Operation Dixie, a broadly conceived CIO drive to organize the South. Textiles was at the heart of this effort, as it was the largest southern industry and one that posed a particular threat to the CIO's northern base. Between 1946 and 1953, intensive efforts were made to organize textiles, and the failure in textiles was what doomed the drive to failure. To date, Operation Dixie has been the subject of only one major work, Barbara Griffith's *Crisis of American Labor: Operation Dixie and the Defeat of the CIO*. This work was intended, moreover, "to open up the topic by setting in place the broad historical framework" rather than "to 'wrap up' the many social and cultural trends that intertwine in Operation Dixie." Griffith's work does indeed open the subject up by providing an overview of the campaign in all the different industries, but as a result, it only gives limited attention to textiles. She made use of the huge archival records of the drive donated to Duke University, but before they had been fully catalogued. These records, now fully processed, offer a richly documented record of the southern drive. It is important to follow Griffith's lead and use these records in providing a fuller study of the campaign in the vital industry of textiles, and that is what Chapters 2 and 3 attempt to do.[4]

This period also witnessed a general strike in the South that historians have neglected. This 1951 strike involved over 40,000 workers in seven southern states, making it the region's second largest strike ever. The strike is crucial to the TWUA's history and to understanding the broader failure of textile unions in the South. It involved most of the local unions that the TWUA had managed to establish in the region. Its failure weakened and destroyed many of these locals, and those who were involved felt it was a turning point for the union's fortunes in the South. The 1951 strike is also important because it marked an attempt by the TWUA to raise southern union wages above the level of nonunion wages. Throughout this period, unorganized companies matched the pay and fringe benefits won by the TWUA in the organized sector. This tactic proved an effective method of preventing unionization, especially as nonunion workers were able to share in the tremendous pay increases won in the unionized mills. The union's attempts to make organized mills grant a union pay scale that would not be copied were consistently hindered by the competitive nature of the textile industry, which made companies unwilling to assume wage costs ahead of their competition. The constraints placed on textile unions by the structure of the textile industry played an important part in causing them problems in the South—a factor that has been obscured by the prevailing emphasis on worker culture.[5] Thus, the impact of higher wages resulting from the war and the structure of the industry worked together to thwart the TWUA. The union's attempt to establish a union wage scale, and the fallout from the failure of the ensuing strike, will be discussed in Chapters 5 through 7, along with a case study of the strike in its most important location, Dan River Mills in Danville, Virginia. These chapters exploit sources that have seen little use until now.

This study also examines issues of community and state hostility, race and gender, and the decline of the company-owned mill village. The union conducted a high number of strikes in the South in this period, the overwhelming majority of them unsuccessful. Given the existing historiography, these strikes clearly pose fundamental questions about militancy, worker culture, and community support. Existing explanations of the failure of unionization in textiles have stressed the hostility of the community and local state power. Southern mill owners' dominance of the community and close links to the political power structure have been contrasted to northern industrial communities, where, it has been argued, local political protection and community support helped workers to win strikes and form unions. In Chapter 4, the southern strikes are examined as a whole in the light of these issues, followed by a case study of a 1949 strike in Tarboro, North Carolina. The Tarboro strike produced good written records because of the extensive involvement of the National Labor Relations Board (NLRB). Together with interviews with participants in the strike, these records allow for a close exploration of a typical postwar southern textile strike. The Tarboro strike is also emphasized because it was felt to be a test case for southern unionism by the union, management, and the press.[6]

Issues of race and gender also shaped the TWUA's experiences in the South. The issue of civil rights was central to the experiences of the TWUA in this period. The union struggled between its ideological commitment to civil rights and the practical problems that this caused within its membership, which was overwhelmingly white. Indeed, before the 1960s the southern textile industry itself was predominantly white, with African Americans confined largely to nonproduction jobs. But although they were only a small percentage of the workforce, African Americans played an important role in the TWUA, especially through segregated local unions that existed across the South. Very little is known about these separate locals or about the way that the racial balance of the industry affected unionization. This study attempts to examine these issues.

In contrast to black workers, women were integrally involved with the events described. At this time, women represented approximately 45 percent of the workforce in the southern textile industry, and they participated in all of the strikes and organizing campaigns of these years. Women were particularly active in the TWUA, and this study examines the role of women in closer detail throughout the story.

Self-destruction plays a role in explaining the TWUA's failure in the South in these years. Historians have ignored a major internal dispute in the union—the battle between the union's two top leaders, president Emil Rieve and vice president George Baldanzi. The Rieve-Baldanzi split did tremendous damage to the union, especially in the South, and this study examines the causes of the battle and its consequences.

Because so much of the TWUA's history in this period is one of failure, it is important not to overlook the differences that unionization made in communities where the TWUA did become firmly established. Finally, in Chapter 8, a case study of Rockingham, North Carolina, primarily approached through oral histories of retired workers from Aleo Manufacturing Company, examines the social and economic changes that took place during this period. It is especially important to examine the relationship between unionization and the decline of the company-owned mill village. Extensive use of oral history in one location also allows for an insight into the impact of higher wages and the rise of consumerism at the local level, allowing us to measure the degree of social and economic change that was taking place.

chapter one

Workers, Mills, and Unions

before 1945

In 1993, eighty-six-year-old Solomon Barkin, looking back on a long career as research director of the TWUA, thought that the vital period in the union's history was the decade after World War II: "The period of 1945–55 is the most critical for it was during these years that the union's efforts were the most futile in the South and it never recovered from the stagnancy which set in during that period." Others who were active in the TWUA in these years shared the view of the sophisticated Jewish intellectual, pointing out that because the union launched major offensives in the South during these years, the defeat of these efforts were huge blows. Indeed, these years were central to the history of textile unionization in the South. The TWUA began to lose members at a time when other industrial unions were consolidating earlier gains. Its failure to organize the South compounded the problem of operating from an economically declining northern base. While the 1940s and 1950s were "years of advance" for organized labor as a whole, the TWUA anticipated the decline of the American labor movement by dropping from over 400,000 members in 1945 to 176,000 in 1957.[1]

A Small-Town Industry

Historians have recognized a number of factors as central to the failure of southern textile organizing before 1945—employer opposition, worker culture, union ineptitude, and the ineffectiveness of federal protection. What they have overlooked, however, is the role played by the structure of the textile industry, despite the fact that its competitive nature has posed continual problems for unions.

The southern textile industry developed in the years between 1880 and 1910, when the New South's cotton-mill campaign went into full swing.[2]

The expansion of the southern textile industry continued at a steady pace between 1910 and 1945, weakening the New England textile industry and establishing the South as the home of the American textile industry. The South's share of the spindles in the cotton textile industry increased from 5 percent in 1880 to 39 percent in 1910, 72 percent in 1930, and over 80 percent by 1945. Aggressive community support, favorable labor legislation, and, crucially, lower wage levels were largely responsible for the ascendancy the South achieved over New England.[3]

Technically, the textile industry was not one industry but several. Among its subdivisions were carpets and rugs; hosiery; and silk, rayon, and other synthetic fibers. The largest subdivision, however, was cotton spinning and weaving, known as primary textile manufacturing. This industry dominated the South. In 1947, the region had 801 plants engaged in cotton spinning and weaving, and these plants employed nearly 400,000 workers. Plant size, therefore, was small, with the average mill employing around 300 workers. The majority of these mills, moreover, were located in small towns in the Piedmont section of North Carolina, South Carolina, Georgia, and Alabama, with North Carolina being by far the leading textile state. This story concentrates on these states and this industry.[4]

The southern cotton textile industry comprised mills that performed one or more of the functions involved in the preparation of raw cotton for processing, the spinning of cotton fibers into yarn, and the weaving of yarn into cloth. Southern cotton textile mills were thus involved in the stages of production from the opening of raw cotton bales to the placing of cloth in the hands of a finisher. Illustrating the fragmented nature of cotton textile production, spinning and weaving represented only the first, basic part of a four-stage process. The other three stages were finishing, distribution, and cutting. Finishing occurred largely in the North, although some southern plants were beginning to finish their own cloth in the postwar period. Through the cotton exchanges of Worth Street in New York City, cotton textiles were distributed to the cutting trades, which manufactured the fabric into apparel. This process occurred in the garment districts of cities located, again, largely in the North. The apparel industry was a separate industry from cotton textiles and had its own union, the Amalgamated Clothing Workers.[5]

Spinning and weaving were the fundamental processes of cotton textile manufacturing, and all other processes, such as picking, carding, combing, slashing, and beaming—involving the straightening of fibers and the preparation of yarn—were related to these two functions. Spinning and weaving were both classified as semiskilled operations and were jobs that workers could easily be trained to do. By the postwar period the majority of southern mills both spun and wove. The significant feature of primary textile production was the fact that, unlike the manufacturing of steel, automobiles, and iron, and the refining of oil, no single manufacturing process needed to be performed on a large scale in the interests of efficiency. It was this feature that kept mills small and helped make the industry competitive.

In addition, textile executives emphasized how easy it was for new firms to enter the market, making the industry further prone to overproduction. The small unit investment needed to get into the textile industry induced a wild expansion of capacity, originating in the boom of World War I and persisting for two decades thereafter. Because of the industry's fragmented production process and its small-town location, mills produced in an isolated position from immediate markets. Inventories began to build up on wholesalers, garment makers, or converters, and before this information reached the mill owners, they had massively overproduced. Moreover, with prewar wages low, many mills kept on producing to cover overhead costs. As a result, throughout the 1920s and 1930s, selling prices were very low, which in turn meant low wages for the workers and low earnings for investors. Mills faced strong pressure to sell in order to rid themselves of inventories and prevent others from taking their trade. Whenever there was a hint of price improvement, production increased, exacerbating the tendency to build up surpluses and depress prices. Profits were minuscule or nonexistent throughout the 1920s and 1930s; the industry as a whole was experiencing substantial losses as late as 1938. Between 1923 and 1940 the cotton textile industry's cumulative net income before taxes barely balanced its total losses, while over the same period the industry sustained a net decline in assets upward of $580 million. For most mills in the 1920s and 1930s, a net of 2 percent on sales was a good year. Between 1926 and 1932, less than half of southern mills paid a regular dividend. Other studies have pointed out how the textile industry as a whole lost money between 1926 and 1939.[6]

World War II transformed the fortunes of the cotton textile industry, and as in other areas, its impact had significant consequences for the TWUA's hopes of organizing the South. During the war over 80 percent of cotton textile production in the South was for military orders. By 1945, only 2 percent of the industry's output went for civilian use. By the end of the war there was a massive pent-up civilian demand for textiles, especially as many other workers had earned higher wages during the war and wanted to spend their money on consumer goods like textiles that had been unavailable during the war. The textile industry took over three years of full production to satisfy this demand, during which its high profits caused the union to dub it "The Nation's Most Prosperous Industry." The complete turnaround that took place in the industry's fortunes was illustrated by the leading southern company Dan River Mills, which made a loss of over $1 million in 1938, and small profits of $446,727 and $390,870 in 1939 and 1940 respectively. During the war, profits averaged well over $1 million per year, and they steadily rose to an unprecedented $15.1 million in 1948. Thus, the war provided the textile industry with highly profitable operating conditions for nearly a decade. Based on full capacity of two forty-hour shifts, the industry never exceeded 90 percent production in the six years prior to 1939, and in some years production dropped to 57 percent. During the war, capacity utilization based on this same measure averaged 133.2 percent. A study by the TWUA in 1948 found that textile manufacturing profits increased 1,000 percent between 1939 and 1947, rising from $186 million to $2,020 million. The textile industry epitomized the way that World War II restored prosperity to American business far more successfully than the New Deal had.[7]

The war also generated structural changes in the textile industry, stimulating integration. The most common type of integration was vertical: that is, weaving and spinning mills started to usurp the other stages of textile production, encompassing every step from cotton bale to ultimate consumer product. Many southern mills grew through integration during the war. Integration reached its peak in 1946, when 123 mills changed hands. Major chains such as Avondale Mills of Alabama used integration to effect closer links with selling agencies and thereby earn larger profits. The TWUA made much of these changes, arguing that the textile industry was becoming increasingly monopolistic. The union hoped to eliminate the argument that had held back its progress in the South—that the industry was too competitive to support higher wages.[8]

The union's hope that integration would work to its advantage did not materialize. Integration failed to alter the intensely competitive nature of the textile industry. It remained easy to enter the industry, especially during World War II, when selling textiles was no problem. Indeed, the number of participating companies in the cotton textile industry increased by 20 percent between 1945 and 1954. Despite integration, in 1947 no single textile company was able to sell more than 3 percent of the total capacity of the textile industry. A recent study of North Carolina's textile industry in the immediate postwar years concluded that it "met the classic definition of a competitive enterprise" because "while a giant like Burlington Industries could grow and establish a modern corporate structure, hundreds of small family-owned mills continued to operate in North Carolina." Integration was only sustainable in specialized mills, such as shirts, sheets, and towels, in which style was not a big factor. Large mills working outside these markets continued to emphasize their vulnerability to smaller operators. Indeed, large southern companies were no larger in 1955 than they had been in the 1920s.[9]

The severe depression that hit the textile industry when the postwar boom ended confirmed the fact that the industry had changed very little from its prewar patterns of behavior. While the outbreak of the Korean War temporarily restored full production, by the end of 1951 the industry was hit by a full-scale depression that lingered throughout the 1950s. By January 1952, large southern companies were once again delivering orders below the cost-price, and the *Southern Textile News* reported "stagnation in textile markets" due to overproduction.[10] Many executives claimed that the depression of the 1950s was even worse than that of the 1930s.[11] Due to overproduction, prices of many fabrics dropped 40 percent in the space of one year, and profits evaporated. Large and small mills were equally affected by this depression.[12]

This persistence of competitive patterns does not mean that the textile industry emerged from World War II unchanged. What integration had achieved in the southern textile industry was a significant concentration of ownership. While the mills were dispersed in small units throughout the southern countryside, ownership and control had passed to relatively few financial interests. In November 1949, forty-two interests owned less than 20 percent of the southern plants, but these forty-two interests employed 45 percent of southern textile employees. This had significant negative consequences for the TWUA, as chain ownership allowed companies to switch production if one of their plants was struck, reducing the union's strategic position in the industry even further. Chain companies also had sufficient holdings so that they could be unaffected by one plant's being down even if production was not switched.[13]

The structure of the textile industry had profound consequences for textile unions. It is clear that in general terms, the position of a union was stronger when it operated in an oligopolistic industry, such as automobiles or steel. First, in terms of the effort spent per potential member, large plants were much easier to organize than small. Second, in some instances concern about adverse publicity did prevent management of large firms from actively fighting union drives. Third, once unions were established in oligopolistic industries, they were rarely exposed to the entry of new establishments or to the danger of runaway shops. Most important of all, however, in comparison with competitive industries, unions in the oligopolistic sector represented both numerical strength (in relation to an industry's workforce) and actual market power. This market power was an important point, for it enabled a union in a highly concentrated industry to play on either the inelastic or expanding demand conditions prevailing in the product market to extract higher wages.

The experiences of the TWUA in the South were shaped by the industry's structure. The large number of mills made organizing time-consuming and difficult. Indeed, even the largest southern companies were composed of small mills. The three largest southern textile companies in 1949—Cannon Mills, Burlington, and J. P. Stevens—collectively employed more than 64,000 workers, but they were divided into eighty-six separate mills. Even when the TWUA managed to penetrate these chains, it still occupied a minority presence. Thus, victory at a J. P. Stevens mill during World War II netted the union representation of only 650 workers out of the 18,600 that worked for the anti-union giant in the South. There was no huge, bellwether plant that the union could concentrate on, knowing that if it were successful, the rest of the industry would fall into line. To unionize the South, moreover, the TWUA desperately needed to establish a wage differential between union and nonunion plants. Organized mills, however, were reluctant to assume wage costs out of line with the mass of unorganized mills. The small profit margins, high labor costs, and intensely competitive nature of the industry meant that these mills consistently claimed that a wage differential would put them out of business.[14]

This argument was bolstered by the experience of the New England textile industry, which had declined while operating under a wage differential and a much stronger union presence. While other factors were responsible for this decline, southern mill owners themselves blamed the higher wage costs forced by textile unions. The vice president of the large (and unionized) Dan River Mills, Basil Browder, typically described New England mill owners as weak-backed men who had "practically liquidated themselves" by granting the union too many wage increases. The sectional competition between the two regions helped to prevent southern mill owners from looking to unions as a means of stabilizing the market, as the ultracompetitive soft coal industry and the needle trades had. As Browder's remarks indicate, however, southern mill owners were also ideologically anti-union, perceiving employers who did deal with unions as weak men who were willing to sign away the rights of management. It could be argued, indeed, that the ideological anti-unionism of southern textile mill owners was much greater than that of other industrialists, particularly the liberally inclined garment manufacturers, who were predominantly Jewish immigrants.[15]

The advantages of operating in oligopolistic industries are illustrated well by the labor history of the 1930s. Because overproduction and overcompetition plagued the textile industry before the war and continued to do so after 1948, it was often cheaper for companies to shut down for a while, as in a strike, than to operate. This was a fundamental problem in the 1934 textile strike, where overproduction robbed the strike of the ability to cripple industry and force manufacturers to deal with the union.[16] By contrast, the sit-down strikes of the late 1930s in the automobile and rubber industries were able to succeed largely because they hurt companies in profitable, oligopolistic industries by stopping production. Moreover, the victory of these strikes provided the breakthrough that left the automobile and rubber industries solidly organized. For example, General Motors, the main target of the United Automobile Workers (UAW), had invested heavily in new technology prior to the strike in Flint, Michigan, and was receiving large orders for its new models. The Flint strike so tied up production that instead of producing 15,000 cars a week, GM was producing 150. This hurt a company that had quadrupled its car and truck sales between 1932 and 1936. The structure of the textile industry prevented the union from forcing recognition, which was frequently the only way of building a secure union against the universal anti-unionism of American business. This was a crucial difference, because the sit-down strike was the breakthrough that American labor had failed to achieve before the New Deal. Prior to the sit-downs, most mass-production unions had failed to organize a significant proportion of their industries. As late as June 1935, the UAW's paid-up membership was only 5,135, and most of these members were concentrated outside of the key state of Michigan. The sit-down strike was indeed deliberately conceived as a way by which a minority could prevent management from importing strikebreakers and breaking the strike as they had in the past.[17]

In the postwar period, the fluctuating market conditions and overproduction that plagued the industry continued to limit the TWUA's fortunes. The mass of small mills posed fundamental problems for the impatient strategists of Operation Dixie. The crucial 1951 general strike failed partly because of an unexpected depression induced by overproduction. Other important southern strikes floundered as wartime integration allowed companies to switch production. Sectional competition between New England and the South conditioned the TWUA's repeated attempts to unionize the South in the immediate postwar years and ultimately had tragic consequences for a union that had established itself before World War II in the declining sector of the industry.

"The Food Never Came": Textile Unions before World War II

Prior to the 1930s, the textile industry was never more than 2 to 3 percent organized. This low representation largely followed the pattern prevailing in other mass-production industries, however, for organized labor as a whole was very weak before the New Deal. There were sporadic strikes by unorganized workers in textiles, as in other industries, but these produced few lasting institutional gains.[18] Even the timing of unrest in the textile industry largely followed national trends, with major strikes between 1898 and 1900 and between 1919 and 1921. It was only during the New Deal that the experience of textiles differed from that of other mass-production industries. Unlike other mass-production industries, the textile industry was not solidly organized during the New Deal. Therefore, the immediate postwar years became vital for the TWUA.

The failure of textile unionization in the 1930s was due in large part to the General Textile Strike of 1934, a grave defeat that set the cause of unionization back for many years. Southern textile workers had responded enthusiastically to the early New Deal; more than 200,000 walked off their jobs when the strike began on September 1, 1934.[19] Despite the determination of the strikers, the abandonment of the strike by the United Textile Workers (UTW), an AFL predecessor of the TWUA, provided management with the opportunity to fire and blacklist union supporters and to impose increased workloads on those who remained. For example, the *New York Times* estimated that 72,000 strikers were locked out of their jobs after the strike. The New Deal apparatus that was set up to prevent this victimization proved ineffective.[20]

This wave of discrimination, and the inability of the New Deal to prevent it, set the cause of unionism back tremendously. The 1934 strike showed that government protection needed to be far more stringent and coercive in order to be effective. The strike also highlighted the importance of relief in southern textile strikes. When the UTW called the strike, it had promised to support the strikers, hoping for assistance from New Deal relief agencies. In reality, no such assistance was secured, and the UTW, a small and poorly financed union, was unable to provide the effective relief that it had promised. The failure of the union to deliver on its promises of relief proved particularly galling for southern workers. Scott Hoyman, a missionary's son who worked for the TWUA in the South between 1950 and 1985, felt that workers "remembered the strike in the organized plants, but they really remembered it in the unorganized plants. They always say 'Lord, we don't want to get into that union and have happen to us what they did to our mothers and fathers in 1934.' About that they had promised in the '34 strike that food would come and the food never came." During Operation Dixie it was so common for organizers to mention 1934 as a problem that one organizer wrote from a campaign in Bristol, Tennessee, "This is one of the few cotton mills where you don't have the 1934 strike to contend with." As the *Greensboro Daily News* wrote in 1950, in the minds of many workers, textile unions were "still associated with trouble" because of the 1934 strike.[21]

The 1934 strike, therefore, is vital to understanding not only the failure of southern textiles to organize during the New Deal but also the postwar organizing problems of the TWUA. The size of the strike made it a catastrophic defeat that cast its shadow over future organizing attempts. Although a few workers kept their faith in unions after the strike, most vowed never to associate with organized labor again.[22] Moreover, the themes that the strike highlighted—the role of protection from the federal government and the relief issue—were to remain of central importance in determining the success of organizing the southern textile industry in the postwar years.

Following the 1934 strike, the biggest effort to organize the textile industry was the drive of the Textile Workers Organizing Committee (TWOC) between 1937 and 1939. Because the UTW was in disarray following the 1934 strike, the TWOC, a CIO-funded body, took over the task of organizing; it was headed by the respected leader of the Amalgamated Clothing Workers, Sidney Hillman. The TWOC drive concentrated heavily on the North. It was based in New York City, and Hillman's declared policy was to organize the North first. Those efforts that were made in the Piedmont failed as a result of a sharp textile recession combined with determined employer opposition. The two factors worked together: the downturn in the market encouraged mill owners to fight the union. Once again, New Deal labor legislation proved no match for southern textile mill owners, who overcame the drive through discriminatory discharges, threats, evictions from mill-owned houses, and a variety of other techniques. Through this formidable response to the TWOC drive, southern textile management cemented their reputation for virulent anti-unionism. The drive produced only one union contract in North Carolina, one in South Carolina, and nine over the Piedmont as a whole, bringing no more than a further 2 percent of active spindles under union contract.[23]

The TWOC drive affected the future prospects of southern organizing in a number of ways, however. It led to the founding of the TWUA: in May 1939, 302 new locals from the TWOC merged with 126 former UTW locals to form the TWUA-CIO.[24] The TWUA's president, Emil Rieve, and vice president, George Baldanzi, both came to prominence during the TWOC campaign. They were heads of independent federations that made up the UTW; Rieve came from the hosiery federation and Baldanzi from the dyers. During the TWOC drive, they joined forces to campaign successfully for a national union with greater centralization. The TWUA was to have a very low turnover at the top in the 1940s and 1950s. Rieve was to remain president until 1956, and Baldanzi vice president until 1952.

Like many labor leaders, both men came from ethnic backgrounds in the North. A short, squat man, Rieve was born in Zyradow in Russian Poland in 1892 and emigrated to the United States at the age of twelve. He began work in a Pennsylvania hosiery mill and rose to the presidency of the American Federation of Hosiery Workers (AFHW) by the age of thirty-seven. By World War II, Rieve had become one of the leading figures in the CIO, serving on both the National Mediation Board and the National War Labor Board (NWLB). Baldanzi, unlike Rieve, was American-born, the son of an Italian-American coal miner. He was born in Black Diamond, Pennsylvania, in 1907, and followed his father into the mines before securing work as a textile dyer in Paterson, New Jersey. Baldanzi differed greatly from Rieve in appearance and character. With dark black hair and a prominent nose, he was frequently referred to in employer propaganda as "a hook-nosed Italian."

From the early days of the TWUA, Rieve and Baldanzi failed to work together very effectively, a problem based largely on differences in character. Baldanzi was a far more flamboyant character than Rieve and an excellent speaker, and these talents won him a considerable following in the South. Baldanzi's strengths lay in organizing, Rieve's in administration. Rieve led the union where it was firmly established, in New England, and rarely visited the South, whereas Baldanzi concentrated on strike and organizing situations in the South and was well respected there. The union managed to contain these personality differences until the failure of the 1951 strike led to open warfare between the two leaders and their supporters. Rieve prevailed in this battle partly because he maintained the support of William Pollock, the TWUA's secretary-treasurer from 1939 to 1956. Viewed from the South, Scottish immigrant Pollock was a distant and anonymous character who concentrated on administration and rarely visited local unions. His loyal support of Rieve ensured his succession to the leadership, a move that horrified many southern activists, when Rieve retired in 1956.[25]

The TWOC drive was also important because it was successful in making large organizing gains in the North, especially in New England. Northern mill owners did not oppose the union as virulently or successfully as their counterparts in the South did. They were unable to label organizers as "outside agitators," because many TWOC staff had worked in the northern textile industry.[26] This northern success meant that future organizing drives, unlike the TWOC, would concentrate exclusively on the South. The TWOC largely established the postwar pattern of a strong northern union laying siege to the South with financial reserves that the UTW had never been able to secure. Indeed, because the TWOC had established a strong northern union without making comparable gains in the South, organizing the South became the primary objective in the postwar period, ensuring that the "turbulent years" in the South would be 1945–55. For the TWOC's successor, the TWUA, raising southern wages took on an added importance. As the new union operated from an economically vulnerable northern base, it was vital to raise southern wages and protect the economic interests of its northern members. The dilemmas faced by a northern union that desperately needed to organize the South and protect its northern membership left the TWUA vulnerable to destructive regional tensions in the postwar years.

TWUA'S Heyday: World War II

In vast contrast to the 1930s, during World War II the TWUA was able to make considerable progress both in organizing and in raising wages in the South. This wartime progress was to have a large influence on the union's immediate postwar history and provides the key to understanding many of the TWUA's problems in the South between 1945 and 1955.

The union reported "substantial net membership gains" between 1943 and 1946 despite the fact that the industry lost over a quarter of a million workers between 1942 and 1945. For the first time, the TWUA won contracts in some of the biggest and most important chains in the South. These included gains at the Cone Mills chain, based in Greensboro, North Carolina; at Dan River Mills in Danville, Virginia; at a Cannon Mills plant (the only time a union has ever penetrated Cannon), and several mills of the large Georgia-based A. D. Julliard chain. Between March 1, 1943, and February 15, 1946, the TWUA won 436 contracts, covering over 100,000 workers—an unprecedented rate of organizing progress. The union's progress in the South during the war was illustrated by the fact that in April 1946, just over 20 percent of southern cotton workers were under contract, a figure considerably higher than ever achieved before.[27]

The 1934 strike and TWOC drive had failed largely because the governmental protection offered by New Deal labor legislation had proved insufficient against determined employer attack. In particular, even if workers successfully managed to organize and win an election, it was possible for companies to stall the bargaining process and prevent a contract from being signed. Between May 1939 and May 1941, for example, the TWUA won fifty-one elections in southern cotton mills but secured contracts in only twenty-nine.[28] During World War II, the strict protection provided by the National War Labor Board (NWLB) overcame management resistance by the only possible means—by compelling them to accept union contracts. As labor had made a no-strike pledge for the duration of the war, the board adopted union security provisions as standard in these wartime contracts.[29] Due to the problems that the TWUA had endured in winning contracts in the South, especially over union security issues, these provisions led to the signing of many contracts that undoubtedly would not have existed otherwise. While studies of labor in World War II have often argued that this strict regulation absorbed worker militancy, in southern textiles, only such intrusive government action could overcome management intransigence and tip the power balance in the union's favor. Meanwhile, the no-strike pledge protected the TWUA from the necessity of having to strike to try and win a contract—a considerable advantage, because these strikes were on the whole unsuccessful.[30]

TWUA organizers who had worked through the 1930s remembered the war years as the most productive in their working lives because of the strict protection offered by the NWLB. Don McKee, a red-haired college graduate who worked as an organizer in South Carolina between 1937 and 1948, thought that "the War Labor Board, that was the time when we had the most success negotiating contracts in the South." If management refused to sign a contract, "it would go to the War Labor Board, and the War Labor Board would ensure a minimal, fairly decent contract which management had to put into effect as part of the war effort." Emphasizing the massive improvement over prewar bargaining, McKee added, "It was a minimal sort of contract, but it was super compared to what we were getting." If a company still refused to obey the contract, the federal government could actually seize the plant and run it, a scenario that did occur in the textile South.[31] Another TWUA representative who worked the South during these years, Alabama native Julius Fry, recalled the way the war alleviated workers' fear of being fired for union activity: "The climate during World War II was ripe for organization. . . . We were more bold during the war years because you were frozen on your job, and supposedly you couldn't quit. And people didn't give a damn sometimes, under those conditions." Another TWUA staffer in the South, Scott Hoyman, pointed out that "almost every bargaining relationship that this union has ever had began in World War II."[32]

The war is therefore crucial to an understanding of the union's postwar history in the South. The long-term problem for the TWUA was that its wartime gains were more extensive than the union or the UTW had consistently been able to win under normal conditions. They thus placed the union in a position where it was stretched beyond its natural power. For many who worked in the South, the union's priority during the immediate postwar years should be to defend the gains it had made during the war rather than attempt new organization. Indeed, despite the union's attempts to organize new plants, a large amount of its energy in the postwar period was expended defending its wartime gains, especially in the large anti-union chains that had been penetrated for the first time during the war.[33]

The war years are also central to understanding the TWUA's postwar history in another sense. In order to eliminate the long-standing North-South wage differential and protect the interests of its northern members, from its foundation the TWUA was devoted to raising southern wages. During the war, the union achieved enormous success in this area, using federal bureaucracy to win wage increases. The union took advantage of a NWLB ruling known as the "hold the line" order of April 18, 1942. While designed to halt inflation, the order decreed that NWLB could order wage increases that were "clearly necessary to correct substandards of living." The TWUA began a successful and sophisticated campaign to prove that southern textile wages were "substandard." Rieve led the union's effort from his position as a NWLB member, calling for "a decent, American standard wage." The union's efforts achieved fruition in the "Big Cotton Case" of February 1945, when the TWUA successfully

Table 1. Wage Increases in the Textile Industry, 1941 and 1945

	January 1941	June 1945	% Increase
Average hourly pay	48.80 cents	75.90 cents	55.50
Average weekly pay	$18.01	$31.67	75.69
Average weekly hours	36.90	41.80	13.40

Source: "Fisher and Rudge Brief for Negotiations, Summer 1951," folder, Dan River Mills Company Papers.

won a sixty-cent-per-hour minimum wage for the textile industry plus a range of other fringe benefits.[34] By the end of the war the minimum wage in cotton textiles had been raised to sixty-five cents an hour, a huge improvement over both the twenty-five-cent minimum of 1937 and the thirty-eight-cent minimum prevailing in the industry in January 1942.[35]

In the months immediately after the war, textile wages continued to rise quickly. On average, wages for southern cotton textile workers more than doubled between 1941 and 1946, rising from forty-two cents an hour to eighty-six. Southern textile workers received eight separate pay increases between January 1, 1941, and August 1, 1946, around the time that Operation Dixie began. In percentage terms, their wartime pay increased more than that of any other group of mass-production workers. These great increases resulted not only from the role played by the TWUA but also from the wartime shift of workers into higher-paying industries, which forced southern textile mills to raise their wages. The war also saw the introduction of incentive plans and a considerably longer working week, which meant that take-home pay increased more than even these huge hourly increases indicate. Moreover, these gains were not wiped out by inflation: even allowing for the rise in consumer prices, the real wages of southern textile workers increased by over 50 percent between 1941 and 1945.[36]

In the immediate postwar years, national union leaders imagined that wartime progress meant that the time was ripe for further organization. Those who worked in the South had a different understanding. The TWUA took considerable pride in its record of progress during the war as a whole. Echoing Rieve's claim that wartime progress was "phenomenal," the TWUA's 1946 Executive Council Report boasted that "no union has ever done more to raise the economic standards of its members than has TWUA." These gains were particularly important because they meant that the mood in the TWUA was optimistic. Because such progress had been achieved during the war, the union's leaders imagined that this record of progress could be carried forward into postwar organizing in the South. Illustrating the union's confident mood, Secretary-Treasurer William Pollock boasted in 1946 that "it has been in the last four years a

Table 2. Comparison of Textile Wages with Steel and Automobiles,
1941 and 1951

Industry	Average Hourly Wages		
	1941	1951	% Increase
Automobiles	1.042	1.869	79.4
Steel	0.953	1.885	97.8
Textiles	0.526	1.322	151.3

Source: "Negotiating Data 7-51 thru 4-52 Negotiations" folder, Dan River Mills
Company Papers.

relatively simple matter to organize plants and get them under contract."
This optimism and self-belief were crucial in making the immediate postwar years a time of intense and continued organizing activity.[37]

Adding to the significant wage increases of the war years, between
1945 and 1950 the union's pressure for increased southern wages brought
rich dividends. The industry was so prosperous that nonunion manufacturers followed wage increases won in the union sector, meaning that the
TWUA was able to successfully protect its northern membership. Indeed,
the New England textile industry shared in the prosperity and did not experience substantial mill closures in these years. Between 1946 and 1951,
textile wages continued to increase more than those of any other industry. Even allowing for postwar inflation, these were substantial wage
increases. At Dan River Mills, wages increased 185.5 percent between
January 1941 and August 1948, well ahead of the 73 percent rise in the
cost of living. At Burlington Industries, a prominent southern textile
company, the company reported that pay had increased by 233 percent
between 1940 and 1950, representing a 92 percent rise in real wages. For
the southern textile industry as a whole, "real" average weekly earnings
increased from $13.83 in October 1939 to $29.32 in October 1950.[38]

World War II and the Southern Mill Village

The prosperity that World War II generated for the textile industry was
crucial in causing social change and drastically altering the organizing
climate. Clearly, it was the textile industry's long history of low wages
and small profits that caused these changes to have a disproportionate
impact for both workers and management. Workers experienced great
economic and social improvements through the operation of the wartime
economy. Similarly, companies experienced unprecedented profits. This
dramatic change of fortune caused both to abandon prewar concepts and
to move toward a new relationship with one another—a relationship that
had profound consequences for unionization prospects.

This new relationship is illustrated by the economic impact of improved wages on the company-owned mill village. Originally, owners built company houses as a means of securing labor and encouraging the whole family to work in the mill. They set low rents as an inducement and included electricity and water in the rent.[39] The higher wages of the 1940s put pressure on this system and influenced the decision of many southern mill owners to sell mill houses to workers during the 1940s and early 1950s. In addition, some companies wished to free up the capital that they had tied up in housing, real estate that was sometimes more valuable than the mill and its equipment.[40]

The change in mill-village housing was explored by one of the most active investigators of mill-village life, Harriet L. Herring. Herring was a mill-village social worker and colleague of sociologist Howard Odum at the Center for Social Research at the University of North Carolina. She noted in her classic 1949 study of mill-village decline that one of the main reasons for selling was "higher textile wages which make home purchase feasible." Higher-paid workers were reported to want "better cottages—ceiled and then plastered, running water taps on the porch, and presently inside toilets and baths." In a wide-ranging survey of the southern textile industry, the industry journal *Daily News Record* described "a new pattern of living" among southern textile workers. During the war, increasing numbers of textile workers had left the industry and switched to the higher-paying industries that were beginning to locate in the South, such as the chemical industry and the paper industry. These industries did not provide housing. The *Record* noted that "the daily increasing employment of these new industries has been itself a powerful influence impelling cotton mill workers to leave the mill village for their own homes." At the same time, higher wages had made home ownership realistic, especially as many workers now owned cars and could therefore live farther away from the plant. The *Record*'s conclusion—"No matter how fine the houses, how modern their conveniences, how many prerequisites their occupants receive from the mill management, the mill village is still a paternalistic institution, and will probably be increasingly recognized as such by the cotton mill worker as his education continues to improve and his industrial experience broadens"—symbolized the abrupt change that the industry had made in relation to company housing.[41]

Higher wartime wages put pressure on the company-owned mill village in other ways. One study, for example, found that companies could no longer afford to provide free electricity because "increased wages enabled mill village families to purchase electric irons, refrigerators, washing machines, electric ranges, fans and heaters," whereas when the houses had been built families had had only "three or four 40 watt incandescents." Mill owner Caesar Cone recalled that Cone Mills decided to sell their houses to workers in the 1940s because "originally, when the houses were built, there was maybe a 40 watt bulb in each of the four rooms. And it didn't cost a hell of a lot to absorb that juice. . . . But, then as electrical appliances came along and people wanted irons and stoves and bought all these items, it was patently unfair. . . . We just decided to abolish the whole smear."[42]

At the end of World War II another contemporary observer of the textile industry, Mildred Gwin Andrews, sent questionnaires to a wide variety of southern mill owners to find out more about the reasons for mill-village decline. This enquiry was significant because Andrews was a representative of the North Carolina Textile Manufacturers Association and was employed as a spokesperson for the southern textile industry. Hence, she was trusted by management, who freely shared developments at their mills with her. The responses that she received indicated not only that home ownership was becoming the norm but that management was encouraging it. Many were consciously turning their back on paternalism and encouraging their workers' desire for independence. Albert Spaugh of Washington Mills in Winston Salem, North Carolina, for example, reported that between 50 and 60 percent of his company's employees lived in their own homes. He explained, "At the present time many employees, especially former servicemen, are building small homes in and around our towns." A wide range of other companies reported that at least 50 percent of their employees were now home owners. Ironically, many companies reported that mill workers were moving into rural districts and engaging in part-time subsistence farming, a move back to the practices of the first generation of mill workers that hinted at the strength of mill workers' rural traditions.[43] Since eight-hour shifts were the norm during this period, workers, especially those on the second and third shifts, were reported to have "plenty of time" to farm.[44]

Management supported these changes by either loaning their employees the money to build or purchase homes or helping them to secure such loans from commercial or governmental institutions. Southern textile management quickly abandoned the company-owned mill village as they witnessed the effects of home ownership on workers. Indeed, all the evidence suggests that home ownership had beneficial results from the company viewpoint. One manufacturer wrote privately to Andrews that "based on the survey which I made of home ownership in other villages as well as from our own experience, I am confident that home ownership rather than mill village ownership is a wonderful thing both for the company and for the employees. There is probably no one thing which contributes more to a person's pride than home ownership." Home ownership was reported to make a huge "psychological difference" to workers, stimulating responsibility, stable employment, and interest in self-advancement. Company-owned mill villages had been built originally partly as a means of securing stable employment. Now, with workers earning enough to own homes, their sale was the best way of achieving the same result. As Paul Redmond of Alabama Mills in Birmingham, Alabama, wrote, "The encouragement of home-ownership is, in my opinion, a great deal more important than undertaking to house all of our employees and encourage the paternalism that goes along with it because in this way we will certainly have a great deal more stable employment."[45]

The lifestyle of the postwar southern textile worker was radically different from that prevailing in the prewar company-owned mill village. Wartime wages led to rising living standards and new opportunities. Even for workers who continued to rent from the company, considerable improvements were made to mill villages. The war stimulated companies to make these changes, because, as the *Daily News Record* wrote, "During the war, so many other industries not only paid higher wages, but furnished more pleasant employment which gave workers a higher social status, that it was necessary to make the mill villages pleasanter places in which to live." During and immediately after the war, many companies launched beautification and modernization projects, the most common involving the installation of indoor plumbing and bathrooms and improving the underpinning of mill houses. Many companies financed these improvements by raising rents to "the going community rate," which itself signified a more commercial relationship between workers and the company, given that prewar rents were very low.[46]

Many observers remembered the way that wartime prosperity transformed the textile South.[47] Junius Scales, a Communist who organized textile workers in High Point, North Carolina, shortly before the war, vividly recalled the way the mill villages changed while he was away in service. On returning to visit workers, Scales felt that there was "a whole new atmosphere. . . . Nobody had a car before, and cars were springing up all along the street. It was touching to see all these people who had lived in terrible conditions for so long experiencing these conveniences." Scales remembered that items such as washing machines and refrigerators were multiplying rapidly. He characterized the social changes taking place as "consumerism with a vengeance. . . . As soon as they could, they grabbed everything they could."[48]

These changes taking place in southern textile communities represented a dramatic shift from the low living standards of the prewar period, but at the same time, they were only a reflection of broader changes taking place in American society. As southern textile workers bought cars, homes, and other consumer items, they were taking part in a national movement toward consumerism generated by the higher wages of World War II. In the five years after World War II, consumer spending increased 60 percent, and the amount that Americans spent on automobiles rose 205 percent. In the four years following the end of the war,

Americans purchased 21.4 million cars, 20 million refrigerators, and 5.5 million stoves. The interest that southern mill owners noted among their employees in beautifying and investing in their homes was typical of these years, when investing in and improving a house was seen as the best way to plan for the future.[49]

This shift to consumerism and home ownership had profound consequences for unionization. For years, textile unions had complained that the absolute control of the company-owned mill village was the main obstacle to organization, a point developed by historians. By this reasoning, the sudden collapse of this system should have been of great benefit to textile unions. The continued failure of unionization in the postwar years seemed to indicate that little had changed in southern textile communities, explaining why historians have repeatedly portrayed southern textile communities as distinctive, static communities that managed to remain outside of the American mainstream.

The key to understanding the apparent paradox of social change and the continued failure of unionization lies in two aspects of the changes taking place. First, the changes were economically generated by World War II and shared by union and nonunion workers alike. It was not necessary to join a union to share in the improved standard of living. Second, it is important not to see the shift from the company-owned mill village simply as liberation for southern textile workers. As workers became home owners, they took on new, restrictive responsibilities. Most textile workers, despite their improved pay, still did not earn enough to buy large items outright. Across the South after World War II, textile workers bought items through installment plans. In southern textile towns, the press contained numerous advertisements by department stores that offered to finance the purchase of cars, washing machines, and other consumer items through plans that required only a small down payment, or sometimes none at all. Throughout the 1940s and 1950s, southern textile workers constantly owed money and thus had more to lose by joining a union and risking the loss of income through strikes or job loss. Joining a union could actually threaten the "new pattern of living." The breakdown of the mill village also had other negative repercussions, since it meant the end of the close-knit, cohesive communities that had served as a basis for worker militancy, as well as a shift to a more fragmented and isolated workforce.[50]

The large and rapid social changes that World War II brought about are thus particularly significant in the light of the overwhelming emphasis that historiography has given to continuity in the textile South. As workers received higher wages and became the owners of homes and cars, they entered the American mainstream in a way that has not been recognized. This change is particularly significant, because historians, sociologists, social scientists, and many others have been consistently fascinated by southern textile workers due to their apparent status as a subclass outside of the American mainstream. These workers have been persistently described as a people apart by a wide variety of observers. Early observers described overworked and despondent mill workers with low social status. In 1941, Wilbur Cash's classic study *The Mind of the South* noted a wide gulf between the mill worker and other groups of southern society. Mill workers formed a "separate community" and were looked down upon by other sections of southern society, who regarded them as "cotton-mill trash" and "lint-heads." [51]

The company-owned mill village was at the center of southern textile workers' powerlessness and social isolation. As Harriet Herring noted in 1930, "It is . . . obvious that the owner can largely prevent organization if he chooses," for he knew everything that went on in the villages. The TWUA itself claimed that the company-owned mill village was "the fundamental obstacle to labor organization" because of the "total power" it gave to mill owners.[52] Not surprisingly, Herring and other contemporaries believed that the breakup of the mill villages would liberate southern textile workers and break the bonds of the paternalistic system. They assumed that unionization would follow. For example, John Kenneth Morland, who studied mill workers in 1948–49, predicted that unionization would replace the declining paternalistic system. This failed to happen, however, in the years following the sale of mill-village houses.[53]

The failure of unionization does not mean, however, that southern textile communities were static and conservative. Largely due to the continued failure of unionization, modern scholars have stressed continuity with these early writings by continuing to probe the distinctive culture of the southern mill worker. Most modern writings have also accepted the idea of a poorly educated, economically insecure, and socially isolated cotton-mill class, even in studies of textile workers written in the 1970s and 1980s. Others have stressed that while houses were sold off, much remained the same, especially the mill owners' power and dominance of textile communities, the endurance of paternalism, and the workers' psychological inability to challenge the system. In his study, for example, James Hodges noted that the overall conclusion of those who had studied postwar southern textile workers was one of "continuity" between the workers of the 1930s and those of the 1980s. Another historian, David Carlton, noted in 1982 that "the hostilities of the period before 1920 produced an antipathy toward the town that is still discernible in south-ern mill centers, and the grievances of the operatives of that age against farmers live on in the present-day distrust of unions and liberals." Similarly, Barbara Griffith sees the static cultural climate of the South and its villages as one of the central reasons for the failure of postwar unionization.[54]

The continuing failure of unionization, indeed, seemed to indicate that little had changed in the textile South. In fact, workers and others associated with the industry in these years remembered them as a time of tremendous change, when established patterns of company control were broken and tremendous economic advances made. They consistently made statements to the effect that during these years textile workers were "coming into the real world" and "starting to live a normal life." Thus, it was the separation from other groups in southern society that observers have persistently noted that began to change in these years. The first opportunities workers had to trade outside the company store, own homes, or even afford to go to a diner were simple yet important changes that have been overlooked and that need to be recognized and explored. Yet rather than helping unionization, such changes actually contributed to its failure. The reasons for this result need to be explored in greater detail.[55]

chapter two

Cracking the Textile Industry

Operation Dixie, 1946–1953

In the summer of 1946, the CIO launched an intensive organizing drive in the South. Realizing the threat that an unorganized South posed to its recently acquired northern bases, the CIO set its sights high, declaring that its goal was the complete organization of the South's major industries. No union understood the dangers of a nonunion South better than the TWUA. The South had become the home of the textile industry, yet the TWUA's base was still in the declining New England area. For this reason, and because textiles comprised the largest southern industry, organizing the textile industry was at the heart of Operation Dixie's efforts. The TWUA invested a great deal in the drive. George Baldanzi declared, "We who have 80% of our industry in the South that is completely unorganized and which threatens our very existence . . . would be betraying the interests of our membership if we did not throw . . . everything we have to organize the textile workers of the South." Measured against its ostensible aim of bringing extensive unionization, the drive was only partially successful in most industries; and its failure was particularly noticeable in the crucial industry of textiles, where many campaigns were abandoned and only one-quarter of all elections were won.[1]

Traditional accounts of the failure of Operation Dixie stressed corporate and community opposition to the drive, along with financial constraints. Barbara Griffith's recent study has stressed the culture of the mill workers and its role in the union's failure in textiles. In a study of the important Cannon Mills drive in Kannapolis, North Carolina, Griffith stresses workers' "fear" and loyalty to the company and mill owner les Cannon. She concludes that the drive failed because "workers in ny-owned mill villages in the American South lived under the most ¿ kind of police tyranny." Griffith also argues that Operation ¹ ended by the winter of 1946, a claim that ignores the fact that the drive made a determined effort to organize southern textile workers until 1953 and was greatly affected by factors that only came into operation after 1946.[2]

"A Spirit of Victory"

Given the acute problems that thwarted Operation Dixie, at first glance the launching of such an ambitious campaign may appear strange. In 1945 and early 1946, however, the mood in the TWUA and the wider union movement was an optimistic one. Many unions had made great strides during the war and immediately afterward, and the climate seemed to be ripe for organization. A healthy economy made wage increases possible and seemed to bode well for future organization. The success of the 1945–46 strike wave, the defeat of Fascism, and Roosevelt's unprecedented fourth term also lent encouragement to the union movement.[3]

This optimism clearly had a considerable influence upon the launching of Operation Dixie, a broadly conceived campaign that targeted all major southern industries in twelve different states. The CIO decided to embark on the drive at an executive board meeting on March 15–16, 1946. President Philip Murray cited the CIO's recent "tremendous victories" and record-breaking series of wage increases, claiming that they would ensure the success of the drive by serving as "a beacon light to all unorganized workers." TWUA president Emil Rieve claimed that his union's record of wartime progress showed that the TWUA was capable of organizing the South. Many carried this optimism into the early stages of Operation Dixie, believing that workers would respond to the campaign. For example, one of the leaders of the drive, William Smith, claimed that there was "a spirit of victory" among southern textile workers.[4]

The CIO appointed Van A. Bittner of the United Steelworkers to head the campaign, with the TWUA's George Baldanzi as deputy director. A veteran union leader, Bittner was seen as a good choice because of his ability to combine an affable exterior with internal toughness. Balding and bespectacled in appearance, he was described by *Business Week* as "poised, shrewd, and articulate" and well-schooled in the realities of industrial conflict. Beneath Bittner, state directors were appointed with the responsibility of coordinating the campaign on the ground level. Although the drive was conducted in twelve southern states, in many of these states, such as Texas or Arkansas, there were very few textile plants. Surviving records provide a detailed insight into the drive in three southern states with a large number of textile plants—North Carolina, South Carolina, and Tennessee—but they provide only a glimpse of the campaign in other states, including the important textile states of Georgia and Alabama.[5]

The directors appointed in the textile states came from a variety of backgrounds, but most had considerable experience in the labor movement. In North Carolina, the drive's director was William Smith, a forty-two-year-old Californian with a union background outside the textile industry. Like Bittner, Smith combined a personable exterior with a quiet passion to organize the South, particularly the textile industry. In South Carolina, the drive was headed by Franz Daniel, a graduate of Union Theological Seminary in New York City who became active in the southern labor movement through the Highlander Folk School in the 1930s. Daniel brought experience and proven ability to the operation. Similarly, Tennessee director Paul Christopher was one of the most able and respected southern union leaders at the time Operation Dixie took place. He was a native of South Carolina who entered the mills before his labor activism brought him employment as a textile organizer in the 1930s. Christopher was one of Operation Dixie's most colorful characters, an alcoholic who admonished and encouraged his organizers more than any other state director did. He worked tirelessly for Operation Dixie, and his detailed reports provide a rich documentary record of the campaign.[6]

The way that Bittner began Operation Dixie typified the confidence and optimism that had generated the campaign. He issued dramatic releases to the press and his staff calling the drive "a great crusading movement on behalf of humanity" and claiming that "nothing under God's sun is going to stop this mighty movement of ours from doing this job." Both Baldanzi and Bittner argued that southern workers were essentially the same as other American workers, that they fervently wanted unions, and that if a large enough campaign could be launched they would respond. Bittner claimed that organization would inevitably come to the South through hard work, commitment, and organization. This could best be achieved through the assignment of "energetic boys from the North," reflecting the view of South Carolina director Franz Daniel that "southern situations need the drive and energy of northern industrial workers." Educational and political programs aimed at bringing about long-term change in the South were seen as unnecessary. Bittner dismissed the CIO's Political Action Committee (PAC) as "about as useful as Bill Green [the elderly AFL statesman] as a CIO organizer." On race, the drive was quickly distanced from progressive movements. Operation Dixie was to be all about winning elections, and winning them as fast as possible: "All of our people should devote themselves to just one thing that is winning elections."[7]

The emphasis on winning elections reflected the fact that the goals of Operation Dixie were primarily economic. More than anything else, leaders wanted to raise southern wages through unionization, so the TWUA and other unions could protect their bases in the North. Told the TWUA's 1946 convention that Operation Dixie was necessary because "as long as wages remain low in any one section of the country, there is always the threat of sweatshop competition with other areas." Confirming the drive's rejection of political action, he added that "all freedom begins with economic freedom." These comments also reflected the belief that only through economic improvement could real political change be achieved in the South. Thus, CIO president Philip Murray called Operation Dixie "a simple, pure, unadulterated campaign of trade union organization" and argued that higher wages would set in motion positive political changes such as the removal of reactionary politicians. This economic approach was universally supported when the drive began.[8]

Thus, the organizers who went south in the summer of 1946 were keen to emphasize the economic benefits of unionization. Organizers stressed that if wartime prosperity was to be maintained in the South, it would have to be maintained through a high-wage economy.[9] The press saw the CIO's strategy as sophisticated, and, reflecting the optimism of the time, few predicted failure.[10]

Until his death in 1949, Van Bittner was stationed in Atlanta, whereas Baldanzi operated from Greensboro, North Carolina, a location he chose specifically because of its proximity to a large number of textile plants. On a day-to-day basis, it was Baldanzi who ran the campaign in textiles. Early on, indeed, he laid down the basic principles that were to guide the textile campaign. Textile organizers were told that the groundwork of any drive should be to get in-plant committees set up before a widespread organizing campaign was launched. Although many textile organizers came from the TWUA, Baldanzi made it clear that they were employed by the coordinating body of the drive, the Southern Organizing Committee (SOC). If an election were won, the organizers would withdraw and the TWUA would be responsible for the negotiation of a contract.[11]

The structure of the textile industry posed particular problems for the strategists of Operation Dixie. The sheer number of plants—in 1946, North Carolina alone had more than 1,000—meant that there was no effective hellwether plant that could set a pattern of unionization for others to follow, as had happened in far less competitive northern industries such as automobiles and rubber in the 1930s. From the outset, the structure of the textile industry made the kind of sweeping unionization that Operation Dixie envisaged very difficult to achieve. SOC leaders generated a considerable volume of correspondence debating how best to tackle this problematic structure. They decided that unless they concentrated on large plants, the drive would dissipate. In the main textile state, North Carolina, this decision meant that the vast majority of resources and personnel were sent into two locations—the Cannon Mills chain in Kannapolis, and Gaston County. In the latter location, efforts centered on the huge Firestone plant, located in the old Loray Mill, which had been the scene of a dramatic strike in 1929. The logic behind these campaigns was to target locations where the industry was as concentrated as possible. Cannon Mills was the largest textile company in the South, employing 41,000 workers in twenty mills. Gaston County, with 104 mills, was a major center of the industry. Although these locations were described as "the two most important drives from the angle of largeness," the number of mills present in these two locations alone hinted at the impossibility of implementing a concentrated strategy in the textile industry. Similarly, in South Carolina, the drive was concentrated in the Greenville-Spartanburg area, where that state's textile industry was clustered; in Georgia, around the large Bibb mill chain; and in Alabama, in the huge Avondale Mills based in Sylacauga.[12]

The efforts to unionize these large chains constituted round one of Operation Dixie's textiles branch. Launched in July, the Cannon, Avondale, Bibb, and Firestone campaigns had all collapsed by November, none of them having secured enough signed cards to petition for an election. These failures were decisive in ending the hopes of achieving rapid unionization, especially as they resulted in the CIO's decision, made at its Atlantic City convention in December 1946, to drastically curtail the drive. The fact that international unions were funding the drive meant that there was a pressure for immediate results, and Van Bittner was unable to satisfy this desire, especially in textiles. At Atlantic City the CIO decided on huge cuts. In textiles, they reduced state budgets and the number of organizers by 50 percent. For Barbara Griffith, these cuts marked the end of Operation Dixie, because they made it clear that wholesale unionization of the South would not be achieved.[13]

The Atlantic City convention, however, cannot be viewed as the end of Operation Dixie in textiles. None of the drive leaders or organizers viewed it this way. Organizing attempts continued for another six and a half years in textiles, generating a rich body of neglected records. In addition, at the end of 1946, organizers were transferred into textiles from other industries, particularly tobacco, partly off-setting the 1946 cuts. Union leaders were motivated by the feeling that textiles, if nothing else, had to be organized. William Smith, for example, wrote that "unless we crack some of the major textile mills . . . the rest will not mean too much." These sentiments marked a major shift from the early days of the drive, when Bittner made it clear that there was to be no emphasis on "any one specific industry." Operation Dixie thus shifted from its multi-industry emphasis to concentrate almost exclusively on textiles.[14]

Smith's comments about winning "major" mills were indicative of the way that the drive's leaders stuck to their big-plant strategy after 1946. Indeed, the official reaction to the early failures was that they had "wasted" too much energy on small, insignificant mills. The concentrated strategy must be intensified, and organizers were told that "no work is to be done among any of the small plants." This strategy had always been attractive to the drive's cost-conscious planners, who, aware of the enormous task of organizing textiles, were eager to maximize their limited resources. As budgets became tighter in the later stages of the campaign, therefore, the strategy seemed to make more sense than ever.[15]

New campaigns aimed at organizing the textile industry were launched in 1947 and succeeding years, and many of these campaigns went on for several years.[16] The Standard-Coosa-Thatcher drive, for example, lasted more than four years. The campaign that consumed the most time and energy, however, occurred in Anderson County, South Carolina, where the CIO repeatedly struggled to overcome one of the South's most antiunion strongholds. Indeed, most residents of Anderson County still associated unions with a violent shooting that had occurred there during the 1934 strike. Six strikers were killed by dozens of "loyal" workers and overseers who had armed themselves in reaction to news that strikers might try to close the Chiquola Manufacturing Company in Honea Path. The Anderson campaign showed that the SOC leaders regarded the organization of textiles as paramount and were prepared to dig deep to achieve it. Indeed, as Operation Dixie went on, leaders shifted their goal from rapid organization to a more gradualist view, realizing that organizing the South was a long-term commitment.[17]

Clearly, in terms of effort and organizing activity, Operation Dixie in textiles was a seven-year campaign. The question remains, however, how much was actually achieved following the cuts of December 1946. Election results show that victories dropped off after 1946, but the difference was not enormous. It may also be that, as the union leaders themselves argued, the drop in victories after 1946 was largely the product of the Taft-Hartley Act. From May 15 to December 31, 1946, the SOC won twenty-one textile elections and lost twenty-six. From 1947 onward, fewer elections were won, but gains were still made; in 1947, fifteen elections were won and twenty-two lost. In some ways 1948 was an improvement: it was the SOC's only "winning season," with a record of fourteen victories and twelve defeats. Consistent gains were also made in 1949 and 1950. A noticeable drop occurred from 1951 to 1953, reflecting the fallout from the failed 1951 strike.[18]

The number of election victories seems high considering the drive's failure in its major campaigns. Indeed, the real failure of Operation Dixie in textiles was its inability to achieve its professed aim—to organize the major plants in the industry. Ironically, the elections that the SOC won consistently occurred in much smaller plants than the elections it lost. Thus, the twenty-one victories of 1946 covered only 4,279 workers, while the twenty-six defeats covered 11,847. In 1947 the twenty-two defeats covered over 20,000 workers, while the fifteen victories covered only 4,118. A testament to the competitive nature of the textile industry was the fact that the biggest plant the SOC was able to win in 1946 covered only 800 workers. Moreover, sixteen of the twenty-one victories occurred in plants employing less than 250 workers.[19]

The SOC was able to secure small but consistent gains in textiles. By the time Operation Dixie was officially terminated by the CIO in April 1953, it had won 64 out of the 232 elections it contested. As a result, many in the TWUA felt that Operation Dixie was not a complete failure.[20] Nevertheless, it was the organizers' continual inability to penetrate large plants that troubled national CIO leaders, who had hoped to use these victories as a springboard to complete unionization of the South, and it was on this failure that the SOC judged Operation Dixie.[21]

Exploring the reasons for the campaign's failure to crack the major chain mills is, therefore, a central question. Given the seven years of effort that textile organizers devoted to the campaign, however, and the fact that election victories were well spaced out, it is also important to examine the SOC's problems over a wide time span and from as many campaigns as possible.

"The NLRB Is No Damn Good"

From the outset, it was clear that government protection was going to play a central role in determining the success of Operation Dixie. Union growth between 1935 and 1945 had been linked to the willingness of staff members of the National Labor Relations Board (NLRB) and the National War Labor Board (NWLB) to take steps to actively assist unions. Government protection was especially important in efforts to organize the southern textile industry. Organizing drives in the 1930s had met determined resistance from anti-union mill owners, and it was only under the more stringent protection of the NWLB that textile unions were able to make real strides in the South.[22]

The NWLB, however, stopped operating at the beginning of 1946, and national labor relations reverted to the control of the NLRB. This put the TWUA on the defensive, in a position where it needed to protect the gains had made through the NWLB. The storm clouds loomed ominously for ʼoung union whose only real organizing had been performed during ld War II, especially as the last years of the war had seen a growing ce of the board by flagship anti-union textile employers.[23]

reports from organizers showed that many campaigns were ru-
liscriminatory firings and open defiance of the NLRB. This was
true of several drives in the Deep South states of Georgia and
ʼcluding the crucial Bibb and Avondale campaigns. Alabama
und J. Ryan, for example, reported that at Avondale the
ʼng liquidated" while awaiting investigation of unfair labor

practices against the company, including "discharge cases, demotions, company interference and everything in the book." The company acted in a similar fashion in the Bibb campaign. Leading union member Charlie Busbee, for example, testified that "they were firing everyone that belongs to the union."[24] Many textile organizers recalled that immediately after the war, companies began to deliberately flout the NLRB to destroy organizing drives. Joel Leighton, an organizer in Tennessee and North Carolina, recalled that companies would "deliberately fire union leadership" as an effective means of killing drives. Many reports confirmed the damage inflicted by these tactics.[25]

Although some organizers claimed that this opposition was greater than before, to a large extent these tactics represented a continuation of prewar tactics. It is clear, however, that these problems were greatly compounded by the passage of the Taft-Hartley Act in June 1947. This act significantly reduced the amount of government protection that unions received. Its central purpose was to reform federal labor relations policy by recasting the nature and functions of the NLRB. Whereas the New Deal's Wagner Act (1935) had sought to encourage workers' right to form unions, Taft-Hartley aimed to balance this right with the interests of the general public and, more particularly, employers. It has been argued that the act merely formalized long-term changes in NLRB practices, as the board had already taken steps away from its pro-union stance of the 1930s. However, for unions such as the TWUA, whose progress was so linked to federal protection, and who faced a huge organizing task, the act had a particularly jarring impact. As the TWUA leaders argued, it was weak unions such as the TWUA that were most affected by Taft-Hartley.[26]

Several provisions of the Taft-Hartley Act were particularly important in hindering Operation Dixie. Especially damaging was the "free speech" or "captive audience" clause, which expanded the rights of employers to express their views on the eve of elections. Other important revisions changed the definition of "employer" in such a way as to remove antiunion citizens' committees from the NLRB's jurisdiction and increased the time required for representation elections by repealing the prehearing election procedure.[27]

These provisions worked together in a way that greatly strengthened the hand of southern textile employers during Operation Dixie. The ability to delay elections, often by taking advantage of the repeal in the prehearing election procedure, was to prove particularly damaging. Delays were also the product of an underfunded and understaffed NLRB that worked more slowly than before, especially as it was burdened by the legal complexity of the Taft-Hartley Act. By October 1947, the NLRB had the greatest backlog of cases in its eleven-year history. Its case load was increased by new provisions allowing employers to charge unions with unfair labor practices and to seek to decertify unions. By March 1948, it took almost twice as long for the board to conduct an election as it had in 1946.[28]

Organizers' reports from a wide variety of campaigns highlighted the problems caused by NLRB delays. Many drives fell apart while organizers waited for election dates. From Republic Cotton Mills in Great Falls, South Carolina, for example, Harvey Mayo wrote, "Interest is at a low ebb and nothing will happen so long as month after month passes without board election."[29] Indeed, the universal problem was that it was very difficult to stop campaigns from disintegrating during long delays. As William Smith described it, "In most cases, card signing stops after we petition for an election." Workers found it hard to deal with delays. Many of them reasoned that the majority of them wanted a union, so why was there a delay?[30] SOC directors complained that organizers themselves were guilty of thinking, with disastrous consequences, that the campaign was over once an election was petitioned for.[31] Many organizers described how hard it was to maintain interest over an extended period of time. Many workers wanted to take matters into their own hands and strike for recognition. These strikes usually failed and added to feelings of powerlessness and frustration. Other workers became disillusioned and despondent, because the delay seemed to illustrate the union's ineffectiveness.[32]

These problems in maintaining morale over lengthy campaigns played into the opposition's hands, leaving workers vulnerable to company propaganda in the preelection period. During Operation Dixie, employers used their newly enshrined rights to "free speech" successfully. Thus, the Taft-Hartley provisions complemented one another, creating both the delay and the means to exploit it. Countless textile elections were lost because of the employers' effective use of the preelection period.[33] At Dacotah Mills in Lexington, North Carolina, William Smith reported that well over 50 percent of workers had been signed up. In addition, "good committees had been set up and it appeared to be an excellent situation." However, "a day or two before the election was held, the company sent out a vicious anti-union letter . . . and we were overwhelmingly defeated the election." In a 1950 election at Mooresville Cotton Mill in Mooresville, North Carolina, the union received only 492 votes, although it had collected 977 cards. Despite repeated defeats, it took a long time for the union to realize that new organizing tactics were needed. A frustrated organizer wrote in the fall of 1949 that "time and time again, we have been carried away by the false notion that because people sign cards, they vote for us. In almost every election I have been in, the TWUA received 30% less votes than it had signed cards." He argued that the union had to wake up and realize that it needed more than expressions of interest in elections.[34]

In many campaigns, companies utilized delays to do far more than simply send out letters. They stepped up their use of intimidation and discriminatory discharge, knowing that the NLRB was too slow to be effective. Companies worked on the principle that "justice delayed is justice denied," as Isadore Katz, the TWUA's leading attorney, called it. Katz was a Jewish New Yorker who authored the TWUA publication *Taft-Hartleyism in Southern Textiles: Feudalism with a New Face*, which detailed the union's problems with federal labor law. Many campaigns were destroyed because of delays. George Johnston, a young veteran who worked as an organizer at Swift Manufacturing Company in Columbus, Georgia, remembered clearly his unhappy experiences with the NLRB. Having successfully signed up a majority of the workforce, union activists were fired. Once the activists had been fired, it was very difficult to rebuild the campaign through the NLRB. The length of time it took the postwar NLRB to deal with the case destroyed the campaign: "Had the NLRB decision been made within weeks after the discharges, we might have announced victory, told everyone that 'the federal government is behind you . . . let's complete the organizing.' But the law's delay had contributed to killing the union." [35]

The provision of the Taft-Hartley Act that removed anti-union citizens' committees from the NLRB's jurisdiction also had an impact on the drive in textiles. The use of these committees—usually led by the local chamber of commerce and other business groups—only occurred in a handful of drives, indicating the wide variety of employer responses to Operation Dixie. Where they were used, however, they played a central role in thwarting unionization, especially in the important Anderson drive. Baldanzi claimed that in Anderson "there seems to be a concentration of the most reactionary and bigoted people in the South. This bigotry and this prejudice seems to be confined chiefly—as is usual in the South—to the Chambers of Commerce, Kiwanis and Lions Clubs, and to the supervision of all factories." The Anderson drive illustrates well the type of extreme emotions that Operation Dixie generated in some textile communities. For example, when Lucy Randolph Mason, the CIO's southern community relations representative, visited the Anderson Chamber of Commerce in 1950, she reported that the secretary's eyes "froze over" when she mentioned that she was from the CIO. The secretary "simply and flatly stated there would be no unions there, *whatever* it might take." It is clear that in addition to their ideological hatred of unionism, Anderson's leaders feared that CIO influence might prevent them from continuing to attract new plants to their community. The citizens' committee was decisive in defeating the CIO at the town's Fiberglas textile plant, the closest the CIO came to taking a mill in Anderson.[36]

The inadequacies of federal protection during Operation Dixie led to a strong sense of disenchantment and frustration with the NLRB.

Organizer Helen Gregory, for example, wrote, "I am fully convinced that we must rely solely on our economic strength in the future, because our experiences of the last few months show conclusively that we cannot rely on the NLRB to carry the ball for us." Another organizer simply declared that "the NLRB is no damn good." Paul Christopher, like Gregory, struggled to find a different way of organizing without relying on the NLRB. He suggested more long-term, educational work that would "thoroughly indoctrinate" workers into unionism, thereby providing them with the psychological strength to resist last-minute attacks. A similar type of approach was belatedly suggested by other strategists.[37]

This type of internal debate showed just how damaging the Taft-Hartley Act and the changed nature of the NLRB were. Publicly, the TWUA and many other unions constantly attacked the act as a "slave labor law" and campaigned for its repeal. However, the amount of private correspondence between union officials showed that behind the rhetoric, they genuinely believed that the act really did hurt Operation Dixie.[38] Lucy Randolph Mason, for example, visited a large selection of the drive's textile campaigns in her work as a CIO community relations representative. The small, gray-haired woman had worked tirelessly to increase acceptance of the CIO in the South for over twenty years and was an experienced and perceptive observer of southern organizing conditions. Mason wrote her friend Paul Christopher in 1948 that "the Taft-Hartley Act is doing just what it was meant to do—slow down, hamper, annoy workers who are trying to build unions." The minutes of the meetings of Tennessee SOC staff reveal frequent references to the Taft-Hartley Act and the weakness of federal protection. In one meeting in 1951, for example, organizer John Brownlee "pointed out that Taft-Hartley was still very much with us, that election delays now give companies the chance to destroy our efforts . . . and that charges do not mean anything." The damage inflicted on Operation Dixie by the slowdown in NLRB procedures is vitally important, especially in its connection with an ongoing historical debate about the contribution of federal labor law to the decline of organized labor.[39]

The Taft-Hartley Act, therefore, was an important factor in the failure of Operation Dixie. However, it should be remembered that the act only came into effect in September 1947, by which time the drive was already in serious trouble. What the act did was create new problems in the latter part of Operation Dixie and provide new weapons for those companies that chose to flout an already-underpowered NLRB. Many companies chose not to take advantage of the act when faced with union campaigns, but even in these cases, Taft-Hartley was important because of the psychological encouragement it gave to anti-union forces. Nowhere was this more important than in the South, where government protection in the 1930s had helped union membership because many workers genuinely believed that the president wanted them to join a union, especially in the 1934 uprising. The Taft-Hartley Act, in contrast, symbolized the national shift to the right that made the organizing climate more hostile than union leaders had imagined when they launched Operation Dixie.[40]

"Everytime We Have an Election in the South, the Race Issue Is Used"

While the Taft-Hartley Act clearly encouraged corporate opposition to the drive, it was not solely responsible for the effectiveness of that opposition. Employers were also able to exploit other powerful issues, especially the race issue. Race was a major problem in textile campaigns, despite the fact that Operation Dixie tried to take a soft line on the issue. Van Bittner's early press releases avoided any lengthy pronouncement on race, saying only that the drive aimed at organizing all southern workers "because they are all God's human beings." This followed the CIO's declared policy of organizing workers regardless of race, creed, or color. Typical of the optimism that accompanied the launching of the drive, Bittner declared confidently that "as far as the South is concerned, we have no negro problem."[41]

The textile industry might have appeared to provide some grounds for the belief that race would not be used to hinder unionization. The southern textile workforce was overwhelmingly white, with blacks confined to nonproduction jobs such as sweepers or janitors. This racial balance came about as the southern textile industry developed after the Civil War by drawing on an abundance of cheap white labor from nearby agricultural areas. The promotion of the industry as the salvation of poor whites, and white workers's resistance to the introduction of blacks into the mills, also contributed to blacks' exclusion. In the 1940s, blacks only made up between 2 and 6 percent of the textile workforce in the main southern states in which the industry was based.[42]

Nevertheless, organizers found that employers used this racial balance to scare workers: managers would claim that the union would threaten their job security by integrating the mills or even by evicting whites altogether. Given that textiles was a low-skill industry where even the most complicated jobs could be easily learned, this threat had some potency. Indeed, the willingness of white textile workers to respond to racial propaganda is central to understanding the problems the CIO encountered during Operation Dixie. Don McKee, who ran Operation Dixie's important textile campaign in Rock Hill, South Carolina, had no doubt about the importance of race to the drive's failure: "The main thing that hurt the CIO drive to organize Dixie at this time was the race question." McKee thought that the race issue was particularly powerful because of its appeal to the workers themselves, a point made by many others. He remembered how employers circulated interracial pictures from CIO publications in several campaigns just prior to the election. He recalled vividly when this occurred in an important defeat at Aragon-Baldwin Mills in Rock Hill in December 1946. Local union workers came up to the young McKee afterward and asked angrily, " 'Why in the hell did you send that pamphlet out?' That was a difficult question to answer because obviously the CIO national policy was nondiscrimination. . . . But how do you explain that to textile workers who are highly racially prejudiced?" Other mills were to repeat this tactic throughout the drive "so that the CIO had to make a policy to be very careful in sending out pamphlets." Many other organizers and TWUA staffers involved in Operation Dixie remembered the damage inflicted by the race issue.[43]

The racism of white workers that was evident in these campaigns illustrated the importance of an independent racial identity among many southern textile workers. This confirms other recent studies, for it is clear that notions of "whiteness" were a central part of the class consciousness of southern textile workers, challenging earlier studies that disputed the autonomy of race from class.[44]

Employers understood how explosive the race issue could be in an industry based on a social, unwritten exclusion of blacks from the mills.[45] Thus, anti-union attorney Frank Constangy, who worked for a large number of anti-union corporations and played a crucial role in formulating their strategy against Operation Dixie, felt that one of the CIO's biggest "mistakes" in textiles was its failure to see the way that even a cautious stand in favor of racial equality threatened the white textile worker: "The race issue is still a strong factor in all considerations. . . . White textile workers are antagonistic, inherently, to organizers, and particularly CIO organizing, because they have a sub-conscious realization that, whether the CIO organizer advocates it or not, that nationally the CIO is committed to the breaking down of the racial barrier." [46] The prominent employer journal the *Textile Bulletin*, whose distribution reputedly included thousands of textile workers, chose to attack Operation Dixie repeatedly on the race issue. Its savage editorials were written by David Clark, a man with a long history of using his publication to advance a variety of conservative causes that he believed in, including opposing the candidacy of Frank Porter Graham for the U.S. Senate in 1950. Clark was an influential conservative, experienced in helping textile manufacturers fight unionization. He constantly portrayed the CIO as an organization primarily interested in integrating the mills. The success of Operation Dixie among black workers in the tobacco industry was used to bolster its claim that the CIO was a black-rights institution.[47] Although it is difficult to substantiate the claim that workers read the *Bulletin* on a regular basis, clippings of its racist editorials were posted on mill bulletin boards in a number of campaigns and were reported to have had a significant effect in the union's defeat.[48]

Faced by this onslaught, textile organizers exercised extreme caution, often at the expense of African American workers, when confronted by racial situations in their campaigns. It was clear that the racial antagonism of white workers to black participation presented organizers with a difficult dilemma. Several drives were held back by the reluctance of organizers and their superiors to base them around black workers, who frequently responded to the CIO more enthusiastically than white workers.[49] Thus, in a drive at the Werthen Bag Corporation in 1950, Christopher reported that excellent progress had been made "among the Negroes employed in the used bag plant." However, he continued that organizers could not build a campaign around these contacts because "by moving into the open first with the Negroes we will be too vulnerable to the charge of being a Negro union. . . . Reports are that not too many of the white workers in the big plant . . . are favorable to organization." [50]

As the campaign progressed, a few more progressive organizers became openly critical of the campaign's attempt to downplay race and avoid the PAC. One of the most vocal critics was David Burgess, a labor intellectual raised in China who was attracted into the labor movement partly because of its progressive racial stance. Working first as an organizer and then within the PAC, Burgess argued that one of the key weaknesses of organized labor in the South was its lack of political power, the product of low political participation among African Americans and poor whites. Indeed, low political participation in the South robbed southern workers of politicians accountable to a labor vote. This was a crucial difference, given that actions by political figures had proved central to labor progress in a number of labor conflicts in the North in the 1930s.[51]

Others outside the drive also criticized the CIO's racial policy. Leading Communist Junius Scales, who in the 1940s led the party's half-hearted efforts to organize textile workers in the Carolinas, thought that "the most fateful decision Van Bittner had to make in that operation was to play it soft on the race issue." In the *New Republic*, A. G. Mezerik claimed that "Operation Dixie failed because it failed to face up to the fact that segregation is the issue of the South." If the campaign had been based on the abolition of segregation, Mezerik argued, at least "a sound, if small, corps of dependable and informed workers would now exist." [52]

Although these were isolated voices, they were supported by the fact that despite all the efforts to downplay the race issue, it was still used very effectively by southern textile employers. Whatever public stance the CIO sought to take, as an institution it was perceived as a threat to segregation. Although organizers were informed that they must not approach the race issue in such a way as to allow "reactionary anti-labor forces to take advantage," these forces managed to inflict great damage anyway. Illustrating the damage that had been done, Paul Christopher wrote Franz Daniel, for example, that an election had been lost at Fair Forest Finishing Company in Spartanburg, South Carolina, because "evidently you were unable to overcome the anti-union prejudice which developed over the race issue." Reports from other campaigns told of similar problems. At Patterson Cotton Mill in Roanoke Rapids, North Carolina, R. C. Thomas reported that the company had stirred up the race issue and divided the campaign, with the result that "the white workers will not meet with the colored workers." Helen Gregory, like other organizers, found workers at DuPont bothered about the "Negro issue."[53]

Above all, the cautious racial approach made no difference to the Ku Klux Klan, which was reborn in many textile towns where organizing campaigns were launched. Journalist and maverick liberal Stetson Kennedy infiltrated the Klan for the SOC and found that it had considerable influence among textile workers, illustrating again the willingness of workers themselves to respond to the image of the CIO as a threat to segregation.[54]

Klan opposition was instrumental in defeating several textile campaigns. Its success in opposing Operation Dixie rested on the involvement of both company representatives and rank-and-file workers. Its greatest contribution came in the Bibb Mills drive in Macon and Porterdale, Georgia. Kennedy's reports from the meetings that he attended described how a Klavern that was set up in Macon quickly attracted new members. At one meeting in the summer of 1946, a group of men from Bibb Mills, including the police chief, were inducted into the Klan, and at subsequent meetings they reported back on their efforts to destroy the Bibb drive. Having been instrumental in destroying the Bibb campaign, Macon Klansmen helped revive the Klan in Knoxville, another important center for Operation Dixie. Kennedy traveled to Knoxville and found a resurgent Klan that "is giving Bittner and the entire CIO hell." In South Carolina, a state investigation revealed that the Kleagle of the Carolina Klan had solicited contributions from textile manufacturers to organize working crews to break up organization.[55]

In Tennessee, the Klan's opposition was led by Kleagle J. B. Stoner, who told Klan members that "Operation Dixie will be all right if we can work into them and take it away from them." As Kennedy's 1946 interview with him makes clear, Stoner was virulently antisemitic, describing Adolf Hitler as "too moderate" and declaring that his own neo-Nazi party would eliminate Jews via gas chambers, electric chairs and "whatever seems most appropriate." Later, Stoner set up the National States Rights Party (NSRP) and ran for governor of Georgia in 1970 on the

NSRP ticket. During the 1940s, Stoner emphasized the large numbers of Jews active in the labor movement and fought hard against Operation Dixie, establishing strong Klan chapters in several towns where campaigns were in progress. Several union campaigns in Tennessee were indeed thwarted partly through the active support of workers, often union members, for the Klan. These members often saw no contradiction between their membership in the Klan and in the union. One of the most disturbing Klan-related occurrences was its role in defeating a CIO drive to organize the American Bemberg plant in Elizabethton, Tennessee. This plant employed large numbers of women and had been the setting for a major strike in 1929. Organizer Dorothy Daniel reported that "KKK, which has not been active in Elizabethton in many years, has been revived within one week of the beginning of our membership drive. They are making shows of morality by burning crosses before homes of sexually immoral [*sic*]. Most workers think well of KKK." The drive in Elizabethton petered out, according to Daniel and fellow organizer Helen Gregory, because the Klan had helped produce a feeling among women workers "that the CIO is not respectable." A Klan revival also greeted a textile drive at the American Enka plant in Lowlands, Tennessee.[56]

The drive at the Standard-Coosa-Thatcher mills in Chattanooga illustrated both the subtle ways that the Klan could have a negative influence on a union campaign and the fact that this influence was strengthened by workers' racial fears. The race issue began to pose problems in the fall of 1946 when the union lost its hall, which it had been renting from the Junior Order of the United American Mechanics. Organizers reported that they had lost the hall because of pressure from the Klan: "the Klan meets in the same hall and they met this past Friday night and we were told on Sunday that we could no longer use the hall. I think the Juniors and the Klan are working together and along with the company to do all they can to cause us to lose the Thatcher election." In addition, many union members—"the Klan group"—were also members of the Klan. The loss of the union hall turned out to be a bigger problem than it might appear. A new hall was found, but most workers refused to go to it, because "the members did not like the location because of the amount of Negroes in that neighborhood and that was the reason they would not go to the meetings." Given that meetings were central to the success of any campaign, this was a major problem. The opposition of the Klan prevented the SOC from getting its own union hall back, and workers continued to refuse to come to the new center. By the fall of 1948, meetings had been reduced to a farce, "not attended except by one man, now and then," and the Standard campaign petered out.[57]

It is important not to exaggerate the influence of the Klan during Operation Dixie. Its role was confined to specific campaigns, and in many areas, particularly in the crucial textile state of North Carolina, there was no mention of it. Its influence was geographically limited, but it was important within these confines.

While employers consistently utilized prejudices against African Americans during Operation Dixie, their use of racism was not confined to issues of black versus white. Company letters that workers received on the eve of elections repeatedly emphasized the ethnicity of the TWUA's leaders and suggested that this in itself constituted a strong enough reason to stay away from the union. These letters took on a standard form, with the most exotic names from the TWUA's executive council plucked out and listed. The names were often misspelled, sometimes by mistake and in other cases to increase their "foreign" sound. In a typical letter, for example, workers at the Virginia Cotton Mills in Swepsonville, North Carolina, were asked, "Here are the names of some of the main leaders of this union—Reevie [sic], Baldanzie [sic], Schaufenbil, Unger, Chupka, Sgambato. Where do you think these men came from? Are their backgrounds, their beliefs, their faith and principles anything like yours and mine?" In one 1948 speech, Baldanzi referred to this type of opposition, much of which was directed at him: "We have been confronted with all kinds of vicious, fascist propaganda[,] . . . racial bigotry of all descriptions. . . . We have had them tell the workers 'If you vote for TWUA, they will put Negro foremen in every department, because it is a Nigger union.' We have literature all over the South with Baldanzi's picture, pointing out the big, long nose, the way he looks, that he is a foreigner." [58]

Much of the employers' material was also antisemitic. Ironically, this literature was even circulated in campaigns where the mill owners were Jewish, particularly in the mills of the Lowenstein and Cone families, both of which owned large mill chains in the South. On one occasion, when the CIO was trying to organize a Lowenstein mill in Anderson, the plant manager made a preelection speech calling on workers to "keep the CIO kikes out of this county." Baldanzi wrote to company president Archie Joslin about this. Baldanzi admitted that the TWUA "might make more headway were I to instruct my staff to engage in an antisemitic campaign directed at your company." This letter had little effect, however; organizers at Jewish-owned firms continued to complain to their leaders that antisemitic literature was being used. At Cone Mills, organizers wrote that supervisors were distributing *Militant Truth* and other anti-union publications that were virulently antisemitic, with the apparent consent of the Cone family, who lived in the area.[59]

The type of literature used, and its damaging impact, illustrates the explosive nature of the race issue at this time. Employers used the issue, and many workers responded, illustrating how embedded racism was in all strata of southern society. Even some southern organizers opposed the CIO's racial policy. There was brief talk of a separate southern union, known as the Dixie Organizing Committee, to be led by organizers who claimed that "instead of $1 million and two years to organize the South, it will take $5 million and they still won't succeed if they don't leave the Negro out of it." [60] The severity of the problems posed by the race issue were frequently apparent at TWUA conventions. The 1950 and 1956 TWUA conventions saw demonstrations and impassioned speeches by southern delegates when even weakly worded civil rights resolutions were debated. At the 1950 TWUA convention, for example, many southern delegates spoke against a resolution supporting civil rights. Ed Kirkland, a business agent from Columbia, South Carolina, opposed the resolution "on the grounds that this type of resolution is what is making the organization drive in the South as hard as it is today." He explained that when a drive was launched, "the first thing they put out is leaflets saying the CIO is in favor of the FEPC," and he added that "even if the FEPC is passed, in my local and in the mills where I come from, we probably will defy the law." [61] At a later convention condemning White Citizens' Councils, many southern representatives also spoke out. Rene Berthiaume, the TWUA's director in Rock Hill and a northerner, declared that "every time we have an election in the South, the race issue is used." He added that a recent issue of *Textile Labor* "caused us all kinds of hell in the South." A dramatic speech by business agent M. L. Wood illustrated how civil rights could trap TWUA leaders between local and national priorities. Seventy percent of his local belonged to the White Citizens' Council, Wood explained, and "my own wife . . . calls me a Nigger lover. . . . I assure you that if you pass this resolution, that tomorrow morning's newspapers will have something on it and our members will drop out of the union." A lively debate ended when the resolution was passed narrowly, with "confusion in the hall." [62]

Given the strength of racism, the CIO also deserves some credit for the limited stance it took. The TWUA itself, while hardly the most progressive CIO union, made a repeated commitment to support civil rights against the wishes of many of its southern staff and membership. Similarly, in 1950, Lucy Randolph Mason wrote to all major southern churches for statements opposing discrimination and asking for interracial pictures. She hoped to put together a pamphlet to show workers that the CIO's race policy was not as isolated as employers might have them believe. The responses she received provide an indication of how progressive the CIO's policy really was, as most churches admitted that they were "not entirely free from race discrimination," and none provided interracial pictures. These responses show how little support the CIO's racial policy could find and illustrate that it was progressive by the standards of the late 1940s.[63]

Overall, the race issue was clearly an integral part of Operation Dixie's failure in textiles, although the drive's leaders did not claim that it was the most important factor in this failure. As Franz Daniel concluded, "I do not think you should over-play the race prejudice, but it certainly deserves some space in any story of the job here." [64]

"The Commies Are Always in Our Hair"

The race issue was a powerful obstacle to overcome partly because of its ruthless and repeated use by employers. With equal frequency and ruthlessness, employers also used the slur that the CIO was dominated by Communists. In the immediate postwar period, indeed, there was an upsurge in anticommunism that had grave consequences for Operation Dixie. The CIO itself became divided between left- and right-wing forces, culminating in the expulsion of the federation's left-wing unions in 1949–50. Great damage was thereby inflicted on the prospects for southern organizing, because many of the unions that were expelled had been the most successful in the South, particularly the Food, Tobacco, Agricultural, and Allied Workers Union (FTA). Operation Dixie lost unions that had been "a beacon" for unorganized workers, as well as many dedicated personnel.[65]

The impact of anticommunism on the textile drive is, however, less obvious than that of race. The TWUA was completely unaffected by the battle between left and right in the union movement. One of the CIO's more conservative unions, the TWUA was fiercely anticommunist. Communists had never penetrated it, largely because a clause in the union's constitution barred them from membership. The only location in the textile South where the Communists had any influence was at Erwin Mills in Durham, North Carolina. Here Junius Scales, the Party's chairman for the Carolinas, maintained a small cell and published a paper that was covertly distributed to workers in bathrooms and on windshields. Despite these efforts, Scales, an amiable man who was imprisoned for his beliefs during the McCarthy era, admitted that the Communists never made any real headway in Durham. The TWUA's top leaders—Rieve, Baldanzi, and Pollock—were committed anticommunists. As Scales remembered it, "They saw Communists under every loom and every spinning frame. If there was militant action, they suspected Communists of being in there, and unfortunately they did us too much honor because we didn't have that many connections." Scales thought Baldanzi was so anticommunist that he was "really warped." The southern press, indeed, never attacked the TWUA along these lines, and the union was also undisturbed by the Taft-Hartley Act's requirement that union officials sign non-Communist affidavits.[66]

What made the race issue particularly damaging in textile campaigns was its proven ability to strike a chord among many workers and divide them from the union. Textile organizers' reports bore testimony to these problems. Those same reports, however, did not cite anticommunist propaganda as having the same effect.[67] In general, it is clear that the race issue had a far more powerful appeal to southern textile workers than the Communist issue. Bill Evans, a CP member and shop steward at Erwin Mills, remembered these problems in his attempts to increase Communist membership in Durham: "There were workers in Erwin Mills who didn't know the difference between Communism and rheumatism. . . . All they had to do was raise the race issue; it would create much more interest and excitement among workers than the Communist issue."[68]

These problems did not mean that the Communist issue was irrelevant to Operation Dixie in textiles. Employers used anticommunist propaganda heavily in the preelection attacks that were so effective in defeating textile campaigns. The Communist issue was useful because it dovetailed very conveniently with other issues that were used, particularly the race issue. Junius Scales remembered that "from the company side it was a perfect two-pronged offensive: everybody knew that a Communist was a Nigger lover, so they were able to play on the racism of white workers." Thus, anticommunism was important on a general level, providing extra rhetoric with which employers could attack the textile campaigns, but it did not figure as a component by which workers themselves rejected union representation.[69]

Thus, a mix of anticommunism, racism, and Christianity was exploited by several scurrilous publications that appeared in many textile drives. An Evall G. Johnston, otherwise known as "Parson Jack," produced a viciously anti-union publication titled *The Trumpet*, which was circulated mainly in Georgia. Johnston had links with the Klan and tried to organize a White Protestant Christian Party in 1947. After Operation Dixie, Johnston continued his racist ministry through publication and touring sermons. Sherman Patterson produced *Militant Truth*, described by author John Roy Carleson as "a combination of . . . Bible-belt fundamentalist, Flag-waving, and Red and labor baiting." It was a widely circulated pamphlet by another racist demagogue, however—Joe Kamp's *Communist Carpetbaggers in Operation Dixie*—that best illustrated the linkage of Communism with the race issue. Kamp argued that the South "has been selected as a battleground of the revolution" because it had "an enormous Negro population and the Communists have found their agitation is most effective among the Negro people." "Un-American" agitators would therefore incite not only a "class war" but "a bitter and vicious race war."[70]

It is important to try to ascertain the amount of damage that these publications caused the textiles arm of Operation Dixie. The strongest case in which one of them contributed directly to an organizing defeat was the Bibb Mills drive. The company chose to respond to the CIO drive by mailing a special edition of *The Trumpet* to all of its 8,000 employees. *The Trumpet* obliged by threatening workers with discharge and violence if they signed union cards, and it clearly played a role in the way the Bibb drive petered out after a promising start. Thus, the NLRB mentioned *The Trumpet* as influential in the union's defeat when it found the company guilty of unfair labor practices.[71] The negative influence of *Militant Truth* was mentioned in several different reports, particularly in campaigns in Tennessee where the Klan was also active.

The financial resources of men such as Patterson and Johnston made their publications a real threat. Parson Jack, for example, had the financial backing of enough southern textile manufacturers that he could mail his publication to workers in any plant where the SOC was planning to organize. In 1949 Patterson wrote privately that he had a circulation of 50,000. He added, "We do reach all Congressmen and Senators and feel that we carry considerable weight." These right-wing forces were well-financed and closely connected. In contrast, the CIO never had enough personnel or money to counter the influence of these publications as it hoped to. Lucy Randolph Mason, who spent a considerable amount of time trying to win community support for the SOC, complained to a friend that "nothing has ever been done to really unearth and uncover *Militant Truth* and the *Trumpet* because of the pressure of other work." She explained that the CIO needed "at least one person in each state who does all the things that organizers don't have time to do." She admitted that all she could achieve was to "make a hit or miss at doing that here or there." Meanwhile, Mason's colleague John Ramsay was still collecting information on his own for a pamphlet that would attack *Militant Truth* long after the major textile drives had collapsed.[72]

Large sections of the press, employers, and the AFL also repeatedly attacked the CIO as Communist. Bypassing the less controversial TWUA, these sources emphasized that it was the CIO that was being offered to textile workers. The spirit of McCarthyism permeated many campaigns, and even organizations whose connections to the CIO were tenuous came under attack in campaign material.[73]

The effect of all this propaganda was to ensure that the CIO clearly lost the public relations war in Operation Dixie. From the beginning, an important part of the campaign was to promote the idea that the CIO was a mature organization and to cultivate powerful allies such as businessmen and clergy who were vital to the CIO's future in the South. Lucy Mason and John Ramsay were employed permanently in visiting community leaders, primarily those in textile communities. Both of them described a shift to the right in public opinion in their reports, a change that made it increasingly difficult to disassociate the CIO from Communism. It was the progressivism of the early CIO that had attracted many and continued to do so. Yet this progressivism became a burden in an era where many were unable to distinguish it from Communism. As Mason wrote with frustration, "The CIO does not follow the Communist party line. . . . If the Communists also happen to believe in some of these measures, the rest of us Democrats cannot reject our beliefs because Communists may think the same way." The prevalence of the association was depressing. Mason wrote that her own pastor, who was "supposed to be one of the most liberal ministers in Atlanta," was himself guilty of "unconsciously linking the labor movement with other movements he fears." She added, "This is all too typical of the church, or its representatives, pretty generally." [74]

Indeed, the work of Ramsay and Mason to win the support of the clergy yielded few results. Both came across many ministers who associated the CIO with Communism.[75] What was more significant, however, was that even when they encountered favorable ministers, most of them preferred to stay neutral in textile organizing campaigns, while anti-union preachers took an active role in defeating the union in several textile campaigns.[76] Ramsay felt that his inability to make more progress was related to the effective postwar propaganda put out by his opponents, which had helped to erode the ties between the church and labor.[77]

Clearly, the shift to the right in national public opinion and the rise of anticommunism had an impact on the textiles efforts of Operation Dixie, providing new weapons for opponents and preventing the CIO from gaining legitimacy in the South. While organizers failed to mention anticommunism as a specific factor in textile election defeats, it was always an important background issue that the SOC was unable to throw off. As Paul Christopher complained, "The Commies are always in our hair." [78]

Thus, the organizing climate in which Operation Dixie functioned did not prove as favorable as the CIO's leaders had anticipated. Unforeseen events—including the passage of the Taft-Hartley Act and the start of the Cold War—equipped opponents with new powers to defeat organizing efforts. Faced by determined opposition, the drive needed to muster its resources wisely. However, sporadic feuding with the AFL wasted valuable resources and yielded few gains.[79] Moreover, from 1947 onward, SOC staff were increasingly used in a variety of roles, especially in nurturing established textile unions, which were desperately short of resources themselves. In doing so, they achieved a great deal to help the labor movement in the South and provided a positive epitaph for Operation Dixie. As Paul Christopher wrote, during much of Operation Dixie his staff members spent up to 40 percent of their time on vital non-organizing work, especially working in strike situations where elections had been won but no contract had resulted. He added, "To those of our colleagues who criticize and favor folding up the southern CIO drive, complaining about a lack of progress, I would say that they should pause to consider where our Southern CIO movement would be today if the CIO Organizing Committee had not been in existence." [80]

chapter three   **"What Do We Need a Union For?**

We've Never Had It So Good"

The Problem of Rising Wages

in Operation Dixie

The race issue, the Communist issue, and the impact of the Taft-Hartley Act were all major components in the failure of Operation Dixie and have been recognized as such. However, their relevance is limited to campaigns where employers chose to fight unionization attempts by deliberately flouting the NLRB, utilizing the race issue, and so forth. Taken as a whole, they do not fully explain the reasons for the collapse of the organizing campaign in textiles, for in many cases textile employers chose to fight the drive by keeping wages up with the union pay scale. This tactic proved to be very effective because it harnessed specific social and economic changes originating in World War II and used their power against the union. It proved very difficult to sell southern textile workers the economic benefits of unionization, as the drive aimed to, because of the significant economic advances that workers had made during the war years and continued to make thereafter. Thus, Operation Dixie's textiles campaign failed because of the combination of general factors already discussed with economic and social changes specific to textiles.

What makes this interpretation particularly compelling is the wide variety of evidence supporting it. The negative effect of rising wages is repeatedly described in the accounts of both labor and management sources, as well as in the contemporary press. Rising wages, in particular, were the factor that most organizers and TWUA participants identified when they analyzed the drive's failure. Despite this widespread testimony, the role of wages has not been recognized at all in existing historical accounts.[1]

Free-Riding in Operation Dixie

Organizers who worked in textile campaigns during Operation Dixie remembered vividly the effect that the increased standard of living had on their efforts. Joel Leighton was a young, idealistic New England schoolteacher who began organizing for the TWUA shortly before World War II. A tall man of slender build, like many TWUA activists Leighton was attracted into the labor movement by the labor upsurge and optimism of the New Deal. He worked on many of the union's most successful campaigns, including the unionization of the huge Dan River Mills in Danville, Virginia, in 1942. Because of his successful record, Leighton worked on some of Operation Dixie's most important campaigns, including the Cannon drive and the Standard-Coosa-Thatcher campaign. Looking back over his lengthy involvement in southern textile organizing, Leighton observed that the war was a watershed in the TWUA's fortunes in the South. Shortly before the war, the union "really had some momentum in organizing the South." During the war, this momentum was continued through the framework of the NWLB. Once the war ended, however, the union had lost this momentum because the organizing climate had been transformed by wartime wages. Leighton explained, "Daddy came back from the war and started to organize again and found people saying 'Well, we have a car now, we've never had an automobile before, we have indoor plumbing, we have better housing, we have better wages. What do we need a union for? We've never had it so good.'" The situation was particularly problematic for organizers, because workers felt that "we don't need a union to do this, it just happens." As Leighton explained, "They'd never had to strike or anything, Uncle Sam took care of them." Organizing became particularly difficult because increased wages had enriched workers' lives in so many different ways. Leighton remembered, for example, that on trips into textile towns on a Saturday or Sunday he would see "the women nicely dressed in good, clean print dresses, whereas before the war mostly they would look a little ragged." The "socially primitive" living conditions of the prewar years had begun to change; workers now had their first disposable income to support their church or engage in new leisure pursuits. Leighton felt that these improvements led to "an underlying feeling that a union was not necessary." In a 1994 interview, he added, "It has always been my feeling" that it was this change that was responsible for the failure of Operation Dixie in textiles, because it was prevalent in every campaign that he worked on.[2]

What made rising wages especially damaging for the TWUA was that union and nonunion workers were able to share in them equally. During

Operation Dixie, nonunion manufacturers continued their wartime practice of matching union pay scales and benefits to forestall organization and secure labor in the booming postwar textile economy. The lack of a pay differential between union and nonunion plants effectively destroyed Operation Dixie's attempts to emphasize the economic benefits of unionization. Don McKee, like Leighton, was an Operation Dixie organizer who had also had experience before the war. McKee remembered the problems caused by nonunion workers receiving pay increases. When he tried to sell a union-led wage increase to unorganized workers in Rock Hill, he found that they had already received it. Most questioned why they needed to pay union dues to receive what they were already getting, while often, even as they refused to sign union cards, they thanked McKee for the union's efforts in fattening their pay envelopes. Others asked when the union was "going after" its next wage increase. The impressions of McKee are supported by another Rock Hill organizer, David Burgess, who expressed the belief that pay raises given to unorganized workers "constituted an effective method of weakening our organizing campaign in Rock Hill."[3]

Written reports from textile campaigns confirm that the central problem was rising wages coupled with the lack of a pay differential between organized and unorganized workers. In many cases, unorganized workers made it clear that they were very aware of conditions prevailing in union plants. Organizer John Neal, for example, reported from a losing campaign at Standard Knitting Mills in Knoxville, Tennessee, that workers claimed "that they did not need a union at the Standard Knitting Mill, that the union couldn't give them anything that the company hasn't already, they get wage increases every time the union gets one." Other organizers who worked on the Standard campaign reported the same problem. Orvill Munzer told fellow organizers at a Tennessee staff meeting that "this is a long campaign as the wages were not too bad and they are getting other benefits similar to a union contract. Of course not as good, but they are hard to be convinced. They are slow to sign cards." So slow, in fact, that the Standard campaign, into which the drive's planners had invested a great deal of time and resources, was abandoned without an election.[4]

The same problems were reported by organizers in a wide variety of plants, both big and small, and in several different states. Thus, one organizer wrote from a campaign at a relatively small mill, Roxboro Cotton Mills in Roxboro, North Carolina, that organizing was at a standstill because workers had "union wages, vacations with pay, and two paid holidays." One of the largest and most important textile campaigns, the Avondale Mills drive, was suffering from the same problem. Alabama director Edmund J. Ryan reported that only 1,000 out of 7,500 eligible workers had been signed up after four months of intensive organizing.

The main reason for this was that "Comer [referring to mill owner Donald Comer] is still paying 17% above our wage scale . . . so that we are unable to advance or get much interest." The local newspaper, the *Pell City News*, reported that Avondale workers were "unwilling to trade their higher than union wages, bonuses, and hospitalization facilities for a scale far below that to which they are accustomed." Ryan made clear, however, that Comer's high wage policy was not the only method being used to fight the union. He wrote that along with its wage policy, the company was using "a very vicious system of outright firing, discrimination, and every conceivable way to terrorize workers whom he finds belong to the union." At Avondale, as in other campaigns, companies used two very different tactics side by side to destroy the union's campaign—high wages to reduce the desire for organization, and discrimination against union members to frighten workers away from the SOC.[5]

In many instances, companies clearly preferred to match union conditions rather than have a union. The economic boom engulfing the southern textile industry in these years was decisive here, for mill owners could grant large wage increases and still make substantial profits. The prosperity of the industry gave mill owners considerable freedom of action, making it easy for them to grant union wages and benefits en masse when an organizing campaign was launched at their mill. Paul Christopher reported from a lost drive at the Southern Webbing Company in Greensboro, Tennessee, that on the eve of the election, 80 percent of workers were signed up. However, the company promptly granted workers "everything that union contracts have [and] the committee disintegrated." Timely wage increases also played a role in defeating several campaigns in the important Gaston County area in North Carolina. Organizer Jim Prestwood reported from Bloom Mill in Gastonia, for example, that "the interest in Bloom is bad at present. It seems the ten cent raise the company put into effect has served its purpose." Similar reports came from other Gaston County locations.[6]

One of the central goals of the textile campaign was to target workers in chain mills where the TWUA already had a foothold among some plants. A number of large southern companies, most notably the Cone Mills chain of Greensboro, North Carolina, had been penetrated by the TWUA during World War II, but due to the structure of the textile industry, many more plants remained to be organized within these chains. Organizers found, however, that not only did companies copy union conditions in their nonunion plants but that workers there were especially likely to compare their own conditions with those prevailing in the union mills. Thus, in a drive at an American Thread Company plant in Tennessee, workers told the organizer that "unions would not help them because they have practically the same benefits" as workers at the company's unionized mill in Dalton, Georgia. Similar problems dogged the

SOC's repeated efforts to complete unionization of Cone Mills. Organizer Jim Fullerton reported, for example, that workers at a Cone plant in Salisbury, North Carolina, received "union wages, vacations with pay, and have two paid holidays." They were "well acquainted with our Greensboro situation and even our contracts." At one point the TWUA's director in Greensboro, Bill Billingsley, explained that the main reason most of Cone was nonunion was that "the company takes care to extend all of its nonunion employees every significant gain made by the union and so there is much less incentive for these employees to join the union than would otherwise be the case." Companies also proved willing to match the pay of a unionized mill if it was close to them geographically. Thus, Paul Christopher complained that he was unable to make any progress in textile campaigns in the Knoxville area because companies matched "all benefits TWUA-CIO local 513 members have at Brookside Mills in Knoxville." [7]

The improving wages that southern textile workers were enjoying tended to reinforce their reluctance to embrace unionism and could also solidify their identification with the company, a factor historians have often viewed as a block to unionization. The TWUA's own publication, *Textile Labor*, viewed the granting of increased wages to unorganized workers in this light. An article in 1949 claimed that "since the start of the war, paternalism rather than violence has been the South's best weapon against TWUA. Wages were kept close to union levels. Working conditions were improved." Similarly, Edmund Ryan characterized Comer's high-wage strategy as "very paternalistic." Organizers indeed frequently complained that these tactics increased company loyalty. One TWUA official, for example, remarked after a wage increase put into effect at Cone Mills's large nonunion plant, "White Oak workers think that Clarence Cone and his brother are still their father and keeper." [8]

Organizers often came across individual workers who rebuffed their efforts on the grounds that they considered their pay good. Organizer H. V. Batchelor, for example, talked to a worker in Newberry, South Carolina, who "said union couldn't do anything for him as he was already making $1.05 an hour." Another "said he wasn't interested in the union, he said he had a good job and the company was good to him, he said he made $48.70 per week for 36 hours." Workers reasoned that their deal was a good one, and they saw no reason to take the considerable risk of joining a union. One loom fixer told Carl Holt that he "could not see the need of a union because the workers made good money." Like many other workers that organizers encountered, this fixer used purely economic rather than ideological grounds to decide against the union. He even informed Holt "that he did not have anything against unions. He gave me names and addresses of other fixers at the plant." It is clear that while some workers may have had a variety of reasons for being reluctant to sign a union card, the impact of higher wages reinforced this reluctance.[9]

Southern textile workers, however, were still paid considerably less than workers in other mass-production industries, as the TWUA repeatedly pointed out. While textile wages were still low, it was the rate of increase that was fatal for the TWUA. In percentage terms, textile wages had increased far more than those of other mass-production workers between 1941 and 1947. Ten years before Operation Dixie most southern textile workers had been making less than twelve dollars a week. The rate at which wages increased, and its impact on organizing, was explored well by a number of press articles on the drive. A New England journalist named Howard S. Rains toured the South in the early 1950s to observe the reasons for the failure of Operation Dixie's textiles campaign. He concluded that "the main explanation is that most mill workers have improved themselves tremendously in a financial way over the past few years." In New England there had also been wage boosts, "but the gains have not been so sharp." Rains stated that the rate of southern increase was "very important" because "the worker who feels content— whether he should or not—is difficult to organize." [10]

The southern press followed Operation Dixie keenly, and several of the larger papers probed the reasons for the failure of textile organizing. They, too, emphasized the fact that southern textile workers' standard of living was undergoing a dramatic increase independent of unionism. The *Charlotte News*, for example, quoted a textile union official who claimed that "the biggest obstacle his organizers have faced is the memory of the worker himself. The average worker, he reported, remembers the day when he worked sixty hours a week for $15 and less. Now with higher pay—about $1.26 an hour—and higher living standards, he gives little thought to joining a union." [11]

The *Greensboro Daily News* examined management's perspective and found that managers tended to agree with this view. In a series of articles exploring the failure of textile organizing, an anonymous "leading textile manufacturer" claimed that the most important factor was the rise in workers' economic standards. Since the war, "workers have had full time occupation and full pay. A labor union just can't win under those conditions." Interestingly, this industrialist also specifically rejected the idea that the failure of textile organizing was the result of worker culture: "he tended to discard the conclusions . . . which suggested that the major reasons for the failure are worker individualism and distrust of the outsider. The net purchasing power of the worker has risen, he says." Manufacturers also pointed out that mainly due to the New Deal, a large part of the textile unions' program had been usurped by government: "we now have minimum wages and laws providing good working conditions. The wage and hour law is an example." [12]

Southern organizers were not used to confronting the problems caused by rising wages. In the past, southern organizing had met with violent resistance. As *Fortune* magazine pointed out, in contrast to the organizing drives of 1934 and 1937, in Operation Dixie there were "no road barricades to halt the union flying squads" and no machine guns perched on top of mills. Southerners reacted to Operation Dixie with apathy because of "the golden salve of prosperity." Wage gains given to unorganized workers had put unions organizers on the defensive, forcing them to emphasize the "less tangible benefits of unionization."[13]

Given the violent resistance to the southern campaigns in many communities, *Fortune* clearly exaggerated the break between Operation Dixie and earlier textile drives. Nevertheless, there was such a break. Although the thinking of management during Operation Dixie is far less documented than that of the union, this break can be traced in the changing nature of industry publications such as the *Textile Bulletin* and the *Southern Textile News*.[14] These publications remained anti-union, but they began to show an increased sensitivity to labor relations that indicated why so many companies fought Operation Dixie through wage increases rather than open resistance. Management indeed claimed that Operation Dixie would fail because they had evolved "a healthy labor relations formula that precludes unionization. This formula includes adequate and just wages, bonuses, paid vacations and paid holidays." This approach was typified by Burlington Industries, an industry leader in personnel matters. Under the pioneering leadership of founder and president J. Spencer Love, in 1954 Burlington became the largest textile company in the world. Burlington exemplified not only the phenomenal changes in economic standards that were taking place but also the way that the industry increasingly publicized the increases to promote a more modern image, moving away from the traditional association of textiles with poverty and substandard living conditions. Burlington, like other large companies, also recognized early on the role that rising wages could play in keeping their workers nonunion. Burlington's approach involved granting wages higher than those prevailing in the union sector, extending fringe benefits, and offering a modern employee relations program. This approach helped the company to retain labor and avoid unionization throughout the 1940s and 1950s.[15]

Management journals of this period illustrated that manufacturers were willing to use the postwar economic boom to make improvements in working conditions. They were also driven to these changes by the need to make the textile industry attractive to workers in an era of labor shortage. Articles urged management to become sensitive to workers' needs because the availability of work meant that workers "no longer fear the boss, nor worry about his displeasure." New techniques were needed, as "the day when a department head is chosen because he is big enough to lick everyone else in the room is passing." Feedback from different mills revealed various schemes, including suggestion boxes, increased use of the open-door policy, and a greater emphasis on encouraging promotion from the ranks. Many of these changes were undertaken consciously to resist unionization.[16]

It is clear that many southern textile executives enjoyed the opportunity to use the postwar boom to raise wages. Nathaniel Gregory, a young management trainee who was later to become vice president of Erwin Mills in Durham, remembered that during the 1930s many executives were ashamed of the industry's "horribly low" wages but were unable to raise them because of the depression. In the postwar years, the industry was anxious to shake off its reputation for exploitation and low wages in order to attract good workers.[17] Signifying this change was the newly formed Textile Committee on Public Relations, which handled the industry's press releases and was chaired by prominent southern mill owner Charles Cannon. The main theme of the committee's arguments, and a central argument of southern management in this era, was that "we are no longer the sick man of industry, employer of child labor, low wages, and can be used as a whipping boy by anyone who may wish to come along." The committee chided mill owners who wrote to it calling for a more confrontational position against the CIO, telling them that although they "shared the desire to slug it out and undertake a direct challenge to an organization such as the CIO," it was better to raise wages and fight unionization through constructive means. Utilizing these ideas, textile campaigns in Operation Dixie saw the blanket use of preelection letters as management's most consistent weapon. These letters cited the wage gains that workers had been able to make, along with the fact that these gains had occurred without a union. Workers were repeatedly informed that they were already receiving the benefits that the CIO was promising them. Thus, management's new approach tended to encourage workers' sense of identification with the company, in line with wider industrial-relations thinking of the 1940s.[18]

Rethinking the Cannon Campaign

It is difficult to place enough emphasis on the importance of the campaign to unionize Cannon Mills to the overall fate of Operation Dixie. George Baldanzi, for example, declared simply that the Cannon drive was "the most important and the most significant in the South." The unions saw the Cannon campaign as vital primarily for strategic and economic considerations. The Cannon drive was central to Operation Dixie's strategy of winning the biggest plants in the textile industry. During this period, Cannon Mills was the largest textile company in the South, employing 25,000 workers in seventeen mills. Its size dwarfed other major southern companies; it employed more than twice the number of workers as the biggest southern mill the TWUA had under contract, Dan River Mills in Danville, Virginia. Moreover, its operations were concentrated exclusively around the company-owned town of Kannapolis, situated some twenty miles north of Charlotte in North Carolina's industrial Piedmont. This concentrated location was unusual for a company of Cannon's size and increased its attraction as an organizing target. Union leaders knew that if they could organize Cannon, they would have captured a strong foothold in the South that would greatly help them to organize other mills.[19]

These economic and strategic factors cannot alone explain the fascination—perhaps the obsession—that textile unions, particularly the TWUA, have had with Cannon Mills. Until the 1980s, Kannapolis was an unincorporated company town par excellence, the largest in the world. Cannon Mills, which was family-owned, controlled every conceivable aspect of life in Kannapolis. This gave the town enormous symbolic significance for the TWUA. *Textile Labor*, for example, described Kannapolis as "the domain of King Cannon," a place where "the mill guards are cops" and where every aspect of life was controlled by a company that workers both identified with and feared. The most prominent member of the Cannon family in this period, Charles A. Cannon, was a short, plump, middle-aged man. Despite his rather genial appearance, Charles Cannon was probably the most powerful southern textile manufacturer at this time, regarded by many in the TWUA as the voice of the southern textile industry. In seeking to unionize Cannon mills, the TWUA sought not only to conquer the largest southern textile company but to topple the whole structure of the paternalistic mill-village system.[20]

The commitment of textile unions to organize Cannon Mills is clear. In 1921 and 1934 the mills experienced major strikes, both of which were unsuccessful. In addition, during World War II a major organizing drive at Cannon failed. After the collapse of the 1946 campaign, there were repeated organizing attempts in the 1950s and 1960s. The TWUA's successor, the Amalgamated Clothing and Textile Workers Union (ACTWU), continued the tradition of defeat by losing a close election in Kannapolis in 1991.[21]

The 1946 drive thus fits into a whole history of attempts to organize Cannon. It was launched on June 28, 1946, and ten organizers—half of the total number of textile personnel in North Carolina—were assigned to Kannapolis, with Dean Culver in charge. A native of Iowa, Culver was a long-term resident of Badin, North Carolina, only a few miles from Kannapolis. He had an impeccable organizing record in the steel and aluminum industries and seemed an excellent choice for the job.[22]

From the beginning, the Cannon drive found its progress hampered by the problems of trying to organize in a community where company control was so pervasive. The SOC was unable to secure radio time on a local station; Culver and another organizer were arrested for violating a "local ordinance" when they tried to operate a loudspeaker; and, most important of all, the SOC was unable to rent an office in Kannapolis and had to run its campaign from nearby Concord. Organizers also reported that the corporate dominance of the Cannon family had adversely affected the psychological attitude of workers. There was "a general pattern of rationalization built around the prestige of Charles Cannon" that made it difficult to sell unionization, and, this factor, it has been argued, doomed the Cannon campaign to failure.[23]

The paternalistic system does not in itself explain the Cannon drive's failure, however. Organizers made clear, for example, that the paternalistic psychology was not a monolithic one that affected all workers alike but one that was most effective among women workers. All organizers reported that women were particularly difficult to sign up, and they cast around for a way to appeal to them. Nancy Blaine, a young TWUA staffer assigned to "crack the women," reported that it was "difficult to sign up women. They give names but don't want their names used because they are afraid because of housing, and are waiting on their husbands." In other reports, women were described as "waiting to see what the men would do." Dean Culver wrote that "women's influence is against us," and he listed a number of causes for this fact. At the root of their reluctance was economic insecurity. Cannon Mills gave women work that was "better paid than any other occupation for women." Consequently, women workers "are afraid of losing the feeling of superiority over other workers." Organizers complained about women working, because Cannon families where both husband and wife worked had a high income. This made it difficult to produce any sense of dissatisfaction over wages, especially among women. Reviewing the SOC's inability to appeal to women, Culver recommended "that we advocate high enough wage scales that only one member of the family would need to work." This approach was fraught with danger, however, because women clearly *wanted* to work. As one organizer wrote, "We must be very careful not to be interpreted as advocating that other members of the family be denied work." Cannon Mills had a long-standing policy of "developing Cannon families in which two, or more, members of the family are employed." The SOC was trying to sell the idea of an individual, male wage in an industry and region with a history of family work.[24]

Equally problematic for the SOC was the sense of importance and purpose that company paternalism reportedly lent to many women workers. Nancy Blaine investigated the popularity of the town's massive company-sponsored women's clubs among Cannon women. She concluded that the women's clubs were important in taking away potential union leaders: "the women's clubs provide an outlet for those women who are organizationally minded, and as such they infringe on our membership." She attributed the prestige that women drew from their activity in clubs to the fact that the main club "includes people from uptown Kannapolis as well as Cannon mill workers." In all, the clubs had over 10,000 members.[25]

Dean Culver complained in several lengthy reports that one of the main problems in Kannapolis was that Cannon "knows how women's minds work" and had constructed Kannapolis accordingly. He described it as "a show town, an effective background for women to feel important in. Women are proud to live in Kannapolis. It is clean, broad streets, unique, cute, and is probably the nicest stage for a cotton mill employees' wife or daughter to act upon." He concluded that Cannon's control of women was "his very best defensive mechanism," "an effective way in which he handles them and their thinking." Recognizing the size of the problem, Culver admitted, "I really would like help and suggestions on the proper approach to women. . . . I am groping for the answer in my own mind."[26]

This groping was part of a wider attempt that Culver made to try to explain the SOC's problems in Kannapolis. Going beyond the spartan reports required of him by William Smith, Culver wrote a series of lengthy analyses of the Cannon situation. His description of the way that Cannon wages reinforced female workers' resistance to unionism was part of the central problem that he diagnosed in Kannapolis—the way that relatively high wage levels acted to take away the union's economic appeal. Generally, accounts of the failure of Operation Dixie in Kannapolis have emphasized workers' reluctance to embrace unionism based on their dependence and fear of the company. *Textile Labor* indeed claimed that the failure of the organizing efforts of the late 1940s was due to Cannon's "vast power," a conclusion supported by Griffith's recent case study. However, the significant body of records generated by the campaign indicate the importance of specific economic and social changes rooted in World War II. Rising wages and a dramatically improving standard of living gave paternalism its hold, reinforcing the company's position as workers realized that their living standards were improving without a union.[27]

The dominance of the Cannon family over Kannapolis meant that it was crucial for the SOC to have a strong message to sell to Cannon workers. It was the union's weak selling position that organizers, especially Culver, continually returned to in their reports and correspondence. The problem in Kannapolis was that workers felt they had a good deal because their pay and conditions were generally equal to or better than those in the southern mills that the TWUA had under contract. This left the union with no economic base on which to build a campaign. Culver wrote, "Cannon is very careful not to allow broad issues to grow in his working force. He will meet union standards almost as soon as they are established in this industry." There were no "short range popular issues" on which to build a campaign, because wages were "higher than in other textile mills" and the mills were "clean and comparatively comfortable." Consequently, the union had to fall back on trying to sell noneconomic benefits, such as "the idea of a written contract, guaranteeing seniority and other articles of security." With pay levels higher than ever before, however, it was not surprising that Culver complained that the emphasis on noneconomic benefits was getting nowhere; workers felt that "right now they have no pressing need for these things." Even Culver himself saw the rationale of the worker's reasoning: "Cannon employees actually feel that they have a superior deal, and they may have."[28]

The available figures on wages paid at Cannon highlight the union's difficulties. Cannon Mills had a declared policy of "advancing wages when conditions in the industry justified it." With textiles booming, Cannon workers received four major wage hikes between January 1944 and the launching of the drive in the summer of 1946. The minimum paid at Cannon rose from 42.5 cents an hour in 1944 to 73 cents in July 1946. In April 1946, cotton-mill workers in the Concord area were the highest paid in the southern textile industry in terms of average hourly earnings, according to the Bureau of Labor Statistics.[29]

Joel Leighton, who took control of the Cannon drive after the removal of Culver in October 1946, agreed that the central problem was rising wages. Due to the war, Cannon workers' standard of living "had increased 100% in the space of four years." This caused workers to question why they needed a union. Leighton felt that the problem of rising wages, which affected textile organizing campaigns across the South, was "particularly acute" in Kannapolis because of Cannon's historic position as a wage leader.[30]

The responses that workers gave to the campaign illustrated this problem. Not surprisingly, many who had lived through the long hours and very low pay of the industry before the war were cautious about endangering their relative prosperity. It was very difficult for the union to overcome the feeling that given the vast improvement that was taking place, a union was unnecessary. As one Cannon worker explained, "I know that when there is a time for better pay, Cannon is always ready to start better pay first. . . . I make more money now in nine and a half hours than I made in 120 hours when I first came here. So you can see why I don't want a union." Illustrating the tendency of wage raises to strengthen paternalism, many workers viewed them as the product of Charles Cannon's personal benevolence rather than economic conditions.[31] Moreover, the union found that its lack of economic appeal actually increased the importance of the issue of Cannon's popularity. As organizer Ruth

Gettinger wrote, "The workload is up to standards set in many union contracts. The only issue we have is freedom from Cannon domination, and Cannon is very popular."[32]

In their correspondence both Culver and Leighton expressed the view that because the union lacked an economic appeal, a new approach was needed in Kannapolis. Culver wrote, "I am convinced that we must change tactics in some way in order to organize this community. . . . The workers have no pressing reason to join the union and we must give them some, some issue in their behalf that they see as practical and that they really want." Writing with increasing frankness to Smith, by September he complained that "there are no hot issues here. We must make our issues. . . . This, coupled with the fact that we are going to have to do it in a place where the workers are probably better treated than in most organized plants makes the problem one which I know of no approach to except a costly one."

This "costly approach" entailed long-term, educational work that he, like many others in Operation Dixie, recommended. His main solution for the Cannon drive, and for the southern drive generally, however, was for the union to dramatically raise pay in organized plants, putting it on a par with the pay of northern unionized workers. Since unorganized textile plants had matched union pay, the CIO had to seize the initiative by giving "wide publicity" to the fact that it wanted to establish an "Industrial Master Agreement" that would put the average wage in the textile industry on a par with the average wage in steel and automobiles. Such an agreement would overcome the TWUA's inability to establish a pay differential between union and nonunion plants, which was responsible for its problems in the South. Indeed, Culver diagnosed the TWUA's central problem in the South in these years. He described the union's position as "like the chicken and the egg. We just can't set high union pay scales in an industry until you represent all of the workers in that industry. . . . On the other hand, it is very difficult to organize workers without being able to promise them, in terms they can understand, this kind of economic justice."[33]

Culver imagined, however, that the TWUA could establish a union pay scale if it was ambitious and seized the initiative in the South. The TWUA should launch a "crusade . . . to advance the wage levels and standards of these workers up to the better paid workers of American industry." These suggestions were natural for a man who had extensive experience in the steel industry. In textiles, however, the competitive nature of the textile industry made companies reluctant to assume a wage differential. Nevertheless, the need to establish a wage differential was crucial. As one organizer wrote after Cannon Mills implemented a pay increase during the 1946 campaign, "It is my opinion that we will have to raise our sights somewhat in all of these textile mills—the fact that a lousy eight cent raise has put us on the defensive is bad—why not shout for $1.18 minimum in textiles." [34]

Despite the symbolic significance of Kannapolis as a company town, the failure of the Cannon drive had very little to do with company opposition. The reaction of the company to the drive was never mentioned in written reports. Similarly, community opposition apparently did not play a decisive role in defeating the drive. [35]

Organizers frequently described the way that the organizing climate had been altered by higher wages. Far from being isolated in a company town, Culver explained, these workers, because of their disposable income, "can and do read. They own radios and many automobiles. They have traveled and visited around considerably." Overall, "the actual physical isolation from outside influence and contacts is considerably less than in the average mill village." Organizers found that, rather than helping them, these changes presented them with new obstacles. The prevalence of car ownership made workers hard to reach, for example, as many workers parked their cars inside the mill gates, thereby avoiding organizers who had anticipated that they would come in on foot. Many workers drove in from surrounding communities, making it hard to contact them when their shifts finished. The campaign lost momentum when Cannon workers took their two weeks of vacation soon after card-signing began. Organizers expressed surprise that the majority of workers were leaving Kannapolis for holidays on the coast or in the mountains, trips that would likely have been out of their parents' reach. Thus, social changes that were the result of improved wages hindered the campaign. [36]

In Kannapolis, as in Operation Dixie generally, particular emphasis was placed on veterans. It was believed that because veterans had left the mill villages and served overseas, they would be more responsive to the message of unionization. However, for Cannon veterans as well as other Cannon workers, the postwar period opened up new opportunities without having to join a union. Under the GI Bill, a piece of legislation that was to prove extremely beneficial for many southern textile workers, GIs from Cannon Mills were able to attend nearby Belmont Textile School, where ambitious workers learned the necessary skills for management. This school was one of the many that were set up during this period, as a new emphasis was placed in management circles on promoting workers from the ranks. Due to the large enrollment from Cannon Mills, it was necessary to keep the school open year-round. Cannon Mills also constructed over a hundred new homes for veterans, and the union had particular problems finding support in "GI Town." [37]

Thus, in Kannapolis, an isolated mill town and one of the South's last mill villages to be sold off, issues of social change were at the heart of the union's failure in its campaign of June–December 1946. Indeed, the Kannapolis drive showed that the huge wage increases generated by World

War II affected a wide variety of communities, and the drive illustrated in close detail the devastating effect such wage increases could have on an organizing campaign.

The Internal Debate over Wages

The slow progress of Operation Dixie inevitably produced a considerable degree of self-analysis by textile leaders. When top officials of the TWUA or SOC discussed the reasons for the drive's failure in textiles, they always came back to the same set of problems. The drive's Georgia director, Charles Gillman, for example, wrote privately in 1947 that textile elections were being lost because "the workers have been treated so good, so they claim, by the companies in the past several years, and too, their wage rates are exceedingly high." From the TWUA's important Greensboro-Burlington Joint Board, Director Bruno Rantane wrote a lengthy analysis on the failure of textile organizing. Rantane identified the problem as the fact that "in an inflationary period such as the one we are confronted with, the average worker who is gullible and ignorant falls prey to the 'how good the employer is to you' type of propaganda." He argued that the union had very little chance of success in this economic climate. It desperately lacked "issues," because "workers working overtime hours earning the highest wages they have ever known and experiencing a false sense of prosperity are hard to get aroused to the needs of organization." He argued that greater progress would only come when there was "economic dislocation." [38]

A wide range of other union figures wrote in a similar vein. George Baldanzi, for example, told the TWUA's 1950 convention that the drive had failed because of how nonunion employers had matched union benefits. He argued that the drive "will have to have some economic base if we want to appeal to workers to join the union, because you can't have them join the union by asking them to fall in love with its democratic virtues." A TWUA report in 1948 concluded that Operation Dixie had failed because "workers were earning the highest wages they had ever known and the great demand for labor gave them a feeling of security." [39]

As a natural consequence of this self-analysis, criticism of the drive's current approach emerged. Some were prepared to describe why the campaign was going wrong, but a few really put pen to paper and argued that a different approach was needed in order to end this failure. In the summer of 1947, for example, Lucy Randolph Mason corresponded with many of Operation Dixie's textile organizers and staff heads about the need to change the drive's basic approach. She sent them an eight-page article she had written espousing her ideas. It was significant that Mason, a diminutive gray-haired woman who worked tirelessly for the

CIO in the South for over twenty years, led this initiative: she was a senior, respected member of the CIO whose work as a community relations representative gave her close insight into the problems dogging a wide variety of textile campaigns. In her article, Mason argued that the CIO must stress to workers that it was because of the TWUA's initiative that wages had risen so much. Workers could not rely on the company for security, especially as these companies had a long history of opposing decent wages. Companies were only granting union conditions because there was a threat of unionization, she warned; "textile workers, remember that what is given can be taken away. It is only when a strong union has won benefits that its members can keep those benefits." Mason also argued that Operation Dixie's economic approach was neglecting the noneconomic benefits that only a union could secure, such as the dignity that workers attained through seniority and through protection from unjust discharge. These noneconomic benefits had a strong appeal among workers, yet they were not generally emphasized by organizers. However, their benefit was difficult to appreciate before a union had been established. As former organizer Don McKee remembered, "That's the hardest thing of all to sell, the way in which the union gives workers a voice. . . . You can talk about the union getting a 10% wage increase, that you can see, but when it comes to workers having some say, they have to experience it." Thus, if the drive wished to achieve large-scale organization quickly, this sort of approach was equally problematic.[40]

Nevertheless, it was symptomatic of the frustration that existed among textile staff that Mason found a lot of support for her ideas. Citing a long list of organizers who agreed with her, Paul Christopher wrote Mason that "more than ever" it was time for a "new approach to textile organization." Many southern staff favored a change because it was clear that the economic approach was going nowhere. One person who agreed strongly with Mason was John Ramsay, her colleague and fellow Christian in the CIO's community relations department. He wrote that the drive had reached an impasse because of the gains nonunion workers had been granted voluntarily. What made this tactic particularly damaging, argued Ramsay, was that "the workers themselves are very unaware of the immoral position in which they are placed. They accept those benefits offered by management but do not join and participate in the union in order to maintain these gains which have come only because of the struggle of unions in other mills." Many TWUA staffers hired for the SOC felt that the whole approach of Operation Dixie was wrong. Joe Pedigo, a dark-haired Virginian who was one of the TWUA's most successful southern organizers in the 1940s, felt that the economic approach failed to address the right question: "they [unorganized workers] were making more money than the organized plants. What have you got to sell? It all boils down to the question of human dignity. No matter how good the company is, do you want to be in the position of having to depend on somebody to be good to you?"[41]

Like Pedigo, many who had worked in the South for a long time before Operation Dixie felt that the drive should emphasize noneconomic benefits. Even though this promised to be a slower approach, they felt that the South could be organized only through long-term, educational work. The Operation Dixie strategy, on the other hand, which anticipated rapid gains, seemed to be dictated from the North. Pat Knight, a native of Burlington, North Carolina, who worked as a TWUA southern staffer between 1943 and 1950, asserted, "I think the whole concept of calling it Operation Dixie was not the way. . . . I think they needed to have a lot more patience." The top strategists of the drive reminded Knight "of what Congress is like now, if you didn't succeed and cure all of the ills of Latin America in five years, then it was a failure."[42]

The slower, educational model was in fact adopted by the TWUA in the early 1950s. In 1953, when the union launched its own southern organizing drive following the termination of Operation Dixie, its approach was very different. As *Textile Labor* wrote, "There's no flavor of Operation Dixie in the new southern organizing set-up. . . . We're all sadder and wiser than we were in 1946; we know that hard work—basic educational work—is the only road to unionism in the South. That's the sort of work we will be doing." Many in the union felt that the early strategy of the drive had vastly underestimated the difficulties involved in organizing the South. The emphasis on economic benefits had left the union exposed to the situation where management matched union wages, a tactic that the TWUA's research director, Solomon Barkin, called the "great play" of the industry in these years. Moreover, the drive's early strategy had concentrated exclusively on these benefits, arguing that organizing and educational work were contradictory. This tension between the need for organization and the need for broader change ran throughout Operation Dixie. Van Bittner was adamant that the two issues could be separated. At the end of 1947 he admonished William Smith to detach his staff from all PAC work because the drive's resources must be used "strictly for organizing." At the same time that Van Bittner directed this policy, however, TWUA southern activists continually emphasized that the PAC was central to their progress in the South. Indeed, Baldanzi told the TWUA's 1946 convention that there was "nothing more important" than the PAC. The importance of the PAC was maintained by many TWUA southern staffers because, unlike the early strategists of Operation Dixie, they felt that political change had to precede, not follow, organization.[43]

Despite the damage that the economic strategy caused, it did not prove to be completely misguided. Ironically, the very factor that helped to defeat the drive—the granting of wage increases—had a positive side. The main reason for launching the campaign had been to raise southern wages and eliminate the threat that a low-paid South posed to organized workers in other areas. Operation Dixie was successful in achieving this goal, especially in textiles. This vital achievement ensured that the drive was not an unmitigated failure. Thus, the fate of Operation Dixie revolved around the ambiguous role played by wages.

Indeed, both the SOC and the TWUA derived a sense of progress and achievement from their role in raising southern wages. Contemporary issues of the CIO's official mouthpiece, the *CIO News*, illustrate this point very well. The *News* explained that "coincident with the beginning of the CIO organizing drive in North Carolina, unorganized cotton mills in that state followed the lead of unionized mills" in raising pay. While this had prevented unionization, the *News* was also able to report with pride that the drive had won "millions of $'s in Dixie," including the virtual elimination of the North-South wage differential in textiles.[44]

The fact that wages were increasing was particularly important to the TWUA. Emil Rieve, like most of the top officers of the union, hailed from the northern section of the textile industry and was particularly aware of the need to protect his vulnerable northern members from low-wage southern competition. His speeches continually referred to the importance of raising southern wages. The wage raises that were granted to forestall unionization during Operation Dixie allowed Rieve to report triumphantly to union conventions. Indeed, the way that nonunion companies followed the TWUA's wage scale gave the union an influence in the region beyond its size. This new clout provided the union with a sense of progress and gave it an important psychological boost. *Textile Labor*, for example, boasted in 1948 that the TWUA had "no counterpart in labor history" because it had repeatedly secured universal gains in an industry that was only partially unionized. The wage gains, in particular, meant that the union was able to gain a sense of positive achievement from Operation Dixie. As Baldanzi boasted at the TWUA's 1948 convention, "Bear in mind that as weak as we are in the South, the employers in the South have had to give every wage increase and every other benefit that you have received, because they were afraid if they didn't do it, the workers would join the union." He added that "in terms of gains, we have raised the wages of every organized and unorganized worker in the whole textile industry in the South." Convention delegates in the late 1940s frequently cited these wage increases, and they were a key component in maintaining an optimistic environment in the union during these years. In the 1950s, when the union lost the ability to move southern wages, convention gatherings became far more gloomy affairs.[45]

The consequences of World War II also had an important impact of textile organizing in another form. The war saw the large-scale entry of women into the labor force: the number of female workers grew from 12 million in 1940 to 18 million in 1945. On the whole, this influx only had a limited impact on textiles, an industry that traditionally employed large numbers of women. However, several of the large rayon mills of eastern Tennessee hired women in large numbers during the war. Indeed, around 75 percent of new workers that the Tennessee textile factories hired during the war were women. Because of the prevalence of women in these mills, the drive's planners assigned most of its female organizers, including Dorothy Daniel and Pumell Maloney, to these campaigns. Their reports often described the problems that they were facing in gender terms. Dorothy Daniel, for example, reported from the American Bemberg plant in Elizabethton, Tennessee, that women workers told her "that we don't have much of a chance to get in because there are too many women working in the mill." Purnell Maloney also wrote that one of the main obstacles facing the campaigns she was working on in eastern Tennessee was women workers. They were variously described as self-effacing, frightened, reluctant to assume leadership of the union, and lacking belief in collective action. Many organizers expressed open frustration with female workers. Daniel, for example, wrote of the Elizabethton workers, "These women are mice. Even the women leaders are mice in both plants. I have found practically no one with real leadership ability." [46]

It is clear that these women textile workers were particularly cautious in their attitude toward Operation Dixie because of the insecurity of their employment. While for workers as a whole the war tended to increase their feelings of security, making it more difficult to sell unionization, for newly hired women workers, the end of the war created great fears of job loss. Women had mainly been hired as temporary workers, and their tenure became precarious when GIs began to return home. Women came to be seen as a threat to union wage scales, and in many industries, such as automobiles, inequitable seniority agreements gave men the right to "bump" women in the event of transfers or layoffs. Studies have shown that even when women constituted a significant membership of the union, industrial unionism was unable to live up to its promise of organizing workers regardless of sex, color, or age. [47]

In the eastern Tennessee campaigns, newly hired women workers were reluctant to join the CIO. The fear of these women workers was clearly a product of the war, as women textile workers in other southern locations, who had not been hired in the war, played a central role in strikes and union activity. [48] Helen Gregory, indeed, reported that "after V-J

Day, hundreds of women were laid off so returning GIs could have their old jobs back and brand new women were hired to take their places. Fifteen year workers see young people advanced over them." Because layoffs without regard to seniority were common, most women were reluctant to form plant committees: "they are very much afraid of being laid off if they have anything to do with the CIO." Gregory explained that newly hired female workers in centers such as Elizabethton, Knoxville, and Old Hickory viewed the CIO warily because "the women know that new machines will eventually cut their departments and some of them believe that signing a CIO card will cause them to be laid off."[49]

While fear of lost employment was the main problem, organizers also complained about the inexperience and ignorance of newly hired female workers. Purnell Maloney, for example, claimed that at Standard Knitting Mills in Knoxville, "men workers are ready and willing but the problem is women, many recently hired and of high school age. There are some 70% women throughout the entire mill." Maloney claimed that these workers "do not know much about how or what a union is supposed to accomplish" and were unable "to proceed without running into reprisals from management and the company." In the DuPont campaign in Old Hickory, organizers complained that women workers, especially those hired in wartime, were particularly vulnerable to company paternalism, a criticism also voiced in Kannapolis. This problem was acute in the important DuPont campaign, because the company sponsored an elaborate system of worker councils and social and recreational activities. The detailed reports that Maloney produced from Old Hickory indicate that the CIO was unable to lure young women workers away from a network of company-sponsored activities. For example, in May 1949 Maloney wrote, "Meeting arranged for this night fell through when a competitive soft ball game was scheduled between the girls in Winding and Reeling Areas. Girls in these 12 Textile areas had planned a group meeting." Another meeting only attracted four men from a small department; that night women workers were participating in a beauty contest, a revival in the Baptist church, and a baseball game with an "out of town ball team."[50]

Despite the importance of gender to these campaigns, on the whole organizers rarely described the problems they were facing in gender terms. Moreover, where women were more established members of the workforce than in eastern Tennessee, they often gave strong support to union activity, especially during strikes.[51] The evidence from the Tennessee campaigns, however, is valuable in throwing further light on the importance of the war's impact on Operation Dixie's textiles arena.

The textiles arm of Operation Dixie failed for a variety of reasons. This failure cannot simply be explained by employer opposition, worker culture, or postwar anticommunism, important as these factors were. It was also the specific impact of the war in generating social and economic changes of far-reaching significance, especially by dramatically raising the wages of southern textile workers. The scale of this change had a profound effect on Operation Dixie, and on other postwar initiatives launched by the TWUA. While the amount of lasting cultural and social change the war produced is contentious, its role in dramatically raising wages and kick-starting the economy is not. Other studies have also illustrated the dramatic economic effect of the war on different regions, especially in states whose prewar economic level was a low one.[52]

The war was also crucial for the TWUA because of the assistance and protection it gave the union in organizing the South. Union leaders imagined that this record of progress meant that the time was ripe for southern organizing. They could not have known that the 20 percent of southern workers the TWUA had under contract in 1945 would be the most it ever achieved. By the end of Operation Dixie, however, some union leaders had realized that the war's legacy was to make organizing harder, not easier. As Paul Christopher wrote in April 1951, "I am rapidly coming to the conclusion . . . that we are going to have to resign ourselves to a lot of legwork, that is not going to pay off in the first campaigns. In many ways, it can be said, by the time the southern drive started in 1946, we had already organized the so-called cream of the southern crop. What we had left to organize was tough."[53]

chapter four

"Winning Elections Isn't Enough"

Postwar Strikes

Operation Dixie was all about winning elections. According to the strategy of the drive, once an election was won, the Southern Organizing Committee withdrew from the situation and allowed the respective international union to negotiate a contract. Southern staff soon began to realize, though, that in textiles, winning an election was often only the first difficult step of the union's battle to obtain a recognized existence. As one organizer wrote, "It seems that winning an election does not necessarily mean that we have been successful in establishing a union." Indeed, *Textile Labor* reported that after a year of Operation Dixie, there were some thirty southern mills where elections had been won but no contract had been reached. The journal concluded that "winning elections isn't enough. If management refuses to bargain after a TWUA election victory, every triumph will be a potential financial drain until a contract is signed." In most cases, this inability to secure a contract led the TWUA into strikes. Thus, the story of Operation Dixie's failure was not simply an inability to win elections but also involved an inability to turn these victories into lasting institutional gains. In a two-year period after the start of the drive, the TWUA was involved in thirty-six southern strikes, many of them following an organizing campaign. In other cases, even when a local had a contract, the yearly negotiating sessions were often a tense period and led to many strikes. The high number of strikes that occurred in the South during these years was important in determining the union's failure in the region, as most were lost and drained the TWUA of resources and membership.[1]

Nationally, the immediate postwar period saw strikes among workers in the major mass-production industries, such as automobiles, steel, rubber, and meat-packing. These strikes generally occurred for more wages. They also occurred, unlike earlier strike waves, among secure unions. Indeed, it was a sign of the maturity of unions in these industries that these strikes largely achieved what they wanted.[2] In contrast, the southern strikes that the TWUA went through concerned not wages but issues of union security and the contract. Not only did they pose a threat to the existence of the locals involved; in many cases the union ceased to exist because of their strike's failure. Through strikes, often forced against its will, the TWUA was dismantled a local at a time in the South between 1945 and 1955. The postwar years were turbulent ones for the TWUA as it battled to secure recognition in this region. Despite the importance of this period, though, very little has been written about these strikes.

The failure of southern textile workers to win their postwar strikes poses fundamental questions, because it was part of their broader inability to form cohesive unions in the same manner as most northern industrial workers in the 1930s and 1940s. What were the reasons for this difference? Many historians have emphasized how difficult it was to sustain unions in company-owned southern mill villages. The whole issue of the distinctive character of southern textile workers, and its responsibility for the failure of the industry to unionize, is at the heart of the debate. In analyzing the failure of the TWUA's southern strikes, it is crucial to determine not just the reasons for failure but especially the role played by worker militancy and culture.[3]

A central theme of the strikes was companies' determination to reverse the progress the TWUA had made during the war. As in other areas, the TWUA's strikes between 1945 and 1955 were greatly influenced by the impact of World War II. The fact that most southern strikes occurred over the issue of union security indicated that the TWUA had not secured any kind of acceptance in the South by the end of World War II. Pat Knight, a slim young woman who worked for the TWUA's Education Department in the South between 1943 and 1950, remembered that she spent most of these years in strikes. While many TWUA activists grew up in liberal environments outside the South, Knight was a native North Carolinian whose father was a company doctor for Burlington Industries. Describing herself as "idealistic," Knight became interested in the educational side of the labor movement, feeling that mill workers needed the opportunities for self-development that a union could provide. Knight felt that the prevalence of strikes was due to the fact that when the war ended, management began "trying to break the union. I think in most places they accepted that they had to deal during the war with the government orders and so forth, but generally the idea was not to have to continue once the war was over. Go back to the status quo." This management offensive put the union under severe pressure in the South almost as soon as the war ended. As Ross Groshong, a young Quaker who also worked on the TWUA's education staff in the South, recalled, "In this period the right of the union to exist was the continual and major problem." Managers' actions were determined by the progress that the union had made during the war: in general management had a desire to claw back the ground that it had lost.[4]

The NWLB ceased operating at the beginning of 1946. The situation in Gaffney, South Carolina, exemplified what happened when the protective environment provided by this agency ended. In 1944, Gaffney Manufacturing Company had refused to accept a NWLB contract, objecting strongly to the checkoff and maintenance-of-membership provisions. Due to the wartime emergency, the federal government seized the plant in May 1945 and operated it for over three months. Immediately after the plant was returned, the company ignored the contract and refused to recognize the union. Although the TWUA was trying to get the company to follow a NWLB order, without the wartime emergency the union had no power of enforcement except its power to strike. Thus, on September 11 a strike began. Union leaders had no doubt that the company was trying to break the union. Local representative Charlie Puckett, for example, reported that the company wanted "a fight to the finish hoping to destroy the union."[5]

The Gaffney strike was a pivotal event in the TWUA's postwar history. The strike exemplified many of the features common to the postwar strikes, not least of which was the virtual impossibility of union victory. Above all, the strike showed that worker militancy was not sufficient to ensure victory. Gaffney workers showed remarkable determination, striking for an incredible twenty-two months. Even when the strike was finally abandoned, very few of the original workers had returned to work. All those involved in the strike praised the militancy of the workers. After fourteen months on strike, Puckett wrote, "It is remarkable to see a group of workers remain on strike for so long a period, with so few breaking rank and returning to work." In Gaffney, as in many postwar strikes, the determination of the workers had a dramatic quality. Puckett described how strikers brought their children to the picket line and "formed a V through which the scabs had to pass, sung songs, repeated the Lord's Prayer, which was very effective, in fact, some of the scabs went into the mill crying." These tactics were so effective that the company secured an injunction preventing children from picketing, on grounds of "juvenile delinquency."[6]

The Gaffney strike was still broken, however, because the company gradually recruited outside labor and, with protection provided by a strict injunction, brought them into the plant. The union had little defense against this strategy. As Puckett admitted, "The union is in a very unfavorable position as a result of the company being able to hire new employees." On July 15, 1947, the TWUA had to abandon both the strike and the local union. By this time the company had been able to get two full shifts running with outside labor; thus the Gaffney workers, despite their determination and unity, were frozen out of the equation.[7]

Union leaders knew that the Gaffney strike had cost the company money. Yet Gaffney Manufacturing Company was part of a chain of mills controlled by the Deering-Milliken company based in New York City. The company could easily switch production to other plants. Deering-Milliken was, moreover, fervently anti-union: it confirmed this with its labor relations tactics in the 1950s, when it closed a mill in Darlington, South Carolina, after the workers had voted for TWUA representation.[8] The Gaffney strike was an important precedent for such acts of union resistance because it proved that it was possible for a company to break a union, especially in a chain mill. This lesson was not lost on southern textile manufacturers, who regarded Gaffney as a test case of how far they could go in their postwar drive to restore the status quo.[9] Thus, while TWUA leaders tried to blame the loss of the strike on the Taft-Hartley Act, the real truth of the Gaffney strike, as the company pointed out, was that it was lost without the help of the act. All the Taft-Hartley Act did was give companies extra weapons and confidence with which to attack the TWUA's southern locals. Moreover, its passage, which occurred simultaneously with the loss of the Gaffney strike, provided a double blow for the union.[10]

Many features of the Gaffney strike were repeated in other situations. Encouraged by the test case established in Gaffney, many strikes that followed had similar themes—company intransigence over union security and the checkoff; dramatic striker militancy for the right to have a union; the breaking of strikes through the importation of outside labor; the importance of chain ownership; and the lack of a level playing field between management and labor. As at Gaffney, these strikes generally involved refusal to continue to implement NWLB contracts, because manufacturers were keen to regain the ground they had lost during the war. Illustrating the way that the union was suddenly put on the defensive, the TWUA's George Baldanzi declared that manufacturers were launching a conscious offensive to recover ground: "the military war is over, but our war to protect and extend the gains we have made is only starting." [11]

Refusal to bargain was the most common cause of the strikes, and the issue that caused companies' most fervent resistance was the checkoff of union dues and other similar union security provisions. This issue led to many strikes, because the TWUA had a declared policy of not signing a contract in the South without the checkoff. This policy was guided by the experience of previous textile unions, particularly the UTW, which had won sporadic mass support in the South but had failed to build secure, dues-paying local unions. The TWUA's insistence on the checkoff put it on a collision course with management, many of whom were fundamentally opposed to it. At Royal Cotton Mill in Wake Forest, North Carolina, the mill's owner, B. Everett Jordan, a prominent politician who later became a U.S. senator, refused to sign a contract with the checkoff, and in 1951 his stance led to a strike. Using an argument that would be repeated elsewhere, Jordan stated, "We have no objection to workers belonging to a union, but it's not the company's duty to collect union dues." Many companies argued that the checkoff had only been given to the union during the war in return for the no-strike pledge. Hence, with the war over, companies argued, as one mill manager put it, "that the union should not expect us to continue union membership and the check-off." [12]

Contemporary management publications confirm the determination of southern textile employers to remove the checkoff from union contracts immediately after the war. The employer journal the *Southern Textile News*, for example, repeatedly attacked the checkoff of membership as undemocratic means of maintaining union membership and claimed that the CIO was forcing workers to strike in order to obtain "the four pegs of puppet government[:] . . . maintenance of membership, the check-off, union shop, and closed shop." The influential journal issued a call to arms against these provisions, boasting that southern mill owners could "break the back" of the CIO if they agreed not to sign any contracts containing the checkoff. [13]

The importance of the checkoff as an issue of conflict was also stated by TWUA staff who worked in the South. Walter Orrell, a small, slender man who worked as a TWUA representative in Salisbury, North Carolina, in the 1940s, remembered that "management always used the check-off for a bargaining point because they thought they could bust the union if they got rid of the check-off." The union, in turn, "felt like they had to have the check-off to survive." Pat Knight also felt that during this period union security was the central issue concerning the TWUA's southern locals: "Their chief thing in bargaining would be the whole issue of union security. We were asking for union maintenance, and that was what they were totally opposed to. That was the issue and it was true generally all over." [14]

This concern with union security does not fit in with the established wisdom of postwar labor history that wages were the central grievance between workers and management. This wisdom, however, is clearly more applicable to northern industrial workers whose unions were, by this stage, firmly established. In southern textiles, the TWUA's insecurity made union recognition the key issue; indeed, wages rarely appeared as an issue in negotiations.

In contrast to management's hope that workers would not respond to union security issues, however, workers' basic determination to have a union was a common feature of the strikes. Partly because management strategy in the South was to give union wages to unorganized workers, those workers who did organize, often conscious of management's strategy, looked to the union for noneconomic rather than economic benefits. Noneconomic benefits were also stressed because workers showed a strong desire to break free of company control and establish justice in the workplace through seniority and the grievance procedure. These noneconomic benefits were, indeed, greatly appreciated by workers who had worked under a union contract.[15]

Southern textile workers showed remarkable militancy in fighting for these noneconomic benefits. One indicator of this militancy was the length of many strikes. Textile workers across the South showed a determination to strike for long periods in an effort to get a union. A strike in Athens, Georgia, lasted for twenty months, and one at Amazon Cotton Mill in Thomasville, North Carolina, for seventeen months. A strike at Dallas Manufacturing Company in Huntsville, Alabama, lasted over a year. Very few strikes were less than six months long. In no case, thus, did workers quickly crumble and abandon the union. In most strikes, the simple desire for some kind of voice in the workplace was what sustained workers in these bitter strikes. Pat Knight, for example, recalled that "in several of the strikes there would not be a real issue about wages which could be settled or negotiated, or workloads, it was this more, really abstract concept of the right to have a union, that was what people really cared about, even though in the short term they were losing money every day." She added that it was "really inspiring" that workers were willing to make such sacrifices for their basic rights.[16]

This determination took place in the face of tremendous odds, often in plants where managers made it clear from the beginning that they had no intention of recognizing the union. At a strike at Hadley-Peoples Manufacturing Company in Siler City, North Carolina, workers sustained a solid strike for over six months although the mill owner had announced at the start of the strike, "You can take what I have offered you or you will never get a contract." At the beginning of a lengthy shutdown at Clifton Manufacturing Company in Clifton, South Carolina, owner Stanley Converse told the union "that he was going to drive the union out of his plant." Yet when company supervisors "visited" strikers to try to recruit a back-to-work movement after four months on strike, the vast majority refused, telling their bosses that they would only work under a union contract. Many workers' responses showed that they were conscious that their battle was one of collective needs, not individual self-interest. Nellie Frady, for example, told a manager who was pressurizing her to return to work "that she was not ready until a contract had been signed as this was the only thing left for the working class of people." State director Charles Auslander described the Clifton strikers as "very determined . . . willing to suffer hardships and in particular, a bleak Christmas."[17]

Very few strikes actually failed because of large-scale defection by workers. What was more significant was the wide-ranging variety of powers that management was able to use to bypass the workers' militancy. The prevalence of chain mills in the South after the war made it easier for particular mills to withstand long strikes and force the union into submission. Again the war years proved influential, because they saw an increasing concentration of ownership in the textile South, with large chains such as Deering-Milliken and J. P. Stevens assuming an increasing importance in the region. While the industry was still very competitive, most of the strikes occurred in large chain mills because of the union's desire to organize the major plants in the industry. It was very difficult to win a strike against these mills, because they could switch production to a nonunion mill within the chain. In a 1947 dispute at Highland Park Manufacturing Company in Rock Hill, South Carolina, a TWUA representative reported, "The company owns and operates fifteen plants in North Carolina and one in Rock Hill. The company can use its plants in North Carolina to produce while it fights the union at Rock Hill." The Deering-Milliken chain, which controlled twenty-one southern mills by 1946, even had a policy, declared only at covert management meetings, that it "will not operate a union mill." Thus, after destroying the Gaffney local, the company went after the union in the Dallas plant in Huntsville—the only remaining union in the whole chain. TWUA representatives in the Dallas plant knew they were in trouble from the start and feared a strike. Union representative Roy Lawrence summed up the fear of Dallas's TWUA staff when he wrote, "We are fearful that the Dallas strike may prove to be something similar to the Gaffney situation, in as much as both mills are owned by the Deering-Milliken interests." These fears proved to be justified: the Dallas local was forced into submission after a lengthy strike. In contrast to the union, these chain companies had little to fear from a strike. In one private meeting of southern executives, for example, a representative from the Lowenstein chain declared that he was "ready to take a strike at Rock Hill[,] . . . take work to Lyman." [18]

Even when mills did not belong to large chains, the TWUA found that manufacturers often supported each other in their efforts to oust unions. In this sense, the union became a victim of its own weak representation in the South, for many lone locals had been established among a mass of nonunion mills. Regarding a strike at the isolated union plant Woodside Mills in Greenville, South Carolina, state director Charles Auslander pointed out that the 1950 strike had been planned by the company, "who, conspiring with the other textile manufacturers is seeking to wipe out the remaining hope for the textile workers in this area for just treatment." This charge of collusion occurred frequently in reports from strike situations. The charge had some truth because the removal of a union freed manufacturers from the need to provide union wages and conditions, which they did as a way of preventing unionization.[19]

Manufacturers broke most strikes by the same method as that used at Gaffney—they recruited outside labor. This tactic was a potent management weapon because, as at Gaffney, the union had no power to stop it. For example, at the Hadley-Peoples Manufacturing Company in Siler City, North Carolina, on April 19, 1948, the strike was reported to be progressing "very well," with only eleven of the original workforce of around five hundred having broken the picket line. During the first week of May, however, local TWUA representative Bruno Rantane reported that "the strike took a decided bad turn" when strikebreakers entered the mill; he explained, "The company has been advertising all throughout the state, South Carolina, and Virginia." Although Rantane repeatedly emphasized that "none of our people have broken ranks," reports from the Federal Mediation and Conciliation Service (FMCS) showed that increasing numbers of workers were imported after this, causing the strike to be lost.[20] Many other strikes were broken after management made a determined effort to recruit strikebreakers. Most companies went to great lengths to find strikebreakers, traveling large distances and offering them free transportation and a variety of bonus payments to enter the mills. TWUA representative Nancy Blaine reported that a strike at Highland Park Manufacturing Company in Rock Hill, South Carolina, failed because "company representatives spent everyday after work, and every weekend, scouring the countryside for scabs."[21]

The way that outside labor was brought in began to follow a standard pattern in this period. Larry Rogin, the TWUA's education director throughout this period, recalled that immediately after the war, southern companies evolved a strikebreaking formula. It involved forcing a strike over an issue the union could not agree on—namely, the checkoff; leaving the plant closed for several months while a back-to-work movement was recruited; and, finally, importing labor with the help of an injunction limiting the union's ability to picket. During these strikes companies increasingly relied on sophisticated attorneys who specialized in breaking unions. Robert Cahoon, the North Carolina attorney who handled TWUA's southern legal cases in these years, felt that anti-union lawyers such as Frank Constangy and Whiteford Blakeney "devised a strategy that you had to be very sophisticated to counter." He described this strategy as one of "continual delay," a tactic that involved exploiting the ineffectiveness of the NLRB. This use of legal means to break unions originated in this period and was to play an important role in thwarting later campaigns, particularly the J. P. Stevens case of the 1960s and 1970s.[22]

These lawyers exploited the NLRB in such a way that the agency became a weapon that they could use against the TWUA, rather than a protective agency for the union. The union found that the NLRB offered little effective protection during its postwar strikes and, in fact, provided another obstacle that made it very difficult to win strikes. In 1950, for example, an internal TWUA report concluded that the NLRB had not protected it at all during its recent southern strikes: "In no case has the NLRB, still supposedly the defender of workers, gone into action until long after a strike has been lost and the local union destroyed."[23] The main complaint was the board's slowness, for in 1949 the average interval between the filing of a charge and the decision was five hundred days. The union's gripes about the ineffectiveness of federal protection increased after Taft-Hartley. The union claimed, with some justification, that the law encouraged southern textile employers to force strikes. Several provisions of the act inflicted quantifiable damage on the union— particularly its ruling that workers who had been replaced in strikes could not vote in subsequent elections. This clause led directly to the loss of four local unions in North Carolina and one in Georgia. In the late 1940s, the TWUA's legal team, headed by Isadore Katz and southern attorney Bob Cahoon, led a vocal campaign against the Taft-Hartley Act, claiming that it was "forcing unions into organizational strikes."[24]

In reality, however, Taft-Hartley was not the decisive element but simply another management weapon that made it even harder for the TWUA to win strikes. It was the intrinsic weakness of the union that was the continual problem. Thus, when interviewed forty-five years later, Cahoon, still a practicing lawyer at age seventy-eight, explained that "my real feeling was that it was sort of beside the point. The problems were more fundamental than Taft-Hartley. Taft-Hartley was just a symptom of the political trends at the time. It didn't help but it was beside the point." Cahoon, echoing the view of Pat Knight, felt that the real problem was that the TWUA was too weak even before Taft-Hartley and needed strict government protection to win contracts in the South. Another union representative, Dick Conn, felt that with or without Taft-Hartley, TWUA could not win strikes because employers "had so many weapons."[25]

The weak strategic position of the TWUA was also illustrated by its financial inability to compete with southern textile companies in a strike situation. Past strikes, particularly the uprising of 1934, had shown how vital relief was to success, and this was even more true in the postwar period. In 1947, Emil Rieve told *Textile Labor* that the "vital factor" in southern strikes was money. He added, "So long as TWUA is able to guarantee benefits to strikers it need not fear being forced into strikes." Many strikes were weakened by the inability of the union to do this. TWUA had a declared policy of providing only food relief, and this policy was strictly enforced by the union's fiscally conservative treasurer, William Pollock. This policy proved inadequate in the postwar period because workers had many extra financial responsibilities that the union was unable to cover. Thus, the higher standard of living generated by World War II not only hindered Operation Dixie but also made it harder for the union to win strikes and continued to blight its fortunes in the South.[26]

With their higher wages, workers had begun to buy consumer goods such as cars, washing machines, and furniture through installment plans. This increased wealth increased the economic pressure on workers in a strike, as installment companies dunned them for payment almost immediately. One southern business agent, E. T. Kirkland, told the union's convention in 1954 how difficult it was for southern textile workers to strike due to this financial pressure. He explained that strikes had been easier in the 1930s: "The cost of the strike in 1937 and 1938 was very simple because nobody in the strike had anything to lose, so you didn't have to finance anything." Rising wages had produced a very different situation: "today they own their own homes, their own refrigerators, automobiles, everything, but in the case of a strike they take them within two months." He explained how in many strikes companies put pressure on credit agencies as an effective means of frightening workers. He added, "The only way to organize the South today is by having lots of money. . . . We have had situations where we have stayed on strike for ten, twenty, and twenty-five weeks and then because of the financial condition we have had to tell these people to go back to work, there was no money."[27]

As in Operation Dixie, the union found itself confronted with new problems caused by the improved standard of living that World War II had brought to the textile South. Strike records highlight many cases in which the union's relief policy was inadequate to cope with the financial responsibilities of postwar workers. In a strike at Clifton Manufacturing Company in Clifton, South Carolina, state TWUA director Charles Auslander reported that tremendous pressure was being placed on strikers because of the national union's reluctance to help with installment payments. Illustrating the new importance of credit to workers, the company tried to break the strike by offering to meet workers' payments if they came back to work. It was reported that "as soon as they returned to work, they seemed to have plenty of money to pay all their bills and get their cars out of the finance company's hands. One person when he returned to work the first day paid $125 to get his car from the finance company." Most workers remained on strike, however, both in Clifton and in other locations, despite the risk of losing major purchases; this highlights the strikers' determination and militancy. As Auslander wrote, "Just to show you some of the spirit we have here, we have had five members who have given up their automobiles and have not crossed the picket lines."[28]

Similar relief problems occurred in other strikes. Companies consistently showed an awareness of the power that credit companies had over workers by pressuring installment agencies so that workers would lose their newfound possessions. Workers, moreover, repeatedly showed a great reluctance to jeopardize their new possessions—items that were a product of wartime prosperity—through strike action.[29]

Because companies were forcing strikes in order to break unions and making an effort to import labor, violence between strikers and strike-breakers became a common feature of the strikes. The strikes generally had an enormous impact on the communities in which they took place, as many became the scene of continuous violent incidents. The violence that occurred between workers was another problem for the TWUA to deal with. Strike-related violence tended to be used to discredit the union cause, and in several cases it provided the justification for the strict injunctions that helped to break strikes. In addition, such violence clearly inflicted damage on workers themselves, as close communities were split and friendships ended forever. Several reports illustrated just how divided and polarized workers became during strikes. According to stories from other strikes, violence was related to the desperation of workers who were conscious that they were defending wartime gains. For example, Nancy Blaine wrote from a strike at Highland Park Mill in Rock Hill, South Carolina, that "there has been a feeling of desperate urgency as if time were running out and the fight was now or never." Workers were "afraid of the future. They are afraid the laws protecting workers will be crippled and that the companies will rule again, as they did before the war."[30]

In many cases, women, who played a central role in the strikes, were often at the heart of strike activity and violence.[31] In several strikes, the central involvement of women brought comment from the press. In the 1947 strike at Amazon Cotton Mill in Thomasville, North Carolina, the *Thomasville News-Times* headlined one report of strike violence "Women Furnish Most Excitement in Textile Strike." The paper added that with the strike crumbling, "there is a lot of hard feeling evidenced away from the mill, particularly among the women." Clearly finding the involvement of women unusual, during the court cases for women the *News-Times* repeatedly reported on how the women looked and how attractive they were.[32]

The closest insight into worker division, however, is provided by detailed reports that supervisors made during the Clifton strike. They illustrate how the community became seriously divided between strikers and nonstrikers, with the issue of crossing the picket line becoming one of public morality. One management report stated, "Pickets are saying pretty nasty things—such as: 'which man are you going to sleep with tonight'— that's the woman that lives with a man without marrying him." Reports were full of pickets exposing, or threatening to expose, nonstrikers' supposed sexual immorality. Much of the abuse was led by women, who repeatedly shouted out the names of nonstrikers who were patrons of black prostitutes. One report noted, "One car came in and one of the women hollered and asked him about that woman you sleep with." Women also acted with ferocity against one another at Clifton, as in other strikes. A report from the end of the strike described how women camped outside the home of female strikebreakers and used "profane language." The morality of crossing the picket line was illustrated by strikers' repeated use of biblical language and the way they likened non-strikers to Judas. The moral pressure worked, as many strikers that the company tried to entice back to work refused for fear that their moral standing in the community would suffer. For example, striker Scouel Baker told a visiting supervisor that he could not cross the picket line because "he had two girls and he did not want anyone calling them names on account of him returning to work." [33]

The postwar strikes hurt the TWUA in a number of ways. The most obvious effect was lost locals. Among the local unions that were destroyed completely were those at Gaffney, Huntsville, Rockingham, Thomasville, Siler City, and Rock Hill. Thus, the union's biggest strikes were all failures. Locals were also lost through strikes in a variety of other locations, including Athens Manufacturing Company in Athens, Georgia, and Pacific Mills in Rhodiss, North Carolina.[34]

The strikes also hurt TWUA financially. Despite some problems in getting relief to its striking workers in the South, the union did spend a vast amount of money on southern strikes. In the two years between 1946 and 1948 the TWUA spent over $500,000 in direct strike support in the South. The Gaffney strike alone cost over $75,000.[35] The strikes seriously debilitated the union, robbing it of the reserves it needed to protect southern locals against a determined employer attack. Many in the union clearly became frustrated with the South, seeing it as a continual financial drain that yielded few returns. Rieve himself complained in 1950 about the prohibitive cost of southern strikes. The TWUA's failure to secure contracts out of its southern strikes was crucial, because it was in these years that the northern textile industry went into a rapid decline. Thus, the union was unable to build a secure, dues-paying South to replace its declining northern base.[36]

Lost strikes also clearly damaged the union's broader organizing prospects. Given the commitment and violence that accompanied postwar strikes, it is not surprising that the failure of strikes generally left workers bitter and disillusioned. Organizers' reports continually highlighted how difficult it was to win elections in plants where a past strike had failed. It was no coincidence that the plants where the TWUA lost major postwar strikes were never subsequently organized. Strike defeats were publicized across the South and did little to inspire workers who were thinking of organizing.[37] Sometimes the link between strike defeats and election de feat was very direct. Shortly after the unsuccessful strike at Woodside Cotton Mill in Greenville, South Carolina, the TWUA went through an election at the company's plant in Easley, South Carolina, and suffered an enormous defeat. Auslander wrote, "The election is over and we took a terrific beating of 435 to 79. There is little doubt but what with the election following on the heels of the Woodside strike in Greenville we were in a vulnerable position, particularly where we were not able to gain anything as a result of the strike." [38]

Many in the union felt that the strikes helped establish a legacy of de feat in the South that made workers reluctant to unionize. Larry Rogin, for example, felt that workers became more cautious because "they had seen strikes lost in all their neighboring mills like Tarboro, like Hunts ville, like Gaffney. . . . These things were known, you couldn't keep them secret." Rogin felt this position was understandable, because in asking workers to strike, the union was asking them to fight against enormous odds. As he put it, "We were asking the workers to take on too unequal a struggle," given the enormous advantages held by the manufacturers.[39]

It was, indeed, the amount of strikebreaking power available to manu facturers that made postwar strikes so difficult to win. It was not that southern textile workers lacked militancy but that they had precious lit tle else. The TWUA lacked effective governmental protection, sufficient finances, and simple economic power to win strikes. In several strikes, workers who were ably backed up by their union sustained a solid shut down for long periods of time but still could not win. The TWUA's own analysis of the Gaffney strike, for example, was that the effort repre sented "an inspiring demonstration of solidarity and courage; unfortu nately it proved fruitless in the face of unlimited company resources and ceaseless community hostility." To understand these problems more closely, however, it is necessary to look at one particular strike in closer detail.[40]

Solidarity in Tarboro, North Carolina: A Case Study

In the 1940s, Tarboro was a flat, dusty town of around six thousand in habitants, located in eastern North Carolina away from the state's textile belt. The town's main enterprise, however, was Hart Cotton Mill. The five hundred workers of this mill spent most of 1949 on strike trying to gain a union contract. This strike of a small mill in a small town at tracted a considerable degree of national attention and publicity. Colum nist Murray Kempton wrote about the strike in the *New York Post*, while TWUA staffer Dick Conn, whose brother Lewis played a leading role in the strike, was inspired to write a labor novel based on the strike's events. Governor Kerr Scott made repeated attempts to settle the strike, as did national organizations such as the National Religion and Labor Foundation. Tarboro workers traveled to their nation's capital to testify before a congressional hearing. The strike also became the subject of a lengthy and public legal battle, involving first the NLRB and then the circuit court.

Like earlier southern textile strikes, such as Gastonia in 1929, the Tarboro strike interested a wide range of groups because it was a classic struggle of southern labor. Indeed, for many the Tarboro strike came to symbolize the struggle for unionism in the South. This was especially true for the TWUA's North Carolina director, Lewis Conn. A tall, dark-haired man, Conn, like many other TWUA officials, came from a Jewish background and was attracted into the labor movement as an idealistic young man in the 1930s. He was active in the union movement in his native Kentucky before starting work for the TWUA in the South in 1939. Well-respected within the union, Conn had been involved in several other postwar contract strikes in North Carolina before the Tarboro strike, and he quickly recognized the dispute's importance. Describing the strike as "the most widely publicized labor dispute that has occurred in North Carolina for many, many years," he added that "the importance of victory in the Tarboro strike cannot be overstated. The strike must be won if our union is to go forward."[41]

The strike was so important because it was seen within liberal circles as an archetypal postwar union-busting attempt. Union president Emil Rieve declared that "in reality, this dispute involves far more than 500 Tarboro workers. The outcome will affect the welfare of workers throughout North Carolina and in other states as well." If the company succeeded in breaking the union, "the same tactics will be followed by other mills. Textile workers will be back where they were a decade ago." A similar sense of importance was felt by the union's southern attorney, Bob Cahoon, who led the TWUA's legal battle in the strike. In October 1949, this thirty-four-year-old North Carolinian called the strike "the most important case that we have had anywhere in the United States." He added that the strike was "a focal point of interest in the entire textile industry of the nation, as both management and labor recognize that there is being fought a fundamental issue[:] . . . whether or not the employer is required to bargain in good faith, and whether or not the laws provided are effective to compel employers to respect the rights of employees." Despite its fundamental importance, the Tarboro strike, like most postwar contract disputes, has received no historical attention.[42]

Hart Cotton Mill was organized by the TWUA at the end of World War II. The roots of the 1949 strike were evident in 1946, when the mill's absentee owners, Ely and Walker Dry Goods Company of St. Louis, Missouri, fired local plant manager Mr. Youngblood and replaced him with Marcus Carter, an outsider from St. Louis. The issue of chain ownership, a common theme of the postwar strikes, was at the heart of the Tarboro dispute. Youngblood's removal was clearly connected with the fact that he had settled a short strike with the union in 1946, an action that anti-union Ely and Walker disapproved of. Supervisor L. D. Lilley, for example, testified before the NLRB that Youngblood told him, "I settled that strike, but I didn't last long. Carter might as well 'satchel up' and get ready to go if he settles this one, because he won't last long."[43] With Youngblood's removal, there was a clean sweep of all management personnel; new staff members were brought in from outside. At the same time, there was a dramatic change in the company's attitude toward the union. Local union president Charlie Stancil testified that overseer John Umphlett told him, "I can tell you now, Charlie, that's a union-busting committee that's being sent here." Evidence of this was provided by Carter, who shortly after taking over simply refused to meet with the union and settle grievances.[44]

These events showed the important role played by the St. Louis owners of the mill, who through these changes took charge of the Tarboro situation. Plant manager Youngblood and most of his supervisors were local and popular, with a reputation for respecting the workers with whom they had been raised. In contrast, Marcus Carter was a stern and distant outsider who was never popular among Tarboro workers. This change in personnel ensured that Ely and Walker had men running the plant who were answerable to them. Illustrating Ely and Walker's control over events in Tarboro, during the 1949 negotiations Carter spent a great deal of time on the phone, clearing all decisions with his supervisors in St. Louis. At the congressional hearing, it was established that Carter decided labor relations policy "with members of the staff of officers and directors of the St. Louis dry goods house."[45]

As in many other postwar strikes, the TWUA found itself dealing with a powerful chain company with a variety of interests in the South. The strategic weakness of the union's position in the Hart Mill was glaring from the beginning. Ely and Walker, a wholesale dry goods house that substantially controlled Hart mill, used the mill to produce cloth that was then processed separately and sold. The company's holdings were vast. It directly controlled 250,000 spindles, and it had a stake in 530,000 more through substantial minority ownership of Pacific Mills and Woodside Mills, both South Carolina–based chains. The Tarboro plant was therefore only a small part of its overall operation. The company's labor relations policy was largely controlled by its president, E. P. Cave, a rotund sixty-seven-year-old executive with a fanatical hatred of unions.[46] Cave's role in the Tarboro strike was a strange one: he never made a public appearance in Tarboro, yet clearly exerted a huge influence on the company's conduct in the strike. But for the TWUA, the determination of distant outside ownership to break one of their local unions in the South was what made the Tarboro strike epitomize this period. Lewis Conn, for example, thought the strike illustrated the determination of "absentee owners . . . to crush the union of their employees."[47]

The way that the strike began was also seen by the union as typical of many other postwar conflicts. Negotiations for a new contract reached a standstill in May 1949. With time running out, the union dropped its initial proposals for improving the contract and proposed that it would be willing to renew without any changes. The company, however, insisted on three changes: a no-strike clause, removal of a clause protecting workers from wage reductions when workloads were changed, and, most important, removal of the checkoff. Lewis Conn, who handled the negotiations for the union, claimed that these demands typified the way that recent antilabor legislation allowed employers to bust unions. Indeed, of these three contract issues, two were the direct product of the Taft-Hartley Act. Under Taft-Hartley the no-strike clause that the company proposed would have made the union liable for unauthorized strikes, even if they were initiated by workers who were not union members. Taft-Hartley also decreed that state right-to-work laws took priority over its own union security provisions. In North Carolina, as in most southern states, this meant that the voluntary checkoff was the only form of union security available; both maintenance of membership and the union shop were prohibited.[48] Hence, attacks on the checkoff took on a new potency. Collectively, these three proposals made up an excellent union-busting formula. The company could weaken the union by removing the checkoff; then, by arbitrarily changing workloads, it could force a strike for which the union would be liable. The NLRB itself concluded that these proposals left the union in "an impossible position," especially as the removal of the workload protection clause gave the company "the perfect means of precipitating a strike."[49]

That the company wanted to force the union to strike was clear from its behavior in the negotiations. The NLRB called the company's positions "ephemeral" and added that "this is one of those occasions where the Respondent 'lacked a sincere purpose to reach an agreement.'" Marcus Carter introduced these three issues only twenty-four hours before the contract was due to expire, having earlier proposed a list of different changes, which were now dropped. When Conn asked if the company was serious in injecting these proposals so late in the negotiations, Carter replied, "Of course I'm serious. The contract is going to expire tomorrow night, isn't it?" Federal mediator Seth Brewer spent several hours with Carter trying to convince him to renew the contract. Carter told Brewer that he knew that refusal to do so would mean a strike. This possibility did not worry him. He said, "Well, the gates will remain open. And the people are welcome to work without a contract." This reaction typified the way that chain mills had no fear of a strike. Once the strike began on May 12, 1949, it was Conn who tried to set up further sessions with Carter, who told him that he could not meet for at least a month and that "it was going to be a long strike." When a session was finally set up for June 2, the union, realizing the seriousness of the situation, brought in George Baldanzi, who had a lot of experience dealing with tough southern executives. The exchanges between Baldanzi and Carter did not lack color, but they achieved nothing. At the close of the meeting, Baldanzi screamed, "Listen, you are not fooling us, we know what you are thinking, you are thinking you are going to take advantage of a slump in the market and beat the union." Carter "turned red in the face" and retorted, "It's none of your damn business what I am thinking."[50]

As Baldanzi's remarks indicated, the willingness of the company to force a strike was related to poor market conditions in the textile industry: 1949 marked the end of the postwar boom that had brought the industry its considerable prosperity. Cave's St. Louis office instructed Carter to take a firm stand against the union because of the contracting market. The company's economic position was important in determining its strike conduct. The way that this downturn in the market put the squeeze on the union reflected a long-term problem for all textile unions. In the past, it had proved difficult to win textile strikes because of fluctuating market conditions in this intensely competitive industry. Overproduction had plagued the industry before the war and continued to do so after 1948. In the overcrowded market of the 1920s and 1930s, it was often cheaper for companies to shut down for a while, as in a strike, than to operate. This had been a fundamental problem in the 1934 uprising. A similar situation faced Hart Mills in 1949. The company emphasized that the mill no longer made a profit and that it was cheaper for them to remain shut down than to operate. In last-minute negotiations in Tarboro, Carter told the union that he was "indifferent as to whether or not the union struck, as he could sell all the cotton he had in the warehouse and make more money than by operating the mill with it." Not surprisingly, the meeting ended without further agreement.[51]

The company's fear of increased competition was crucial in guiding their strike strategy. The correspondence between Cave and Carter showed that they felt the mill needed modernizing, and they worried that the union would hinder this. Like other southern companies that the union had under contract, they worried that unorganized mills, which outnumbered unionized mills four to one, could undercut them and force union mills out of the market. Unionized mills, aware of their minority position, were reluctant to allow their costs to increase ahead of non-union competition. They also wanted a free hand to change workloads as economic conditions varied. This was a central problem for the TWUA in this period, and it resurfaced continually in the union's dealings with organized plants. A product of the textile industry's competitiveness and the union's inability to organize a majority of firms, it prevented the union from establishing superior conditions in organized plants, which would aid further unionization. In negotiations, Carter continually referred to the fact that "only 20% of the textile mills in the South were organized." He also claimed that "we felt it would certainly be to the advantage of the workers to be in a mill which was competitive and operating." [52]

Apart from these legitimate economic fears, the company's claim that the union would prevent them from remaining efficient also illustrated an ideological annoyance with the union's influence in the plant. It is clear that the company felt threatened by the union, feeling that it was wrongly usurping the rights of management in the plant. Like many other U.S. executives, these managers believed that they had unilateral control of the mill and that a union should not infringe on this power. Carter claimed that the union was not cooperative: "we have seen no indication that the union would assist us in many problems in the mill." He complained about the union "intimidating workers when they didn't desire to join," which "seemed to demoralize morale and certainly didn't add anything to the efficiency." Carter's superior Frank Leslie claimed that relations with the union had been marked by "constant bickering, unreasonable complaints and demands" and that the union's decision to call a strike was "the 'oak tree that broke the camel's back.'" Carter was also reported to have displayed "considerable personal pique" over an arbitration decision he lost to the union in 1948, and this was clearly influential in forming his decision to fight the union in 1949. [53]

The belief that the union was not cooperating also influenced the company's refusal to grant the checkoff. Carter claimed that in previous years "we stated that we were willing to check off union dues, hoping that the union would co-operate and assist management in running the mill efficiently." Now Carter claimed he was unwilling to "take positive action in helping to continue the advancement of a group that was out to destroy him." The NLRB concluded that this remark constituted "eloquent evidence that Carter had determined to eliminate this 'group.'" The checkoff was at the center of the Tarboro strike, as in many other postwar strikes. The company's other main objection to the checkoff was also a common one. They viewed the checkoff as a concession that the NWLB had forced upon management and that should now be taken back. [54]

When the strike was called on May 12, 1949, Tarboro workers walked out en masse. The strike quickly took on the character of a siege, with the company making repeated efforts to break the morale of workers and get them into the plant. These attempts included the threat of eviction from company housing, a tactic that had been used successfully in other strikes. [55] Supervisors also visited strikers to try to induce them to return to work. In all of these activities, the NLRB ruled that the company overstepped its legal rights. The company was found guilty of offering individual workers better conditions if they returned to work than they had offered to the union as a whole and of threatening to close the mill if strikers did not return. That September the company was also successful in obtaining a harsh injunction that drastically restricted picketing.[56]

The Tarboro strikers clearly faced enormous odds, confronted by a company that had deliberately precipitated a strike and was willing to break the law to beat the union. In addition, the market position of the mill robbed the union of any economic leverage. Nevertheless, the workers had many forces in their favor. Not only were they militant; they also received support from a wide variety of sources, including the wider community and state politicians. This support was unusual, given that historians have generally emphasized the hostility of these groups and their role in breaking southern textile strikes. Indeed, the role of community opposition and local state power has figured prominently in both traditional and recent historiography, which has stressed the mill owner's dominance of the community and close links to the political power structure. By contrast, in northern industrial communities it has been argued that local political protection and community support helped workers to win strikes and form unions.[57]

Very few Tarboro workers crossed the picket lines at any time during the strike, which lasted nearly seven months. TWUA Local 316 was a strong and cohesive unit. When the strike began, of the 550 workers employed, less than 60 were not union members. The strike was eventually abandoned by the union because the company had succeeded in getting over 200 workers into the mill and had one full shift running. Most of these workers had been brought in from outside, however; less than forty were union members at the time the strike began. As former union secretary Mae Dawson remembered, "It was just a handful of our people that went into work. . . . I could almost name them on my ten fingers."[58]

Those involved in the strike praised the militancy of the strikers. Indeed, for most of the strike Lewis Conn, the main TWUA representative in Tarboro, was convinced that this militancy would ensure a victory. After a month he wrote privately to Rieve that "the morale of the workers is excellent. There is no production going on." He was confident about the outcome of the strike, describing workers as "extremely militant." Even when the company secured an injunction in September, normally an ominous sign, Conn wrote, "My belief is that an injunction will not break the strike. . . . I do believe we can win this strike." He cited the continued high morale of the strikers and the failure of the company's attempt to recruit a back-to-work movement. Once the strike had been abandoned, Conn made it clear that this move had nothing to do with the spirit of the strikers. Indeed, just before the strike was called off he wrote that strikers were still "holding firm and after half a year on strike

are exhibiting admirable spirit and determination." Overall, Conn concluded that "there have been few strikes in the history of North Carolina
where the workers have held their ranks so solidly." [59]

Many strikers reacted to the visits they received from "bossmen" with
considerable bravery, especially considering that the men who were visiting them had the power to fire them. Striker Gurney Mitchell, for example, told a supervisor, "Mr. Fowler, I will be glad to go back to work
when Mr. Carter decides he will bargain on a contract with the union. I
won't go back until then." Many workers showed a spirited resistance to
the company's attempt to break down the strikers' collective stance and
deal one-on-one. Walter Aldeman, for example, told Carter, "I think I
know the facts. I have followed the papers and attended my union meetings. . . . Mr. Carter, I cannot bargain for myself, or for the other employees in this matter. We have a union committee and union representatives to do the bargaining for us." Aldeman even offered to make Carter
an appointment with the union committee. Most workers refused the
company's attempt to break the bond between them and their union.[60]

Tarboro workers were indeed determined to fight for their union. In
this classic postwar textile strike, worker militancy sprang from the simple desire to have a union. Workers showed that they were aware of the
company's intention to bust the union and were fighting to continue to
have a voice in their conditions. Dignity, protection, and workplace
democracy were cited by many former strikers as their goals when they
recalled the strike. Many explicitly rejected economic considerations as a
rationale for the dispute. Mae Dawson, a small, determined woman who
played a leading role in the strike, felt that "we weren't striking for more
money, we were striking for rights, things we wanted to have. The company that owned it was determined on doing away with the union, that
was their main object. . . . We knew what we were fighting for." Gerald
Worrell, a thin young man of twenty at the time of the strike, recalled
that "it really wasn't that we wanted more money or anything, we
wanted to be treated fair." Calm great-grandmother Madelin Wells remembered the turbulent events of the strike, and her participation in it,
very clearly. She felt that she was striking for "a better place to work . . .
better times for lunch, or supper, because lots of times they didn't stop
for nothing, didn't have no lunch break, you ate on your job. . . . Sometimes, if you talked to them, it made them mad." Many felt that money
was not the issue because their wages were already higher than most
other jobs available in Tarboro, such as working in a retail store. The
comments of Vivian Gurkins typified the lack of agitation over the wage
issue: "we weren't asking for more money, because they paid us pretty
good at that time, we were making more than the telephone company
were, we got real good money compared to what other people got." Bill

Hoard, a big man with a deep voice, remembered the union-busting nature of the dispute quite clearly: "We had a union contract, and they didn't want to sign it, they wanted to bust the union."[61]

Despite the lack of economic appeal, many workers provided vivid evidence of this desire for the protection that a union offered in written sources as well, especially those workers who described their motives for striking before the NLRB. These workers described unfair company treatment and the way that the union had begun to alleviate these problems. Like workers in other locations in the textile South, they enjoyed, and did not want to lose, the freedom from humiliating company control that the union gave them. Local union president Charlie Stancil testified that "the union made a big difference in the way the overseers acted toward the people." He described how the union had ended the very unpopular practice of replacing regular workers with "spare hands" at times when work was slack. Others testified about the enormous difference that seniority had made to them.[62] Most workers were mobilized behind the union because of the voice it gave them to overcome years of company dominance. This sentiment was best exemplified by a forty-two-year-old striker, Lester Matthews, who gave remarkable testimony before the NLRB. He explained that "I am on strike because I have been a textile worker since before I was big enough to leave my mother." He added, "I think I know pretty well what this dispute is all about. We are trying to keep our right under the law to have a union so that we can have at least something to say about what rules we will work and live under, and try to build a union strong enough that our kids won't have it quite as tough as I had it." The company was "trying to split us up and . . . take from us our only real protection, our right to stand together in a union. We resent that, and we do not mean to be beat down."[63]

These responses also show the sense of collective strength and empowerment that many workers drew from the strike. TWUA's southern attorney Bob Cahoon remembered vividly that during the strike Tarboro was "really a revolution. These people who had always been on the bottom and taken orders were saying 'We're not going to take orders.' It may not have been against any written law but it was against the law that everybody knew." Many workers took pride in the way that they were able to run the strike themselves. They formed strike committees, and members of those committees proudly described how "we textile workers have trained men and women out of our own ranks to administer our programs." The picket line became the center of a new community, and the whole community became involved in the strike. Strikers fixed up a special amplifying system on the picket line and sang songs; their favorite was "Solidarity Forever." Many recalled how the community became closer during the strike and how this new closeness sustained strikers.

Others remembered the strike as an educational experience they were glad they had been through.[64]

Pat Knight, who worked closely with the strikers, remembered that she was able to achieve a great deal of educational work during the strike because strikers were so focused on union business. She too recalled the militancy and spirit of the Tarboro strikers. Strikers met every night in emotional meetings that kept morale high. When Knight herself suggested meeting twice a week rather than every night, they refused and continued to meet every night until the end of the strike. The meetings always began with a prayer and were strongly influenced by religion. Knight felt that prayer was useful because most strikers were church-going, and "the shiest kinds of people find it very easy to get up and pray and really talk on strike subjects with the Lord's blessing." The way that religion sustained strikers suggests parallels with the civil rights movement, where religious faith was also crucial in aiding grassroots resistance. Many of the strongest strikers were women, and they played a crucial role in keeping spirits up. Knight remembered it was the female strikers who kept up her own morale, even though she was supposed to be helping them.[65]

The strike also received a considerable degree of support from the town as a whole. On May 21, for example, the strikers were given permission to use Tarboro's historic town common for a giant cookout. A local department store provided all the food, while the drinks were donated by a local retailer. Town leaders gave the strikers many expressions of support. A local teacher, B. J. Mickelson, told strikers that "the entire community is behind you." Many former strikers remembered sympathetic acts from merchants. Former striker Ray Holland, for example, recalled one store that allowed strikers to buy new clothes for their children on credit, knowing that many would be unable to repay him: "a lot of folks said if it wasn't for Mr. Shugar, a lot of children wouldn't have had clothes to go to school with."[66]

It would be misleading to imagine that all merchants and other townspeople supported the strike. The attorney for the town during the strike, Herbert H. Taylor, recalled that in reality the town was ambivalent. A respected member of the "uptown" community, eighty-two-year-old Taylor, still a lawyer in the same office he used during the strike, remembered that although they helped the union, merchants also "played both sides of the fence." He explained that "the merchants would complain, not publicly, but privately, and explain their gifts by saying that these people were their customers, and that if they didn't support them they'd lose them. At the same time they would say that the police and courts were not protecting them by letting the strike continue." It is clear, however, that in Tarboro mill workers were not looked down on as "lintheads." Taylor felt, for example, that many townspeople supported the strikers because they knew them well and "were highly regarded in the community." Similarly, Pat Knight remembered that many members of the "uptown" community went to the same churches as strikers and consequently were sympathetic to their struggle. This support the strikers received from familiarity with the town was clearly helped by the fact that the company was owned by outsiders and its top managers all lived out of state.[67]

The Tarboro strikers also received support from North Carolina governor Kerr Scott. During previous strikes in the state, governors had generally taken the company position, often providing troops to help break strikes. Liberal Democrat Scott, however, openly criticized the conduct of the company and publicly intervened in the dispute. He called both sides to the governor's mansion for a meeting on October 6. At this meeting, Scott clearly felt alienated by the attitude of the company. When the company prevented a settlement by rejecting his proposal for arbitration, Scott remarked that the company wanted to "bust the union." This tense relationship was revealed more starkly in a second meeting on October 19, when Scott traveled to New York to meet with company chief Frank Leslie and TWUA president Rieve. According to Leslie's private account of the meeting to E. P. Cave, Leslie and Scott had gotten into an argument, and Scott had called the company's attitude "inflexible," "uncompromising," and "adamant." Scott emphasized that "absentee ownership had the same moral responsibility as local ownership," to which Leslie later remarked, "I did not consider it relevant whether or not the Hart Cotton Mills was owned by the Soviet ambassador." This meeting, the last major attempt to settle the Tarboro strike, ended in a shambolic manner. Rieve and a Mr. Crane, a conciliator for the North Carolina State Labor Department, withdrew to leave Scott and Leslie alone. According to Leslie, Scott misunderstood this move and spent "at least forty-five minutes" talking with Leslie about "Foreign Affairs, the Notre Dame–North Carolina game, and the difficulties in trying to chew tobacco in New York City where there were not sufficient receptacles for spitting." Not surprisingly, "it was generally agreed that the forty-five minutes had been largely wasted," and the meeting ended with little achieved. Scott emerged from this tête-à-tête to say that "fundamentally, the trouble is that the company just doesn't believe in unions, and the union does"—a deceptively simple statement that summed up the basic truth of this postwar textile strike, and many others as well.[68]

Scott's intervention, and his public call for arbitration, helped to broaden the knowledge of the strike. Papers across North Carolina also began to cover the dispute. In general, press opinion was favorable to the strikers. The *Raleigh News and Observer* was the most vociferous in its criticism of the company, echoing Scott's call for arbitration. Like Scott, the paper concentrated on the absentee ownership angle. It claimed, for example, that "no mill owned by outside capital . . . has a right to insist upon prolonging serious trouble by declining arbitration."[69]

With this coverage, the strike also became increasingly important for the union. Signifying this, the TWUA started to picket Ely and Walker's headquarters in New York. According to the *Tarboro Daily Southerner*, this was "just another indication that the strike, which first attracted the attention of North Carolina, is now taking a nation-wide prominence." The TWUA's commitment to the Tarboro strikers is difficult to fault. Realizing the crucial importance of relief, the national union poured money into Tarboro, going beyond its normal relief policy. The *Raleigh News and Observer* sent reporter Simmon Fentress into Tarboro, and his detailed report highlighted the role of the union's relief effort in maintaining workers' spirits. High morale was maintained partly because the union proved willing to make payments on strikers' installment plans. One striker "told how a necessary payment on his house had been met, strike or no strike. Another said the notes on his new refrigerator and washing machine are being extended and the extension fees paid." In Tarboro, the fact that the union fulfilled workers' obligations kept them faithful and determined. Many workers also cited the satisfactory nature of the union's relief effort as their reason for refusing to go back to work when the company visited. Even after forty-five years, most former strikers praised the backing they had received from the union, although they remembered the amount of grits and fatback they had to eat during the strike.[70]

Thus, in Tarboro a militant and determined workforce was sustained by the active support of their governor, a large section of the community, the press, and their international union. However, this backing was not enough to force the company to change its position. What was crucial was that the company never showed any interest in reaching a settlement. This was made abundantly clear in the closing days of the strike, when Carter was called to testify before a congressional committee, which concluded, "You don't lead us to believe here that even now, in spite of any severe or tense situations, that you would enter into an agreement."[71]

It was in the light of this intransigence that Lewis Conn made his decision to call off the Tarboro strike at the end of November. In explaining this decision, Conn cited the fact that "the company had made it clear that it would not sign a contract even if the union surrendered all its demands." He pointed out what had happened to the union in other southern strikes when it had tried to fight a chain company to the finish. He mentioned the strike at Amazon Mill in Thomasville, North Carolina, where the union fought Cannon Mills for over a year and had to call off the strike with "no organization left." In Tarboro, he reasoned that if the union called off the strike with its membership intact, it would be in a position to rebuild the union in the mill, while pressing charges with the NLRB.[72]

The Tarboro strike was a victory for economic power, and this was the way it was interpreted by those involved in it. Even without the downturn in the market, it is doubtful whether TWUA could have won a contract in the Tarboro strike. Pat Knight, for example, felt that the strike

was a good example of the way that the union was outgunned in many postwar strikes: "they had a lot of interests, and it was very easy for them just to shut this mill down and forget it. . . . they could live with a nonproducing mill for a long time." Former strikers remembered that they supported the ending of the strike because they realized that they were unable to stay on strike as long as the company could stay shut. Gerald Worrell, for example, thought that "the union that we had just wasn't big enough to fight the mill company. . . . They didn't mind losing money because they had other plants that were still running." Catherine Hathaway simply stated, "They could afford to stay shut down better than we could afford to stay out of work"—a point of view that was echoed by others.[73]

The strike also showed that union victory was not guaranteed even with strong support from the NLRB, despite the faith that the union placed in the board. Pressed by the TWUA, the board ruled quickly on the Tarboro case: it found the company unequivocally guilty of unfair labor practices. Conn was triumphant. He wrote Rieve that "the NLRB hearing . . . was all our show. . . . Company witnesses, Carter in particular, were terrible—evasive, dishonest, and caught in lie after lie. We have, of course, great loyalty among our members here." Conn saw this NLRB victory as the platform on which to rebuild the union. Hart Cotton Mills saw it rather differently. Like many companies, the mill showed a flagrant disregard for the NLRB and ignored the decision. It also hired notorious anti-union lawyer Whiteford Blakeney and appealed the NLRB decision to the U.S. Circuit Court of Appeals. Its reliance on legal methods was typical of the methods southern textile companies increasingly used to fight unions after World War II.

Indeed, the company's economic power continued to determine the union's fate after the strike. It is clear that once Hart Mill was running again the company had much greater control over workers, especially in the area of job security. Former strikers remembered that when they returned to work, the company used its economic power to kill any union spirit. Floyd Morris, like others, recalled clearly that many of the union leaders were fired in the first few months after returning to work: "Carter would find some fault against a person because of the strike. He done that until he cleaned them out, because he couldn't fire them, he had to find some fault." Conn complained in April 1950 that in spite of the NLRB order, "the company is . . . weeding out some of our good union members." By November, he reported that "the company is playing tough and refuses to comply with the strong NLRB order handed down in our favor." Describing the way that the situation had deteriorated, Cahoon wrote that the company had launched a "campaign to persuade its employees that no union activity will be tolerated" and added that workers were "completely fed up." Thus, it was very difficult for the union to devise a winning strategy.[74]

The remaining hopes of saving the Tarboro local were firmly dashed on July 31, 1951, when the U.S. Circuit Court of Appeals set aside the NLRB's order and dismissed its petition to enforce. Leaders of the TWUA reacted with disbelief and anger. Cahoon wrote, "The decision stinks." Conn found the decision shocking because "in all my experience in the labor movement I have never seen a more blatant violation of the act than that committed by Hart Cotton Mills. They set out deliberately to destroy a local union." The court based its decision on the fact that the company had met its obligations of bargaining with the union, and it upheld the company position that the union should have signed a contract with no checkoff. The decision showed how much extra power the Taft-Hartley Act gave employers, especially if they went through the motions of bargaining. In fact, an internal NLRB memorandum discussing the case had declared that the Tarboro case "is not a strong one particularly in view of the Taft-Hartley definition of collective bargaining. The company has very skillfully gone through the motions with Blakeney plotting the course."[75]

With the TWUA unable to overturn the court decision, the only option left was to try and reorganize the plant. The union sent organizers into Tarboro in the summer of 1952 and managed to secure an election in December. The company launched a big campaign prior to the election, placing a three-page letter in the *Tarboro Daily Southerner* informing workers that if the union returned, there would be another strike. On December 19, 1952, the Tarboro story finally came to a close as workers voted against the TWUA by 357 to 236. No union has ever reorganized the mill, although it has changed hands several times since the strike.[76]

The rejection of unionism by Tarboro workers in 1952 reflected the profound impact that the failed strike had had on their lives. In contrast to the national union, which reasoned that the battle for a contract had not ended with the strike, strikers viewed the return to work as the end of the road. Indeed, the memories of former strikers reveal a hidden history of the strike that starkly contrasts the impressions gained from the perspective of the national union. While Lewis Conn may have been optimistic, Arky Andrews remembered the despondent mood at the end of the strike—the time when, as a young woman, she began a lifetime of work in the mill: "people knew they had lost what they were striking for. They had lost the union, that's what they were striking for." The union decision was inevitably viewed by some as a sellout. The anger of Gerald Worrell was still evident after forty-five years: "we found out the union wouldn't back us up all the way. The union come in and told us, if you want your job, go on in and get it, because we're leaving. That was it. The money run out, they run out." When it came to the 1952 vote, former strikers stressed their fear of another strike and of losing their jobs, as the company had made clear that it would not tolerate unionism. Floyd Morris, for example, felt that the strike killed the possibility of any future activism because "people had it rough" and took many years repaying their debts. The mood of the workers was best remembered by Arky Andrews: "People were afraid of their jobs, that's the whole thing, and rather than to have what they went through when they had a union and the plant didn't support it, they were better off not to have it." She added, "The company came round and told you how . . . to vote, remember who you were working for. I don't know if I'm supposed to say that, but that's the truth."[77]

The strike also left many painful memories that led to a social amnesia concerning unions and the strike itself for many years. According to one former striker, "union was never talked. You didn't speak of a union in any way. That was just a known fact." The number of Tarboro workers who broke the picket line may have been small, but it was enough to cause lasting divisions within a very close community. Mae Dawson, like many others, was never able to feel the same about those she knew who crossed the picket line, even those who were members of her own family: "Some of my close friends, I even had a cousin who went through the strike line, and there was a bad feeling there for a long, long time about these people. . . . I didn't hate them, but I just had a different feeling for them, because they did not stick together, and if you don't stick together you're going to die separately." Vivian Gurkins, normally an ebullient and bright woman, explained sadly how the strike had affected the community: "It was a lot of hard feelings with people, some of them I reckon still don't like each other. . . . A lot of people never, ever had anything to do with them [the nonstrikers]." Floyd Morris, who himself broke the picket line at the end of the strike, vividly remembered the hard feelings this caused. Gesturing with his hands, he stated sadly that "the people were crossed up like that. After the union a lot of people that belonged to the union wasn't friendly like they were before. It went on, but it finally wore out." Many stressed the lasting impact of the strike by providing examples of workers who went to the grave without speaking to one another again. For many others, the legacy of social division was one of their most lasting memories of the strike.[78]

The pain that the strike left was typical of labor conflict in small southern communities, where union allegiances were taken seriously. This grim legacy appears to seal the fate of the Tarboro strike as a depressing story of union defeat that was all too typical for the TWUA in these years. The national union certainly did not gain anything from the strike. The Tarboro defeat was a major one that was repeatedly used against the union in organizing campaigns. Surprisingly, however, very few former strikers felt that the strike was a waste or a negative experience. The main reason for this was that once the union was defeated, conditions at the mill improved considerably. Many felt that the strike had finally earned them the company's respect because they had stood up for their rights and struck for far longer than the company had imagined. The company granted better conditions because it, too, wanted to avoid a repeat of the strike. Madelin Wells typified the positive feelings former strikers drew from their militancy: "we stayed out and showed them they couldn't run over us that much, they thought we would turn around and go right on back. I think we did real good staying out as long as we did, I sure do." Like most other strikers, Bill Hoard "never did regret" the strike because the company maintained union benefits after the union had gone: "the company found out something, we earned respect. They respected us more." Others also stressed the strike's long-term, positive results. Mae Dawson explained, "I never have regretted it. I think it did some good because it taught a lot of people to stand up for their rights. Of course I always have, but there were a lot of people who learned." Gerald Worrell felt that things improved because supervisors had tried to run production jobs during the strike and had found out how hard they were. Even those who had not been keen on the strike felt that it was responsible for winning better conditions. Anna Edmondson said, "I think it was better afterwards, things was better because of the strike." [79]

Among the improvements that workers received after the strike was the introduction of vacation pay. Catherine Hathaway, who like most former strikers worked at the mill for the whole of her working life, recalled that "after the strike we began to get vacations, and we would get raises more often, they tried to keep us up. We didn't win it, but it made the company start doing better, because they had to." After the strike the mill also introduced a profit-sharing plan, which was popular with many workers. A common complaint of workers had been that the company offered no transportation to the mill. Gerald Worrell remembered that after the strike "everything improved over there, we got transportation back and forth from our homes, the mill company furnished a bus or a flat-bedded truck after the strike." Worrell thought that "the company realized that it should give the people a voice in what was going on" because "they wouldn't have another strike if they treated people fair." For workers who had emphasized dignity and fair treatment as their reasons for striking, these changes were clear victories. Mae Dawson, herself a keen unionist, recalled that "after the strike we got bonuses, Christmas parties, vacation bonuses. They were really better to us than if we'd had a union." [80]

Many also drew comfort from the fact that those who returned to work before the strike had been called off did not receive any special treatment when everybody returned. Indeed, many who had been hired from outside were laid off, and old workers were given their jobs back. This was viewed as a major triumph and another sign that the company respected strikers. Bill Hoard remembered, "When the strike was over, they took every one of us back and let them go. They really appreciated them, didn't they?" Meanwhile, the local workers who had broken the picket line did not get treated any better by managers, and they got the cold shoulder in the plant. Madelin Wells felt that nonstrikers "thought they were going to profit by it [but] they didn't have it a bit better than we did." The strike was also remembered as a positive event because of the unusual experiences it provided. Some, for example, had fond memories of meeting "Governor Kerr" and finding out he was "for the people." [81]

The positive way that former strikers recalled the Tarboro strike contrasts greatly with the way the strike's defeat was viewed by the union at the national level. For TWUA leaders, and for other liberal observers, the strike was a tragedy. The union had designated the strike as a vital test case, and its loss showed just how difficult it was for the TWUA to overcome determined corporate resistance and win a contract. Murray Kempton concluded in the *New York Post* that the Tarboro strike illustrated the classic "losing strike" described by the proletarian novels of the early 1930s. He wrote that "history and the labor triumphs of the last fifteen years" were supposed to have made the proletarian novel obsolete. However, in Tarboro one of its "traditional scenarios" was played out in "all its depressing purity." The significance of the strike defeat was also grasped by the *Raleigh News and Observer*, which commented that "the Hart Mill strike showed that in North Carolina it is still possible for a determined employer to break a strike—if the employer is willing to pay a big price." It added, "To understand the significance of this trial before the NLRB it is necessary to remember that it was not conducted under the old Wagner Act, but under the Taft-Hartley Act." Both of these reactions described a feeling that the clock had been turned back in industrial relations, that the balance had shifted back to the employers. Indeed, defeats such as Tarboro showed that employers had regained the initiative they had lost during the New Deal and, more crucially in textiles, during World War II. It was clear that weak unions such as the TWUA could no longer rely on government to help them make organizing gains: in the postwar period, this government protection was not sufficient to ensure unions' survival. As Lewis Conn concluded from the strike, "The tragedy rests in the fact that the workers . . . have no recourse under federal or state law which can effectively preserve their basic right to organization. . . . For all practical purposes, the employer is unhampered by any labor legislation." [82]

Recent studies of southern textile workers have concentrated heavily on worker culture, on the workers' distinctive nature and its consequences for unionization. The Tarboro strike illustrates, however, that the issue of worker culture and militancy was not necessarily decisive or relevant. What the determination of the strikers did bring them was important gains that can easily be missed if one studies only written sources. These gains occurred, however, at the expense of the union's survival. The Tarboro strike therefore illustrates the central problem facing the TWUA in this period—the union helped all southern textile workers because its presence in the South influenced manufacturers, as in Tarboro, to raise pay and improve conditions. As a result, living standards improved considerably. However, these economic gains hindered the union's long-term progress, because, as in Tarboro, companies preferred to pay union wages than have a union. The gains thus occurred at the expense of the survival of local unions. This dilemma was crucial, because the TWUA urgently needed to establish secure southern locals to replace its declining base in New England. Without such locals, the union would be trying to organize the South from an ever-smaller, and ever-poorer, northern base.

chapter five   **Moving Southern Wages**

The 1951 General Strike

            In the spring of 1951 the TWUA called a general strike in the South. This strike was the largest the union ever conducted in the region and, by its own admission, the most important. In terms of numbers involved, it was the second largest strike ever to occur in the South, following only the uprising of 1934. It involved 42,000 textile workers in seven states; the union pulled out all of its major southern locals plus many smaller mills. However, the general strike tactic was unsuccessful, as the one in 1934 had been, and the union suffered a major defeat.[1]

In many ways, the comparison between the 1934 and 1951 strikes is misleading. The 1934 strike involved huge numbers of unorganized workers who sought the right to organize and union recognition. In addition, it has been argued that the strike was forced on a small and poorly equipped AFL union from below by southern workers eager to test the rights given them by New Deal labor legislation.[2] In contrast, the 1951 strike, reflecting the development of the labor movement, was conducted by a secure CIO union trying to raise the wages of workers it already had under contract. The strike, indeed, reflected the priorities of the national union rather than agitation from southern workers and illustrated what problems could result from the efforts of the union's northern base to penetrate the South. Issues generated by rising wartime wages were also at the heart of the strike, especially the pressing need to establish a wage differential between organized and unorganized workers, thereby preventing nonunion workers from sharing in war-induced prosperity and holding back southern organizing.

Despite these differences, both strikes had a very similar impact on the workers and unions involved, representing central defeats that set back the cause of textile unionism in the South for many years. The strike of 1951, like that of 1934, was regarded as an important turning point by many, including most of the TWUA's leadership. Research Director Solomon Barkin, for example, felt that the strike was "crucial" and represented "the death of the union." Barkin's emphasis on the importance of the strike is particularly significant because the labor intellectual from New York spent more than forty years both working for the TWUA and examining the fate of textile unions in the South through a variety of academic publications.[3] Similarly, Ken Fiester, editor of *Textile Labor* throughout these years, felt that the 1951 strike was "very damaging" and "the worst thing that happened to us." Sol Stetin, a plainspoken Jewish New Yorker who was a member of the union's executive council in 1951 and became TWUA president in the 1960s, felt that the 1951 strike "had a very demoralizing effect on our union in the South." He added that the 1934 and 1951 defeats had similar effects: they both helped to create a "legacy of defeat" that made further unionization very difficult. In 1979 he reflected, "I've developed the belief that you're not going to make a breakthrough in the South until the labor movement can declare, and the people accept, the idea of winning. A success leads to lack of fear. There was the defeat in '34, and then the defeat in '51. . . . They created an aura of fear in the South."[4]

What the two strikes have in common, therefore, is that they are the only occasions when southern textile workers really took management on and tried to reshape the status of unions in the southern textile industry. Because both of these efforts were clear failures, they were key moments in deciding the fate of unionization in the southern textile industry. As such, they both represent pivotal events in southern labor history. But while 1934 is recognized as such and has received considerable scholarly attention, the 1951 strike has been completely overlooked and received no historical treatment. Consequently, this account uses new archival sources to tell the strike's story.[5]

The Setting

The TWUA's demands in the 1951 strike were bold and wide-ranging, indicating their desire to reshape the union's progress in the South. They were formulated by the union's newly formed National Cotton-Rayon Policy Committee, composed of delegates from locals across the South, at a meeting in Washington, D.C., on January 4, 1951. The basic demand was for a 12 percent base pay raise and a minimum rate of $1.19 per hour, representing a 20 percent increase on the minimum prevailing in many union plants. In addition, the union demanded a controversial "cost-of-living escalator" that automatically tied wages to the rise in the cost of living; employer-paid pensions with a minimum of $100 a month; a minimum of eight paid holidays per year; and company-paid medical insurance for workers and their dependents. The union decided to demand these changes in a large number of its southern locals simultaneously because many mills had contracts that were due to expire at the same time in the spring. In many other cases, contracts had clauses that allowed them to be reopened if the union wanted a wage increase. This was the first time that the union had made demands on the industry as a whole rather than bargaining with individual companies, and it clearly represented a decisive attempt to introduce industrywide bargaining of a type used by northern industrial unions.[6] Indeed, many of the changes demanded by the union mirrored the sorts of gains that had recently been won by northern industrial workers through industrywide bargaining.[7]

In several different respects, this program, while supported by southern locals, was one generated by the union's northern base, and it reflected the long-term interests of the northern-based national leadership in raising southern wages to the level of northern industrial workers. Throughout these years Rieve was committed to raising the wages and fringe benefits of southern textile workers up to the level of workers in other unionized mass-production industries such as steel, rubber, and automobiles. Like Dean Culver in Operation Dixie, he wanted to establish a genuine union wage scale that would put southern textile workers on a par with workers in northern mass-production industries and end free-riding. In 1948, for example, Rieve expressed dissatisfaction with the tremendous progress in wages that his union had helped to bring about in the South because "even though we have gained magnificently, we have not as yet reached the level of wages that other workers enjoy in other industries, and we shall not rest until we have brought that about." In 1951, Rieve justified the strike because southern textile workers earned "thirty-five cents an hour below the average for all manufacturing."[8]

In addition to the desire to win benefits for their members, the TWUA also had more compelling economic reasons to want to raise southern wages. The precarious status of the New England textile industry, where the vast majority of the union's locals were based, made raising southern wages and reducing southern competition of paramount importance. The need to raise southern wages became especially intense after the spring of 1948, when the New England textile industry entered a decline from which it never recovered. Between 1945 and 1948 the American textile industry had been protected by a booming market, as consumers were eager to buy the textiles that had been in short supply throughout the war. When this boom ended, however, the poor competitive position of many northern mills became apparent. Mill closings and mass unemployment followed, putting tremendous pressure on the TWUA. As a TWUA Executive Council Report concluded, because most TWUA members worked in the New England textile industry, "our members were the chief sufferers from the slump." Thirty-seven New England mills were liquidated in 1949 alone. Leading northern manufacturers such as Seabury Stanton, of Hathaway Mills in New Bedford, Massachusetts, blamed the decline on southern competition and claimed that unless southern wages and fringe benefits were raised considerably, "many mills are facing permanent liquidation." They pointed out that although the TWUA had virtually eliminated the wage differential, northern mills still faced crippling disadvantages because they had to pay for pensions, insurance, and many other fringe benefits that were largely absent in the South.[9]

The paramount importance of raising southern wages to protect New England was keenly felt by Rieve, who repeatedly declared war on the long-standing North-South textile wage differential. In one 1948 keynote address, Rieve revealed the roots of the 1951 strike by stating his determination to eliminate the differential and his willingness to strike the South, if necessary, to achieve this: "Our firm contention is that there should be no such differential. . . . I have a hunch that Southern employers are going to resist—and we must be prepared. We are known throughout the country as a peaceful union . . . but that was only possible because we were prepared for strikes if they had to come." Moreover, the union's own report on the strike asserted that it was called to eliminate regional wage competition. Many union activists also recalled the strike as compelled by the precarious economic condition of the union's northern base. Research Director Sol Barkin, who was also a respected economist, felt that the strike "was really stimulated, impelled, by the economic interests of the locals in the North. . . . The survival of the union was at stake in this wage battle, and the hope was that we could achieve our economic goals through a strike, and of course we didn't." The TWUA's drive to establish uniform labor standards and eliminate southern competition against their northern base had also been an important aim of the UTW in the 1934 strike. It reflected the fact that both unions had the majority of their membership in New England and that, therefore, protecting the interests of these members remained a priority.[10]

Through the TWUA's determined efforts, coupled with a booming postwar textile economy, the union was able to come close to eliminating the North-South wage differential by the end of 1947.[11] The amount of progress that had been made in raising southern wages was a major victory for the TWUA, and the union took considerable pride in this achievement. Wages were raised through a mechanism that was also driven by the union's base in the North. The union would negotiate a wage increase in the North, usually with the pattern-setting New Bedford–Fall River Manufacturers Association. They would then petition key southern employers, such as Dan River Mills in Danville, Virginia, and Cone Mills in Greensboro, North Carolina, for the same increase. These companies had become pattern-setters for the whole South: their increases were usually put into effect by other union mills, and also by nonunion mills as a way of forestalling unionization. On February 22, 1947, for example, TWUA negotiated a 10 percent increase; Dan River and Marshall Field, another major unionized chain, were the first to sign. Within two weeks, this increase had been copied by virtually all union and nonunion mills, so that in all, 550,000 southern workers received pay increases. Similarly, on November 8, 1947, after a northern increase, TWUA and key southern mills agreed to a 9 percent increase. Dan River was again first to sign. *Textile Labor* reported that the Dan River agreement had been "pivotal" as it had "cracked resistance elsewhere"—the increase had quickly been copied by other union and nonunion companies. Dan River was indeed the mill that most frequently set the wage pattern.[12]

The union consistently used this same mechanism to raise southern wages from 1942 to 1951. It achieved a solid record of winning better wages and conditions for its members, and for many nonmembers as well. This mechanism was crucial in providing the union with a replacement mechanism for industrywide bargaining in the South, thereby giving it a way of protecting its base in the North. It was also vital in giving the union a sense of influence and progress in the South. After one increase, for example, *Textile Labor* boasted that TWUA "has no counterpart in labor history" because its influence over the industry was so great in relation to its numbers. The winning of wage increases for organized and unorganized workers also won the union praise from sections of the southern press and public opinion who appreciated the prosperity that increased purchasing power was bringing to the South.[13]

The Showdown

Clearly, the demands of the union in 1951 reflected long-term goals of raising southern wages. The question remains, however, why the union chose to raise the stakes in 1951, going for a bigger increase than it had ever won before, plus other fringe items that were also cost-based, and presenting these demands to the industry as a whole. Several factors help to explain this change. Of central importance was the outbreak of the Korean War in June 1950. The textile industry had been in depression since March 1948, but when the Korean War began, the economic position of both workers and the industry changed overnight. As in World War II, textile plants were an important part of the war effort, and war orders kept them humming in 1950 and early 1951. The prosperity of the textile industry seemed to justify an ambitious wage program, especially given that mill margins were the highest they had been since the 1947–48 boom. The union pressed for its demands because they believed that their goals could be achieved even under a national stabilization program, with the cost of wage increases met from profits without an increase in prices. As one executive who negotiated with Rieve explained, "In Rieve's mind, the industry was in a position to absorb much higher wage and benefit costs. In one stroke, he wanted to wipe out any differences between North and South as well as a big chunk of the differential that existed between textiles and major hard goods industries."[14]

Rieve's push for these wage demands was also influenced by his relationship to the Wage Stabilization Board (WSB), the Korean War's equivalent of the NWLB. The WSB was part of the wage- and price-control regulations that President Truman established to hold down war-induced inflationary pressures. It was composed of industry, labor, and public representatives, and Rieve was one of the original labor members. On February 15, 1951, the WSB adopted a policy that limited wage increases to 10 percent between January 15, 1950, and July 1, 1951. Labor members immediately withdrew from the board, charging that the board was biased because the public members consistently voted with the industry members. It claimed that the 10 percent order typified the way that the board was helping industry profit from the wartime economy, ignoring "the necessity of equality of sacrifice." On February 27, 1951, the labor boycott of the stabilization program was extended when labor representatives resigned from all mobilization agencies. Union leaders demanded a new board, one that was fair to labor and that had the power to settle disputes, as was stipulated by the Defense Production Act (DPA) of 1950. Rieve's push for wage increases in 1951 was greatly influenced by his hope that a new board would be set up with the power to decide on the union's case, thereby averting a strike. In executive council meetings, he continually referred to the imminence of a "dispute section." On the eve of the strike, Rieve told management that "all we say is agree with us. Sign an agreement subject to the approval of the proper government agency and we'll take our chances to get it approved, either wholly or partially." Rieve was clearly influenced by his experiences in World War II, when he had been a member of the NWLB that the TWUA had used so successfully to win pay increases. He hoped that the fact that a government board would decide on the pay dispute would make it easier for management to make an offer.[15]

Following the Washington conference, the Cotton-Rayon Policy Committee met in Danville, Virginia, on January 14, 1951, to present its wage program to the southern membership. Meanwhile, a conference of state directors and top union officials decided on a March 15 strike deadline if the demands were not satisfactorily met. The immediate cause of the strike was the fact that southern management resisted the union's proposals wholesale, while New England employers did not. It is crucial to explore the reasons for this important shift, because it constituted an important turning point, breaking the wage pattern that had functioned for whole of the union's existence. On March 15, just as a strike vote was about to be taken, northern employers settled with the union. The TWUA did not win all of its demands, but it did secure major concessions, including a 7 percent wage increase and a cost-of-living escalator clause. With southern negotiations deadlocked, the TWUA extended the strike deadline for two weeks. The union's position was that if an agreement could be reached with one southern employer, this would be enough to avert a strike, as precedent showed that other companies would follow. They therefore targeted attention on their most important southern mill—Dan River. Rieve came south in an effort to, as he boasted, "mop up" southern negotiations with this key mill.[16]

The New England settlement left the TWUA in a very awkward situation. This was especially true as northern manufacturers had made clear that their settlement was conditional on the union's winning similar terms in the South. As Solomon Barkin remembered, "The union was caught in a vice. It had successfully concluded a wage agreement in the North and had as part of that agreement committed itself to achieve a similar wage increase in the South. Despite its weaknesses in the region it had to proceed with the commitment." Rieve himself admitted privately that "we have engaged ourselves in the North for good or evil" and added that he was "very much worried" about whether similar terms could be won in the South. Both management and union recognized that the stakes involved were high. In fact, New England management argued that the outcome of the southern negotiations would determine the survival of the New England industry, since a further widening of wage costs would force many northern mills out of business.[17]

In the week before March 31, the Federal Mediation and Conciliation Service (FMCS) intervened in the TWUA's negotiations with leading southern mills. The central negotiations were at Dan River, where Rieve had taken control, but talks were also in progress with the Marshall Field, Lowenstein, Cone, and Erwin chains. These were the companies known in the union as the "Big Five"—those that the union traditionally used to set southern wages. The FMCS reports from these talks indicated that management had similar objections in all locations. One major stumbling block was the confused wage and price situation resulting from the Korean War. Southern textile workers had received an 8 percent increase in September 1950, so the maximum increase they could receive under the 10 percent formula was 2 percent. This made settlement in the South harder than in the North, where there had been no increase since 1948. The northern offer did not, therefore, break the 10 percent formula. Most southern textile executives argued that they were unwilling to break this law and propose a bigger increase. This position was spelled out by A. D. Elliott, manager of Huntsville Manufacturing Company, part of the Lowenstein chain, who called the union's demands "against the law. . . . The company's position in this matter is that, as a legally responsible corporation, it cannot be placed in the position of failing to comply with the laws of our country." The greatest offer the union ever received was indeed 2 percent, the maximum allowed under the prevailing setup. Dan River made this offer on the eve of the strike. It was put into effect by all southern mills and was the only pay increase that the TWUA won from the 1951 strike.[18]

Many executives also used the price situation to justify their refusal to settle. The price situation was in a state of flux at the time of the negotiations. On January 26, 1951, the newly established Office of Price Administration (OPA) announced a General Ceiling Price Regulation (GCPR), which provided for a maximum price based on the maximum price of goods delivered by the manufacturer during the period from December 24, 1950, to January 25, 1951. Because these dates were used as the starting period, considerable inequities and distortions of the price structure came about. Those manufacturers who had cooperated voluntarily found their prices frozen at a lower level than those who had ignored the requests. Because of this confusion, shortly after the announcement of the GCPR, the cotton exchange closed and all textile-selling houses withdrew from the market. Through February, March, and April 1951, manufacturers awaited the announcement of a new price regulation to end the confusion. Due to the lack of price clarity, many executives claimed they were not in a position to give a wage increase. The head of Marshall Field, for example, asked, "How can we agree with the union on a substantial increase in our costs until the OPA announces what the government policy will be on prices?"[19]

The central argument that management used, however, stressed the competitive nature of the textile industry. The structure of the industry made it difficult for the union to achieve its wage goals and make southern textiles an industry with wages similar to automobiles or steel. A central problem for the TWUA in these years was the unwillingness of unionized southern companies to establish pay scales and benefits well above those in unorganized southern mills. The TWUA needed such moves so that it could protect its northern base and unionize the South. While the union constantly compared southern union wages to those in the North, however, organized southern mills were always aware of the mass of unorganized southern competition and feared that they would be forced to assume higher wage costs that unorganized mills had no obligation to follow. Many unionized companies already claimed that they paid wages higher than those prevailing in the nonunion sector. The FMCS reported that Erwin Mills refused to break the 1951 deadlock because "the company stated that it could not risk entering into an agreement of this nature since it was exceedingly doubtful that in doing so, it would have effect of influencing the balance of the southern textile industry, its petition, to follow such a wage pattern, and the company would be left in an unfavorable competitive position." The company emphasized that "only approximately 20% of the southern industry is unionized." The TWUA's treasurer, William Pollock, told the executive council that employers were resisting, especially on the cost-of-living escalator clause, because "they have the fear that non-union employers will not follow them." Similarly, the head of the Lowenstein chain reasoned that "if his company were to effect a general wage increase along with improved fringe benefits, . . . the risk other employers would not follow suit was too great." [20]

Management emphasized that it was inaccurate to compare the wages of southern textile workers with those of northern industrial workers because of the labor-intensive nature of the textile industry. The president of Dan River Mills, Russell B. Newton, declared that "the conditions in the other industries mentioned [automobiles and steel] where a large portion of total production is concentrated in comparatively few companies, make for an entirely different competitive and bargaining situation." Mills such as Marshall Field stressed in the press that given the number of producers, they could not take on the extra costs the union program demanded "and still remain competitive," especially considering that they had no assurance the competition would follow. Indeed, the FMCS reported that the company would "take a strike before agreeing." Likewise, Cone Mills claimed that the union's proposals would put them ahead of their competition and prevent them from "remaining in business." As Baldanzi himself admitted, textiles was "a highly competitive industry, where a quarter of a cent a yard means an awful lot in terms of millions of yards." Several of the big chains, with whom the union had established their most valuable and constructive relationships in the South, complained that the union was victimizing them with this program, especially in the light of the union's continued failure to organize the South. As Baldanzi reported from negotiations at Marshall Field, "They are afraid that we're driving constantly to improve standards with our people that we have organized, but not extend organization." [21]

These fears of unorganized competition reflected the real stumbling block in the 1951 negotiations: after all, this argument was most often heard in private negotiations, while the "confused price and wage" argument was put forward in the press, where the companies could portray the union as trying to break the law and sabotage the war effort. Indeed, the crucial factor was the very different position of strength in the two regions. The union's ability to secure a settlement in the North, and its inability to do the same in the South, were part of the same problem. In the North, the union had real economic leverage over management, because around 85 percent of the industry organized. In February 1951, predominantly northern-based woolen workers, who were also solidly unionized, had struck successfully for four weeks over the 1951 demands and won a settlement by maintaining a solid strike. This was seen as a precursor of what would have happened to northern cotton workers if they had struck, and it influenced the cotton manufacturers to sign with the TWUA.[22]

In the South, by contrast, the union's position was radically different, with at best only 20 percent of workers organized. In the past, southern management had voluntarily followed northern increases, especially just after the war, when the threat of organization seemed greatest. The failure of the 1951 negotiations was important because it broke this wage mechanism. The strategy of resistance was clearly finalized at the annual meeting of the American Cotton Manufacturers Institute (ACMI), which conveniently met in White Sulphur Springs, West Virginia, on the eve of the strike deadline. The gathering had a "record attendance," with over 90 percent of the southern industry present. Not surprisingly, the "strike threat" made up the "principal topic" of discussion. Speaker after speaker argued that the general strike would not work because of the TWUA's weak representation in the South. As a result, they anticipated that the effect of the strike would be to victimize union workers while their nonunion counterparts could carry on earning wartime wages. Many executives argued that a strike would be unpopular both with workers and with public opinion. The public would see it as sabotage of the war effort, while workers would not want to miss the chance to earn the highest wages the industry had ever known. Many southern executives also perceptively realized that the strike would be deeply unpopular because union workers would risk losing the consumer goods that they had recently bought on credit, while nonunion workers could go on making their payments. This was crucial, because management understood the way that war-induced prosperity made strikes more difficult to sustain, and this realization helped ensure victory in the strike. As the leading trade paper, the *Daily News Record*, reported from the conference, "The vital factor is that a major portion of the Southern mills are not unionized, and their employees would continue to be working, at the same time paying off on installment purchases of automobiles, homes, refrigerators, and other items." The overall conclusion of southern management, therefore, was that the union's weak representation and the strikers' economic vulnerability made a solid strike impossible. As the general manager of Fieldcrest Mills, Harold Whitcomb, declared, "This will not be a general strike. . . . If our mills are closed, our workers will lose their pay while the non-union mills throughout the South will continue to run."[23]

On the eve of the strike, therefore, management had a strong sense of the kill, sensing the inability of individual workers in the South to withstand a strike. In contrast, their own position meant that economically, they had little to fear from a strike. At the end of March 1951, the government suddenly halted the purchases of cotton goods. This coincided with an easing of civilian demand. This "unforeseeable turn of events," as the union called it, wrecked the union's strategy to capitalize on the industry's prosperity. To a large extent, it doomed the strike, because mill owners had accumulated inventories; thus a strike would not hurt them. Well before the strike, the *Textile Bulletin* reported belligerently that "the mills can close their doors and make money selling off their inventories." It added that the strike was "unfortunate for the workers because we rather suspect that the mills are in better shape to stand a prolonged strike than the workers, most of whom will be behind by the time they have missed one or two pay-days." A survey across North Carolina conducted by the *Southern Textile News* revealed that most mills could operate for an average of three or four months before their inventories of cotton ran out.[24]

Given the weak position of the TWUA and the enormous gamble that a general strike in the South represented, one must question why the union pressed ahead and called the strike. Those involved in making the decision all stressed the influence of the internal political situation within the union. The period between the 1950 and 1952 conventions was, indeed, one of intense politicking and scheming between the supporters of Rieve and Baldanzi. Baldanzi had survived the attempt by Rieve's supporters to oust him from the vice presidency at the 1950 convention. As a result, both sides were making preparations for an expected showdown in 1952, when Baldanzi was expected to (and did) challenge Rieve for the presidency.[25] The result of this situation on the strike call was that neither faction felt it could argue for caution because of the danger of being labeled nonmilitant. Council member and Rieve supporter Sol Stetin recalled, "It was an unfortunate experience. Neither side wanted to strike, but neither side was going to appear to be soft." Others also expressed regret in hindsight, feeling that political rivalry prevented sound judgment.[26]

Not surprisingly, accusation and counteraccusation surround the strike. According to those in the Baldanzi faction, Rieve, jealous of Baldanzi's influence in the South, wanted to prove to southern staff that he could do a better job than Baldanzi. Up to 1951, indeed, Baldanzi had built up a considerable following in the South and had been responsible for the negotiation of prior southern wage agreements. In 1951, however, Rieve pushed for the extensive wage demands and personally conducted the unsuccessful southern negotiations, despite his inexperience in dealing with southern employers. In turn, Rieve's supporters cited the support of many of the Baldanzi faction for the 1951 demands. Indeed, several of Baldanzi's leading supporters in the South supported the strike, claiming that through its ambitious demands, the union's organizing prospects in the South would be given a boost.[27]

Despite the influence of the political situation on the calling of the strike, many in the union emphasized that the strike would have occurred at some time during this period even without the split. The TWUA needed to try to establish a program like the one they adopted in 1951 in order to force unionized southern mills to set wage scales that nonunion mills would not follow. It was the same type of program that Dean Culver and many other organizers had advocated during Operation Dixie. The strike thus reflected not just union politics but a fundamental issue that dogged the TWUA in the South throughout these years. According to executive council member Larry Rogin, "the union faced a test, divided or unified it would have faced that test, could it move Southern union wages that much?"[28]

"These Guys Have a Timetable"

The strike began on April 1, 1951, when mass meetings across the South ratified the Cotton-Rayon Policy Committee decision to launch a general strike. Around 45,000 workers—just over half of the total number that TWUA had under contract in the South—were immediately involved. The strike was particularly important and risky, however, because it involved the union's most valuable southern locals, the big chain mills that had been used in the past to set southern wages. Indeed, all of the Big Five were struck. The most important location was clearly Dan River Mills, the biggest mill the union had under contract and the most important pattern-setter. Over 12,000 workers struck Dan River on April 1. The strike also affected many smaller locals. In North Carolina, for example, locals were struck in Charlotte, Henderson, Goldsboro, Brookford, Rockingham, Wake Forest, and High Point. Locals in South Carolina, Georgia, Alabama, Tennessee, and Louisiana were also involved.[29]

From the first shift after the strike began, most struck plants made no attempt to operate, while at Dan River Mills, intensive efforts were made to import labor. This move surprised union leaders. It was clearly influenced by the economic conditions prevailing in the industry. As the *Textile Bulletin* explained, "How many mill executives are anxious to run their mills when there is a shortage of orders for yarn or cloth?" It was also standard in most southern strikes of this period for companies to shut down for the first couple of months to give themselves time to weaken the strike and recruit strikebreakers.[30]

Union leaders, however, claimed throughout the strike that this move reflected a clear management strategy that had been established earlier: break the strike by smashing the union in its most important southern ion.[31] Baldanzi, who was closer to southern textile management than any other member of the union, reported to the panic-stricken executive council, "I am firmly convinced it is part of a well-laid plan, between Erwin, Fieldcrest, Cone, and Dan River, but specifically Dan River, and Marshall Field. Marshall Field did not open the gates, but Dan River stationery has flooded Draper and Spray." Evidence from Dan River company records supports this analysis. North Carolina textile towns such as Leaksville, Draper, and Spray were less than twenty miles from Danville, so Dan River had a large pool of idle labor close by. As Baldanzi indicated, the company sent hundreds of letters offering jobs to "unemployed" textile workers in North Carolina; the letters were mainly targeted at skilled textile occupations that were needed for production.[32] Their actions typified the way that postwar southern textile manufacturers acted with a close degree of cooperation in union affairs, even between organized and unorganized companies.[33] Baldanzi claimed, "These guys have a timetable and Danville is the first target. Maybe Fieldcrest is the next. Don't think you can measure the situation on how strong a local is at the moment, because if this is part of an overall campaign on the part of the employers, we're going to have a rough situation." He added that employers wanted "to knock off a few of these outfits that have symbolized our union in the South as Dan River has."[34]

Although efforts to break the strike were concentrated in Danville, the strike was important in other locations as well, and one of its major elements was the battle of words that was carried on between the two sides. Southern textile management across the region chose to fight the strike through a sophisticated public relations campaign aimed at familiarizing public opinion with their arguments and discrediting the strike. This emphasis on public relations showed how southern textile management had evolved from its confrontational tactics of the prewar era. A newly formed body, the Textile Committee on Public Relations, handled the industry's press releases during the strike. Its chairman was Charles Cannon, probably the most influential southern textile executive of this period. The committee's influence is illustrated by the fact that all three of the major wire services—the Associated Press, the United Press, and International News Services—used the committee for information on the 1951 strike. Indeed, Cannon's secretary admitted, "The press is now printing practically everything we put out from day to day."[35]

In most of the locations where management shut their plants, they repeatedly put their case before the public in almost identical full-size advertisements in the press. Their central argument stressed the amount that textile wages had risen. Once again, the union found that its own record of raising southern wages made it harder to achieve progress in the South. The union tried to sell the strike around the slogan "A Living Wage." However, companies hit back by stressing the unprecedented amount that wages had risen in the postwar period. Local papers provided a forum for repeated attacks on the "living wage" idea—attacks that often came from members of the public. Many observers were particularly conscious of the rising living standards of textile workers. A Betty Gentry, for example, wrote to the *Leaksville (N.C.) News* that "most of the workers have fine automobiles, TV sets, and their own homes. If this fact means that living conditions are low, then it is time to strike."[36]

Management also repeatedly claimed that the TWUA was unpatriotic in striking during the Korean War and was seeking to bully the government into changing its stabilization policies. The strike occurred at a time when the Cold War and anticommunism were intense, and as a result the union found itself heavily criticized from across the country for calling a strike while the Korean War was in progress. The war had an especially strong mobilizing effect on American public opinion, because it was seen by many as a "Third World War" and a war against the Soviet Union. The war's impact was even greater for the many Americans who had relatives fighting in Korea. As the numbers killed in Korea increased, workers in many major industrial centers began to take matters into their own hands: they frequently took such actions as beating up alleged radicals and pressuring their employers to fire workers with unusual or unpopular opinions.[37]

In this environment, it is not surprising that most press coverage that the strike received was unfavorable. The TWUA received attacks from across the country for its lack of patriotism. For example, an Alabama newspaper, the *Lanett Valley Daily Times-News*, wrote that the strike ignored the fact that "American husbands, fathers, and sons are fighting a terrible war, dying horrible deaths in Korea." In Georgia, the *Albany Herald* wrote that the TWUA was "subversive" and obviously lacked "a spirit of patriotism," because it had chosen to strike at a time of "high international tension." A marine in one struck town wrote to his local paper claiming that "it was the timing of the strike that was wrong. The lives of our young men and the freedoms they enjoy should by all means come first." He added that he wondered what would happen if the strikers "talked against management in Russia."[38]

The press coverage of the 1951 strike was truly national in scope. It was particularly revealing of the strike's aims that the only papers that supported the strike were from New England. The *Brockton Enterprise and Times*, for example, wrote sadly at the end of the strike that "Massachusetts mills would have benefited were the strikers to have won the higher pay and other benefits sought by them." As it was, the strike's failure illustrated the union's weakness in the South "and explained why ome of New England's textile business has gone south."[39]

A lot of publicity was generated by the strike's violent nature. The cen- of strike violence was, not surprisingly, Danville, which resembled a war zone for much of the strike. The strikes at Cedartown Mills in Cedartown, Georgia, and Royal Cotton Mill in Wake Forest, North Carolina, also witnessed serious violence. In both of these cases, the strikes were the product of long-term efforts to establish unions rather than the 1951 pay demands. The union had decided to involve plants such as these in an effort to strike as many plants as possible at once; ultimately, though, violence grabbed headlines and discredited the union's wider pay demands.[40]

The most serious incident of violence occurred at Royal Cotton Mill on the night of April 27, when "hundreds of shots" were fired in a pitched battle between strikers and nonstrikers. Nonstrikers, who had been openly carrying guns through the picket lines for over a week, fired at the picket line from positions within the mill. Three people, including a reporter from the *Raleigh News and Observer*, were seriously injured. Other incidents of violence followed this pattern: they largely represented violence between workers rather than violence inflicted on workers by authorities. This marks a break from prewar textile strikes—especially the 1934 strike, to which many mill owners reacted violently. While many incidents probably involved a large degree of management collusion, the sheer number of assaults and fights between union and nonunion factions, even in plants that were not attempting to operate, indicates that violence between workers had an independent momentum. Indeed, in several cases management criticized law enforcement agencies for not quelling the number of incidents—another shift from the prewar period, accounts of which have emphasized the subservience of local authorities to the mill owner.[41]

The strike's violence, especially such dramatic incidents as the Wake Forest shooting and an organized laydown of pickets at Dan River Mills, brought it increased press condemnation from an ever-wider audience. The laydown was particularly criticized because it was planned by union leaders. The *Chattanooga News-Free Press*, like many others, attacked the laydown because it was viewed as an attempt to prevent workers from exercising their "right to work," a right that was keenly protected during this period. Even though many incidents were clearly initiated by nonstrikers, it was the union that inevitably suffered. The *Fort Worth Press*, for example, warned that "labor should remember that only strikes which have the backing of public opinion are successful strikes." By this criterion, the 1951 strike was in trouble.[42]

While the TWUA certainly lost the public relations war, it was the battle to run a solid strike that was crucial if it were to have any chance of success. After two weeks on strike, TWUA representatives from the different strike situations met for an emergency session in the O'Henry Hotel in Greensboro, where Rieve had established the strike headquarters.

They determined that the strike was solid in most locations, the vast majority of companies continuing to make no attempt to operate. There were, however, two acknowledged "weak spots": in Danville, and at Cone Mills in Greensboro. The strike's collapse at Cone came as little surprise to Rieve and other TWUA leaders; it reflected the union's low membership in the Cone chain. As a result, most TWUA leaders were philosophical about the Cone situation.[43]

The Danville situation, in contrast, was a major shock to the TWUA's leaders. Within two weeks of the strike, more than 6,000 of the 12,000 workers had broken the picket line. By early May, nearly 9,000 had gone back, according to union figures. This occurred in a union widely regarded as one of the strongest that the TWUA had. Because Dan River was the biggest single textile company in the country (and the world, no less), the TWUA had poured money into Danville to try to make the union as strong as possible. These efforts seemed to have paid off, for the Dan River locals were widely regarded as TWUA's southern showcases. Few anticipated that a strike could be broken at Dan River. The *Greensboro Daily News*, for example, reported from Danville on the eve of the strike that "if a strike were to develop here, it is understood that the mills could not function on the basis of a proportion of local non-union workers."[44]

The TWUA went into the 1951 strike with its fortunes inexorably tied to Danville, the trump card that would allow the union to break the deadlock as it had in the past. Illustrating the importance the union attached to Dan River, Rieve frequently compared the company to pattern-setters in northern, mass-production industries—a false comparison, given that these companies operated in oligopolistic industries.[45]

The union's reliance on Dan River, which had proved to be so beneficial before 1951, also played a big part in causing the failure of the 1951 strike. If one location was acknowledged to be crucial, it could also inhibit the union's chances in a general strike situation, because if the strike were broken in that crucial location, the union could not keep pressure on management by utilizing other centers where the strike was still solid. The effects of such a defeat would also have a negative impact on the union's general progress in the South. Indeed, in the meeting of April 16 and in all subsequent meetings, TWUA's leaders discussed the question of what Rieve called "the effect it would have on your strike situations" if the TWUA decided to "liquidate Danville." The response from various union representatives was unanimous: if Danville were liquidated, their local unions would also be under the risk of collapse. As Baldanzi made clear, "We have 15% organization in the South. If we liquidate chunks like Danville, because representing some kind of pattern and stronghold, they are going to remember Dan River. Wherever we have organization they are going to try to wipe out our union completely." It was agreed that "if we have the kind of pattern which means the liquidation of the strike, it would encourage the other employers to carry on the war to the bitter end."[46]

It was clear that the situation in Danville could not be recovered. Because the strike had effectively been broken by the fourth week of April, the attempts of the FMCS to settle the strike by negotiation received a hostile response.[47] Thus, even though there were few signs of weakness elsewhere, the seriousness of the Danville situation meant that the union had to find a way to end the strike gracefully and maintain some dignity. In sharp contrast to his public posture that the strike was a "victory," Rieve told strike leaders in a private meeting in Greensboro that the union "should get some kind of government agency involved and ask us to return to work with some kind of face-saving device" because "we are in it up to our necks and there is no going back."[48]

This decision was consistent with the way that Rieve looked to the government throughout the strike. He told the strike's leaders that "even before the strike we were trying to induce some government agency to intervene in the hope that the strike could be prevented." His original decision to call the strike had been strongly influenced by his belief that labor's boycott of the mobilization program would lead to a new WSB, with a dispute section that could settle the TWUA's pay dispute. At the end of the strike, he admitted that "from the beginning I didn't have any hope from the employers. But I did have hope from the government." During the strike, indeed, Rieve traveled between Greensboro and Washington to lobby for his case, but his efforts got him nowhere. He reported, "We have seen everybody we could see in Washington," including Economic Stabilization Director Eric Johnston and Bill Boyle, chairman of the Democratic National Committee. The central aim of getting the dispute before the WSB, when and if such a board was set up, ran into a number of objections. It was argued that a dispute could not be certified through an agency that was nonexistent, and that there was no transmission agency. Another major objection was that under the executive order setting up the WSB, the dispute could be certified to the WSB only by the president, if he felt that the strike was substantially affecting the defense effort. However, the FMCS never contacted Truman to recommend this action, because, as they told the union, "the impact of this dispute upon the defense program is not such as to justify the procurement agencies to call upon the President to refer the matter to the board."[49]

Given the union's weakness, Rieve's eagerness to use the government is understandable. Moreover, the TWUA had made its biggest gains through federal protection in a booming wartime economy. Nevertheless, the use of the 1951 strike as a means to pressure the government into changing its stabilization policies was an extremely risky tactic, to say the least, especially for a minority union.[50] Rieve's eagerness to participate in a federal bureaucracy and to use the government to win wage increases is reminiscent of the behavior of the 1934 strike leader, Frank Gorman, who has also been criticized for being too eager to win acceptance with the federal government at the expense of the true interests of southern textile workers.[51]

The way that the 1951 strike was called off also bore similarities to 1934. In both cases, strikes were abandoned when the federal government intervened with the promise of new bureaucratic machinery to resolve the dispute. While the UTW placed their faith in this offer, however, private TWUA records show that the union's leaders never expected very much to come out of the tripartite panel that they accepted when they called off the strike on May 5, 1951. The suggested panel in 1951 was the result of Rieve's pressure on the Truman administration and, consequently, Boyle's putting the case to Truman. Rieve emphasized the board's weaknesses to the strike leaders, pointing out that "it does not have the power to direct the case to the WSB. . . . There is no promise or a hint of a promise that the case will go to the WSB or to anything else." As Rieve pointed out, the panel's powers were very limited: its main role was to engage in mediation efforts. Most managers made clear, however, that with a broken strike that had no effect on the defense effort, there was "nothing to mediate."[52]

The strike's leaders agreed to accept the offer for a number of reasons. Several mentioned the importance of salvaging something from the Danville situation on the belief that if the strike were continued there, the union would be destroyed completely. Rieve also made clear that if the union rejected this offer, the next opportunity for federal assistance might be months away. In several strike centers, there were signs that the companies were recruiting back-to-work movements. This led to concerns about whether the union could meet the relief bill of a strike that had already cost over $1 million. TWUA staffer Howard Parker, for example, explained that in Erwin Mills, "as far as relief goes we have been able to stall off car payments and rent. But right now the strike is going to start costing us $500 a week and in two weeks it will be $1000." These concerns were also influenced by Danville, for the union was now very aware that it simply did not have the financial resources to support a strike among more prosperous postwar workers, who had a greater variety of financial obligations than ever before.[53]

Not surprisingly, few in the industry or press were fooled by the ending of the strike. Indeed, it was widely seen as a major setback for the TWUA. The *Textile Bulletin* accurately forecast the board's ineffective future when it wrote, "We doubt if the mediation panel will accomplish much." It pointed out that the board had no power to order arbitration, to conduct open hearings that might provide a "sounding board for union oratory," or to publish a fact-finding report that could place employers under public pressure. The mood of the *Bulletin* at the end of the strike was triumphant: the editors wrote, "It did us good to observe the general solidarity of management," and they poked fun at union leaders.[54]

Thus, because the union needed to cripple the defense effort to ensure certification to the WSB, the guiding reality of the 1951 strike was the lack of any real economic power, the central requirement of any successful strike. The union was just not big enough in the South to conduct a strike that could cripple the industry. Larry Rogin, for example, felt that the strike was a mistake because "we could shut down what we had organized, and the industry could go on." Rieve himself admitted that TWUA was "a bantam union in our industry. There are more workers . . . outside of our union than there are inside of the union." Norris Tibbetts, a TWUA business agent in Danville who was closely involved with the running of the strike at Dan River, wrote privately shortly after the strike had finished that "I have learned a great deal in this strike. We have made many mistakes. We made our first mistake in trying to make noises like an industry-wide union, which we are not. We have about 15% organization in the South. A solid strike among what we have organized would affect only 10% of the cotton industry." He added that the union was "locked into this industry-wide pose" but scoffed, "Who the hell are we to act like the UAW and GM?"[55]

In addition to this tactical mistake, the strike's inability to be an economic nuisance was also the result of soft market conditions in the textile industry, which were themselves a consequence of the industry's competitive structure. The strike's failure can really be explained by the combination of the union's lack of power and the prevailing economic conditions. Many sources cited the poor market conditions as central to the strike's failure. The *Textile Bulletin* wrote that in future the union "should pick a better time to strike" because "considering the currently poor market, there are not many mill executives who regretted, from a financial standpoint, having their plants shut down for a while." The *Greensboro Daily News*, a more impartial observer, commented when the strike finished that "management itself could probably have chosen no more acceptable a time for a shut-down." Baldanzi and other TWUA leaders also blamed the market conditions as a major factor in the strike's defeat.[56]

The mood in the union turned gloomy as union leaders, on the verge of calling the strike off, began to grasp the size of the damage it had caused. Sensing the strike's fallout, Rieve said that by calling off the walkout "the national union is going to be a bastard. And I'm not talking politics, I mean right up and down the line. I don't know if we can hold the loyalty of the people. They will think they were sold down the river." He also sensed the damage the strike had done to the union's southern organizing prospects: "we had hopes when we started this strike of using it to help us organize. But I guess there is mighty little chance of that now and we'll be lucky if we can organize anyone for a while." It was the consequences of the union's failure to move southern wages for the New England locals, however, that was particularly disturbing, given that over 80 percent of the union's members were in the North. As Baldanzi told his colleagues at the end of the strike, "I am frank in saying to you that in all my years in the South, our union has never been in such a critical position. . . . The whole organization in the North is involved. We'll be in a hell of a shape when we go into the North the next time unless we can do something down here." [57] In the months and years that followed, the fallout from the strike proved to be even more damaging than these gloomy prophecies imagined.

chapter six

Losing on the Relief Line

The 1951 Strike in Danville, Virginia

The 1951 strike in Danville was a dramatic event that left behind a rich body of records. Clearly influenced by a sense of the importance of the events in which they were participating, two of the strike's union representatives, Boyd Payton and Norris Tibbetts, kept detailed diaries about it. While company records are absent from many areas of textile labor history, this is not the case in Danville. Indeed, the company's records provide a revealing and detailed insight into Dan River's conduct and attitude regarding the strike. The company tape-recorded all of its negotiations with the union, providing a word-for-word account of the issues at stake. Other company sources, such as reports from supervisors on the picket line or from "stooges" who infiltrated union meetings and reported back to the company, provide a unique and telling insight into the dynamics of the strike. Press coverage of the strike was detailed and colorful. In addition, those who took part in the strike remembered its drama clearly, even after forty-three years. Taken as a whole, these records provide the detailed insight needed to explore many of the central questions of the strike—why Dan River broke the wage mechanism of the previous twelve years, why the company decided to operate, and why the strike collapsed. The quality of the company's records is especially valuable, because many of these questions can clearly be answered only through detailed access to the company's thinking.[1]

The strike's failure is particularly instructive because of the light it throws on the difficulties of sustaining strike action among postwar workers with a rising standard of living. Indeed, in accounting for the failure of the crucial 1951 strike in Danville, the wage raises generated by World War II are again central to our understanding. Rising wages also played a central role in establishing the union in Danville before the strike.

Throughout its history, Dan River Mills has been a crucial location for textile unions seeking to organize the South. Indeed, the mills were at the center of most of the major organizing drives and strike waves that affected the textile industry before World War II.[2] Dan River played a major part in the unrest that swept the textile South between 1929 and 1931; in 1930–31 it witnessed a long and violent strike. The TWUA also made Dan River one of its first southern targets after its establishment in 1939. It was not until World War II that the TWUA finally achieved what previous unions had failed to do, however, when it established a lasting presence in Danville following an election victory in June 1942.[3]

Unions were particularly keen to capture Dan River because of its size and its prominent role in the industry. Even at the turn of the century, Dan River was a major southern textile company. By 1930, it had become the largest textile company in the South, employing around 5,000 workers. This position was maintained as the company continued to grow in the 1930s and 1940s, and by the time the TWUA was voted in, it employed over 13,000 workers. The company was therefore consistently seen as a prize catch for textile unions. In addition to size, this was also partly because of location. Situated on the North Carolina–Virginia border, Danville was at the head of the southern textile industry, the first major obstacle that northern unions faced when they came south. If they cracked Dan River, however, major North Carolina textile centers such as Burlington, Durham, and Leaksville were all less than sixty miles away. Dan River was seen by unions as the "gateway" to the southern industry, a vital foothold geographically and psychologically in their plans to organize the southern textile worker.[4]

The Danville that the TWUA penetrated in 1942 was a town of around 40,000 inhabitants. Between 10,000 and 14,000 of this population worked at Dan River, so the mills dominated Danville. Dan River itself operated twelve weaving and spinning mills, together with dyeing, bleaching, finishing, and power plants. All in all, these mills had nearly half a million spindles. Although some operations were based downtown at the company's Riverside division, the vast majority were located in Schoolfield, a mill community located two miles outside downtown Danville. Schoolfield was a community apart from Danville; indeed, it was unincorporated until 1951. Danville retained a different character from Schoolfield, its streets festooned with majestic southern mansions rather than mill houses. These had been built for wealthy tobacco merchants, for in the nineteenth century the town was an important center of tobacco trade and manufacturing. Schoolfield, by contrast, was a landscape of smokestacks, huge red-brick mills, and rows of small mill houses. The location of the mill community away from the town proper, even when it was such a big employer, was typical of the layout of many southern mill towns.[5]

The NWLB played a crucial role in establishing the TWUA in Danville, directing a contract that contained the checkoff of union dues, a clause the company bitterly opposed.[6] Dan River's opposition to union security, and the fact that the union was established in large part through the NWLB, was representative of the TWUA's experiences across the South during World War II. What was not typical was that after this difficult beginning, the union and company quickly developed a model relationship based on trust. In part this was due to the care and attention that the national union took in building the union in Danville. From an early stage, Dan River, the biggest southern mill the TWUA had under contract by far, was recognized as vital, and it never lacked capable staff or funds.[7] During these years the director of the Pittsylvania County Joint Board, of which the Dan River locals were the major part, was Emanuel "Slim" Boggs. Born in 1907 in Louisville, Kentucky, Boggs was a tall, thin man, even in his eighty-seventh year—hence his nickname. Boggs was an experienced union leader who had been active in the UAW in the 1930s. Like other TWUA activists such as Lewis Conn and Joel Leighton, he had been active in the Socialist Party and had come into the labor movement during the New Deal years. An amiable yet perceptive leader, he certainly helped to develop the union's relationship with the company during his long stay in Danville, and he remembered that he and his staff were able to develop an excellent working relationship with the company.[8]

The company representatives who were responsible for union relations in these years were Vice President Basil Browder and Industrial Relations Director Malcolm Cross. Cross was an articulate, college-educated young man in his early thirties who had come down from New Jersey to join Dan River in 1949. Browder, by contrast, was an older, local man from the tiny town of Horsepasture, Virginia, who was well known and influential in the wider Danville community. Browder cemented this reputation through a considerable amount of company-sponsored charity and philanthropic work. His Southside Virginia accent and down-to-earth character also made him popular with many workers. According to one union representative in Danville, Browder "was the guy you wanted on your side." Transcripts of the negotiations between company and union illustrate that the union did indeed establish a very constructive relationship with Browder between 1946 and 1951. After contract negotiations in 1946, 1947, and 1948, all of which produced pattern-setting wage increases, both sides praised the other for the patience and constructive spirit they had shown in the negotiations. In 1951, for example, Browder related how proud he was of the company's relationship with the union, adding, "Our attitude towards the TWUA is not one of just tolerating them. It is an attitude of full acceptance." In the wider climate of labor relations in the textile South, this public acceptance of the union was remarkable. It helped the union to settle grievances satisfactorily and thus to grow in popularity among the workers. Between July 1945 and October 1948, TWUA membership in Danville doubled. At the time of the strike, more than 75 percent of workers belonged to the union.[9]

The relationship between the TWUA and Dan River was particularly important because Dan River consistently set southern wage patterns, thereby allowing the union to protect its locals in the North. On the whole, the competitive nature of the textile industry made companies reluctant to lead wage movements for fear that they would be put at a competitive disadvantage. Dan River, however, proved willing to take the initiative on a number of occasions, partly because the company shared fully in the tremendous prosperity that prevailed in the textile industry between 1945 and 1950.[10] As Browder told the union in 1952, "I know in a good many cases when we did give wage increases of 8%, that other mills gave 6%. As long as we could sell goods, we could make goods and sell them at a profit; it wasn't too much of a worry to us; it wasn't too much of a bother. . . . We were so prosperous at that time, we were glad to be in a position to share our benefits with our workers." [11] The company's willingness to give frequent wage increases under these conditions illustrates how the unprecedented prosperity of the 1945–50 period caused companies to lose some of their competitive fear and explains why so many fought Operation Dixie by raising wages.

This prosperity cannot fully explain why Dan River proved willing to be a pattern-setter, however. After all, the prosperity was industrywide. On several occasions in negotiations, Browder made clear that he had agreed to be a leader in the interests of building a constructive relationship with the union. The role that the company played was not an easy one. In 1951, company attorney Frank Talbott admitted, " 'Pattern-setter' has been applied to us by friends and competitors as a derogatory epithet." Browder also described how the company's willingness to set wages had brought it criticism and pressure from other sections of the southern textile industry, but he explained that the company had been "forward-looking" in the hope that the union "would stand by us when the pinch came and when we needed stability on your side of the table." [12]

One of the union's business agents, Norris Tibbetts, who participated in all the negotiations during these years, wrote, "I think Dan River people really felt they were in the vanguard of a new approach to labor relations in the South." Browder, indeed, was proud that the union-management relationship at Dan River had, as he put it, "enabled the South." In one bargaining session with the TWUA leaders, he added, "We were proud of it progress. We were glad to be a part of it. We have bragged about it selves. You folks have used it in the South in your organizing campaigns because some of you have told me about your references to 'look at what the union and company are doing in Danville.' " Indeed, Danville came to be seen as the future for the union movement in the South, a sign that management and unions could work together in the southern textile industry. For many in the TWUA, Danville was the union's southern "showcase."[13]

The union's record of constructive bargaining even brought it praise from sections of the community in Danville: the local press praised the TWUA for its efforts in raising wages. This praise was as remarkable as the company's open acceptance of the union, because it was unprecedented for the anti-union southern press to praise the union movement.[14]

The acceptance of the union in Danville was noted and publicized by a wide variety of observers. Prominent labor journalist Mary Heaton Vorse visited Danville for an article she wrote for *Harper's* in 1949. Vorse was a keen observer of southern textile workers, an interest that dated back to her novel *Strike!*, a fictionalized account of the famous 1929 strike in Gastonia, North Carolina. Her 1938 book, *Labor's New Millions*, had done much to capture the energy and optimism that accompanied the foundation of the CIO, and in the 1940s she continued to travel and write revealing studies about workers and strike situations across the United States. Vorse's 1949 article about Danville captured the degree of social change taking place in the postwar textile South, changes driven by the way that higher wages had integrated textile workers into the wider community. She wrote that "the South has changed": in southern towns where unions had been established, "the industrial hands who were once the lowest paid workers" had become "buyers and voters of consequence" who were "in good standing" in the community. Danville typified this change. Comparing the situation to the 1931 strike, when the community had been violently opposed to the union, she noted that Danville had changed so much she could hardly believe it. Vorse described how the union hall was now on the main street of town. Higher wages had radically changed living standards and had won merchants and farmers over to the union cause. Southerners had finally realized, Vorse asserted, "that good wages mean good business." The CIO's Lucy Randolph Mason reached similar conclusions when she visited Danville in 1947. Little did Mason and Vorse know that the higher wages that had achieved so much improvement for Danville workers would also contribute to the union's destruction.[15]

Danville was vital to the TWUA because although efforts to unionize southern textile workers had largely failed, positive examples like Danville provided, as Mason and Vorse argued, "a nucleus which cannot be ignored." The TWUA also imagined that it could continue to use Danville as a platform for its progress in the South. Thus, Rieve came to Danville on March 22, 1951, looking for a settlement for the whole

He was clearly confident that Dan River would break the ice, as it
[d]ne in the past, even though this was his first major visit to Danville
[since] World War II. Nine days of colorful negotiations followed Rieve's
[arriv]al.[16]

[" . . . R]ieve Came In and Started Shouting and Pounding on the Table"

[T]he 1951 Danville negotiations illustrated in close detail the central prob-
[l]em facing the TWUA in these years—that unionized companies were
reluctant to increase their wage costs significantly above those of their
nonunion competition. Dan River continually argued that they were only
a small part of a very competitive industry, the vast majority of which
was unorganized. Given this situation, the company would not risk another increase in light of the soft conditions within the industry, the unprecedented size of the union's demands, and the wage and price confusion. The risk that the mass of unorganized competition would not
follow the increase was too great. Whereas Rieve and other members of
the union delegation claimed that southern textile wages were inadequate
because they were below textile wages in New England and wages in
other mass-production industries, such as steel and automobiles, the
company continually emphasized unorganized competition in the South.
Dan River's tough attorney, Frank Talbott, told the union, "You know
from past experiences with us . . . [that] as a matter of life and death, we
must be acutely sensitive to the competitive situation. The companies
that we have to compete with lie to the South of us and you also know
that the greater part of it is unorganized." Browder also explained how
the company felt constrained by the competitive nature of the textile industry. He claimed that "every spindle of the textile industry is a potential competitor for us. And these are things we can't overlook. Dan River
can't expect to be the smartest managed mill in the country." He pointed
out that despite its size, Dan River had "only 2%" of the total spindleage
of the American textile industry. The company had to keep its wage costs
in line with unorganized competition because "we are just one little bitty
unit in the textile industry." [17]

Dan River officials based their case on two points—that they were in
direct competition with hundreds of unorganized mills, and that their
wages were already higher than these competitors'. The company paid
wages almost on a par with New England but had to "sell our fabrics
[m]ore in competition with the Southern industry than the North." [18]
[W]age costs were crucial for Dan River, as for other textile companies,
[be]cause they comprised at least 30 percent of total costs; on the eve of ne-
[go]tiations, due to the slump in business, they rose to 39.5 percent. For in-
[dus]tries such as automobiles, the comparable figure was around 5 per-
[cent]. Because of this difference, the company concluded that "it will have

a serious effect on our sales if our wage costs continue to get out of line." These arguments showed how, unlike the situation for unions in automobiles or steel, the structure of the textile industry made it very difficult for the TWUA to gain industrywide wage increases.[19]

Nevertheless, Rieve tried to answer these arguments by claiming that Dan River was a pattern-setting company, "just like the steel industry has got the U.S. Steel Corporation that makes a pattern. Whatever happens there usually sweeps their industry. In the automobile industry, the General Motors Corporation sets the pattern, and it sweeps their industry." Browder emphasized that the union's relationship with Dan River was not comparable because the company's market share was much smaller and nonunion companies remained the majority: "You were talking about in the motor industry, that GM sets the pattern and the pattern sweeps the industry. I will tell you quite frankly that if we could set the pattern that would sweep the whole Southern textile industry, we would be less concerned about this situation than we are." He added, "In the first place, you have a little over 15% of the Southern industry organized. . . . When you get all those folks lined up here and doing as well as Dan River does, then we would be able to talk to you about doing more." TWUA representative Ken Kramer, a close associate of Rieve who was also unused to negotiating in Danville, argued that the company had nothing to fear, because if unorganized companies failed to follow Dan River's lead, the union would organize them. It is clear, however, that by 1951 the union's failure to achieve organizing gains had made unionized companies like Dan River very cautious. Thus, Browder hit back at Kramer, "I don't understand it—you talk about if we don't put it in, you are going to organize them. There are mills to the South of us whose wages are twenty cents an hour below ours and you can't get those folks interested in joining the union." To Kramer's reply that these were small mills, Browder retorted angrily that they included "some mighty good-sized units, brother, some mighty good-sized units."[20]

Browder indeed asserted that the competitive nature of the textile industry made the comparison with oligopolistic industries such as steel inaccurate. When Rieve asserted that the average textiles wage was low because it was still below $1.56, the hourly average for all manufacturing industries, Browder replied, "Well, compared to Motors, it may be, but after all, I don't think we can compare Dan River Mills with General Motors." These industries enjoyed a much larger market share and were far more profitable than textiles. Textiles, in contrast, had a long history of intense competition and overproduction. According to Browder, "the automobile industry is a baby, comparatively speaking, that has grown up overnight, and it is a profitable one. I wish we could operate as well as they do." In addition to the differences in profitability, however, Browder also argued that textiles could not be compared to these industries because it was a lighter industry that employed large numbers of women. Indeed, the gender composition of the workforce seemed to make a difference to Browder, who argued, "Our wages—$1.33 is not too far below that for an industry that is not a heavy industry. Now, of course, Motors and Steel and Mining and all those are heavy industries. Your high wages are strictly a man's industry. The textile industry is not."[21]

Dan River's concerns about unorganized southern competition also conditioned their rejection of the union's argument that southern textile wages should equal those found in New England. The TWUA always found it difficult to sell this argument in the South but felt compelled to protect its northern membership. Dan River, like most southern companies, reacted strongly to the idea that New England was some kind of model that they should follow. Frank Talbott told Rieve bluntly, "We don't propose to have New England tell us what to do." The company argued that the New England textile industry "is a liquidating industry. . . . 80% of the spindles are in the South, against 17% in New England." The South was "where our competition is." Browder, like many southern textile executives, saw New England mill owners as weak-backed men who had let the union get on top of them. He insisted, "We don't want to maneuver ourselves into a position of self-liquidation here such as New England has done over the past twenty-five years or so."[22]

The tragedy of the Danville negotiations was that despite their objections, the company indicated repeatedly that it did not want a strike. In the light of the confused stabilization picture, company officials proposed that negotiations be postponed until clarification had been reached.[23] Local union leaders such as Boggs and Norris Tibbetts themselves had serious reservations about the strike but agreed to go ahead out of what Tibbetts called "a sense of obligation to our brothers in the North." It is also clear, however, that the union's refusal of Dan River's request and the way that the 1951 negotiations were conducted were influenced by the political situation within the TWUA. Danville had become TWUA's showpiece largely through negotiations conducted by Baldanzi, and union leaders in Danville were identified as Baldanzi supporters. Hence, Rieve's determination to come to Danville and secure a settlement was clearly politically motivated. According to Boggs, Rieve was jealous of Baldanzi's influence in the South and wanted to prove his militancy. The way that Rieve conducted the 1951 negotiations played a crucial role in alienating Dan River management. Rieve had very little experience working in the South. Boggs recalled that the Polish-born Rieve "was never able to communicate effectively in the South. He had this thick accent and brusque personality that made it extremely difficult for him to understand southerners or for southerners to understand him." Boggs claimed that Rieve's tough northern negotiating style backfired in Dan River, where decorum and respect characterized union-management relations: "Rieve came in and started shouting and pounding on the table, and management got worked up. They said, 'Mr. Rieve, we are southern gentlemen, we are not accustomed to conducting business like that,' and they walked out."[24]

Other sources support the conclusion that Rieve's decision to lead negotiations was a mistake. Company transcripts from the negotiations indicate that Rieve's confrontational style annoyed Dan River officials, who clearly preferred dealing with Baldanzi. Dan River personnel manager Malcolm Cross recalled that management did not like the way that Baldanzi was kept out of the important negotiations. He explained that "Baldanzi was the guy that southern management looked to. . . . We felt that he had a better understanding of the southern textile worker than Rieve had, or Rieve's chief lieutenants." He added, "I personally liked Baldanzi."[25] At an early stage, Browder asked Rieve what he knew about the chances of future price clarification from Washington. Rieve replied, "That is management's problem. Our problem is wages"—a phrase that Browder repeatedly used against Rieve, arguing that if the union showed no interest in the company's price position, the company would not help the union regarding wages. It was also important that Rieve came South having already declared that there would be a strike if no agreement was reached. Personnel Manager Malcolm Cross recalled that "the biggest mistake in bargaining with a company like Dan River is saying you're going to strike. It may have worked in New England, but it was absolutely the wrong tactic in Dan River, absolutely." In negotiating sessions, the company referred to the union's tactics as "bargaining with a gun to our heads" and claimed that they were shocked because it marked such a break from the polite way negotiations had been conducted before.[26]

The real damage inflicted was the company's loss of confidence in the union. Dan River officials disliked the way that the union had sabotaged its long-standing relationship with the company and brought outside political issues into the negotiations. It is clear that Dan River felt the union deserved a strike because of its attempts to force Dan River's hand. In a final negotiating session between Browder and Boyd Payton, TWUA's Virginia director, Browder spoke at length about the political situation in the union and explained angrily that "we were absolutely disregarded by the union's national leadership . . . and they were perfectly willing to sacrifice everything that we had done over the past ten years to achieve a point."[27] The feeling that the strike was political clearly influenced the company's decision to operate. Browder explained, "We could have rolled over and played dead and kept the gates shut. . . . But, we were absolutely disregarded by the union's national leadership and we were just one segment in a big wheel here that they didn't care anything about."[28] Browder's attitude was that he didn't want a strike, but "if we are going to have a strike at Dan River, we are going into it on the basis that we're going to do our best to win it." Like most southern companies in this period, Dan River had little fear of strikes.[29]

It is clear that the TWUA's announcing a strike deadline more than a month before the actual strike was crucial in giving Dan River time to prepare to operate. The company made extensive arrangements before the strike began to import nonstrikers into the mills. At a confidential meeting of March 13, 1951, company officials decided to operate. In the next two weeks, Dan River arranged for two nonunion bus companies to pick up and deliver potential nonstrikers. They stocked up in advance with coal and hired a fleet of trucks so that supervisors could transport nonstrikers to the plant. Crucially, they agreed that supervisors and other nonproduction workers "will be asked to perform jobs vacated by strikers." Finally, they concluded that "every effort" should be made to fight the strike.[30]

"The Union Just Frankly Didn't Have a Chance"

When the strike began on April 1, the company began intensive efforts to bring nonstrikers into the plant. It is clear that the strike was broken partly through these efforts. Robert Gardiner, a young personnel manager at the time of the strike, remembered that workers were frightened to walk through the picket lines, which were unruly from the beginning, so management would pick them up in cars and drive them through. Once in the plant, however, many workers were reluctant to go through the daily ritual of breaking the picket line, even from the protection of a car, so Dan River officials quickly evolved a foolproof method for bringing workers in. The company brought over one thousand cots and sofa beds into the mills, enabling many workers to spend the whole strike in the plant. At the same time, those who drove to the mill were allowed to park inside. Management trainees from Dan River's sales office in New York were brought in to direct traffic at shift changes, utilizing the company's sixteen gates to send traffic away from the pickets. The final and most damaging move came halfway through the strike, when management constructed a steel walkway bridge so that workers could park their cars in the company's largest parking lot and walk over the picket line and into the plant. Robert Gardiner himself drove nonstrikers into the mill and recalled vividly having rocks thrown at his car. Gardiner felt that management's tactics were decisive in breaking the strike: "the union just frankly didn't have a chance. There's not much a union can do when a company is as determined to operate as we were, and not to give in to the union."[31]

The private diaries of union leaders Boyd Payton and Norris Tibbetts provide close insight into the company's tactics during the strike. At the time of the strike, Tibbetts was a small, wiry young man of twenty-nine who had come out of the army at the end of the war and been appointed to a position as a business agent in Danville. Although he had been involved in steel strikes in his hometown of Allentown, Pennsylvania, the intensity and violence of the 1951 strike made a lasting impression on him, and this was reflected in his diary, written while he was on night duty at the union hall. An intelligent and perceptive man, Tibbetts devoted a great deal of mental energy to trying to understand the causes and significance of the 1951 strike.[32] Payton, the TWUA's state director for Virginia, was considerably older, an experienced and wise union leader. In contrast to Tibbetts, Payton was a big man, standing over six feet tall and weighing 250 pounds. Due to his size, experience, and calm temperament, Payton was seen by Tibbetts as "a good guy to have around in a strike situation." Like most TWUA leaders who worked in the South for an extended period, Payton was accustomed to industrial conflict and was under no illusions about the necessity of strikes for any local union that sought to establish itself in the South. Despite his considerable strike experience, Payton recognized the Danville strike as particularly significant, and he wrote a detailed forty-page strike diary in which he articulated wide-ranging views on what the union needed to change in order to be more successful in southern strikes. After the strike, Payton was best known for receiving a prison sentence for his role in the violent strike at the Harriet-Henderson Cotton Mills in Henderson, North Carolina, between 1958 and 1960.

The diaries of Payton and Tibbetts reveal that the company resorted to a whole array of tactics to break the strike. Thus, Tibbetts noted on April 4 that company officials were "using everything they can" to get workers back into the plant. The company's supervisors were very active in this effort. Payton wrote that "the company had organized its supervisors to conduct a visiting campaign among all workers. Some people were visited three or four times in one day and conversation varied from begging employees to report, to actually threatening them with loss of jobs if they failed to report."[33] At the same time, supervisors also pushed the company's position in the community, as part of a sophisticated and successful public relations campaign.[34]

Thus, Dan River used a mixture of modern public relations and old-fashioned strikebreaking to crush the 1951 strike. Company records indeed show that while increasingly sophisticated methods were used, such as detailed prestrike surveys of worker and community opinion, Dan River also relied heavily on traditional economic power, forcefully importing strikebreakers and relying on its influence in the community to pressure workers to return.

Intensive efforts were made to recruit outside labor. Robert Gardiner remembered that the company sent its managers out into the countryside looking for strikebreakers: "we'd just go out and we'd replace the strikers. . . . We'd hire replacements for the strikers." Large trailer trucks, with around fifty chairs hastily attached, were used to transport the replacements to Danville. During the five-week strike, the company hired 1,465 replacement workers.[35]

Company sources indicate that the high wages available at the plant during the strike enticed many strikers to break the picket line and made it easier to find replacements. When the strike was called, the average wage at Dan River was $1.32 an hour. During the five weeks of the strike, the average varied between $1.44 and $1.51. At the same time, the average working week increased from thirty-eight hours to between forty-six and forty-eight hours. Malcolm Cross remembered that many workers stayed for long periods in the mills and worked double shifts, increasing the pressure on those still on strike. Baldanzi claimed that enormous pressure was being put on strikers because if they went back they could sleep and eat in the mill for free and earn "as much as $200 per week."[36]

The determination of Dan River to operate placed the union on the defensive from the dispute's beginning. It also helps explain why the picket line was marked by violence from an early stage. The most serious incident occurred on 18 April, when a supervisor fired shots from a car, injuring two strikers.[37] At the same time, violence between strikers and nonstrikers took place throughout the strike, especially in small communities outside Danville that lacked effective police control. It is clear that much of this violence was perpetrated by strikers, although union leaders tried their best to prevent it. During the five weeks of the strike, the company handled eighteen dynamite cases, twenty-one shooting cases, and 610 other acts of intimidation.[38]

The fear of violent attack is central to explaining which workers went back to work. Among culturally homogeneous southern textile workers it is more difficult to detect the defining characteristics of workers who broke strikes than it would be in a more ethnically diverse workforce. Indeed, historians have found it difficult to detect patterns of militancy among southern textile workers.[39] Nevertheless, it is possible to draw some conclusions from the 1951 strike. Company records indicate that throughout the strike, the numbers working on the daytime shift were higher than those on the second or third shifts. On April 8, for example, 41.3 percent of workers had returned to the first shift, compared to 33.4 percent on the second and 28.6 percent on the third. These proportions were maintained until the strike was called off on May 6, when 67.6 percent of the first shift was working, compared to 55.6 percent and 38.1 percent on the second and third shifts respectively. The *Danville Bee* noted this phenomenon and reported that it was due to the fact that first-shift workers were the only ones who could both enter and leave the plant in daylight. Other workers feared attack, as most of the violent incidents occurred under the cover of darkness, especially when nonstrikers tried to come in from outlying communities.[40]

In addition, the support of women for the strike was particularly notable.[41] Women's prominence in the strike was largely a reflection of their representation in the workforce. The southern textile industry generally employed large numbers of women, and at Dan River women made up around 50 percent of the workforce. Women strikers were particularly important on the picket line, regularly turning out in large numbers. The Danville women were following a tradition of female militancy in southern textile strikes. In the 1929 wave of strikes, especially in the 1929 strike in Elizabethton, Tennessee, "disorderly women" played a central role. The involvement of women was also noted in the 1934 General Strike. From the major strike center of Greenville, South Carolina, for example, the *Textile Bulletin* reported, "Particularly prominent in abetting and opposing the strike were the women. Muscular and stockingless, Amazon battalions accustomed to working beside their men headed picket lines at many points and hurled the sharpest taunts at mill guards and militia." In many postwar textile strikes, women continued to play a central role.[42]

The cases of strikers who were particularly abusive on the picket line, or who blocked the gates, went to arbitration immediately after the strike, as the company sought to remove its most militant workers. Arbitration proceedings reveal that many of the most active pickets were women and that women played a central role in the laydown of April 17. The company was particularly eager to remove Doris Nuchols, a shop steward from the sewing room and a picket captain during the strike. A Dan River manager, R. E. Henderson, testified that "at the times I saw her, which was virtually every shift, every day[,] . . . she was very prominent in the front ranks of the pickets during that time." Nuchols achieved considerable notoriety on the picket line. A nonstriker, Eva Woodell, explained that Nuchols "was so much noted that everybody called her 'The Girl in the Red Hat.' The 'Girl in the Red Hat' will go down in history. She had it pulled down, kind of mannish." Nuchols was noted for screaming abuse right into the face of nonstrikers and for stomping her feet at them. Toward the end of the strike, she was arrested for calling a worker "a yellow-bellied scab." One company memorandum that was prepared for the arbitration hearing captured the notoriety that Nuchols achieved on the picket line: "her remarks addressed to workers, as well as to supervisors within the mill gates, soon earned her the nickname of 'Gravel Gertie.' . . . Because of her shrill voice, her abusive and insulting remarks, her prominent position in the picket line, and her endurance, she became perhaps the most notorious picket during the strike."[43]

The company's eagerness to remove Nuchols, however, illustrated how effective a strike leader she had proven. Supervisor John W. Sutton testified that Nuchols "was a leader on the picket line. She carried more weight with the pickets, it looked like, than anybody else on the picket line." Another supervisor, James C. Carrick, explained that Nuchols directed picketing and was "always out in front." Malcolm Cross testified that her actions on the picket line left nonstrikers "personally aggrieved" and reluctant to carry on working: "more than anyone else, perhaps in the entire strike, her actions offended and irritated other employees." They asked "if there was something that could be done to control her." One nonstriker described how "she just put her whole attention on us as we would come out of the gate. . . . She would look at the others that she had around her and say 'There they go, there they go—ain't they pretty.'" Nuchols was at the heart of pickets' efforts to associate nonstrikers with rats. According to Henderson, "she frequently, and almost continuously, used the expressions when people were going in and out, 'There goes two more dirty rats.'"[44]

When Nuchols was called to testify, her responses provided an insight into the motives for her activism, illustrating her alienation from the company and strong commitment to the union. She explained that she carried on attending the picket line even when she had shouted herself hoarse and her husband tried to stop her: "he says 'I don't want you to go even at all.' And I says 'Well, I am going anyway, because I feel like it is my place to be there.'" It is clear that for Nuchols, crossing the picket line was a moral issue, an act that symbolized class betrayal. She agreed that she had "shouted as much as I could" and insulted workers because "I think I would be ashamed to cross the picket line." She made no attempt to deny any of the company's charges, including that she had used the word "scab." She even told the company that the arbitration hearing did not matter "because it seems like that everything around here is run more or less by the company." When Cross asked her, "You called them garbage and rats, didn't you?" she replied, "Oh, yes, I sure did. I yelled a lot. I was very active on the picket line." Frank Talbott then asked Nuchols, "Generally, you don't mind what names people call you?" to which she replied confidently "I know I am a lady and it doesn't make any difference to me. I was called everything out there on the picket line." Indeed, Nuchols resisted with confidence the charge that her behavior was unfeminine, countering Talbott's assertion that "generally, when a person is a lady, they feel insulted when people address remarks like that to them" with the riposte, "I just go ahead and shout it back at them."[45]

Talbott's remarks indicate that Nuchols, confident that her refusal to cross the picket line put her in the right, consciously challenged conventional standards of feminine behavior. In fact, one supervisor's report from the picket line declared, "Some threats were issued in the language that seems to be out of keeping with the way a lady ought to conduct her-

132
The 1951
Strike in
Danville

self." Moreover, Doris Nuchols was not an isolated example. Many other women were also discharged for "unfeminine" behavior on the picket line. According to supervisor's reports, Edith Terry "was another woman who was particularly active on the picket line, and was constantly using insulting and abusive language. On a number of occasions, she called employees 'rats,' 'green scabs,' and 'yellow.'" Other women fired for using abusive language on the picket line included Vera Blackman, Pauline Dawson, Mary Hayes, and Viola Rittenberg.[46] Many of these women, like Nuchols, came from the sewing room, an all-female department of around five hundred workers. Several of them were already shop stewards and had made a name for themselves in the company's eyes well before the strike. Another vociferous picket and sewing-room shop steward was Erna Bray, who was also fired following the strike. It is clear in this case that the company used the strike as their chance to remove one of their most awkward workers. At Bray's arbitration hearing, the union claimed that she had been "deliberately framed because of [her] well-known loyalty to the union and her militant attitude in protecting other sewing room personnel from the perfidious machinations of unscrupulous supervision." Confidential company correspondence showed that the union's charge was accurate. Even publicly, the company cited Bray's past behavior as part of their case. They claimed that "she has been a disruptive force for many years . . . because of her militant attitude and her distrust and suspicion of all things which concern company policy and supervisory action." From Bray's case as from Nuchols's, a strong sense of alienation from the company and union loyalty emerges. At one point in the hearing, the company claimed that Bray "has no feeling of loyalty to Dan River Mills" and spent far too much time in the mill "barging into conversations between supervisors and employees that did not concern her."[47]

The prominence of women on the Dan River picket line was partly due to the fact that the national TWUA sent Lilian Yadon, a TWUA representative from Louisville, Kentucky, into Danville to lead women's picketing. Yadon was an experienced strike veteran and a genuine firebrand. She referred to the female pickets in Danville as "fine women" and explained that her main job was "to see that our women pickets are not pushed around or scared by company efforts to intimidate them." The southern press had a field day with Yadon's arrival. The *Danville Register* reported that a "mysterious red-haired women with a Northern accent" was leading picketing, her main activity "yelling and drawing back her right arm as if she was getting set to toss an object into the cars of workers entering the mills. Those in the vehicles often were fooled by the trick and ducked." Yadon helped inspire the events of the night of April 17, when the union called for volunteers to take part in an organized laydown in front of the mill gates. Many women strikers agreed to participate. Maggie Robinson, another sewing-room worker, said that she took part "in order to show the people exactly how you felt about the scabs going to work across the picket lines." All of the women who took part in the laydown shared this desire to make a point and were willing to take risks to do so. Viola Rittenberg, for example, admitted that she wanted to stop nonstrikers from entering the mill, even "if I wound up in Memorial Hospital or someplace."[48]

"The Union Was Our Only Voice"

Another clear pattern of militancy was the overwhelming support that black Dan River workers gave to the strike. On April 16, at a time when 45 percent of white workers had abandoned the strike, Boyd Payton noted in his diary that 97 percent of black workers were still on strike. The bleachery and dye-house departments, where most blacks worked, were unable to get any production throughout the strike. Even when the strike was called off, with only 35 percent of white workers still on strike, Payton's figures reported that 95 percent of the blacks were still out.[49]

The militancy of black workers needs to be explored, especially as little is known about black workers in the textile industry prior to the 1960s.[50] The fact that blacks were largely excluded from textile mills before the 1960s has also meant that they have been largely excluded from historical writing; recent scholarship has concentrated on white workers.[51] But there are several reasons why black workers are central to the history of the TWUA in the immediate postwar years. First, in the 1940s and 1950s blacks did enter the southern textile industry in increasing numbers, largely due to labor shortages generated by World War II.[52] In addition, despite their low overall representation, blacks were a regular feature of the workforce across the South, particularly in the first stage of the production process—the opening of raw cotton bales.[53] Moreover, there were pockets where blacks were employed in much larger numbers, especially in finishing plants, such as Dan River's bleachery.[54]

Most important, however, the racial balance of the industry has always been of great importance to textile unions that sought to establish themselves in the South. As was evident during Operation Dixie, employers successfully exploited the racial fears of white workers by threatening that the union would force them to hire more blacks if it were voted in. Ironically, in fact, the race issue could be explosive for unions working in an industry with only small numbers of blacks, and there was often more segregationist union activity where there were few black members.[55]

Textile unions generally avoided taking a strong stance on the race issue and made few efforts to organize black workers. When plants with blacks were organized, the segregated local was the norm, and black workers at Dan River themselves belonged to such a local. These segregated textile locals existed across the South and had a long history dating back well before the postwar period, to at least the unrest of 1919–21. In the 1934 General Textile Strike, black locals were formed in most major southern textile centers. Separate locals also persisted during the postwar years, among both the TWUA and its AFL counterpart.[56] Very little is known about these locals—the way that they affected race relations, and the experiences of their members. Given their ubiquity, however, it is vital that we uncover the race history behind these separate locals and, in particular, compare the history of black TWUA workers with that of white members. The Dan River local, one of the largest and most important in the South, provides an opportunity to answer some of these questions.[57]

Textile unions were not unique in having segregated locals in the South. Many other unions also responded to the race issue in this way.[58] Generally, separate locals have been seen as a negative development, for it was felt that only through integration could blacks achieve recognition and progress. Many who worked for the TWUA in the South in these years shared these assumptions and tried to prevent the establishment of separate locals. Most of the separate locals that were formed were thus the product of local objections by white members. The central question, therefore, is whether the segregated local was indeed a bad institution to placate racist whites and consign blacks to the sidelines, or whether it could produce more gains than could be achieved through integration.[59]

When Dan River Mills was first organized by the TWUA in 1942, black and white workers belonged to the same union. Dan River faced serious labor shortages during World War II and, as a result, began to hire black workers. Between 1946 and 1955, the number of black workers held steady at around 1,400, or 15 percent of the workforce. The influx of black workers caused tensions in the plant, leading to a June 1944 walkout by white workers who demanded that blacks be employed in a separate building and excluded from the union. Management acquiesced, abandoning the idea of employing blacks in production jobs and confining them to working in the company's bleachery. This white resistance led to the formation of a separate local for blacks. Pat Knight and other union representatives who visited Danville disliked this solution and felt that it would not help to break down race prejudice. Ken Fiester even remembered that when the local was set up, "we were ashamed of it."[60]

At the same time, Fiester and others recalled that many black workers themselves supported the idea of a separate union: "we had the separate local in Danville not because we wanted it but because the blacks insisted that the only way they would be able to say anything at all is if they had separate locals." It is clear that while the local was partly a product of white prejudice, some black workers grasped its potential for group advancement early on.[61]

Indeed, the separate black local produced considerable self-advancement for African American workers and also helped to break down racial prejudice. African American workers were clearly able to achieve far more recognition in their own local than if they had taken part in an integrated local. These achievements were partly the result of the automatic representation blacks received on the union's joint board. In Danville, the joint board was composed of members elected from two large white Dan River locals and the black local. Because of rivalry between the two white unions, the black local came to hold the balance of power on the joint board.[62]

This position of strategic power meant that whites were forced to recognize and make concessions to blacks. Joe Pedigo, a TWUA southern representative who visited Danville regularly, recalled that "you quickly noticed how people tended to segregate themselves in meetings. Whites would sit in one group and the Negroes in another. It wasn't long before the whites began to realize that here was the balance of power and you'd see a white go over and sit down and put his arm around a black guy's shoulder, and start whispering to them." Pedigo felt that the separate local brought blacks power and recognition they never could have achieved otherwise: "I still think it was the best setup we could ever make, because there were 1,400 Negroes in a plant with 12,000 workers and they would have been completely lost in one unit. Here they were swinging the balance of power in the structure that we set up there. They had more than their numbers by way of power." Their position of power also produced results when the joint board elected business agents, the only paid union representatives in the area. In Danville there were four business agents, and because of the black group's strategic position, one business agent was always an African American. Having a separate local also gave blacks automatic representation in other areas. They sent delegates to every convention and conference as a matter of right. They were represented on all committees. Blacks had automatic shop-steward representation in the mills, both in mixed departments and in those that were predominantly black.[63]

This automatic representation also helped to change the prejudices of whites. Norris Tibbetts wrote, "Because of the fact of the segregated local with Negroes having representation by right, the white leadership of the union has discovered that Negroes have much to offer in the attainment of the common goal." He added, "Negroes have been elected and appointed to positions of responsibility because of the necessities of the situation: the white group has learned by experience that Negroes can perform excellently in these positions, and Negro members have developed themselves personally by finding themselves in positions of responsibility." Similarly, Slim Boggs recalled that "the black workers actually gained more recognition among the white workers as a result of having this separate local and separate leadership because it gave them an opportunity to have a forum in the union where they could display the fact that they had equal ability with whites." He noted that "in many cases, when the white workers within the shop steward area would find that the black shop steward was much more able than the white shop steward in the same area, they would take their grievances to the black shop steward." He called this "a very interesting development in race relations."

Moreover, other evidence exists of changing white attitudes. The elections for business agent show that whites voted for black candidates based on their union ability. In 1950, for example, eight members, one of them an African American, ran for four offices. Fifty-seven votes, or 100 percent of the eligible joint board vote, were cast. Of this number, no more than twelve could have been black votes. Yet the black candidate led the field, obtaining thirty-eight votes, indicating a recognition of merit on the part of the white delegates. In 1948, 1950, and 1952, the elections of joint board officers saw African Americans elected to the finance committee with both black and white votes. In 1952, an African American ran for vice president of the joint board and lost by a vote of twenty-two to twenty-one. This meant that the black candidate had received nine votes from white delegates. Also, each year the three locals elected three members to an executive council. The black business agent, Russell Dodson, was regularly elected over at least three white candidates and on several occasions polled the highest vote.[64]

Due to the automatic representation black workers received through their local, all delegations that the Danville TWUA sent to national conferences were interracial. The experiences of these delegations helped in breaking down racial prejudice considerably. Clyde Coleman, a black man who worked at Dan River between 1939 and 1983, vividly remembered attending the TWUA's 1946 convention in Atlantic City and still had pictures of the interracial delegation on the Atlantic City boardwalk. He recalled that on the way up to New Jersey, whites and blacks sat separately. On the way back, after getting to know one another, the delegation stopped in Baltimore to eat. Coleman remembered that "they wouldn't serve us, said they couldn't do it, they would serve the white in the main cafeteria, but the colored had to go to another section. So instead of eating there we went on further. If we couldn't eat together, we didn't eat separate." This type of incident was remarkable, given the intense hostility that had marked black participation in the union during the 1944 strike only a few years before. In 1955, Emanuel Boggs told a representative from the American Friends Service Committee a whole catalog of similar stories. He explained that union members would travel together only if buses were integrated. He also noted, "As they travel, the whites refuse to eat anywhere that they cannot eat with the Negroes. In a few instances, they almost forced interracial eating by barging into the place in an integrated body and seating themselves without waiting for someone to seat them." Union members also rode together interracially in cars. At the 1950 TWUA convention in Boston, a resolution endorsing civil rights and the Fair Employment Practices Commission was discussed. While many southern delegates spoke in opposition to the resolution, Howard Robinson, a white Dan River shop steward, declared, "We have better relations with the colored people since we organized. They carry a lot of the responsibility. We have 1,200 colored people in our organization, and they do great work in Danville." [65]

Despite these positive results, the union leadership in Danville was not happy with the existence of the segregated local, calling it "an ideological and moral problem, to put it mildly." As most black workers opposed the dissolution of the black union, the TWUA leadership in Danville made determined and remarkably successful efforts to break down segregation in other areas of union activity. Thus, white guilt about the existence of the local actually spurred Danville leaders to push integration in other areas harder than they would have if an integrated local had existed. The union hall and other functions were integrated in a successful initiative stemming from the progress in race relations that the separate local had achieved and from the union's excellent prestrike relationship with the company, which meant that Dan River did not try to stir up the race issue. [66]

The advances that African Americans made through their segregated local were greatly helped by the solid support that black workers gave to the union, providing further evidence that blacks supported the separate structure. On the eve of the strike, Dan River's public relations agency, Fisher and Rudge, interviewed 716 white workers and 159 blacks about their attitudes toward the union and the company. The results indicate a massive disparity between the responses of the two groups. Fisher and Rudge concluded that "Negro attitudes toward Dan River Mills generally were less favorable than the white population. Negroes were more favorably inclined toward the union, and generally viewed Dan River less enthusiastically as an employer." Indeed, only 12 percent of the African Americans interviewed, compared to 48 percent of the whites, described Dan River as an "excellent place" to work. The percentage of blacks who thought the union's position was completely correct in the dispute was six times higher than the figure for whites.

Fisher and Rudge noted that it had problems getting black workers to talk on the record, because they were afraid their views would be reported to the company. Some were willing to talk "off the record," however, and these interviews provide close insight into the daily working conditions at Dan River. The survey showed that the positive response of the black workers to the union came partly from their experience of discrimination in the workplace. Fisher and Rudge noted that many African Americans had "a feeling of resentment over discrimination and poorer treatment." Many described how white workers doing identical work received different pay. There was also "resentment that no training program for Negroes existed." Many African American workers also gave "a negative evaluation of their supervision." These responses offer insight into the widespread discrimination that prevailed on the shop floor after the union had existed for nine years; they also indicate that the union was unsuccessful in solving fundamental problems facing black workers.[67]

Given this failure, the overwhelming support of black workers for the strike was remarkable. It is clear that blacks supported the union because, despite its limitations, it had made a difference in their lives and was the only institution available that offered any prospect for change. As Clyde Coleman recalled, "The blacks were loyal to the union because the union was our only voice. Before we didn't have any voice at all. If you didn't like what the whites did, you didn't have a job." African Americans now had the power to choose shop stewards from among their own ranks and the power provided by the grievance procedure. "The union gave a voice to the blacks. If you were right in what you thought was right, you spoke it. . . . Without the union, blacks didn't have any voice—they didn't hardly have any job." Accordingly, black workers remembered the strike as a more positive experience because it gave them the chance to, as one of them put it, "give management the knowledge of protest." Despite its failure in addressing fundamental problems, the union was important in providing black workers with greater job security and a greater sense of power on the shop floor.[68]

The militancy of black workers in the strike was not wasted. Indeed, the strike clearly played a major role in breaking down segregation and making whites accept blacks as good union members. African Americans played a major role in the strike, and Slim Boggs remembered that this experience was very beneficial in breaking down prejudice: "During the strike, pickets who were off duty—black and white—would come down to the union hall to rest until it was their time again and frequently they would have a bottle of moonshine, black and white tipping the same bottle. The strike had a great deal to do with breaking down segregation." Norris Tibbetts wrote that the strike caused race relations to advance "twenty years" in one move. He added, "The union hall was jammed day and night. Every function, including recreation, was interracial and although it may seem a small point, Negro boys were playing checkers with white girls. I don't consider that a small point." Overall, these improvements were attributed by Tibbetts to the fact that "everyone was so intent on the common goal that they forgot to check the color of the man or woman beside them." Many of these improvements were also sustained after the strike.[69]

The most striking feature of the story of the segregated local in Danville is the doubt it throws on the prevailing wisdom that African Americans could only achieve progress and recognition through integration. It is clear that had the separate Danville local not existed, Dan River's black workers would probably have continued to be relegated to a subordinate position in the union, as they had been between 1942 and 1944. The segregated local gave black workers a degree of power and a structure to work in and thereby brought recognition from white workers in the only way possible—by confronting them with the fact that blacks could perform as elected officers as well as whites could.

The fundamental questions, however, concern the significance and wider context of this progress. There are some indications that segregated locals proved beneficial in other southern textile locations. In 1955, former TWUA staffer Ross Groshong, then working with the UTW, told a representative from the American Friends Service Committee that "often Negroes themselves want segregated unions in order to keep from getting 'lost in the shovel.'" Similarly, the TWUA's Larry Rogin, who claimed to oppose segregated locals, nevertheless admitted that "in places where the blacks were, like Danville and Marshall Field Mills, it usually ended up in a segregated local, and I used to talk with some of the blacks and get their feelings about it, and in general they were in favor of the segregated locals because they would have been lost in large locals, and they got representation on the joint board in this way." Joe Jacobs, the southern director of the AFL textile union in the 1940s and 1950s, remembered that in Winnsboro, South Carolina, a separate black local produced many of the same benefits as in Danville—automatic representation, the consequent development of black leadership, recognition of black ability by whites, and political power on the joint board. Joel Leighton, a TWUA representative in the South, worked in a variety of locations with separate locals. His experiences made him an avid supporter of them, mainly because they "developed black leadership" and helped advance white acceptance of blacks.[70]

The benefits of segregated locals are confirmed by the fact that black workers were completely barred from TWUA locals across the South. This exclusion occurred because the general racial climate among white textile workers was one of extreme resistance to civil rights and integration. Indeed, the benefits of segregated locals can only be understood against this prevalent background of virulent racism. A 1959 study of twenty-three southern TWUA locals, for example, showed that blacks were denied any voice in the union, and in many cases whites prevented them from attending union meetings.[71]

The prevalence of racism in southern society and among textile workers does indeed provide the key to understanding the achievements of the segregated local. Because racism was so prevalent, the segregated local brought African American workers recognition and advancement that in all likelihood would not have otherwise occurred. Moreover, these benefits had wider consequences. On the whole, black workers rarely gained equality, fair treatment, or recognition in mixed CIO unions. Even in industries with large numbers of blacks, it was possible for the union itself to be used to further discrimination against blacks, as Robert Norrell's study of the southern steel industry has shown. Indeed, studies of southern workers who took part in integrated locals have shown that racial accommodation was fragile and limited. Thus, the prevalence of racism across southern society constricted the achievements of integrated locals as well as segregated ones.[72]

It was only in the 1960s and 1970s, partly through the pressure of civil rights organizations, that these fundamental problems of discrimination began to be addressed. In Danville, as elsewhere, black workers increasingly turned to civil rights organizations to tackle the discrimination that they faced in Dan River Mills.[73]

Ultimately, therefore, the story of the Danville local casts doubt on assumptions about the benefits of integration and shows how much rich race history remains hidden in the southern textile industry, despite the small numerical significance of black workers and their frequent "relegation" to separate locals.

"They Were Just Beginning to Get Something to Lose"

Dan River's campaign to break the 1951 strike, both on the picket line and through public relations, was sophisticated and well thought-out, and this clearly helps to explain why the strike failed. Nevertheless, the strength of the company's antistrike campaign does not fully account for why so many workers, many of them union members, crossed the picket line. The company made it easier for workers to abandon the strike, but in most cases, they did not create the pressure that made workers want to go back in such large numbers.

A major problem for the union in Danville arose from its success in raising the wages and living standards of its members in the previous decade. Ironically, this improved standard of living only increased workers' economic vulnerability and their inability to endure a strike. It also created tremendous relief problems in a strike situation. As early as the second day of the strike, the *Danville Bee* was already questioning whether workers could endure a strike, given their newfound prosperity. The *Bee* pointed out that many workers had used the higher wages of the 1940s and "invested in future living comfort which may now have to be sacrificed." The typical Dan River worker had bought items through installment plans, because with Dan River running flat-out, they thought they had an assured income. Many had also started making payments on company houses, which had been sold to workers in two batches in 1949 and 1950. The *Bee* asked, "Who is going to pay the note on the house he is buying on installments? Who is going to meet the monthly payment on the car, the life insurance premium, or the other fixed expenses to which the worker committed himself when there was no strike cloud on the horizon?" [74]

The *Bee*, which was obviously aware of the concerns of strikers, had identified a major problem. As the strike continued, it became clear that inability to make installment payments was the reason many were breaking the picket line. The *Southern Textile News*, which stationed a reporter in Danville throughout the strike, wrote on April 14 that strikers were going back because of "anxieties about the mill-owned houses they are buying on the installment plan but which payments they cannot meet, and this is true of thousands buying cars out of weekly earnings." During the strike, one company that was financing the purchase of five hundred mill houses reported that only 10 percent of these people buying on the installment plan fell into arrears. Clearly, they returned to work in greater numbers than did the workforce as a whole. When their wages had increased, many workers had moved away from the mill village to the outskirts, or even to rural communities outside Danville. Consequently, the *News* reported, "if they lose their cars they would have no transportation each day to and from their mill job." Thus, though the traditional mill village was often itself viewed as a hindrance to union organization, its breakdown presented the union with new problems. [75]

These problems were the product of a dramatic rise in living standards. The 1940s saw large wage gains for southern textile workers as a whole, but in Danville this change was even more acute because of the company's position as a wage leader. Between 1941 and 1951, the wages of textile workers increased 151.3 percent, more than for any other group of mass-production workers. During the same period, however, the wages of Dan River workers increased by 201.3 percent. The real earnings of Dan River workers rose 68 percent between 1940 and March 1951, an increase six times greater than that received by workers at General Motors. Illustrating the progress made by southern textile workers in the 1940s, the differential between the real straight-time earnings of GM and Dan River workers was reduced from 51.6 cents an hour in 1940 to 24.1 in 1951. [76]

Many who worked at Dan River in these years recalled how wages increased rapidly and workers began to buy cars and other consumer items. Melvin Griffiths, who started work at Dan River in 1921 and remembered the low wages of the 1920s and 1930s well, recalled that "the biggest improvement came right after the war." He bought his family's first car on credit and recalled that other workers did the same. His wife Virgil recalled that with higher wages, many workers owed money continually, so that in a strike, "a lot of them would go in debt so far they couldn't be out a day." They remembered that during the 1951 strike, "a lot of them had paid the first payment on these houses on the south side here, and a whole lot of them said they would lose their cars, and lose their homes too, if they stayed out. They almost had to work." Malcolm Cross felt that in these years, higher wages meant that "they were beginning to live the semblance of a normal life." He also recalled that this increased standard of living worked to the company's advantage in the strike, "because if you haven't got anything, you've got nothing to lose, but when you're going to lose these new assets, you've a stake in going back."[77]

Since workers had purchased items through installment plans, their dependence on having a weekly paycheck was actually increased. Thus, after workers received their last prestrike pay check on April 8, a huge relief crisis hit the union. Problems arose because of the TWUA's policy of only giving food relief, because strikers wanted assurances that the union would help them meet their other responsibilities as well. Boyd Payton wrote in his diary on April 10 that the union hall "was packed and jammed from early morning until late at night with strikers who were seeking relief on every possible problem. Many became angry and tore up their union cards when they could secure no clear cut answers on what they could expect by way of relief other than groceries." The union tried its best to alleviate these fears by stating in the *Daily Strike Bulletin* that "the union is on record that strikers will not lose their cars, furniture or homes. Let's get this word inside the mill; those folks don't have to go in. Let's get them with us." Strikers continued to react angrily, however, when the union was unable to keep its pledge of support. Norris Tibbetts noted that workers were "paid yesterday and now have emergency. Won't lose cars, furniture, or homes. Several people have torn up their cards and said they are going back to work." Credit buying was so common that strikers "can't get along—not even for a week." Tibbetts spoke of "the dependency of the mill-worker in Danville on the weekly paycheck, they had to have that money." He wrote that those who were returning to work did not do so out of "love for the boss" but because of crippling economic pressure. He recalled that many union members who crossed the picket line wept, and he added, "What can you say to them? . . . You weep with them."[78]

The union's big problem was the reluctance of strikers to surrender the items that they were just beginning to gain for the first time. Norris Tibbetts, who was responsible for dealing with the union's relief cases, felt that the union was asking workers for an enormous economic sacrifice: "Dan River workers were by no means well off but they were just beginning to get something to lose, a car, a refrigerator, payment on a house." He added, "The union helped bring it about but how can you lean on these people to the point of saying 'you have to give up everything you've gained in eight years under the union in order to pick up another couple of cents an hour?'" The union was asking workers to "risk all" on a stoppage. Many workers reasoned that they couldn't risk everything "but somehow the union will stay even if we go in. They turned out to be right." The economic progress workers had made was difficult to surrender. In the 1920s and 1930s, Malcolm Cross himself called Dan River wages "terribly low." It was very difficult, after these long years of low pay, "to think about having to give it up and have nothing." Indeed, workers feared a return to prewar pay levels, having experienced the freedom that higher wages had brought. One Dan River worker, Shirley Hall, told a congressional committee in 1949 that "our people in the last couple of years have just got a little bit used to making more money. . . . When somebody comes to the door now instead of sending our kids to say 'Mother isn't home,' the head of the house can answer the door because we are not afraid." She added, "Our people are desperately afraid we are going back to the days when I was growing up. . . . When I was a child my mother worked in the mill and my dad worked in the mill, the older kids took care of the younger ones and cooked supper. It wasn't a good way to live, and we are trying to forget about it." Recalling that her family had even worried about paying a one-dollar dog license, she concluded, "I don't want my kids or my sisters kids to be worried about things like that." [79]

The union's relief policy proved to be inadequate when confronted by these problems. Norris Tibbetts complained that "we get money from the national union . . . but we never know how much is coming and when. So there can be no constructive work in planning relief." Strikers asked, "'Can I get my rent paid at the end of the week?' 'Probably, we expect more money in by then.' 'But my landlord must know today.' 'Well we can't be sure.' So another scab goes back into the mills." Both Payton and Tibbetts made clear that it was the inadequacy of the relief effort that was causing the collapse of the Danville strike. On April 9, Payton wrote, "Everyone was agreed that the regular strike activities were being impeded because of the overwhelming relief situation." Four days later, Payton traveled to Greensboro for a special meeting with Rieve. He told the TWUA president, "We are losing the Danville situation on the relief line more than we are on the picket line." On April 25, Payton wrote, "The staff was unanimous in the opinion that Danville could only be held beyond Sunday if we loosened up on relief restrictions." Payton also called TWUA treasurer William Pollock "and requested that $10,000 be loaned to the credit union from which loans might be made for car payments. Became involved in a terrific argument with him over this matter and he refused to comply with the request."[80]

Payton's visit to Rieve and his confrontation with Pollock began a drive from strike leaders in Danville to secure more money from the national union. Payton argued that the TWUA must change its relief policy to meet the needs of postwar textile workers. He wrote that in the 1930s and before, textile unions had not faced these problems. If workers went on strike, they might be evicted from their company house, in which case they would go into a tent city run by the union, but they did not have much to lose. Payton, watching the Danville strike collapse around him and realizing its crucial importance for the TWUA, questioned the union's whole approach to the South. The union, he argued, had "spent millions of dollars in trying to organize in the South and with almost no results because we have never been able to win concessions from our organized mills which would put us far enough ahead of unorganized mills to make the effort of organizing attractive or even to seem worthwhile." The union had been afraid to force its organized mills to assume a clear differential "because we were in a minority position in the South and were afraid to strike for the things to which we were entitled and knew the mills could afford, because of our lack of faith (justified) in our Southern members' willingness to sacrifice and suffer for these things." All previous southern strikes "were conducted on the theory that sacrifice, hardship, and suffering is the only way to win a strike and the only way to build the labor movement." His experience in the Danville strike had indicated that workers crossed the picket line sometimes "because they are in need," but more often "because they have no confidence in the union's ability to protect them from loss of the things which they have bought or are buying."[81]

The alternative that Payton proposed was "a new approach of 'buying' the strength, power, and prestige which might come from winning a strike and gaining the benefits to which our people are entitled." Danville strikers should be given guaranteed strike benefits. The TWUA had a treasury of $4 million. To give strikers confidence, the union should pledge this money to Danville because so much was at stake: "We have four million dollars. If we carry out our present plans of doling out the bare necessities we will lose the strike here and in the rest of the South and wind up with three million in the treasury and no union in the South. Or, at least, with no bargaining power." With guaranteed benefits, Payton argued, "it is my firm conviction that the Danville situation can be saved." Indeed, he maintained that this was the "only way" it could be saved. The consequences of defeat were enormous. Without victory at Danville, "we will never be able to negotiate again in New England before setting a pattern in the South. And there will be no pattern set in the

South because we have no bargaining power." It was a choice between "a strong, united, militant, and confident union," albeit one with less money, and "having a partially broke Northern union and no prospects of gains anywhere in the South." Norris Tibbetts echoed many of these ideas in his diary, arguing that the union needed guaranteed benefits after only a week. He calculated that given workers' varied financial responsibilities, the TWUA needed to spend $232,000 a week on relief. He pointed out that stronger unions had already used guaranteed strike benefits to hold strikes and that this accounted for these groups' apparently superior militancy.[82]

Thus, the relief issue posed fundamental questions about the TWUA's role in the South, especially the central question of establishing a wage differential between organized and unorganized plants. Illustrating the importance of the Danville relief issue, the suggestions of Payton and Tibbetts were debated at length by southern strike leaders in Greensboro. It was clear from these discussions that the TWUA sensed that its whole future in the South was at stake, yet the issue of committing substantial amounts of cash to Danville split the union and prevented positive action. One official who supported the proposal was Baldanzi, who was very familiar with the Danville situation; he spoke in the city on six different occasions during the strike. Baldanzi also emphasized the vast change in living standards that had taken place across the South during the preceding decade and the consequent need for a reappraisal of the union's relief policy: "maybe we have not thought out too clearly the result of building the standards of Southern workers to an increased point. We have put them so much in debt; the car may be the most important thing in a man's life." Baldanzi pointed out, like Tibbetts and Payton, that the advent of credit buying had placed workers in a particularly vulnerable situation: "these people are merely emerging into a period where they have had the so-called fruits of our industrial society in the sense that you and I have had—washing machines, etc., for some time. They are in the middle of this damn thing. Everyone is up to his neck in home appliances, and now they are faced with the stark reality of losing them." He claimed that "because of the evolution in living standards brought about by the union, we are faced with terrific problems. These people are not going to see their cars go and their refrigerators go—they'll go to work first."[83]

Baldanzi went on to highlight some of these cases in detail. He stressed the fact that in Danville strikers were particularly afraid of losing possessions because local credit agencies and merchants had been very unsympathetic to their circumstances. He alleged that the company had put pressure on these agencies. Dan River had indeed written to a variety of merchants and other community leaders as part of its successful public relations campaign. He described the case of one distraught striker who "bought a Henry J. car last month—the CTI [a credit agency] . . . tells him we are sorry, and takes it away from him. . . . We can multiply that 6,000 times." Another striker "had four different loans, one on his home, one on the car, one on the furniture, and one on the washing machine. He said he either gets what he is asking for, or he is going back to work." [84]

Some TWUA leaders, however, opposed the idea of injecting large amounts of cash into the Danville situation. They questioned why Danville seemed to be different from other southern situations, where workers had remained on strike with only food relief. They also doubted whether it was ethical or effective to "pay people to stay on strike." Secretary-Treasurer William Pollock, a union bureaucrat who was always a strong supporter of the TWUA's relief policy, told his colleagues at one meeting, "This isn't the first strike we've had in the South. We've had plenty of them, but none of them have made demands like Danville. Just pouring in money won't win strikes. If this is the only way we can win strikes we've got one hell of a union." Pollock added, "I don't agree with the philosophy that they'll only fight if we buy their refrigerators and their automobiles for them." Many of the strike leaders in other southern centers pointed out that the existing relief policy was working well enough in their localities. For example, E. T. Kirkland, a representative from Pacific Mills in Columbia, South Carolina, claimed that "we're giving them more to eat in one week than we did in nine weeks ten years ago. If we keep on getting that you won't hear us holler for the next six months." Many southern leaders were also concerned about the effect it would have on their local union if a large amount of money was pumped into Danville. Alabama director Julius Fry explained, "While our situations are still solid I am quite sure we will have some embarrassing questions if people find out about a lot of money being given away in nonfood items." These objections prevented the union from changing its relief policy and committing extra funds to Danville.[85]

It is revealing that all of the objections to committing further funds to Danville were made by those who had not visited the city during the strike. In contrast, those who had been to Danville argued that more money was needed there because it was a unique situation. Most strike centers differed from Danville in two crucial ways: the companies made no serious attempt to operate, and strikers were able to hold onto credit purchases because of sympathetic merchants. Louis Hathcock, the strike's leader in Gadsden, Alabama, explained that "on the debts, the merchants have told us 'You people forget your debts until after the strike. After that, start back paying.'" Similarly, South Carolina director Charles Auslander reported that strikers in his state "are assured they won't lose their houses, cars, and etc." Other strike leaders reported the same situation. In contrast, Baldanzi reported that in Danville "there was a complete organization of the community against the union. There was a complete cut off of credit. The company public relations agency had lined up every bank, and every credit agency in town." He asked Kirkland, "Bill, suppose your people couldn't get any extension of credit at all, that would make a problem for you wouldn't it?" Baldanzi argued that Pollock's remarks "display a complete ignorance of what the situation really is. Danville is a situation apart. What we have there is a concentrated attempt to break the union beyond anything in my experience." Boyd Payton's diary described many individual cases of strikers undergoing repossessions after missing just one or two payments. Mary White, for example, lost her car after she missed three payments and refused to go back to work when visited by a supervisor. The car was then sold to another man for $35. On April 13, Payton wrote despondently that it was proving impossible to postpone installment payments and other bills because "the entire community seemed to be solidly organized against the union and we can expect no relief. . . . Very few of the business places in town were willing to extend credit or extend the time for regular payments." [86]

The remarks of Pollock and Kirkland implied criticism of the Danville strikers' militancy. Indeed, it is hard to see that so many people returned to work so quickly without drawing this quick conclusion. Those involved in the strike, however, emphasized the tremendous pressure that the relief situation imposed on strikers and praised the four thousand men and women who stayed out and maintained a hostile picket line until the end. Payton wrote, "It is a mistake to speak of Danville as a weak situation. . . . There are no finer union members anywhere than you will find in Danville." During the strike Boggs told TWUA leaders, "If anybody thinks we have a sewing circle, all they have to do is come up here and look around. I don't think there is a union in this country that, subjected to the same type of pressure we have been, would have made a better showing than we have." Baldanzi too defended the militancy of the Danville strikers in private and public. Some former strikers felt that the strike could have been won if the union had committed more funds to Danville. Elmer Wright, a tall, thin man who was a shop steward at the time of the strike, remembered that "they kept promising to help us, but they never did. If they had got the money it would have been different, there's no doubt." [87]

The failure of the union to win any kind of lasting community support does pose fundamental questions, however, especially considering that before the strike, the TWUA was praised for its work in community relations. The reaction of the local press, which shifted from praise for the union to violent opposition to the strike, illustrates this change in community opinion. The press had supported the TWUA in Danville precisely because it had avoided strikes, especially a repetition of the violent

1930–31 strike. The *Danville Bee*, for example, praised the union after its 1946 negotiations because "most of us remember the tragic days of the strike of 1931 which could have been avoided had the union been in the hands of less virulent and opportunity-seeking ringleaders. The affairs of the union now are being directed by men who are neither headstrong or radical though they are undoubtedly tenacious." Thus, the legacy of the 1931 strike meant that the union would only receive community support if it avoided strikes. When the strike was called, the press immediately attacked by raising the specter of 1931. Slim Boggs mentioned the way that the 1931 strike was "hanging over the town" and providing a "psychological factor the company had to start with." The way that the 1931 strike influenced the 1951 strike demonstrated the lasting impact that strike defeats had in southern textile communities and forecast the lasting damage that 1951 was to leave behind. Even after sixty-three years, the 1931 strike was bitterly remembered by many in Danville.[88]

The rapid swing in community opinion caused some in the TWUA to charge that the Danville locals had been built incorrectly—according to executive council member John Chupka, its leaders had placed "too much emphasis on community relations." This issue divided the TWUA. Many, like Sol Stetin, pointed out how important it was for the union to win respectability in the South and have a visible and successful relationship with a large southern employer. But the strike showed, in graphic detail, the limitations of such a policy. In a moving letter written shortly after the strike, Norris Tibbetts claimed that the main lesson he had learned was that "THE ONLY THING WHICH DAN RIVER MILLS AND MOST OTHER EMPLOYERS UNDERSTAND IS POWER. REASON MEANS NOTHING. LOGIC MEANS NOTHING. POWER AND FORCE MEAN EVERYTHING." He argued, "Organized workers get only what they are big enough to take," and "It is war, and the prefix of 'industrial' doesn't change the character of it." His conclusion was that the union in Danville should "stop, for the most part, this meaningless work in the community. Do some, but at least not kid ourselves about what we're doing. With rare exceptions, cotton mill worker's only friend is his union." In the future, the union should build its treasury and prepare for a strike that "will knock mill on its tail once and for all."[89]

The Aftermath

Tibbetts's remarks illustrate a consistent and simple problem facing the TWUA in the South—the fact that the union could only make real progress in the region by exerting economic power. It was common for those who took part in head-on conflict with management to realize this basic truth about industrial relations in the textile South. To organize the

South, the union had to establish its basic goal of a union wage scale, which southern textile employers were repeatedly unwilling to grant voluntarily. However, Tibbetts underestimated the damage that the 1951 strike had done to the Dan River locals when he argued that the union should rebuild for another strike. Company representatives infiltrated union meetings following the strike, and their reports provide a detailed and fascinating insight into the demoralized and disillusioned state of the workforce. These reports are especially revealing because they dispute the prevailing historical wisdom that corporations no longer engaged in industrial espionage after the 1920s. Thus, one confidential report from July 1951 informed Browder that "the general feeling around the union hall is that more people would work if the strike is called than worked before." The workers who attended union meetings were described as "a pretty sad looking group." Another report described how "there is always a man at the door of the meetings to sign up new members. For the first time for this union not a single new member was signed up at last night's meeting."[90]

Fully aware of the union's position of weakness, the company debated whether it should push ahead and force another strike to destroy the union, or simply reduce it to a position of impotence. The contract was due to run out on July 31, 1951, because the union had struck Dan River on a wage reopener clause. Shortly before the end of July, the company decided not to force a strike. Cross wrote Browder that "a prolonged strike would be necessary to eliminate the union." The company was unwilling to endure the cost of such a conflict, especially given that the 1951 strike had already cost them over $2 million. In addition, if the union were broken, reorganization efforts would inevitably follow: "the nature of Dan River operations is such that it will always be attractive to unions. We would constantly be harassed by organizations attempting to unionize our employees, and who may be more militant if they are successful." The best course to follow, therefore, was to "weaken the union organization" even further. For Dan River, Cross concluded, "a weak union is better than no union."[91]

Thus, the fact that the union survived the 1951 strike was in large part a consequence of this conscious decision by management. The way that Dan River chose to keep the union weak was by proposing the removal of the checkoff. Not surprisingly, the union resisted this proposal, and negotiations were drawn out. The company's central argument for removing the checkoff stressed that it had been granted by the NWLB over management opposition. After the war, the company had gone along with the checkoff in the hope of building a stable relationship with the union, but the strike had shown that the union was not responsible enough to have a checkoff. For Browder, removing the checkoff was a way of both expressing his annoyance and anger with the union for calling the strike and punishing them for abandoning the constructive pre-strike relationship: "over a period of years we made what we thought was excellent progress in building our relationship. . . . And then to have the rug pulled from under our feet and to have ourselves kicked in the face as we were by the action that was taken by people who have no regard to what our situation was locally. That's something that we honestly cannot forget." The company argued that if they continued the checkoff, it could be used against Dan River by the union's feuding national leaders. Consequently, Browder concluded, "We want to be friends, but we are not going to be kicked around by anybody, and want to be in a position when somebody wants to kick us around we will have a chance to kick too." [92]

No agreement had been reached when the contract with Dan River ran out on August 1, 1951. Without a checkoff, the number of dues-paying members dropped from 7,900 to 2,000 at the beginning of 1953. Union members were in no state to strike for a contract, so the Danville locals asked the national union for funds to help them rebuild. In the wake of the strike, however, Danville became what Norris Tibbetts called a "political football," with Rieve forces refusing to send funds into a Baldanzi stronghold. Danville leaders went to the union's 1952 convention hoping to tell their story and enlist the support of the national union. Like other southern locals, they came away disgusted from a convention they claimed was rigged by Rieve to deny Baldanzi supporters the floor. Slim Boggs and many other southern leaders soon decided to take their locals out of the TWUA and into the rival UTW-AFL. Boggs imagined that with a new union, the company might grant the checkoff, given that there was no chance of being caught in the Rieve-Baldanzi crossfire. Browder refused to forgive so easily, though, claiming that "it can happen again." A frustrated Lewis Conn compared the union's situation to a man hanged for "one mistake in an otherwise fairly constructive life." The union had little other choice than to sign a contract without the checkoff in April 1953; from the union's viewpoint, this contract was also considerably weaker in a number of other respects. [93]

Affiliating with the UTW did not solve the local union's problems in securing national support for efforts to rebuild the union. The UTW, a much smaller union than TWUA, spent a lot of money trying to secure as many TWUA locals as possible and faced serious financial problems throughout the 1950s. The Danville locals were consistently unable to secure a significant dues-paying membership or to build strike support. This failure seems puzzling, given that in October 1952, Dan River workers voted for the UTW rather than no union by a substantial margin of 7,689 to 1,624. It was a sign of the TWUA's greatly diminished standing that it only received 230 votes. Local union leaders recalled that the vote illustrated a theme that occurred elsewhere in the South in these years: workers who were used to a union wanted the protection it offered, but only a minority would pay dues voluntarily. After the 1951 strike, workers who wanted to pay dues had to travel to the union hall in downtown Danville—a special trip many were unwilling to make. Dues-paying membership dropped from 2,000 in January 1952 to 900 in June 1955. Slim Boggs recalled, "If they got into trouble and needed assistance from the union they came in and started paying dues again. But most of them didn't get into trouble and didn't pay their dues. The dues-paying membership became smaller and smaller." The low number of dues-paying members also indicated the lasting damage that the 1951 strike had caused. Thus, in 1976, with the Danville locals still operating without a checkoff, the TWUA's education director, Bruce Raynor, described Danville as "a broken union . . . with less than 200 members [out of 10,000 mill workers] who maintain union headquarters as a last bastion of hope." He wrote that this situation was due to the fact that "Dan River workers initiated their 1951 strike with a strong local union, but it ended with a broken organization. The defeat showed Danville workers who held the real power in the South; and it effectively disheartened them, forcing them to conclude that even a strong union was no match for Dan River." [94]

The loss of the checkoff as a result of the 1951 strike was a blow from which the union never recovered. Robert Gardiner, the quiet personnel manager who continued to work for Dan River's personnel department until retirement in the 1980s, recalled that the checkoff was "the big bone of contention" between company and union for the whole of his working life. Indeed, the union tried several unsuccessful strikes to try to reestablish the checkoff. These strikes failed, however, because the company had the union in a situation that worked perfectly for them. As Robert Gardiner recalled, "We had them in a position where they couldn't win a strike. . . . They couldn't win because they didn't have the money, and they didn't have the money because they didn't have the checkoff." Forty-three years after the strike, the UTW still operated a very weak Danville local with around three hundred members and no checkoff. Dan River made no attempt to decertify the union, however, continuing to prefer a weak union to no union. [95]

The 1951 Danville strike was a tragic blow for the TWUA because it destroyed its relationship with a large southern company that openly accepted the union. It was very rare for the union to organize large companies, and even more unusual for these companies to tolerate the union, let alone accept it. In addition to virtually destroying its showpiece union in the South, the 1951 strike defeat had tremendous ramifications for the TWUA as a whole, especially considering that southern employers saw Danville as a test case. Particularly damaging for the TWUA was the loss of Dan River as a pattern-setting wage company. Malcolm Cross recalled that after 1951, Dan River never set a wage pattern again. The union had lost so much influence and power in the South as a result of the strike that Dan River knew it would not make organizing gains. Hence, large nonunion companies would no longer follow Dan River's lead as a way of preventing organization. According to Cross, the 1951 strike "hurt them very badly, and they never made any real progress after that." After 1951, Dan River "followed a nonunion pattern." Slim Boggs considered the strike a "tragedy" because "a union movement was built largely as the result of the success of the union right here in Danville that made enormous strides nationally in the textile industry." The strike "set the economic movement in the textile industry back to the extent that no progress has been made in the South since that fatal strike, and economic losses have resulted in the New England area."[96]

The strike's failure illustrated several broader themes that held the TWUA back in the South between 1945 and 1955. It showed how the competitive structure of the industry hindered collective bargaining, an important point not recognized by accounts that emphasize worker culture as a crucial factor in the failure of unionization. The role of women in the strike illustrated their central involvement in textile strikes during these years. Above all, broad social changes resulting from higher wages were at the heart of this grave defeat. The rising standard of living generated by World War II rather than worker culture or employer opposition played a key role in the strike's defeat. Rising wartime wages had also played a key role in building the union's prestige in Danville before the strike. Even the company's strategy for breaking the strike was greatly helped by the impact of disposable income on postwar southern textile communities. As Malcolm Cross recalled, the company could never have broken the strike unless workers owned cars. Car ownership allowed the company to bypass the picket line, which was well manned throughout the strike: "the union was quite successful at having masses of people at the main gates, and you had to run the gauntlet to get through. But if you can put them in a car you can get five people in and roll up the windows and it's not as frightening an experience." This tactic worked "because of course a lot of them had cars by that time and there was a lot of car-pooling." In addition, car and home ownership meant that by the time of the strike, 30 percent of Dan River workers lived in rural communities outside Danville. It was in these communities that much of the strike violence occurred—violence that brought the union negative publicity and alienated the company. Thus, the TWUA found that economic and social changes set in motion by World War II continued to hinder its progress in the South.[97]

chapter seven   **The Death of the Union**

The Fallout from the 1951

General Strike

           Speaking shortly after his retirement from a lifetime of involvement with the TWUA, *Textile Labor* editor Ken Fiester described what a huge defeat the 1951 strike represented to the union: "It exposed so many weaknesses, it showed us, and it showed the companies just how strong we were down there. . . . The union was exposed really as a paper-tiger, because we not only got whipped, but whipped in a hurry." Indeed, the real legacy of the strike was in how it caused TWUA leaders and southern staff to lose confidence in their ability to really become a major presence in the South. Between 1939 and 1951, the union had been sustained by a self-belief and optimism that it could "crack the South." This sense of self-belief died in 1951, and the strike marked the transition to the 1950s, which were to be a bleak decade of failure for the TWUA in the South. It was because of this change that so many in the TWUA regarded the strike as a watershed. Research Director Solomon Barkin best captured this shift that the strike caused: "It was the last great gasp at being a big factor in the South, it was after that that we began to say 'now what the hell is wrong.' . . . It was the watermark because after that we never dreamed of the South as something we could take over like Sherman marching through Georgia. We became piecemeal about it, couldn't conceive of it as a unified operation." Barkin added, "We had to realize that the assumptions of the early days, of 1937, the War Labor Board, all of this that we could somehow convert the industry would not be possible." [1]

    The fallout from the strike was considerable, affecting the TWUA not only in the South but on a national scale as well. The strike's impact was felt in a variety of different ways—in locals that were involved and in those that were not, in organizing, in the ability to secure wage increases, and in contract negotiations.

"Our Victories These Days Are Only Defensive"

A major consequence of the 1951 strike was the destruction of the pre-strike wage mechanism that had been used successfully to protect TWUA members in New England. With southern manufacturers successfully resisting the wage raise that the North had granted, the union came under intense pressure in the North. This pressure increased as the union failed to move southern wages in the wake of the strike, adding to the economic vulnerability of the New England textile industry, which declined rapidly in the years immediately after the strike.

Because the 1951 strike had resulted in a considerable widening of the North-South wage differential, the TWUA desperately needed to press for a southern wage increase in the wake of the strike. Since problems at Dan River prevented it from setting the pattern as before, the TWUA turned to smaller mills to take the lead. However, the union found that smaller companies were even more unwilling to risk increasing their wage costs above the level of their competitors, especially after the strike enhanced fears that the TWUA would be unable to organize nonunion companies. The depressed market conditions of the early 1950s added to the reluctance of companies to grant a wage increase, especially as the textile industry began to suffer from rising imports, a serious problem that was to plague the industry in ensuing decades.[2] The reaction of management at Kendall Mills in Newberry, South Carolina, whose local had survived the 1951 strike relatively intact, was typical: the company only agreed "to go along with any wage pattern that is established by the industry."[3]

The loss of Dan River was sorely felt by the TWUA. The union finally received a breakthrough in November 1951, when the A. D. Julliard chain of Aragon and Rome, Georgia, broke the wage freeze by announcing an eight-cents-an-hour increase. The following day the TWUA announced that this increase would be extended to all organized southern textile workers. An industry spokesman, however, commented that "Julliard isn't big enough" to set the southern wage pattern and that even if all Georgia mills were to meet the Julliard agreement, it still would not set a southern pattern. In fact, the Julliard increase was never implemented by other organized mills, and southern wages remained frozen.[4]

The Julliard incident illustrated the way that the wage initiative had passed to nonunion companies following the 1951 strike. With Dan River no longer able to be a pattern-setter, and smaller mills unwilling or unable to become pattern-setters, the TWUA failed to move southern wages, despite repeated efforts. The combination of a weakened TWUA and a depressed market thwarted all the union's wage campaigns. Between 1951 and 1955, southern textile workers received no wage increases, while workers in major manufacturing industries received increases totaling from forty-one to forty-six cents an hour. *Textile Labor* wrote in September 1955 that "year after year since 1951, workers in the principal textile divisions have fallen further and further behind other industrial workers in both wages and fringe benefits." It is clear that the strike was largely responsible for this change. In 1955, Solomon Barkin told a congressional committee that "since 1950, the textile workers have not received any improvement in their wage standards or economic benefits. In 1951 the southern textile giants, acting in collusion, defeated the union in a strike, and thereafter have used their powers to prevent any further economic advances by their employees." Thus, the strike's failure helped to establish southern textile workers as the poor stepchildren of American industry—an image that prevailed throughout ensuing decades, as southern textile workers fell further and further behind northern mass-production workers in terms of pay. Thus, while the wages of all nonagricultural workers increased by 463 percent from 1948 to 1978, wages for textile workers increased by only 373 percent.[5]

When wage patterns were set after the 1951 strike, they were set by nonunion chains such as Burlington, Cannon, Springs, and J. P. Stevens. Thus, when the first increase to be granted southern textile workers since October 1950 finally came, at the end of 1955, it was set by Burlington. A 1956 increase was set by J. P. Stevens, and the next major increase in 1959 was initiated by Cannon. This pattern was maintained in ensuing decades.[6]

The TWUA acknowledged that the 1951 strike had ended its ability to set southern wage patterns. Many TWUA members were also aware that this meant the union would not be able to play as effective a role in the South as before. Solomon Barkin felt that "the strike was crucial, it was the change in the tide, I mean the whole concept of unionization and wage programs in the 40s was founded on the fact that the union would lead, [and] the southerners would protect themselves by adopting a comparable increase to that which had occurred in the North." *Textile Labor* wrote that even though the union had managed to set wage patterns before 1951 through "courageous members and sound strategy," the "lesson" of the southern strike was that "forty thousand TWUA members—or even 90,000—just aren't enough in a southern industry employing more than 400,000." Reaffirming the union's new consciousness of its weaknesses, it added, "The tail can't wag the dog if the dog really plants his feet and resists." Dan River executive Malcolm Cross recalled that after the 1951 strike, "Dan River was hesitant to be the leader when

TWUA lost as much influence as it did. . . . The union was very much weaker because of that strike. . . . Dan River couldn't be sure anymore that anybody was going to follow." Before the strike, nonunion companies had followed Dan River's lead because they perceived the union to have organizing potential, potential that it lost in the 1951 strike: "they were making some gains, and they would have made more, but this was such a disaster, they lost all the way round. . . . it just gave ammunition to J. P. Stevens and Burlington." For management, too, the strike vividly demonstrated the true strength of the union and made them realize that it was no longer necessary to respond to union wage pressure.[7]

This shift to nonunion companies was significant because it was largely through seizing the wage initiative that companies such as Burlington and J. P. Stevens came to prominence as anti-union leaders in the 1950s and 1960s. Indeed, by controlling southern wages the nonunion companies placed the TWUA in a desperate position in the region and throughout the nation. The union could no longer promise northern employers that if they gave a wage increase, the southern employers would also come up with one. This put the TWUA under severe pressure from northern employers for much of the 1950s. Indeed, from 1951 onward, the union found most of its energy consumed by fighting hard battles against wage cuts in northern mills. In January 1952, for example, leading New England companies petitioned for substantial wage cuts, citing the TWUA's failure to equalize southern wages and fringe benefits. The TWUA admitted that these demands were due to its failure to raise southern wages, which "has created a sizable discrepancy in wages between the northern and southern mills." Indeed, the 1951 failure produced a widespread frustration with the TWUA among New England mill owners. For them, too, the strike showed clearly that the TWUA would not be able to raise southern wages as it had hoped. One prominent mill owner asked a question that was typical of the time: "how long must New England mills go on being destroyed by a double-standard—one for the South, another for New England? We're tired of union promises, union failure to provide parity, and union double talk."[8]

In fact, the wage cuts that were carried out in 1952 proved to be only the first part of a broad offensive that New England mill owners launched against the TWUA. In the spring of 1953, the union spent over four months successfully resisting an attempted pay cut in Massachusetts' Fall River–New Bedford mills. In the summer of 1955, the TWUA was involved in a bitter strike for thirteen weeks against further pay cuts in New England. This strike was successful in that the union managed to resist further wage cuts. Yet in reality the TWUA was trapped in a no-win situation. Even if it prevented wage cuts, it still lost money and time battling to stand still, and meanwhile it was unable to turn its attention to the ever-more-pressing task of organizing the South. The TWUA publicly acknowledged that because it was unable to move southern wages, "our victories, these days, are only defensive." The TWUA's ability to fight successfully against wage cuts in New England was also counterproductive, because it prevented manufacturers from reducing the wage differential and thus increased the economic handicap under which they operated. Yet if the TWUA had acquiesced in wage cuts, it clearly would have lost face with its members. There simply was no winning strategy.[9]

The wage differential caused by the 1951 strike contributed to the severe economic problems that the industry faced in the 1950s. Manufacturers themselves cited the failure of the 1951 strike as central to their reasons for closing plants.[10] Howard Rains wrote in a 1952 issue of the industry newspaper the *Daily News Record* that "most well-grounded people believe that the setbacks suffered in the South last year is the big reason for closing. . . . The explanation is that many New England firms were marking time awaiting the progress of the unions' efforts to organize the South. Theory was that it may not be worth moving if they were to face the same alleged higher costs and 'union difficulties' they had in the North." Rains added, "It is a fact that some southern mills, particularly in North Carolina, were much in line with the North until the latter area granted its latest wage increase last year." Other sources also cited the strike as influential in convincing many northern mill owners to close and emphasized the difficulties that the TWUA faced in the North, trapped as it was between the need to protect its members and making enough concessions to convince management to run the plant.[11]

Many in the TWUA also felt that the failure of the strike hastened the move of the industry from New England, especially given that the union no longer had a mechanism to control southern wages. Larry Rogin, for example, believed "the union after that could not pressure the northern employers that if they gave a wage increase, southern employers would come up with one. It made employers who were thinking of going South think much more of it."[12]

Apart from deflecting resources away from the vital task of organizing the South, the most damaging consequence of the plant closures in New England was the huge numbers of dues-paying members that were lost as a result. This was fatal for the TWUA because it meant that the union had a shrinking base from which to try to organize the South. One union report at the end of 1952, for example, concluded desperately that "since many of the New England mills are closing our revenue coming from that source has been cut a great deal so we will have to depend more and more on new organization. Since January 1 we have lost an average of $64,000 monthly. . . . We cannot continue to do the things we have." By March 1952, 62,000 of New England's 140,000 textile workers were unemployed. From 1951 onward, the decline of New England absorbed an increasing amount of the TWUA's time, as the union pushed for a variety of initiatives to try to protect their members' jobs. Everybody involved with the union knew that the only solution was to organize the South; but instead, the decline of New England absorbed their energy and robbed them of the necessary resource base for large-scale southern organizing. The TWUA's need to organize the South increased as its ability to do so declined.[13]

The failure to win wage increases in the South also tarnished the union's image in the eyes of its southern membership. The strike's failure led to a large amount of rank-and-file discontent from TWUA southern members, as they too realized the union's weakness and ineffectiveness in the South. For workers, many of whom had struck in accordance with the national union's wage program, a profound sense of despondency set in after the strike. For example, a group of workers from Gold-Tex Fabrics Corporation in Rock Hill, South Carolina, wrote Emil Rieve wanting to know why they had not received any wage increase despite striking: "before the strike, April 1951, we were promised a two cents raise. Not only have we not received the two cents raise, but neither have we received the promised highest wages in textile history. We are beginning to wonder why we are paying union dues each week when the union itself is not coming up to what it stands for." Reports of similar frustration came in from elsewhere. Robert Parker, representative for the North Central Joint Board in High Point, North Carolina, wrote in September 1951 that "the workers everywhere are getting impatient about the slowness of the movement on the wage increase matter. We are trying to explain that it is a real hard fight our union is having with the WSB, as well as the employers, to get the wage increases our workers need right now." Similarly, TWUA representative Harold Griffiths wrote from the Bi-County Joint Board in Leaksville, North Carolina, that "if we could get these wage increases through I feel sure it would help a great deal in securing members and also in organizing campaigns." Other southern representatives reported that workers were withdrawing from local unions because of the strike's failure.[14]

Many workers also felt that the 1951 strike gravely weakened the TWUA and the wider union movement in the South. Ernest Cole, a worker at Aleo Manufacturing Company in Rockingham, North Carolina, which participated in the strike, felt that "it weakened the union everywhere, it's like being in the army, if everybody is not together, you can't do it." Other workers felt, like many members of the TWUA's southern staff, that the strike was doomed to failure because the TWUA was simply not powerful enough to conduct a general strike in the South. Another Aleo worker, John Grant, recognized that the TWUA's intrinsic problem was its lack of power, which effectively doomed its attempt to change the wage stabilization law: "if you've got a law that sets your wages so much and you go on strike to get more, you're crazy, because you're not going to break that law, not unless you've got the whole industry, I mean everyone, then you can break the law. . . . If you shut the whole thing down, they'll listen. John Lewis called every coal miner out, every single one. They listened."[15]

The TWUA found that its inability to move southern wages tended to rob it of appeal and make it seem ineffective and weak. One of the fears of TWUA leaders was that the failure of the 1951 strike would leave the union powerless to stop southern manufacturers from following northern ones in implementing wage cuts. At one executive council meeting where a wage cut at Bates Manufacturing Company in Maine was being discussed, council member Jack Rubenstein told his colleagues that "the last increase in the North was not followed in the South. We were too weak to force the increase there. If we have wage cuts in the North, they will, however, follow through in the South." Echoing the fears of others, Rubenstein argued that the union "ought to resist" these cuts in the South but doubted whether it was in a position to following the 1951 strike. Illustrating the sense of weakness characteristic of the TWUA after 1951, he admitted, "I am scared of a strike. If we know we cannot win, it makes no sense to strike. Naturally we ought to holler. I think we ought to look around for a scapegoat."[16] Indeed, in 1952 and 1953 southern manufacturers did launch a wage-cutting drive that inflicted further damage on the TWUA in the South. The few southern employers who had approximated the northern increase of 1951 moved first for cuts as their contracts expired. At A. D. Julliard in Aragon, Georgia, 750 workers struck unsuccessfully for nearly four months in an attempt to maintain a raise they had won a year earlier. At Pickett Cotton Mills in High Point, North Carolina, workers battled for nineteen weeks against a proposed twenty-one-cent wage cut. In these strikes the workers often turned their frustration against the TWUA, blaming it for its inability to protect their wage scales. At a strike against a wage cut in Thomasville, North Carolina, TWUA representative Robert Parker wrote that "I have heard some bad things said about the union but the remarks of these people topped them all. Their hate was something awful to hear. . . . This cut in wages will leave our union in bad grace in Thomasville and other places." These strikes also gravely weakened the local unions involved and illustrated once more the terrific relief problems caused by credit purchases in the postwar period.[17]

"They Are Apparently Taking Their Cue from the Dan River Mills"

The TWUA also found that the 1951 strike had a very damaging impact on attempts to organize new plants in the South. The strike had a direct effect on a series of defeats that occurred within a year of its failure, especially when elections were held close to strike locations.[18] Thus, despite an encouraging prestrike election campaign, the union lost an election at Halifax Worsted Mills near Danville, Virginia, due to "the economic difficulties which descended upon the textile union workers as a result of their lost strike at Dan River Mills." According to organizers' reports, a campaign to organize the important nonunion Springs Mills plant in Fort Mill, South Carolina, was killed by the failure and violence of the strike at nearby Industrial Cotton Mill in Rock Hill.[19] Harold Griffiths, the TWUA's representative for the Bi-County Joint Board based in Leaksville, North Carolina, reported that the union was having great trouble securing new members in its organizing campaigns in Fieldale, Virginia, and Mayodan, North Carolina, because workers had been "scared by our strike." Similar reports came in from across the South.[20]

Indeed, in the early 1950s, organizing gains in the South dried up completely, and the TWUA lost elections by bigger margins than before the strike.[21] Those involved in southern organizing claimed that the strike had effectively killed the union's organizing prospects. UTW chief Anthony Valente claimed in 1952 that the "strike fiasco has retarded the organizing movement in the South by at least ten years," a point also made by the TWUA's southern director, James Bamford. Bamford reported privately to Emil Rieve that "the recent strike situation has set us back probably for some time in the organizing field."[22] Emanuel Boggs, who organized in a variety of locations after the strike, expressed his belief that "there is no question what the effect was. The effect was that it stopped progress in textile organization in the South and affected progress of organization generally in the South. It caused workers everywhere to wonder 'now, look what happened in textiles. If they couldn't win the general strike, what have we got to gain by joining a union?'" The damage done to the overall cause of southern organizing is borne out by other organizers as well. In the summer of 1951, for example, Edwin Waller, a southern organizer for the United Furniture Workers of America (UFWA), complained that "it is quite apparent that the Southern manufacturers are throwing up every wall of resistance at their command. . . . They are apparently taking their cue from the Dan River mills. . . . However, these are usual occurrences in Southern organizing and all that is usually necessary to overcome the bosses is for organizers to go on a 25 hour, 8 day week."[23]

The strike was particularly tragic because it encouraged manufacturers to go on the offensive against the TWUA, ending the accommodationist tactics that many had used during Operation Dixie. Emanuel Boggs felt that the strike was particularly regrettable because "up to the time of the strike you could see the beginning of an acceptance of unions as a fact of life. It brought about a hardening of attitudes on the part of management throughout the South. . . . I can't think of any other one factor that had as much effect on hardening management attitudes." Speaking in 1981, he added, "This strike is still affecting management attitudes in the South." Similarly, Paul Swaity, the TWUA's director of organizing between 1967 and 1976, was a close friend of federal mediator Yates Heafner, who worked for more than twenty years trying to settle labor-management disputes in the South. Swaity recalled that "Yates and I, when I was southern regional director, would often talk about the problem of the South. He would say to me that it was interesting that the whole direction that southern textile employers took might have been different." Swaity explained that in the late 1940s, textile employers were discussing whether to confront the union or to permit it to organize but try to take away its organizing appeal. This discussion seemed amazing to Swaity, because after 1951 "the opposition to unionism was so strong." [24]

The assertions of Boggs and Heafner are consistent with the way that many southern textile employers chose to fight Operation Dixie with wage increases; with the constructive relationship that was established between the TWUA and a number of southern companies, most notably Dan River, in the 1940s; and with the emphasis that management put on public relations and constructive personnel ideas in the late 1940s. Moreover, management sources from the late 1940s continually stress the threat of organization and the strength of the CIO.[25] After 1951, management did go on the offensive, fighting unionization far more openly and attacking existing locals. They were aided in their attack by an NLRB that, from the unions' point of view, had been further weakened by the Eisenhower administration in terms of unions. Management began this attack by successfully utilizing the 1951 strike's failure as propaganda material in organizing campaigns.[26] Contract negotiations where local unions had long been established also became more difficult. In June 1952 Charles Auslander wrote from Woodside Mills in Greenville, South Carolina, that contract negotiations were very arduous because "following the usual practice since our Southern strike, the employer in this case insisted on the elimination of the check-off." TWUA southern director James Bamford wrote that the TWUA was finding its contracts under attack "throughout the South," especially on the check-off issue, because "employers are already starting to use Danville as an example." The TWUA's 1954 executive council report summed up the tough environment in which the union operated between 1951 and 1954: "during all this time the Southern picture was dark. Disheartened by the unsuccessful strike of 1951, faced by heavier employer and community pressure than ever before, the average local union was simply not in condition to fight for higher wages." [27]

The acute failure of the TWUA's southern organizing drive of 1953–55 highlighted these problems well. Unlike Operation Dixie, which did produce consistent gains in small mills, the drive of the mid-1950s struggled to capture even small plants, where organizers needed to work for far longer than had been the case in the late 1940s. Moreover, campaigns were met by mass firings and wholesale violations of the NLRB. With the union unable to set southern wages, mill owners had no need to match union pay scales, and they had an extra incentive to fight organization through confrontational tactics. Companies repeatedly made open displays of economic force to kill organizing efforts. At a Goodyear plant in Rockmart, Georgia, for example, organizer Purnell Maloney wrote that "the situation is heartbreaking" as she watched her best activists being fired. From Tifton Mill in Tifton, Georgia, another organizer wrote that a drive was going nowhere because the company was firing supporters at the "slightest excuse." He relayed that "there is no talk in the plant (company has forbidden it) about the union. Company bosses and stooges are busy as hell." In part, what made the removal of union activists so effective in the early and mid-1950s was the fluctuating market conditions that characterized the textile industry during these years. This backdrop allowed companies to fire union supporters under the cover of economic layoff and made workers terrified for their jobs.[28]

Finding the task of organizing very difficult, in the mid-1950s the TWUA sent its organizers into many different situations, transferred them frequently, and never mounted the kind of concentrated effort that it had during Operation Dixie. Organizers were told to "check out" particular mills or towns with a view to launching a campaign. Garland Brook, for example, was sent into nine different campaigns in a two-year period between 1953 and 1955. Speculative reports came back from varied locations, including Kannapolis, which was never far from the TWUA's mind. What was noticeable about the period after 1951, however, was the failure of the TWUA to tackle industry giants such as Cannon. This was itself the result of the fact that the union had lost its early postwar belief that it could organize major chain companies. In January 1953, M. W. Lynch reported from Cannon Mills, "I find a lot of sentiment around this area for the union, however, when you consider the size, the number of employees involved and the amount of money it will take to carry on a campaign in the Cannon chain, you wonder how long it would take to bring this to a final conclusion." Instead the union adopted a prudent, low-risk approach of using its limited resources on smaller targets to try to create outposts of unionism. Many in the union realized all along that the union needed to pool its resources, as Boyd Payton put it, "in large, pattern-setting companies rather than small marginal ones which even if organized would have no impact on others." Dissatisfied with the small plant approach, Payton added that "we are quite busy, but I have the feeling sometimes that we are just 'spinning our wheels.' There must be a brighter day coming—somewhere—sometime." Eventually, the TWUA went back to the big plant approach with the launching of the J. P. Stevens campaign in 1963.[29]

"The Strike Is Broken; Return to Your Job before It Is Filled"

That the weaknesses revealed by the 1951 strike emboldened southern manufacturers to resist the union was also illustrated by the fate of the sixteen local unions that remained on strike after May 6 in order to renew their contracts. For these mills, the ambitious wage demands of 1951 switched to a battle for the locals' very existence. Indeed, the common theme of these strikes was the way that manufacturers took advantage of the fact that workers were on strike to make sweeping changes to weaken or destroy the local union in their plant. The story of these locals also provides further evidence of southern TWUA members' despondent mood following the strike, their reluctance to strike again, and, consequently, the free hand that companies had to weaken and destroy some of the TWUA's most important and long-lasting southern locals.

At the Industrial Cotton Mill in Rock Hill, South Carolina, for example, once the wage strike was called off, the union agreed that it would return to work if the contract were simply renewed for one year. The company, however, refused to extend the contract for more than three weeks and refused to give ground in negotiations. It demanded the elimination of the checkoff; the unilateral right to set workloads; and a clause that would make strikes for wage increases illegal. Management stated simply that "workers can return to work without a contract—if they want." That it was the strike that encouraged management to go for the kill was highlighted by the fact that the Industrial local had been in existence for six years before the strike, with few major problems.[30]

The Industrial situation followed the pattern of other postwar contract strikes. Having made its sweeping demands, on July 15, the company moved on to the next stage of its offensive by reopening the mill and starting a campaign to entice workers back. It implemented a wage increase and improved vacation pay for those who returned. It also hired new workers, so that by July 18 one shift was operating with nonunion labor hired from outside. This move led to frequent violent clashes: the *Rock Hill Evening Herald* reported daily "violence and gunfire" between strikers and nonstrikers. By August 2, the strike had been broken; according to the FMCS, around 75 percent of workers were going into the plant. The TWUA finally called off the strike on August 18. Union representative Rene Berthiaume wrote that union members in the plant had been either fired or "forced to quit"—that is, management had made their jobs too unpleasant. Federal mediator Yates Heafner reported that "the terms and conditions did not embrace a contract between the parties." The TWUA was never able to get another contract at the Industrial Cotton Mill.[31]

Other locals were lost in a similar fashion in the aftermath of the 1951 strike. At Huntsville Manufacturing Company in Huntsville, Alabama, the company successfully broke the contract strike with a back-to-work movement in May 1951. Advertisements were placed in the *Huntsville Times* openly recruiting for strikebreakers and offering safe transportation through the picket line. Around 250 new workers were quickly hired, and striking employees were told flatly that "the strike is broken. May we again suggest to you to return to your job before it is filled." A. D. Elliott, vice president, told his employees on May 10 that "striking former employees not working during the strike will be temporarily placed on jobs, subject to being released if necessary to protect Huntsville Manufacturing Company's commitment to . . . workers who returned to work and newly-hired workers." The anti-union press in the South reacted triumphantly when the union was forced to accept these humiliating conditions, and it gave the story much publicity. The *Anderson Daily Mail*, for example, pointed out that "under the return to work program, the 247 who were hired during the strike will not be replaced, but the last 247 hired on the union list before the strike will be abandoned by the union and not have jobs, it was explained. Never before has such a concession been granted by TWUA-CIO or any other union, according to one former NLRB attorney."[32]

The hiring of replacements for strikers proved to be only the first step in the company's campaign to destroy the union. Following the return to work, the company consistently refused to recognize the union in the mill. State director Julius Fry reported in January 1952 that the mood in the plant was a despondent one, reflected by the fact that "our dues-paying membership has declined progressively." By December 1953 the TWUA's representative reported that only fifteen dues-paying members were left at Huntsville Manufacturing Company. The company would only sign a contract that contained super-seniority for strikebreakers and no checkoff. Union representatives and organizers knew that the only hope lay in another strike, but workers at Huntsville, as in other strike locations, refused to show any enthusiasm for this course; they rejected a strike vote on September 27, 1953. By April 1954, only seven dues-paying members remained at Huntsville Manufacturing Company, and the TWUA finally gave up the ghost.[33]

Another of the many casualties of the 1951 strike was the local union at Royal Cotton Mill in Wake Forest, North Carolina. Here the FMCS reported that "management has little desire to consummate an agreement, since practically all of their proposals on various contract sections are designed to maintain the status-quo or spell out the company's unilateral right to control wages, hours, and working conditions." The TWUA called the strike off and agreed to sign a very weak agreement out of "an obligation to employees and the community to arrive at some agreement that would avoid hardship for workers and the community." This agreement, which was not a formal contract, was merely an attempt to save face and did not include the checkoff, because management again refused to yield on this issue. The agreement was subsequently ignored by the company, and the Wake Forest local disappeared.[34]

At Lincoln Mills in Huntsville, Alabama, strikers returned to work on May 28, 1951, with a contract that did not contain a checkoff. This company made it clear that it would not reopen the mill unless the union gave up the checkoff. Alabama director Julius Fry reported that it was the strike that had alienated the company: "relations with the company have always been good but have been a little strained since the wage strike in Spring." Lacking a checkoff, TWUA representatives reported similar problems at Lincoln as elsewhere. TWUA representative Herb Williams wrote in his report for June and July 1954 that because of memories of the 1951 strike, "it is impossible to strike the mill and I would strongly advise against it." Clearly influenced by what had happened to strikers at neighboring Huntsville Manufacturing Company, workers were "afraid to stop their jobs off. They say that if they stop their jobs, someone else will start them up again." The company forced the pace, refusing to settle grievances and increasing workloads, secure in the knowledge that a strike was very unlikely. In April 1955, TWUA representative Herman Mullins reported that "people are getting really fed up with workload increases," but a motion to strike was rejected by the membership. By the end of August 1955, after the contract ran out with workers unwilling to strike to renew it, organizers had given up hope of reviving the local union at Lincoln Mills.[35]

Several common themes characterized the story of these locals that were destroyed by the 1951 strike. Particularly prominent were many of the features that management had exhibited in earlier contract strikes—particularly the refusal to grant the checkoff and the tendency to break strikes by importing strikebreakers. The difference from earlier contract strikes, however, was that after 1951 there was little determination and militancy shown by workers to strike for a contract and the survival of their local union. The failure of the 1951 strike wiped out the ability of many southern locals to endure another strike, leaving workers despondent and disillusioned. Without the ability to threaten a strike, the union was gravely weakened, for TWUA staff and members both knew that the ability to strike was their most effective tool in the South and, in the absence of stringent federal protection, the only hope the union had for overcoming fierce corporate resistance.

What made the 1951 strike particularly damaging was the fact that it
weakened or destroyed the TWUA's best southern locals, especially its relations with large southern companies that had served as showpiece
unions, relationships that demonstrated that it was possible for the
TWUA and these companies to deal constructively. Dan River was clearly
the most prominent example of this, but the events that took place at the
Cone Mills chain in Greensboro, North Carolina, also illustrated the way
that the strike destroyed hopes for a constructive union-management relationship. Before the 1951 strike, the TWUA had developed a solid collective bargaining relationship with Cone Mills. Unlike many southern
textile executives, the leading members of the Cone family, Caesar and
Clarence, openly expressed their approval of collective bargaining and
acceptance of the union. In 1948, Clarence told TWUA representative
Bruno Rantane that Cone mills "sincerely want[ed] to get along" with
the union. TWUA representative Ross Groshong, who knew the Cone
family well, thought that "Cone was among the most decent of the southern mills in their labor relations attitude." The Cone chain was the sixth-
largest textile company in the South and represented a vital location for
the TWUA. Although union membership in most Cone plants was quite
low, it was important that the union conducted stable collective bargaining with this large southern company, and the Cone contracts were among
the best that the TWUA had in the South.[36]

Cone's management, however, was both angered and alienated by the
calling of the 1951 strike. Like their counterparts in Danville, they reacted to these feelings of betrayal by demanding the removal of the
checkoff from all contracts that they had with the TWUA. Ross Groshong recalled, "Clarence Cone was the primary negotiator at that time,
and his reasoning was that he wasn't going to help support a union that
was going to call an industry-wide type of strike that had nothing to do
with his relationship with his employees." Like Dan River, Cone felt that
the strike was forced by Rieve's political objectives and that "they would
not therefore contribute through dues checkoff to the support of that
type of political situation."[37]

The Cone locals were so weakened by the 1951 strike that they were
unable to prevent the loss of the checkoff at all eight union plants. Scott
Hoyman, who worked for the TWUA in New England before being sent
in to try and rebuild the Cone locals, remembered that the 1951 strike
created a sense of hopelessness and defeatism among Cone workers: "if
your plant goes out and half the people go into work, which happened in
the Proximity plant, the leading plant of Cone Mills in Greensboro, you
view it as your own weakness, it made people feel that the union wasn't
as strong as they thought it was." Workers at Cone's Granite plant told

TWUA organizer Garland Brook that their plant "can't be struck." When Brook visited Cone plants in Haw River and Gibsonville, he found a similar pessimism: "general feeling seems to be that a successful strike can't be held at this time." Workers cited many reasons for this, the most common being the "'51 strike" and the fact that "people [were] in debt, having to move out of company-owned houses and paying high rent." Brook wrote that fear of a strike was "awful" and that there was bad feeling in the plant because many had crossed the picket line. When Cone workers voted on whether to accept a contract without a checkoff or strike, they voted to accept the contract against the wishes of TWUA representatives. The union spent a considerable amount of time and resources trying to rebuild the Cone locals but they remained very weak, operating without a checkoff into the 1980s. Between 1951 and 1976, dues-paying membership never comprised more than 10 percent of the total workforce. Thus, another of the TWUA's showpiece southern unions was reduced to powerlessness by the 1951 strike.[38]

Several other important locals survived the strike but found the return to work a painful one. At Lane Cotton Mill in New Orleans, a large branch of the Lowenstein chain, strikers returned to work on May 15, 1951, with a contract that included a new, restrictive no-strike clause. At Pacific Mills in Columbia, South Carolina, one of the TWUA's largest and most active southern locals, workers divided on the issue of whether to return after ten weeks of striking. In what the FMCS described as a "bad situation," a minority favored continuing the strike. However, the sentiments of the majority were reflected by one member who pleaded that "hundreds and hundreds of you people—a lot of you here today— can't go on much longer. We've been out ten weeks and accomplished nothing, we may be out ten more weeks and accomplish nothing." At the A. D. Julliard Company in Aragon, Georgia, strikers returned to work only after the company refused to reinstate many union activists who it claimed had been involved in strike violence. A similar situation arose at Cedartown Textiles in Cedartown, Georgia, where fifty leading union members were convicted for their involvement in violence. The strike weakened the local union and left it in what the FMCS described as "a precarious and embarrassing position."[39]

The Political Impact of the Strike's Failure

The amount of damage the TWUA received from the 1951 strike had enormous political consequences for the union. Most of the TWUA's leaders in the South were Baldanzi supporters, and they felt that the strike was a tragic example of Rieve's poor understanding of the South. Many felt they could no longer belong to an organization that was so inept at appealing to southern workers.[40] Indeed, one of the strike's most important consequences was to widen the gulf between the Rieve and Baldanzi forces to the point where the Baldanzi side concluded that their purposes could be better served in another organization—a decision that had fateful consequences for the cause of southern textile unionism. Shortly after the strike, Baldanzi and his leading southern supporters decided to leave the TWUA and move to their bitter AFL rival, the UTW. They then began a campaign to take over the UTW and make it the strongest textile union in the South, aiming, in the words of Lewis Conn, to "smash the bargaining power of the CIO in the South, and consequently in the North as well." This decision led the two organizations to a decade of fighting throughout the South, ensuring that the fallout from the 1951 strike was even more extended and catastrophic than would have naturally been the case.[41]

The importance of the strike in causing the split was stressed by both Rieve and Baldanzi supporters. Before the strike, personal differences had existed between Baldanzi and Rieve, who both claimed that their personal incompatibility—and not differences over issues—meant that they failed to function successfully as a team.[42] At the same time, Baldanzi's personal unpopularity with the northern-based leadership of the union meant that he worked increasingly in the South, where his charismatic personality and speaking abilities brought him a large following among southern TWUA staff and workers. Rieve concentrated on New England, where his administrative skills and tough negotiating style won him a strong following.[43] Both men thus had independent regional power bases, and in general this separation actually worked very well because it allowed the two men to avoid one another and to work effectively within their own regions. It was because the 1951 strike was such a failure that tensions between the two sides resurfaced and reached new levels as the union sought to explain the strike call. The gravity of the strike's failure thus placed an enormous strain on internal harmony in the union. Rieve himself discussed the strike at length at the convention and claimed that he had "plenty of company" from Baldanzi supporters when he called the strike. Rieve supporter Paul Swaity remembered that "the question of who was to blame for the strike only helped to heat up the conflict that took place. That strike and the tragic losses that TWUA incurred as a result certainly contributed greatly to the internal fight." Indeed, Emanuel Boggs recalled clearly that at the TWUA's convention following the strike, "there was a lot of differences on whether or not there should have been a strike. It developed into a matter of brawling between the people who were supporting Rieve and the ones who were supporting Baldanzi. After the convention, a number of the unions led by Baldanzi withdrew from the union." Another Baldanzi supporter, Joel Leighton, also recalled threats and scuffles between Rieve and Baldanzi supporters over the strike, and he himself was told by Rieve "toughs" from New England not to bring the topic up on the convention floor. The strength of the alienation that southern TWUA staff felt after the strike is indicated by staffers like Boggs, Pat Knight, and Ross Groshong, who even after forty-three years regarded Rieve as "a demagogue" for calling the 1951 strike: "He wasn't particularly interested in the welfare of southern workers. If he had really tried to understand them I don't see how he could have insisted on that strike." For this reason, after the strike it was impossible for most southern staff to remain in the same organization as Rieve.[44]

There was a strong correlation between the locals that took part in the strike and those that switched to the UTW. As a result of the strike, staff and members in these locations were alienated from the union. The UTW won overwhelming election victories over the TWUA in Cone Mills and Dan River Mills, the two locations where the strike had collapsed. Similarly, in the Erwin Mills plant in Durham, North Carolina, the UTW defeated the TWUA comprehensively by a vote of 1,122 to 382. Other Erwin plants also switched to the UTW. In some southern strike locations the TWUA even withdrew from the ballot and encouraged workers to vote for the company. The UTW also made inroads into the Lowenstein chain, winning locals in Rockingham, North Carolina, and in New Orleans. Of the twenty southern locals that switched, sixteen had taken part in the 1951 strike.[45]

The UTW aimed to exploit rank-and-file disaffection with the strike in its secession campaign. Its pamphlets made repeated references to "Rieve's senseless strike" and claimed that the uncaring TWUA leader was vacationing at Daytona Beach during the strike. Other evidence indicates that many workers needed little encouragement to leave the TWUA after the strike. At Erwin Mills in Durham, for example, one union activist, Johnny Burns, claimed that workers were "fed up with Rieve and the CIO's sell out." *Fortune* magazine reported that the UTW was winning elections by big margins because the 1951 strike "was still resented by a lot of mill hands."[46]

The tragedy of the situation was that the Baldanzi group really was, as its leaders imagined, strong enough to make substantial gains in the South. Capitalizing on lingering disaffection from the 1951 strike, the group won control of a core of important southern locals that had participated in the strike. What the group had not anticipated was its inability to extend its gains beyond these locals, or the determined response of the TWUA to win them back. Thus, neither union was able to gain the upper hand in the South but remained locked in a battle that gravely weakened both.

The plan of the TWUA southern group to take over and revitalize the UTW failed. At the time of the split, the UTW was a small union with only 60,000 dues-paying members. It hired between forty and fifty organizers from the TWUA and at the same time, as part of the deal with the

TWUA group, expelled 15,000 Canadian members who had Communist links. According to *Fortune* magazine, the UTW needed to organize at least 75,000 new members to break even financially. It only managed to gain 35,000—about 40 percent of the TWUA's southern membership—partly because some Baldanzi supporters who had promised to bring locals into the UTW failed to do so. One reason for this failure was that Rieve launched a serious counteroffensive to obstruct the secession movement. As a result, the secession movement left the UTW with serious financial problems. These problems were worsened by the UTW's failure to secure a checkoff at Cone and Dan River in the wake of the strike. Loss of the checkoff meant that although the UTW gained bargaining rights for more than 30,000 southern workers, it admitted in 1954 that "less than half are now paying dues to our organization." By the beginning of 1953, the UTW owed more than $100,000, having seen its expenses for organizers increase by more than $200,000 in less than a year.[47]

The union's lack of money encouraged southern employers to go on the attack against the locals that had switched from the TWUA. Ross Groshong, a former TWUA southern staffer who switched to the UTW, remembered that "those unions that did peel off from the CIO no longer had any appreciable monetary support, and the companies knew this." Groshong thought that "all these guys jumped on the bandwagon, they knew we were weak, Cone refused to grant the voluntary checkoff, Dan River refused to grant the voluntary checkoff." In some cases, locals were destroyed completely as a consequence of the switch to the UTW. A notable example occurred at Wade Manufacturing Company in Wadesboro, North Carolina, where the local union had to be abandoned by the UTW during a strike in 1952. As Groshong recalled, "I had to call that strike off. We didn't have any support, monetary support. We could have kept the people out but we didn't have enough money to buy groceries with."[48]

In terms of the number of members lost, the TWUA was successful in limiting the damage from the secession movement; but the movement left it seriously weakened in the South, because it had lost its largest and most important southern locals. The UTW was particularly successful at winning control of the big chain mills that the TWUA had used as pattern-setters in wage negotiations. These mills had been vital to the TWUA, allowing the union to win southern wage raises that protected the union's base in New England. Dan River, Cone, Erwin, and Lowenstein all ranked in the top ten of southern textile companies in terms of market share, spindleage, and employment. Indeed, they were the only mills in the top ten where the TWUA had any representation at all. The fact that the UTW made such big gains among the chain mills was a big blow to the TWUA and, given the inability of the UTW to rebuild these locals, to textile unionism generally. Emanuel Boggs wrote privately of the UTW's capture of the Marshall Field, Cone, and Erwin chains, "Since these three mills together with Dan River have traditionally set the southern pattern Rieve is pretty well washed up in the South since he has forever lost the Big Four." Indeed, the defection of these large mills to the UTW reduced the TWUA to isolated representation in small plants and ensured that it would not be able to reassert control over southern nonunion wages and protect its membership in New England.[49]

In the Erwin chain, two small plants at Erwin and Neuse, North Carolina, stayed with the TWUA. This split the chain, preventing the pattern-bargaining that had brought gains for Erwin workers. As one local union put it, "For eleven years, Erwin workers in Coolemee, Durham, Neuse, and Erwin have bargained together for contracts, struck together and have made gains because of our unity." The same happened to Lowenstein workers. The company's huge finishing plant in Rock Hill, South Carolina, stayed TWUA, while its mills in New Orleans and Rockingham, North Carolina, went UTW. Workers at the company's mill in Rockingham also felt that their gains had come through close cooperation with Rock Hill, especially as all cloth produced at the other mills went to Rock Hill to be finished. When the two plants chose different unions, Rockingham workers felt that it "broke the back" of their union because they could no longer use the threat that Rock Hill would be struck unless the company yielded in Rockingham.[50]

The split was also damaging because the TWUA devoted a considerable amount of time and resources to fighting the UTW in the South rather than addressing the task of new organizing. Scott Hoyman remembered that the day after returning from the poststrike convention to TWUA work in Maine, he was told to drop everything and drive to North Carolina because of the threat of secession. Many other staff members who should have been organizing or doing administrative work elsewhere were, like Hoyman, transferred to secession trouble-spots. Hoyman himself stayed in the South until the 1980s. He remembered clearly how time-consuming the secession battle was: "it was a very bad experience because for the first five years I was down South all I did was try to keep unions from leaving, or get unions back, and then finally to repair the damage that had been caused by the split, and in many cases we were unable to repair it." Hoyman felt that the secession was "a terrible diversion at a period of time that the union, had it not been diverted, might have broken through to another level of penetration in the industry." In Greensboro, North Carolina, the TWUA spent more than three years in a drive to try to win back the Cone locals. At least four organizers were permanently stationed on this campaign, but it yielded few results. Although the TWUA regained several Cone locals in the mid-1950s, it did not regain the checkoff, so these locals remained a financial drain on the national union. In a wide variety of other locations, the union became involved in time-consuming court battles with the UTW over local union funds and property. Both unions used legal obstruction in order to prevent their opponents from establishing successful local unions, even if they had already won representation. The war with the UTW had a lasting impact, especially in that it prevented textile unions from taking advantage of the merger between the AFL and CIO in December 1955. Continued bad relations between the UTW and TWUA meant that even forty-three years after the strike, textiles was one of the few industries where separate CIO and AFL unions still existed.[51]

Both unions used material against one another that was extreme and polemical and that clearly inflicted damage on the image of unionism in the South. One particularly vicious pamphlet distributed by the UTW to Cone Mills workers in Haw River, North Carolina, asked, "Where was Emil Rieve born? In Poland. Does Poland have a Communist government? Yes. Was that where Emil Rieve learned to be a dictator?" *Textile Labor* rightly wrote, "A better question is whether this sort of thing is designed to organize workers or destroy their faith in all unions." Like much of the material generated by the secession battle, this material was almost indistinguishable from employers' propaganda in its attacks on the ethnic origin of union leaders and appeal to anticommunism. However, the TWUA also produced scurrilous material of its own. Illustrating the damage inflicted, employers in fact repeatedly distributed this literature during organizing campaigns in the 1950s.[52]

The split had a debilitating impact on the TWUA. It consumed so much energy that the union lost sight of its most important task—organizing the South. Sol Stetin put the issue well when he stated, "You can't afford to have politics when you've got this big massive job of organizing the unorganized. . . . The bitching and griping about each other hurt us terribly." In late 1952, Stetin spoke of a "lack of spirit, a lack of inspiration and zeal that we need to get back" and added, "It is no secret that the internal fight is, in a large measure, responsible for the conditions we are in today." Others recalled how the battle with the UTW stopped all other union work for most of the 1950s.[53]

Between 1951 and 1954, there was little middle ground in the TWUA, and few managed to remain neutral. One of the few who did manage neutrality, research staffer George Perkel, offered a good assessment of the overall damage that the internal battle caused. From his unique vantage point, Perkel thought the effects of the split were "seriously debilitating because of several things. One is that there were sizeable locals that left the union as a result of the split. Another is the amount of time and resources that were spent by both sides during the three-year period involved obviously had an effect on the performance of the union during that period." Perkel also cited the fact that the public notice of the split and the charges that were made by both sides "fed employers and antiunion forces, so it certainly made organizing more difficult."[54]

Perhaps the greatest damage caused by the internal battle, however, was less perceptible. The loss of Baldanzi from the union meant that the TWUA was deprived of an immense talent. In 1952, Baldanzi was only forty-four years old and clearly was in line to become TWUA president. Even Rieve supporters hoped that Baldanzi could one day become president. His speaking abilities were enormous, as is clear even from the written page. Although Baldanzi supporters exaggerated his success in organizing the South, he had been largely responsible for the TWUA's ability to develop stable collective bargaining with large southern companies, and he had more organizing experience in the South than anybody else. The loss of Baldanzi put the TWUA firmly in the hands of personnel who were inexperienced in the South and who favored concentrating the union's attention on New England. Many TWUA staff recognized the huge loss that Baldanzi represented. For example, in a speech that summed up the fusion of personal jealousy and regional tension that fueled the split, Rieve supporter Ken Fiester expressed his belief that the split was tragic because "George had talents that were useful to the union. If we could have kept these people together we could have moved against the unorganized companies. What would have happened to the presidency I don't know. The Northern people who led the fight against George would not have accepted him as president. I guess what I'm saying is that it was Emil's fault." Indeed, it is clear that if Baldanzi had stayed with the union, the prospects for southern organization would have been considerably brighter. As it was, Baldanzi and many of his supporters drifted away from the union movement following their failure to reform the UTW. Many capable staff, such as Lew Conn, Joel Leighton, and Pat Knight, became disillusioned with the labor movement following the split and pursued other careers for the rest of their working lives.[55]

The loss of these staff members was particularly tragic. If Baldanzi supporters had been distributed across the country, the effect of the secession movement would have been dissipated. However, the vast majority of those who left the TWUA were southern staffers who had been based in the region for a considerable period of time. For the TWUA and other textile unions, one of the key problems in the South had been the organizers' taint as outsiders—that they came into towns as strangers and were easily portrayed in company propaganda as "outside agitators." Between 1939 and 1952, the TWUA had begun to overcome this problem by developing a core of southern staff who were constantly stationed in the region and were respected and known by many workers and employers. Indeed, many of those who left were indigenous leaders who had risen up from the rank and file in southern mills, such as Dean Culver and Jack Crumbley. Others, such as Joel Leighton, Pat Knight, Ross Groshong, Emanuel Boggs, Joe Pedigo, and Lewis Conn, had worked continually in the South for more than ten years before the split and were universally respected. Moreover, men like Baldanzi and Conn had shown that it was possible for union leaders to win some kind of acceptance in the South even if they were from ethnic backgrounds. For example, Norris Tibbetts remembered that managers at Dan River Mills "respected Lew Conn, a man of Jewish background, [and] I think they respected Baldanzi, a man of Italian background, because of their considerable experience in the South." With their departure, the union lost its existing southern staff, eliminating its only personnel who had shown the ability to work effectively in the South. The TWUA was greatly weakened by this loss.[56]

Overall, it is clear that the 1951 strike, an event recognized far less by historians than Operation Dixie, in fact inflicted far greater damage on the cause of southern textile unionism. Operation Dixie has been considered a turning point for southern labor, a time when the failure of the southern labor movement was sealed.[57] However, the evidence indicates that while Operation Dixie failed to achieve its declared goal of organizing the South, it did not, like the 1951 strike, leave the union movement weaker than when it started. TWUA southern staffers and national leaders repeatedly stressed that it was the 1951 strike that represented the watershed for the TWUA. Education Director Larry Rogin, for example, thought this strike was "the signal" of the union's long-term decline in the South "because we came out of that strike weaker than we went into it, and while the CIO drive wasn't a success, we didn't come out of it weaker than before. We had organized some plants, we came out of it stronger." In 1979, Sol Stetin said that the 1951 strike and the secession movement it caused "destroyed the strength and organization we had developed in the Carolinas. . . . It caused terrible, terrible damage. We haven't overcome it since." He added, "That's why J. P. Stevens is so important." Both Rieve and Baldanzi were far more philosophical about Operation Dixie than they were about the 1951 strike. The gains that trickled in throughout the southern drive allowed the TWUA's leaders to argue that organizing would take longer than they had originally envisioned but was worth the work. Rieve declared in 1949, "I am not predicting it will be done in a year or two, but I know it will be done no matter how long it will take." The union kept to its goal of total southern organization but often acknowledged that it was outgunned in organizing campaigns, faced by strong employer and community opposition and a history of past failures. Thus, the gains achieved were a bonus, a boost to the union's morale.[58]

By contrast, it was impossible to salvage anything from the wreckage caused by the 1951 strike, especially as the union itself had precipitated the strike. Local unions were broken; workers were disillusioned and demoralized; employers were encouraged to resist the union even harder;

and all control of southern wages was lost. The strike had cost the union nearly half its total treasury, and after 1951, with New England locals declining, the TWUA went into the red and faced continual financial problems. In addition, the strike had destroyed the union's ability to organize, and TWUA leaders admitted that they did not have the resources to honor all requests from workers who wanted the union to come into their plant. The depressed market conditions of the 1950s also emboldened employers to fight the union, for many had little to fear from a strike. The union's earlier hope that the textile depression might work to its advantage was misplaced, for earlier depressions had shown that unions tended to suffer in economic downturns.[59] Perhaps more telling than these concrete problems, however, was the sense that at bottom, the TWUA had lost the belief that it could, as Sol Barkin put it, "take over" the South as Sherman had eighty years earlier. Without this confidence in its ability to overcome its natural disadvantages in the South, for the first time the TWUA resigned itself to playing a passive and marginal role in the region.[60]

chapter eight

Breaking the Chains of Slavery

Unionization and Social Change

in Rockingham, North Carolina

The major strikes and organizing campaigns that the TWUA went through in the South during these years do not provide a complete perspective of the union's history in the region. It is also important to study a particular community over an extended period, not merely through major events such as strikes and elections but for the long-term impact that unionization had on workers' lives. Indeed, the fortunes of the TWUA were clearly influenced greatly by its ability to maintain its appeal for workers when strikes and union elections were over. To study a community in this way also allows us to examine the broader forces of social change. The postwar period was a time of tremendous social change in southern textile mill villages. The long-established system of company-owned housing was disappearing, and companies were withdrawing from many other aspects of mill-village life. The genesis and growth of the company-owned mill village have been examined in detail by historians. Recent historiography has explored the worker culture that the company-owned mill village produced and the consequences that culture had for unionization. However, the disintegration of this system in the postwar period has received considerably less attention. It is crucial to explore this breakup and the effect that it had on southern textile communities and their workers. It is particularly important to examine the relationship between unionization and the breakup of the traditional mill village, about which little is known.

The recent scholarship that has been produced on southern textile workers has also established clearly that due to the weakness of the written record, oral history is a valuable historical source in understanding worker culture and social change in southern textile communities.

Indeed, written records generated by strikes and organizing campaigns say little about either the impact of unionism at the grassroots level or its relationship to the breakdown of the mill village. Recent studies, however, have shown that it is possible to sustain sophisticated and informative scholarship based largely on oral history, and this study attempts to follow that lead.[1]

The Locale

In the 1940s and 1950s, Rockingham, North Carolina, which is located near the South Carolina state line about seventy miles east of Charlotte, was a major southern textile center. Ten operating textile mills dominated the town's economy. Most of these mills were located close together in East Rockingham, an unincorporated settlement set apart from Rockingham proper. Each of these mills had its own mill village and company store, and workers from different mills had few contacts with one another. The biggest mill in Rockingham was Safie Manufacturing Company, formerly known as Hannah Pickett Number 1, which employed over one thousand workers at this time. Located next to Safie was Aleo Manufacturing Company, formerly Entwistle Manufacturing Company, which employed around seven hundred people. These were the two largest mills in Rockingham, but a few smaller mills, including Beaunit Mills, Ledbetter Manufacturing Company, and Steele Mill, were located close by.[2]

The history of textile unionism in Rockingham prior to World War II was typical of most other southern textile communities: there were strikes by unorganized workers, but no lasting institutional gains resulted. The most notable among these strikes were a thirty-day strike at Safie in 1930 and a longer strike at Entwistle in 1932, both of which were unsuccessful. When World War II ended, no mill in Rockingham operated under a union contract.[3]

This situation was quickly changed, however, by workers at Entwistle Manufacturing Company. They organized during World War II, winning a 1943 election by a vote of 354 to 70. The company, however, refused to sign a contract with a checkoff, and no agreement had been reached by the end of the war. Workers struck on September 17, 1945, and stayed out for over six months. At the time, this was the longest textile strike ever to occur in North Carolina. It ended successfully for the strikers when the mill's local owners—the Entwistle family, who refused to sign a contract—sold the company to M. Lowenstein, a New York–based chain company with mills in several southern states. Lowenstein changed the name of the plant to Aleo Manufacturing Company and signed a union contract containing the vital union security provisions. This change of ownership was crucial to the establishment of a union at Aleo, for it shifted control from a local, anti-union family to the Lowenstein corporation, a northern, Jewish-owned company with a reputation for tolerance of unions. Indeed, the company operated plants in several other southern locations that were also under contract with the TWUA. This change of ownership encouraged many workers to support the union.[4]

This study concentrates on workers at the Aleo plant, largely because Aleo was the only plant in Rockingham to remain organized for the whole of the period under study. The isolation of Aleo as a union plant makes it easier to measure the impact of unionism, because it was closely surrounded by a far larger number of nonunion workers. The Aleo local was also a strong union and therefore affords the opportunity to explore why, in certain locations, the TWUA was able to establish powerful local unions. Moreover, the union at Aleo was an important TWUA southern local, mainly because Lowenstein was one of the largest southern companies that the union had managed to penetrate, and it was central to the union's future in the South.[5]

The Aleo local was strongly supported between 1945 and 1955. Throughout this period, union director Joel Leighton, a young Bostonian who became well respected by Aleo workers, never reported less than 92 percent union membership at Aleo, and at one stage, out of eight hundred employees, every worker except one belonged to the union. *Textile Labor* itself described the Aleo local as "one of the best local unions in the South—militant and self-reliant, thoroughly imbued with trade union spirit." Workers took pride in their militancy. Former worker and local union officer Beatrice McCumbee remembered that "we were good, we had a real union." The history of the Aleo local illustrated a consistent theme of the TWUA's history in the South in these years—the importance of the ability to conduct a solid strike to union progress. For example, Larry Rogin, like other TWUA southern staffers, felt that southern locals could only gain strength through crippling strikes, not by "outnegotiating" the company: "southern textile workers weren't going to get anywhere without striking plants and making it expensive for the industry." Aleo struck frequently between 1945 and 1955, with major strikes in 1945, 1949, 1951, and 1955, in addition to a number of unauthorized wildcat strikes. Many former workers asserted that they could not have built their union without forcing the respect of the company through strikes. John Grant, a weave-room shop steward who was responsible for pulling many of the wildcats, pondered in retrospect whether they had been necessary. His conclusion, however, was emphatic: "I've spent a lot of time wondering whether I should have pulled all those strikes. But the only thing those bastards respected was power, the only power you've got is the power to strike, and you can only strike if the people are together." Between 1945 and 1955, Aleo workers were together. In the words of another former worker, "You'd pull a strike, and the people would beat you out the door."[6]

More significant than this militancy, however, is the way that Aleo workers were able to maintain a strong union for a long period of time, especially considering that they were the only organized plant in Rockingham. Historians have clearly established that southern textile workers have a history of sporadic and determined labor protest, but generally such protest failed to produce secure and lasting unionism. In the postwar period, however, some lasting and strong local unions were established in the South, and Aleo was one of them.[7]

The strength of the union reflected the fact that a large number of workers were active. Good local leadership meant that the grievance procedure functioned successfully, which in turn encouraged union support. Women workers were particularly responsible for the strength of the union; they played an active role in many of the union's affairs. Beatrice McCumbee was one of the many women who held various union offices and was a leader in the formation and running of the Aleo local. A tall, slim, and articulate woman, McCumbee explained her activism by stressing that she had always believed in "standing up for your rights." A lifelong Rockingham resident, like many other retired workers, McCumbee still lived in the mill house she had bought in the 1950s. McCumbee thought that "there were more active women than men. Men sort of shy away from it, I don't know exactly why, but even in church women do most of the work. . . . If it's a group I think women are more conscientious about things." The core of the Aleo local were women. Women like Mary Cribbs, Alice Stafford, Ruby Edwards, Mae Clark, and Cora Langley all held elected office in the union during these years and represented the union on a variety of committees. Women were a strong organizing force. When Aleo workers struck in 1945, many were not members of the new local. This was reflected in the strike vote of August 15, 1945, when 180 workers out of the 466 eligible did not vote to strike. During the strike it was women who signed people up and tried to explain to them why they should support the union. Through this work, they succeeded in greatly increasing the number of union members.[8]

The prominence of women in the union reflected a deeper reality of discrimination. Many men that became especially active in the union were offered managerial positions by the company—jobs that were not open to women. In this sense the Aleo story reflected a wider theme of women's history, for women illustrated greater militancy than men in other locations because they had little access to mobility. There was no competition for promotion and success to undermine the loyalty of women to one another.[9] For example, Beatrice McCumbee remembered that "we had some good men too that worked hard and most of them got to be foreman or overseer, nearly every one of them. The company saw that they had leadership, and put them on. That weakened the union, and helped them too." The most prominent example of this occurred to one L. L. Shepherd, an Aleo worker who was active in starting the union and even worked as an organizer for the SOC for some time. All former workers in Rockingham remembered Shepherd's transformation to "a company man," illustrating the damage that such conversions did to the union.[10]

The union director in Rockingham, Joel Leighton, emphasized that the Aleo local was strong because it became part of the community and that women members were largely responsible for this participation. They organized a Women's Auxiliary known as the Goodwill Club that was responsible for organizing a wide variety of community activities. The Goodwill Club also provided a forum for women to become active in the union.[11]

Leighton also emphasized that the union became part of the community through political action. It is clear that politics played a part in reinforcing Aleo workers' union identity. The national TWUA continually asserted the importance of political action for organized workers as a means of securing favorable politicians to safeguard the labor movement. The Aleo local was able to overcome its isolation in Rockingham and join railroad unions in nearby Hamlet and TWUA locals in Wadesboro and Lumberton in doing PAC work. Joel Leighton reported increased political participation among Aleo workers and described how they played a crucial role in working for liberal candidates. In the primary of May 27, 1950, for example, Leighton wrote that "in this county it is literally true to state that the Union did the greatest part of the campaign work for Senator Graham and Congressman Deane." Aleo workers again showed their commitment to Democratic candidates on polling day: "at least 90% of the registered voters turned out at Aleo and voted for the Union endorsed candidates." In the second primary, the work of the union ensured that Richmond County was one of the few counties that did not succumb to the opposition's last-minute use of racial slurs to ensure Graham's defeat: "In Richmond County, we succeeded in not only improving Senator Graham's numerical vote, but we also increased his percentage of the total votes cast by about 10% over the first primary. I suspect this was the only county in the state that did this."[12]

"It Was the Way They Treated the People"

Former workers remembered that in 1946, when the union came into being, it made a big change in their conditions. The main benefit they identified was the way the union broke the strict and arbitrary control that the company had always exerted over the workforce. They stressed that freedom from this control had been their main motive in organizing; similarly, the most important changes they stressed under a union were those that brought democracy into the workplace, particularly seniority and the grievance procedure. This emphasis on noneconomic benefits was significant, for the national TWUA repeatedly concentrated on economic benefits in its drive to organize southern textile workers. The priorities of Aleo workers, however, reflected postwar workers' broader interest in using CIO representation for control of the workplace through seniority, protection against unfair discharge, and general mitigation of traditional company dominance. Indeed, far from being isolated from national trends, southern textile workers epitomized this struggle for freedom through union representation, because they had endured particularly direct and arbitrary company control.[13]

Former workers vividly remembered injustices that made them strong supporters of the union when it was first organized. Bernice Crumbley, a small, bubbly woman who began working at the plant as a teenager in the 1930s, recalled that like many others, she received no pay for her first twelve months because she was "learning." In addition, the company often refused to provide any work at all: "I walked down there many a time in the rain, snow, any kind of weather, and you didn't know when you got down there whether you was going to work or not." It was this type of injustice that made her and others think of organizing. Beatrice McCumbee also bitterly recalled having to work for an extended period without pay when she started work at Entwistle in 1934. Even when workers got a paid position, it was customary for the company to take them off their job and give it to a "spare hand" or to transfer them to a less desirable job or shift. McCumbee recalled how at Christmastime her job was given to temporary workers who already had jobs elsewhere. She felt that the company "took advantage of people. They would take you out and put someone else on your job." McCumbee thought that the main reason workers organized into a union was "the way they treated the people." Favoritism in assigning work and in controlling access to promotion were common complaints. Former worker Eli Welch, whose fresh features belied his seventy-five years, recalled that "you see a good job in the plant would come open, some overseer or somebody up at the plant would give it to his cousin, uncle, aunt, or kissing buddy. . . . There was no way that you could get a job unless you was related to somebody." Similarly, Loyd Ivey, who held various offices for the union once Aleo was organized, remembered that "before the union come in, if one of the supervisors had a friend that they wanted to give a job, they could just move him in and let you go."[14]

These injustices reflected the unbridled control that the company exercised over workers. Former worker Lee Bateman, a sprightly man of sixty-eight, recalled from his childhood in the 1930s how company control was pervasive even when workers were not at the mill: "they dictated to the people how they raised their children. If I did something wrong . . . the superintendent of the plant would call my father in and say now you've got to go home and punish him." Beatrice McCumbee detailed how the company frequently fired workers who got drunk on weekends, even if they had not set foot outside of their house. These people were often hired back, but the company "liked to show their authority, their control." Others remembered that workers could even be fired for having too much trash in their yard.[15]

For most workers, the embodiment of their servitude was the company store. It was very common for former workers to cite the fact that many people worked at Entwistle for their whole working lives without drawing any pay because they were continually in debt to the company store. Workers were issued special coupon books—or "ducee books," as they were known locally—which were freely distributed and could be used at the company store. John Grant, a tall, forthright man of sixty-nine, explained that "a lot of people who had worked at Aleo for all those years had never drawn a payroll . . . because at the company store you could buy everything you needed, from food to heating oil, coal, clothes, shotguns. That kept you behind all the time. At payday you got a slip showing how much you owed." John Langley, another articulate former worker with strong views about the company store, added that "they would always lend you more money than you had made, so you stayed in debt all the time, and then you couldn't move from place to place." Bernice Crumbley remembered that the company would even deliver groceries and other goods from the company store to workers, most of whom did not have cars: "that big old truck would come out on Monday evening, I can see it now, unloading groceries, that happened every Monday. When payday came, they didn't draw nothing." This control was bitterly resented and caused many workers to compare their status to that of slaves. Addie Faye Wyatt, a retired worker with a lucid memory, felt that "it was complete control by the company. The people were slaves. They owned their homes, they owned their paycheck, we didn't have anything that the company wasn't supplying. We didn't have no money to spend." Lee Bateman felt that "the families [that owned the mills] controlled you, you were almost like slaves, and as long as you were in debt to them at the company store, they could really pin you down."[16]

These remarks are significant because they indicate a powerful sense of alienation, strongly refuting the idea that workers felt any positive identification with the company.[17] Because of this sense of alienation, the most important feature of the union contract for Aleo workers was seniority, which provided them with a fair means of controlling who worked in the mill. Ernest Cole, a union supporter who later became a supervisor, explained that after the union came in, jobs were posted on bulletin boards in the plant, and any worker who was interested could bid. The job was then assigned to the person with the most seniority. He added, "Things like that, it helped." Beatrice McCumbee summarized the empowerment that seniority provided: "after the union, you worked according to your seniority, and then they had to ask you if you wanted off. . . . That was a great change." Similarly, Bernice Crumbley explained that "seniority meant a great deal to me because when I went in there I knew I was going to work. That and the idea that I could go for another job. They couldn't take it and give it to somebody else." Lifelong worker Elijah Conyers felt simply that seniority was "number one in a plant," and Eli Welch felt that seniority was the union's main achievement, because it ended the unfair assignment of jobs by supervisors: "what the union did for the people was . . . it brought in seniority, and that was one of the best things." Seniority, Welch said, "meant a lot to the people." [18]

Workers derived a sense of protection and workplace democracy from seniority. Similarly, many also felt that the grievance procedure was an important change because it provided them with a voice in the mill and thus gave them a sense of dignity and helped to prevent unfair treatment by supervisors. Emsley Phifer, for example, felt that the main benefit of the union was that "people were able to voice themselves if they had a disagreement." Phifer felt that Aleo was a much better place to work after the union because "if you had a second hand and he was giving you a hard time you could say 'hey man, you can't give me all this hell.'" In the words of another, "It gave you the right to say no." Many enjoyed the fact that grievances were taken up through a chain of command rather than remaining between the worker and "bossman." Arbitration was particularly appreciated because it was an impartial way of settling grievances. Minnie Lou Barber, a gentle, soft-spoken woman who came to work at Aleo from the nonunion Safie plant in 1948, found a big difference between the two: "the big difference in the way that Safie was run and the way it was at Aleo," she recalled, "was that you had to listen to what the bosses said, but if they came down on you real hard or anything you could go to the shop steward, you had a recourse, it wasn't like it was at Safie where what the boss said went regardless of whether it was right or wrong, that was one of the big differences to me." Indeed, the protection that the grievance procedure brought was particularly stressed by women workers, who had often faced unfair treatment in the plant. Bernice Crumbley, for example, remembered that in her predominantly female department, "the bossman was different after the union came in. They didn't treat you like a tool. . . . That's what made it so good. They didn't have the last say—you had a say too." Former worker Mary Dennis summed up the psychological difference this protection made to her: "it was just a secure feeling to know that you had someone you could go to. . . . If you had a grievance it was worked out between the shop steward and the overseer."[19]

In addition to the grievance procedure and seniority, workers also cited other union benefits as providing greater freedom and justice in the workplace. The union instituted a defined payroll, in which every job had a clear description and a set pay scale. Many claimed that the job descriptions laid out in a union contract were a huge benefit in that they prevented the company from making arbitrary transfers. Former worker Howard Spivey, for example, described the security brought by these union measures: "For the first time you knew what you were going to do, you knew what you were going to get paid, when you would get paid, and how much. We also had vacations with pay. There's no doubt with numbers you're better off than you are alone." Many others, too, recalled the paid vacation as a particularly important benefit. Even apparently minor changes instituted by the union were greatly appreciated if they broke company control. For example, John Grant and others recalled how for the first time, workers had planned fatigue time during which they were allowed to smoke. Thus, in a wide variety of ways workers appreciated the union because it broke arbitrary company control.[20]

"It Broke the Chain of Slavery on the White People"

Soon after the first union contract was signed, the company store was closed. It is difficult to say definitively that the union was directly responsible for this change. Of equal importance was the change in ownership, for Lowenstein was one of the new breed of integrated companies that ran its mills from a distance, with little interest in company stores set up by local ownership.[21] Nevertheless, the union was also partly responsible for this change in ownership, for the Entwistle family sold the mill because of their reluctance to sign a union contract.[22] Moreover, many former workers felt that the union was integrally involved with the closing of the store, revealing the freedom from company control that many felt a union contract gave them. Minnie Lou Barber argued that the company store "would never have stopped if we hadn't had organized labor because they carried on doing that at Safie for a long time. It wasn't long after we got a union that the company store folded. They showed the people that they could buy their stuff and pay for it a lot cheaper." Similarly, John Grant stressed that "organized labor came in here and done away with the company store" by providing workers with better wages and a greater sense of independence. Addie Faye Wyatt thought that the union had "forced" the store to close. She expressed her feeling that the union "opened a lot of eyes to what the company was doing to them. . . . I think the union showed us we could live without the company store. They made better wages, so they could afford to go and buy like anybody else, they started going to grocery stores and clothing stores, and they had to close the thing down, they weren't getting anyone's check anymore."[23]

Aleo workers also spoke of World War II as integral in producing a desire to be free of company control. Workers themselves recognized that the war was crucial in generating positive social change for southern textile workers. John Langley, for example, declared that "after the war, they [the company] could not control people to the same extent. People started to think about owning their own homes. . . . When that independence started to develop, the mill could no longer control us." For Langley, "it was World War II that was the breaking point," the end of the traditional system of company control. A spirit of "self-determination" arose that, according to Langley, the union helped to nurture but did not produce. This desire fed into the union but also existed independently of it. Minnie Lou Barber remembered that veterans played an important role in forming the Aleo union: "these men had been out and seen the world, and seen how things were, seen how different they were, and they wanted change at home too." One of these veterans, Bill McDuffie, supported unionization immediately on returning to Rockingham because "when you get into service you get an idea of what an organization is, how it works, and you can get more done through it. I guess that's about the biggest reason I joined the union. I'm still union." Lee Bateman, another veteran who took an active role in the Aleo local, thought that "people began to get a little bit more independent after the war [because] they saw what John L. Lewis had done for the coal miners." He remembered that "just about all the veterans supported the union." After living in big cities like New York, he himself had realized that "there was so much freedom in New York that you didn't have in the South, because there was so much pressure on you from the company." Bateman was therefore attracted to forming a union, because "a union contract gives you the freedom to be your own man, and it specifies in a contract what is exactly required of you and what is required of the company." Even workers who did not go into service remembered that they felt differently about the system of company control after the war. Margaret Grant, for example, thought that "everybody was a little more knowledgeable after the war ended, we all heard more things that were going on in the world, it just started improving."[24]

Thus, World War II had far-reaching consequences on the textile South and the fortunes of the TWUA, just as it had on organizing and strike situations. Unlike these other situations, however, in Rockingham the TWUA was able to harness wartime change to its advantage. Workers began to organize to advance themselves, using the union as one, but not their only, tool. Thus, returning veterans led the formation of a men's club in East Rockingham that resulted in many improvements, including the establishment of a voluntary fire service for East Rockingham. Many

Aleo veterans also took advantage of the GI Bill; most of them went to school at night to advance themselves. That the union played a part in this broader process of social change was illustrated by the fact that it was the union that lobbied and helped to secure the building of a separate high school for East Rockingham. The building of this school was a big improvement, because as Beatrice McCumbee remembered, mill children previously had to travel to Rockingham to go to high school and had "seldom made the eighth grade."[25]

The way that the union and wartime change worked together to produce positive social change was illustrated by the impact of the wage increases that themselves resulted from a combination of a booming wartime economy and union pressure. These wage increases were crucial because they were the motor for considerable social change in Rockingham during these years. With increasing amounts of disposable income, workers began to operate as independent consumers, buying washing machines, refrigerators, and other consumer goods from downtown Rockingham merchants. These social changes affected all textile workers in Rockingham, because as in other southern textile centers, wages at Aleo were copied by nonunion mills as a means of forestalling unionization.

Due to the higher wages workers received during these years, significant social changes took place—changes that have received little historical attention. When the war ended, textile workers took part in a national surge in consumer spending, eager to buy goods that they could now afford and that had been unavailable during the war.[26] Although southern textile communities have often been viewed as isolated from national change, southern textile workers were in fact at the forefront of the advent of postwar consumerism, because their wages increased so much. Thus, when Americans were asked in 1944 what they hoped to purchase in the postwar years, they listed washing machines first, followed by electric irons, refrigerators, and stoves—the items that textile workers in Rockingham bought in large numbers. Between 1945 and 1950, U.S. consumer spending increased 60 percent, but the amount spent on household furnishings and appliances rose 240 percent.[27] Ernest Cole, for example, remembered clearly how quickly wages increased and what dramatic social changes this increase caused: "When I went into service in 1944, I was making $21 a week. . . . After I got out in 1946, I went back to work on the same job and I was making $39. . . . And from then, you'd get a little raise every year. . . . People started buying refrigerators, washing machines, regular things." Bill McDuffie remembered that "by the time I got back from service . . . people had bought washing machines, refrigerators, all that stuff. . . . It improved a lot."[28]

These changes had a disproportionate impact on Aleo's textile workers for two main reasons: their prewar living standard had been very low, and they had long lived under the company-store system, which had denied them any economic independence. One indication of the scale of the change was that many retired workers remembered their first purchase of these items clearly. Loyd Ivey, for example, remembered that during the war, consumer goods were unavailable because "everything was defense-geared." In 1947, however, Ivey recalled that he purchased "the first electric refrigerator I ever bought," a big improvement over his old icebox. Similarly, Elijah Conyers remembered that "I didn't get a washing machine until '46 when I came out of service. I didn't have a refrigerator until I came out of service either." Women workers, in particular, remembered the dramatic improvement that these changes made in their lives. Bernice Crumbley remembered buying her first washing machine when she began to receive a regular paycheck right after the war. The machine was a big improvement: "I had rubbed clothes long enough." Minnie Lou Barber remembered that "in 1948 I saved my money and bought Mama a washing machine. I lacked about three payments on it when I married." Margaret Grant recalled that "after the war things started changing" because "we got better pay." There were "a lot of improvements," she explained. "During the war and before the war, women didn't have washing machines. That was a big improvement. I didn't have a washing machine before. Electric stove was a big improvement. I felt like I was really getting someplace getting an electric stove. Radio, all those things." She added, "You could afford to buy better clothes, you just improved yourself all the way round. It was just better."[29]

These purchases were made possible by the spread of credit financing. In the 1940s and 1950s, the local press in Rockingham became full of stores offering "easy" credit terms on furniture and other consumer goods. Emsley Phifer remembered that credit was a necessity for workers who wanted to buy goods such as washing machines and refrigerators: "people couldn't come up with $200 or $300 when they were making thirty-five dollars a week." John Grant explained how credit buying became a way of life for postwar textile workers: "when the company store closed, you had to buy on credit because you couldn't make ends meet. You bought your groceries on credit, we started going to stores uptown. . . . They had trucks that came around and would stop outside your house on payday. You owed money all the time." Indicating the importance of this period in establishing present-day consumer patterns, Bernice Crumbley recalled that "straight after the war it was just like it is now—you could get things, and they'd charge it. They sold clothes and things like that, and you'd pay by the week." When workers fell behind on their payments, "collectors would meet them at the gate when they got paid."[30]

Although many workers constantly owed money to downtown stores after the war, they preferred this system to the old company-store system. Most cited the fact that workers were free to improve and to decide themselves how and where to spend their money. Lee Bateman felt that even though workers were buying items on credit plans, "it meant a better way of life." He felt that the increased wages that had ended the company store "broke the chain of ownership, sometimes I referred to it as the chain of slavery on the white people." John Grant, like many others, felt that the company store was a humiliation because the company was in effect saying "I don't trust you to let you have the money. I'll take it out of your paycheck before you get it. After the union came in, I will have to trust you." He felt that the ending of the company store was "one of the biggest things that really helped the people more than anything else." [31]

Many workers remembered that freedom from the company store and disposable income brought a whole range of improvements and new opportunities. John Langley recalled that after the war, restaurants started to open up in Rockingham. This meant that "for the first time in their lives" workers could go and eat a meal out. Langley explained that "they were only mom-and-pop kind of places," but nevertheless, they offered the first opportunity Aleo workers had to eat a meal out. The fact that workers now went to downtown Rockingham to shop was also a big change. Previously, "mill people never came to town, they had no reason to. It wasn't a race issue, it was a class issue. You knew exactly which class you were in. After the war, we began to start shopping." Stores increasingly began to cater to their new clientele, and as a result, cotton-mill workers became a far more accepted sight downtown. Furniture stores, in particular, began to open up, offering affordable furniture and other household goods that were consciously marketed to the textile-worker clientele. [32]

For the first time, workers started to go to movie-houses that were not controlled by the company. Sports events also began to spring up, replacing company-sponsored events and leagues. Car ownership became increasingly common, allowing workers to attend these new events, travel more, and attend churches of their own choice. The ability to travel, in particular, was a big change, as all workers stressed how little mill workers had traveled during the prewar period, when even the next mill village was considered foreign territory. These changes continued in the 1960s and 1970s, eroding the separate status that mill workers in Rockingham and other southern textile workers had endured for decades. Indeed, former workers described the changes as "coming into the real world" or getting the chance to enjoy a "normal" or "American" way of life. [33]

The opportunities for self-advancement and continued social change increased further in 1949, when, in line with many other southern textile companies, Aleo offered to sell its 193 company houses to the workers. [34] Across the South, companies were selling houses to workers because they no longer needed to provide housing to secure labor and because they hoped that home ownership would produce more responsible workers.[35] In explaining its reasons for selling the houses, Aleo management showed a conscious realization that the relationship between the company and its workers had changed considerably because of World War II. They declared the system to be out of date: "the village had its place in the past." The company claimed that the houses were no longer necessary because workers had "plenty of ways to get around and better wages." Illustrating the amount of social change that had taken place, they compared the decision to sell with the ending of the company store because it signified the integration of Aleo workers into what the company also called "the American way of doing things." They explained, "When the company ceased making store deductions from your ticket this was one step along this line—and now owning your own home and the freedom this will give you is another step in this progress." Indeed, company overseer Bill McAllister remembered that by closing the store and selling houses the company "was trying to do away with the old Uncle Tom feeling. The company didn't want that type of feeling because people are human beings. Forget the power." Thus, the company was conscious that the sale meant the end of its traditional control of its employees and the beginning of their integration into the real world.[36]

For the TWUA, house sales in this period were a problematic issue. The union worried about workers being forced to buy substandard houses. In a variety of cases, the TWUA found companies unwilling to bargain over the sale of houses. Serious and unsuccessful labor disputes occurred at a wide variety of locations because the union was unable to secure terms of sale that it considered satisfactory.[37] The sale of houses at Aleo followed this pattern. The company declared that to buy houses, which were priced at around $2,500, workers had to make a down payment of 10 percent. Workers met this demand with a wildcat strike because they were unable to make such a large down payment. The *Richmond County Journal* reported that workers believed the company was trying to "'sandbag' the employees into immediate purchase of their homes without providing a full opportunity to clear up all questions about the terms of sale and to allow adequate time to raise the money for the required down payment." The *Raleigh News and Observer* supported the workers' position, as did North Carolina governor Kerr Scott.[38]

Although the company made determined efforts to break the strike, workers held firm, and the union was able to negotiate a satisfactory settlement that required no down payment. Thus, at Aleo the strength of the union ensured that the terms of the sale were favorable to workers. Again, the union played an important role in helping workers advance themselves away from the system of traditional corporate dominance.[39]

Former workers universally regarded the sale of company houses as a positive change. Most of them considered the payments manageable and believed the houses represented a good deal, reactions similar to those of workers in other locations across the South.[40] Like the first-time purchase of other consumer items, the purchase of houses was vividly recalled by former workers. Elijah Conyers remembered that "I bought one in '51 and the payment on it was only nineteen dollars a month." Joan Baggett also considered the payments small: "only twenty-three dollars a month for twelve years." And workers found big benefits in home ownership, especially the fact that they were able to improve houses and modify them according to their own tastes. Thus, it was again the freedom from company control that was appreciated. Addie Faye Wyatt explained that many people "put in inside bathrooms. . . . We didn't have an inside bathroom before, ours was on the back-porch." Emsley Phifer typified the prevailing attitude; he explained that selling the houses was "a very good thing" because "people could own their own homes. . . . If you can buy your own home, you know your living is improving." Eli Welch said, "That was great when they started selling the houses, great for the people." John Grant remembered that when the houses were sold, the mill village quickly lost its monotonous appearance as "more contractors came in here than you've ever seen." Many modifications were made, reflecting the attitude, "It's my house, I can fix it up like I want to." These changes were again described as a move toward becoming "normal," like other neighborhoods in Rockingham.[41]

Workers were not unequivocal, however, in their support for the social changes that brought them into the "real world." They agreed that both the opportunity to buy their houses and the improved standard of living that made ownership of consumer goods possible represented a dramatic economic improvement from the mill-village system that had prevailed for decades. For some, though, the downside of this change was that the mill village lost its closeness and sense of community. John Langley remembered that when he was growing up in the 1920s and 1930s, "each mill village was a unit in itself. You didn't go from Entwistle over to Hannah Pickett. We had nothing to do with those people. . . . We never went over the other side, and they never came over to ours." Each mill village was very close—everybody knew one another, and there was a spirit of neighborliness and mutual support. With home ownership and car ownership, this sense of community was lost. Addie Faye Wyatt expressed the feeling that "after the union came in that changed the community-type thing in the village. The wages became higher, people started moving away, the ones who could got out, and it's just now become a place where to me it's just a low class of people who are living in the village." Others also associated unionism with the demise of the mill village into its present state—a dilapidated community with social problems. Minnie Lou Barber explained that many workers bought company houses and "then when they got those houses paid for, and they didn't charge a whole lot for them, then they used that as collateral to get better houses away from here."[42]

Despite this loss of community, most workers felt that the benefits of having the opportunity to make more money, buy a house, and move away were far more important. When former workers looked back on the injustices of the prewar system, none mourned its passing. The sentiments of Minnie Lou Barber were typical of many: "we were closer back then but I really think that the whole community is better off with the way things are now, with people owning their own homes, tending to their own business, and not having the company stand over them and telling them what they can and cannot do."[43]

"Riding a Free Horse"

Despite the strength of the Aleo local, no other textile plant in Rockingham organized during this period, although the TWUA made repeated attempts. In Rockingham the TWUA suffered from the same problem that consistently held back its attempts to organize southern workers— the matching of union pay and benefits by nonunion plants, or "free-riding," as Aleo workers called it. The Rockingham situation, therefore, provides an opportunity to examine in closer detail this central problem, the way it was viewed by union and nonunion workers alike, and the effect it had on the relationship between the two groups.

Rockingham was an important center during Operation Dixie. The SOC launched drives at a number of mills.[44] Early reports were optimistic. As in many other centers, however, few concrete gains resulted, especially after an unsuccessful 1947 strike at the largest mill, Safie Manufacturing Company.[45] Former workers from Aleo felt that workers in other mills failed to organize because benefits and wage increases negotiated in Aleo were immediately copied or bettered in unorganized plants. This was, indeed, a powerful memory for all former Aleo workers. John Langley remembered that "if the union got a five per cent raise, Safie would get six, just to say, 'hey, you can do better without a union.' That happened all the time." Workers universally recalled that nonunion workers from these mills would tell them, as Beatrice McCumbee put it, " 'I don't pay union dues and I get more pay than you do.' . . . They got vacation pay, they got overtime, the same things we were getting without having a union. They could never be sold to join the union."[46]

Written records support the claim that organizing failed because of this free-riding. A lengthy letter sent to Safie workers on the eve of a union election in March 1947 played heavily on the fact that Safie workers would continue to enjoy union pay and benefits without joining and having to pay dues. Mill owner Joseph Safie asked his workers to "look at the Entwistle employees. This union is now drawing money from them at the rate of approximately $13,000 a year. Yet it gets a contract for them at wages less than yours." The monthly reports of the TWUA's director in Rockingham, Joel Leighton, indicate that repeated organization attempts failed because nonunion workers received the same wages as Aleo workers and consequently felt that the union could not benefit them.[47]

The fact that nonunion workers benefited from Aleo's union drove a wedge between the two groups and reinforced the union identity of Aleo workers. Many Aleo workers expressed pride that their union helped all workers in Rockingham, and they took this responsibility seriously. There was a universal pride that the union, *their* union, "helped the whole of Rockingham." Emsley Phifer, for example, recalled that "Safie, Beaunit, J. P. Stevens, those other mills on the other side of town, they would try to keep up with us because they knew that if they didn't the union would come in and organize them. I knew that we were helping the whole town." Yet the matching of union benefits by these plants also exerted enormous pressure on the Aleo workers and made the relationship between the two groups a tense one, with neither side able to understand the other's position. Elijah Conyers remembered angrily that "they wanted us to have it but they didn't want it, they didn't want any dues to pay, but they wanted benefits. We didn't like that. Why should a man ride off what you're doing?" Elsie Hogan, a loom fixer who was union president during this period, also expressed feelings of anger and powerlessness about free-riding: "we carried the brunt of the wage increases for other mills. I got fed up with it, but what am I going to do about it? Ain't none of them would go and help themselves. . . . It was aggravating." Other workers remembered taunts from unorganized workers, especially when Aleo was on strike, with bitterness. Bernice Crumbley recalled one incident vividly: "one man told me when I was out on strike one time for a contract, he said, 'Don't y'all let that thing go dead, because when you get a contract, we get more than you do.' And I told him, 'You ain't doing a thing but riding a free horse.'"[48]

It is clear that many nonunion workers did realize that their benefits came from Aleo, because many Aleo workers recalled how unorganized workers would often ask them how contract negotiations were progressing. The divisions caused by this tension were deep and far-reaching, illustrating how deep an impact unionization made on the community. Loyd Ivey remembered somewhat bitterly that nonunion workers would stop him on the street and ask about contract negotiations at Aleo: "when it came time to renew a contract, I've had a lot of them that lived around me that worked in these other plants, and they'd come up and want to know how *we* were making out. . . . It would have been a whole lot easier on us if some of the other plants would have organized. . . . We were carrying the load for Beaunit, Safie, J. P. Stevens, and Cordova." The problem of contact with nonunion workers increased, moreover, as the Aleo mill village disintegrated and workers began to live in a variety of places and to go to different churches. Lee Bateman explained that "organized labor and unorganized labor begun to tear into families. Brothers, one would work at Aleo and one would not, it deteriorated the families, some got to where they wouldn't speak to one another." He remembered that this division even appeared in churches and other organizations that workers from different plants attended: "can you imagine working at a plant and paying union dues, and the man working at another plant was getting the same benefits you were getting and wasn't paying any union dues? . . . The people that were nonunion were able to buy their own homes, [and] they had cars, . . . so even at church, naturally you were going to discuss things like that."[49]

Most Aleo workers were able to cope with their feelings of annoyance and exploitation about free-riding by realizing that the union gave them some benefits that nonunion plants did not match, especially the grievance procedure. Indeed, it was partly because noneconomic benefits were not copied that they were particularly valued by Aleo workers. Minnie Lou Barber, for example, emphasized that it was the sense of freedom that workers got from a union that divided them from their nonunion counterparts who had never experienced it: "we knew that they were riding in on our coattails, but at least we were better off to have a union. Seniority, and the fact that a boss couldn't just tell you something unfair and you would have to do it. You could go to the shop steward and you could work it out." Aleo workers emphasized their desire to challenge company control as crucial. They stressed that unionism was "in the heart" and claimed that once workers crossed the line and experienced this freedom, they rarely went back. Indeed, nearly all those interviewed were still ardent unionists in 1994, and many supported the closed shop, which had been outlawed in North Carolina for nearly fifty years.[50] The grievance procedure and seniority allowed Aleo workers to feel superior to nonunion workers, who had never known anything but company domination. Aleo workers were free; unorganized workers were not.[51]

Nevertheless, the position of nonunion workers in Rockingham was damaging for the TWUA, especially on the national level. Once again, wartime prosperity was harnessed against the union, as companies proved willing to grant better wages and other benefits because of the war-induced textile boom. As John Langley stated, nonunion workers truly did not need a union. For them the wage increases and increased opportunities produced by the war were enough to bring social and economic improvement: "I think the unions had their best shot when people saw no hope. After the war, people started to own things that they had never dreamed of, automobiles, furniture, for the first time in their lives they could go to a restaurant and eat out." He added, "It was World War II that brought all that tumbling down, but the union didn't fill the void that was left. It was self-determination—'hey, I can make it on my own.' We did not need a union. After all, things were getting better."[52]

"The People Were Divided"

Thus, the Aleo local was the type of vibrant local union that was vital to the TWUA's future in the South. It demonstrated that even when a union plant was surrounded by nonunion mills, the local union could flourish. Pressure was put on the local by the way that unorganized mills matched union pay and conditions, but Aleo workers repeatedly illustrated their ability to withstand this pressure. It is surprising, therefore, that the Aleo local suddenly disappeared in 1955 following a short strike. The 1955 strike was in fact the culmination of three years of factional in-fighting within the Aleo local—a conflict that was directed by the national offices of the TWUA and UTW. Like many other local unions in the South, the Aleo local became a victim of the Rieve-Baldanzi feud, illustrating the role interunion rivalry played in the TWUA's failure in the South in the 1950s.

The roots of the battle lay in the 1951 strike. Joel Leighton, the joint board director in Rockingham, was a strong Baldanzi supporter. Like other southern supporters of Baldanzi, after the strike Leighton took the locals under his control out of the TWUA and into the UTW. For Aleo workers, the switch to the UTW was completed on April 9, 1953, when, disillusioned with the strike's failure, they voted by a margin of 465 to 190 to affiliate with the new union.[53] However, the TWUA bitterly contested these "defections" and made determined efforts to recapture the locals, even when, as in Rockingham, they had lost an election. For more than two years after the change of sides, organizers from the UTW and the TWUA battled for the Aleo workers' loyalty. The result was that workers became tragically divided and lost the unity that had brought them important gains.

The damage and division was inflicted by the almost fanatical desire of both unions to outdo the other, whatever the cost. Both sides used strike defeats of their opponents as part of their propaganda; the UTW, in particular, made capital out of the 1951 General Strike. The language used was polemical and extreme, the UTW referring to "Rieve's Rowdies" and the TWUA accusing the UTW of "complete moral and financial bankruptcy" and claiming that it would give the union "the bum's rush."[54] As in other southern locations, much of the battle centered on a legal fight over the union's property and the right of representation. When the Aleo local first switched to the UTW, the checkoff and union hall remained in the TWUA's hands. As a result, the UTW lacked sufficient finances to process grievances and lost credence with some workers, who therefore began to respond to the TWUA. A lengthy battle also ensued over the union hall. This was "settled" in February 1955 when the TWUA won control of the hall in an NLRB election. The UTW, however, still held official bargaining rights. Not surprisingly, the company was the beneficiary of the feud. When the TWUA tried to secure a contract in the wake of its election victory, the company refused, and the TWUA struck the plant. Almost immediately, large numbers of UTW supporters broke the picket line, and the contract ran out without renewal.[55]

Former Aleo workers remembered that the feuding of the 1951–55 period destroyed the local union, dividing workers and leaving many disillusioned with unionism. Rachel McDuffie, who had been a strong union supporter since starting work in 1947, was one of the many who crossed the picket line in 1955: "I was for the union, and I still believe in them, but when you've got people in there running their mouth, telling you this and that . . . they wanted us to pull out of one and into another, when they want to do it three times, it's just a mess, it gets you down, so I went back to work, said I'd had with it." Many workers compared the situation at Aleo to a divided family or church, arguing that "what was divided would fall." Elsie Hogan, for example, expressed the belief that "if you can get a group of people arguing amongst themselves instead of one accord, something's going to give. . . . Anything you do, divided it will fall." Emsley Phifer remembered the way that the feuding benefited the company: "employees were against each other, they were divided, and finally the company just sat back and let them fight it out, and the company won. . . . The company, they were sitting back clapping their hands." [56]

Many also stressed that the divisions left by the feud were deep and helped prevent the reorganization of the union. Margaret Grant remembered that "people stopped talking to each other. Mothers and daughters quit speaking to each other, mothers and sons quit speaking to each other. One was a good strong union member and they went in there and tried to destroy the union. . . . There was a lot of years they didn't speak to each other." Husband John added sadly, "If you get right down to it, there was somebody in every family it tore up." Even after forty years, bitter feelings over the strike still linger. Thus, as in other southern textile communities, even in defeat organized labor had a huge impact on the Aleo mill community between 1945 and 1955.[57]

Another common theme of this period prevented the reorganization of the Aleo local: the company continued to apply union conditions after the union's defeat. Former overseer Ernest Cole remembered that until the plant was closed in 1978, management kept a copy of the last union contract in their office, and "we went almost exactly by it . . . and a lot of plants in Rockingham went by it too." In particular, the company continued to apply seniority, as well as many other benefits that are still unusual in North Carolina, including double time on Sundays, fatigue time, and overtime pay.[58]

The story of the Aleo local illustrates many of the salient themes of this period, especially the way that the higher wages generated by World War II and union pressure led to significant social changes. These changes belie the image of continuity often associated with southern textile communities. For Aleo workers, unionism fed into and benefited from the social and economic changes generated by World War II; but other Rockingham companies matched these benefits as an effective means of undermining the union's organizing appeal. However, this technique gave organized labor a far greater impact on Rockingham than is apparent from its representation in only one plant. The Rockingham pattern is typical of the TWUA's role in the South during these years: the union brought benefits to all southern textile workers through its presence and the threat of organization but was unable to build a secure, dues-paying future in the region. Moreover, this granting of union benefits has a wider significance, because American companies have used it successfully to weaken the American labor movement as a whole.[59]

The Rockingham story also highlights the role that the union played in bringing about its own failure in the South. The Aleo local was one of many that were sacrificed as a consequence of the TWUA's internal battle. In addition, the importance of noneconomic benefits to Aleo workers calls into question the national union's obsession with wages during this period, a concern driven by a desire to protect the New England textile industry. Organizers and TWUA staffers in the South repeatedly complained that the union needed to base its organizing appeal around the freedom it could offer from unilateral company action, claiming that this approach would be more successful. These men and women realized that for workers who had lived in company-owned mill villages, freedom from arbitrary control was their most important priority. In many locations, the company-owned mill village had produced an accumulation of grievances and alienation from the company, as the sporadic strikes of the prewar period showed. The Aleo story indicates that those who called for a new approach may have been right.

conclusion

───────────┐

The period between 1945 and 1955 was clearly a
good one for southern textile workers but a bad one for the TWUA. During these years the average southern textile worker experienced a rising
standard of living and enjoyed many new opportunities as the traditional
mill village disintegrated. However, the TWUA found that these changes
did not make the organizing climate any easier. In many respects, the experiences of the TWUA in the South between 1945 and 1955 mirrored
national trends. The immediate postwar period was an excellent time for
white blue-collar Americans, who experienced unparalleled wages, positive changes in housing, and the fruits of consumerism, but the period
was a disappointing one for those groups who sought lasting social reform—particularly organized labor, African Americans, and women.
Like the TWUA, these groups had made important advances in the war
and emerged from these experiences with considerable optimism, only to
find they were unable to advance social reform in the postwar period.
This period was one of social change rather than social reform.[1]

General studies of postwar America have confirmed the crucial role of
World War II as a turning point in providing the foundations of postwar
blue-collar affluence but also in dulling the prospects of social reformers.
Nevertheless, the war's impact has not been fully explored by recent labor and social history, which has tended to overlook contingent historical events in its emphasis on wider patterns of social change.[2] The experiences of the TWUA in the immediate postwar years were greatly shaped
by World War II, which generated social and economic changes that had
profound consequences for unionization. It is impossible to understand
the failure of unionization without reference to the war. Textile workers'
resistance to organization in the late 1940s and early 1950s was conditioned by the opportunities provided by the war, by the positive changes
that it had generated in their lives, rather than by a static worker culture.
Similarly, the progress that the TWUA had made during the war also
made employers determined to regain the initiative in the immediate
postwar years.

The war was important because it produced unparalleled economic prosperity for the southern textile industry, an industry that had struggled to make any profit for more than twenty years before the war. This prosperity profoundly altered the organizing climate for manufacturers as well as workers. Before the war, low profit margins and the fact that many manufacturers lived on the brink of economic ruin meant that they violently opposed union drives.[3] When their profits grew large, they were free to raise wages and, indeed, to use raises as an effective means of fighting unionization; this strategy reduced alienation and workers' perceived sense of need for unionism.

This conclusion is particularly significant, because existing studies have explained the failure of unionization by stressing employer opposition and cultural resistance by workers to organized labor. At the heart of these accounts is the assertion that workers had a natural ideological identification with the company, or that company control was too pervasive to allow unions to flourish. This study, in contrast, shows that many workers rejected unionism because of a pragmatic assessment of their position with regard to organized workers and the economic climate generally, rather than their relationship with the company. Indeed, most workers were well aware that it was the union and not the company that was winning them wage increases.[4]

The experience of the TWUA in the South therefore reflected national, not just regional, developments in ways that the emphasis on a distinctive worker culture obscures.[5] This study shows in close detail that the rising standard of living generated by World War II and the difficulties experienced by the TWUA were not simply coincidental but were integrally linked. Very little is known about the way that postwar prosperity affected organizing, because most postwar studies have concentrated on northern industrial workers who were already solidly organized. For groups like automobile workers, postwar prosperity benefited the labor movement. Organized labor entered a period of stability and maturity largely through contract gains negotiated in the prosperous 1950s and 1960s.[6] For the TWUA, however, organizing was its priority after the war. The central problem that prevented successful organizing in the South was the rising standard of living generated by World War II. Rising wages were shared by all southern textile workers, but because the majority of workers were unorganized, rising standards did not benefit the union but, rather, showed workers that things were improving for them without their having to join a union. It proved impossible to overcome the problem of free-riding; nonunion companies matched union pay scales as an effective means of preventing organization. The free-riding problem played a broad and neglected role in weakening the American labor movement.[7]

The problem of free-riding was made more acute because it worked

alongside another factor that historians have generally overloo_
competitive structure of the textile industry. The competitive n_
the industry made union manufacturers reluctant to institute wag_
benefits that nonunion manufacturers would not follow. Small profit _
gins, the high number of competitors, ease of entry into the industry, a_
high labor costs made the organizing climate much more difficult for th_
TWUA than for organizers in oligopolistic industries such as steel or automobiles. The union could not establish a union wage scale that would
revive its organizing efforts without taking on the southern industry in
strike action. The TWUA attempted this in 1951. The failure of the strike
was particularly damaging because it weakened the TWUA's relationship
with the unionized sector of the southern industry, including the companies with whom it had established the most successful relationships.

The fact that social changes generated by World War II hindered the
TWUA in the South challenges the recent historiography that has stressed
continuity and lack of fundamental social change in the textile South.
These studies have denied that national changes altered the fabric of life
in southern mill villages. This stress on continuity of outcome misses the
important social and cultural changes that took place between 1945 and
1955. In fact, the low pay and company dominance of the industry before World War II only increased the war's impact: rising wages and the
consequent breakdown of the traditional company-owned mill village
had a disproportionate impact on southern textile workers, who had for
decades endured low pay and limited opportunities. It was because of
their profound sense of economic and social improvement that these
workers pragmatically reasoned that a union was not necessary. Unlike
unions who had already organized the majority of the workers in their
industry, the TWUA was unable to harness these changes to its advantage,
and it found its appeal dulled by changes generated by World War II. The
union compounded its lack of appeal by continually emphasizing economic benefits and by seeking to organize the South primarily as a means
of protecting its membership in the North.[8]

Because southern textile workers have been considered beyond the
pale of national change, general accounts of postwar American history
rarely cite them as typifying the trend toward consumerism and new opportunities. The move to home and car ownership usually brings to mind
northern-based examples, such as the famous Levittown development in
Pennsylvania, or images of well-paid auto workers in towns such as Richmond, California, or Hazel Park, Michigan. It is clear that textile workers did not move to large suburban developments like Levittown. The
fact that most bought mill houses masked the fact that a significant
change had taken place. As one historian has written, "The mill villages
as such are gone, but the houses remain." It was only contemporaries
who captured the profound social changes that were taking place. TWUA

...rs, in particular, repeatedly described the way that the changing standard of living hindered their efforts. The way that the lifestyle of southern textile workers had changed was described well by organizer Robert Parker, who walked into the mill-village section of the sleepy North Carolina town of Wilson in the summer of 1955. He described how car-owning workers gave the union a hostile reception: "this Wilson plant is some baby. We have to get out of the way of the workers' cars or get run over by them." One married couple "was not interested in the union and didn't care to discuss it or talk about it. A new BUICK road-master was parked in the yard (1955 model)." The view that a union was no longer necessary because of improved conditions was the single most common response that organizers reported. Many workers felt that as the country had now emerged from the Great Depression, a union was unnecessary. Organizer L. A. Gossett, for example, wrote from a failed 1954 campaign in Buford, Georgia, that workers told him, "'[You are] wasting your time. Company pays good and treats its workers good.' None against the union, but says they don't need one like they did back in 1938 and 39."[9]

The scale of the social changes that took place in this period were reinforced by the changing attitudes of southern textile management. Indeed, southern textile management rightly sensed that a workforce with higher wages, good fringe benefits, and greater freedom would be more resistant to unionism. This realization was a remarkable change, given the violent and intransigent way that prewar management had often reacted to unionism. Indeed, it considerably modifies the traditional picture that historians have developed of southern textile manufacturers. Management was able to harness the war-induced prosperity far more effectively than the TWUA was, and it was this ability that accounted for its continued hegemony over the union in these years. Thus, many companies fought Operation Dixie through matching or exceeding union pay and benefits. Management's crucial decision to resist the 1951 pay demands was made because they correctly anticipated that the credit system would doom the strike by making workers unwilling to lose their newfound consumer goods through strike action. Management showed a perceptive understanding of the way that higher wages had changed the industrial relations climate.

Spencer Love, founder and president of Burlington Industries, captured the new mentality of management when he declared in the fall of 1953 that the changes that had taken place in the textile industry comprised "the most amazing industrial transition in the history of mankind." He added, "This industry has evolved from an era of dark and poorly-ventilated plants, peopled by unhealthy looking individuals, to a day of modern and comfortable plants to which some of the most attractive men and women in America drive their automobiles daily to work

for wages that are more than five times what they were twenty-five y
ago." [10] Love's remarks clearly reflected the desire of management to p
mote a positive public image, which was itself a significant shift from
prewar belligerency. Love's own actions, in fact, epitomized the move
that postwar textile management made toward conscious modernization
and the repudiation of prewar company ownership of housing and stores
as out-of-date and patently unfair. During the 1940s and 1950s, all
Burlington plants were air-conditioned, remodeled, and equipped with
the most modern machinery. Particular care was made to provide workers with wages and fringe benefits superior to those in union mills, a
technique that helped keep Burlington nonunion. [11]

Throughout the 1940s and 1950s, management publications cele-
brated workers' newfound independence, their new role as home owners
and American consumers. This change of attitude was remarkable, given
that the industry had developed through mill owners' striving to build
complete communities that catered to workers' every need. Realizing,
however, that the time for such cradle-to-grave paternalism was over,
management now appreciated the importance of consumer independence to southern textile workers. One management publication, *Textile
Neighbor*, repeatedly promoted the cult of home ownership, celebrating
the fact that "the workers in the textile mills are buying their own homes,
often in the country where they can cultivate a few acres of land and
commute to work," a lifestyle made possible by ownership of "good
automobiles." Pictures of a typical textile town on the weekend showed
workers pursuing a variety of leisure pursuits independent of company
control, such as trips to the coast or to the mountains, or tending their
own plot of land. The *Textile Neighbor* spelled out that "even the kind of
recreation that costs money can be had. Good wages make it possible." [12]

Cultural explanations of the failure of unionization in textiles have ignored another national factor that accounted for the southern failure of
the TWUA in these years. Because most studies have concentrated on the
period before World War II, the priorities of national unions have not
figured strongly. Indeed, before the war, most southern textile activism
was generated from grassroots grievances and forced upon a national
union that was ill-equipped to channel it into secure unionism. [13] As a consequence of the New Deal, however, unions made tremendous strides in
the North, and this was particularly true of the TWUA, which was born
following the large northern gains of the TWOC drive. With an established northern membership that was much larger than its southern
membership, the TWUA was always presented with a telling regional
dilemma. Its first duty was to its dues-paying members in the North. At
the same time, however, these members lacked job security unless the
South was organized. Many in the union were also content to raise
southern wages, which helped protect northern jobs, rather than directly

...ing to organize the South. The differing regional priorities that the
...ion faced fed into the 1951 strike, which wiped out the TWUA's
...rength in the South.

Although rising wartime wages brought many positive changes, it
would be misleading to imagine this period as an unmitigated triumph
for the southern textile worker. For American workers generally, the rising wages and new opportunities of the postwar period brought new
problems and contradictions. Studies of auto workers and other northern
groups have shown that despite their increased affluence, blue-collar
workers lacked real opportunities for advancement. In addition, they often became trapped in patterns of credit purchases that took away their
freedom and led to emptiness and dissatisfaction. In 1951, for example,
social commentator Daniel Bell described the way that credit buying increased the financial insecurity of American workers: "in our day . . . it is
not physical hunger which is the driving force; there is a new hunger. The
candied carrot, the desire for goods, has replaced the stick. . . . By mort-
gaging his future, the worker can buy a house, a car, appliances." These
purchases were described by Bell as discouraging militancy, leading instead to "escapist fantasies." [14]

This study shows that these problems, which have thus far been studied mainly among northern, unionized workers, played a key role in
thwarting the TWUA's progress in the South in the 1940s and 1950s.
Like other blue-collar workers, large numbers of southern textile workers began to buy consumer items on installment plans during this period.
The burden of credit purchases was a particularly heavy one for southern
textile workers, however, because unlike most northern workers in secure unions, they had to strike repeatedly without adequate financial
support from the national union. The crucial 1951 strike in Danville
failed because workers were reluctant to jeopardize their new consumer
items through prolonged strike action. Other strikes failed for the same
reason. Historians have asserted that repeated strike defeats in the textile
South established an oral tradition of defeat that discouraged workers
from union involvement. They have usually stressed that workers grasped
that corporate control was too great for a union to overcome. They have
failed to recognize, however, the important role the credit system played
in establishing this acceptance of defeat. Bill Evans, a shop steward at Erwin Mills in Durham, North Carolina, for much of the 1950s, remembered clearly the way that the union remained weak because of the role of
the credit system in the collapse of the 1951 strike there: "it was dead.
The union was almost no union. Essentially it was weak because of that
strike. . . . The typical story was that people bought things on credit, the
houses, they had bought furniture on credit and when a strike came, if a
strike continued for more than one week, they were going to lose all the

furniture in their houses and so people went back to work." Evans recalled that since workers realized they were unable to strike because of the credit system, they were reluctant to strike again to rebuild their union, a scenario common to locals involved in strikes during this period. Thus, for southern textile workers, as for the wider union movement, the legacy of higher postwar wages was a paradoxical one, allowing for individual economic improvement but constraining group advancement for broader gains.[15]

This study also throws doubt on whether the neglect that the new labor history has generally shown for the postwar period is justified. The new labor history has traditionally dismissed the postwar period as a disappointing era when conservatism and Cold War anticommunism sapped the insurgent militancy of the 1930s.[16] It is clear, however, that this argument is not wholly accurate for southern textile workers, who failed to unionize in the 1930s. Much of the 1930s, indeed, represented an exercise in damage limitation for the bankrupt UTW following the disastrous 1934 general strike. It was in the immediate postwar period that the most intensive efforts were made to organize southern textiles. Only in the postwar period did southern textile workers have sufficient financial backing from an international union to demonstrate sustained militancy and form some secure local unions. This study highlights the rich history that southern textile workers left behind in their postwar battle for union representation. In repeated strikes for a contract, southern textile workers demonstrated militancy and a concern for noneconomic goals that belies the traditional picture of postwar workers receiving pay hikes and fringe benefits in contracts from secure and staid unions. For southern textile workers, the most dramatic and important struggles for union security occurred not in the 1930s but in the immediate postwar period.

This conclusion follows an emerging body of southern labor history that has questioned the view that New Deal working-class militancy was tamed by the CIO's wartime bureaucracy and that has asserted the vital importance of the immediate postwar period. Many national unions concentrated on organizing the North in the 1930s and only made serious efforts to organize the South in the 1940s. As Judith Stein has concluded from her research on steelworkers in Birmingham, Alabama, "In Alabama, the 'turbulent years' occurred in the late 1940s and early fifties." It was also in the immediate postwar years that the United Steelworkers (USW) made its most intensive efforts to organize the South. Like textile unions, in the 1930s the USW had concentrated on organizing the North first, and only thought about the South seriously at the end of World War II. The research of Robert Korstad and Michael Honey has also illustrated how important the 1940s were to southern labor, especially as the strict protection provided by the NWLB was crucial to other unions who had been unable to overcome corporate resistance in the South in the 1930s.[17]

By concentrating on the postwar period, this study covers new historical ground. The 1951 strike was a major event that is central to understanding the failure of textile unionization, yet it has received no historical attention. The same applies to the Rieve-Baldanzi split. The rich hidden history revealed by the story of African American workers in Danville illustrates the important contribution blacks made to southern textile history before their large-scale entry into production jobs in the 1960s. The story of Operation Dixie in textiles shows that the campaign's failure is explained more by the unacknowledged role of rising wages, which had a peculiar impact in the low-paid textile field, than by general factors. Moreover, as the experiences of the TWUA illustrate, it was only through the strict protection provided by the NWLB that corporate resistance to unionism was able to be overcome in many southern industries.

A number of recent studies on the decline of the American labor movement in the 1980s and 1990s have begun to pinpoint the failure to organize the South in the immediate postwar years as a crucial failure for U.S. labor. These studies have highlighted the importance of the immediate postwar period to understanding the present-day status of the American labor movement. They have argued that Operation Dixie was a crucial watershed for the labor movement because it failed to organize black and white workers together and to embrace Communist organizers, who arguably had the best track record of organizing black workers. Operation Dixie, they argue, would have had more success if it had been based on African American workers, who responded less to racist and anticommunist propaganda than white textile workers did.[18]

My study shows that this conclusion is not wholly satisfactory with regard to the TWUA's experiences between 1945 and 1955. The detailed and voluminous grassroots records of attempts to organize the textile industry indicate that the most important factor that prevented organization was a rising standard of living, not racist or anticommunist propaganda. It is also difficult to see how the CIO could have achieved a secure base in the South without organizing the textile industry, which was by far the largest southern industry and was a symbol of anti-unionism. Moreover, if there was a vital turning point for textile unionization, it was the 1951 strike, which clearly was more damaging than Operation Dixie. The 1951 strike gravely weakened the union, whereas Operation Dixie did succeed in organizing some new plants. The union emerged from Operation Dixie with some hope for the future. Moreover, TWUA leaders knew that organizing the South was a long-term commitment, and they invested little emotionally in Operation Dixie.[19] Many TWUA leaders were eager to deny that Operation Dixie was a turning point, and they emphasized that organizing was an ongoing effort that continued after the southern drive. The 1951 strike, by contrast, was regarded by TWUA staffers themselves as a turning point because of the amount of damage it inflicted on the union. Despite this evidence, the strike has been completely neglected by historians.[20]

A study of the TWUA's history after 1955 makes it clear why so many saw the 1951 strike as a watershed. Between 1939 and 1951, the TWUA grew in membership; between 1951 and its merger with the Amalgamated Clothing Workers in 1976, it declined. By 1960, the TWUA had lost half of its northern strength, and in 1964 it had only 13,000 dues-paying southern members.[21] The strike was more than a symbolic marker of this shift. The 1950s saw many southern locals, including those that had been its strongest, perish in the fallout from the 1951 strike and the UTW feud. Thus, the TWUA anticipated the general decline of the American labor movement, in that it lost members at a time when others were gaining them. Although some union leaders regarded the TWUA's decline as a lesson for other unions, most contemporaries ignored it by looking at overall growth statistics, a neglect that explains why postwar labor history has until recently been dominated by the picture of affluent workers and stable unions. Only recently has the TWUA's decline been seen as a classic example of the plight of the current labor movement, or, as Robert Zieger puts it, "as American as apple pie."[22]

Moreover, several of the themes that emerged in the immediate postwar period have been central to the failure of unionization since 1955. The 1945–55 period saw the emergence of antilabor lawyers Frank Constangy and Whiteford Blakeney. While moving toward more progressive methods of fighting unionization by equalizing union pay and fringe benefits, companies also relied on lawyers like Blakeney and Constangy to kill organizing campaigns through legal delaying tactics. By 1948, CIO veteran Paul Christopher had already identified the ability of Constangy to destroy organizing campaigns: "I have absolutely no confidence in our ability to win an election in any mill represented by Frank Constangy."[23] The law firms of Blakeney and Constangy were used even more by southern textile employers in the 1960s, 1970s, and 1980s. These firms developed a technique known as "preventative labor relations" that all major corporations used. Its main technique was deliberate violation of the National Labor Relations Act, a strategy based on the fact that the NLRB was too slow to provide an effective remedy. This use of legal methods has been one of the most important reasons for the continued failure of textile unionization efforts since 1955.[24]

The credit system was such a central cause of union weakness that it continued to hold the TWUA back in the South after 1955. This reflected the fact that the credit purchase system that emerged in the 1940s and

1950s has remained in place in ensuing decades. Strikes continued to be lost because of the pressures the credit system placed on strikers. Bruce Raynor, the TWUA's education director in the 1970s, remembered that it was common for the local community to exert pressure against the strikers through credit agencies and other economic means. This tactic was effective because "southern textile workers are some of the most debt ridden people in America, their few luxuries attained through long-term installment purchases." He explained that "cars, furniture, appliances, groceries, homes, insurance, medical care, and even clothes are bought on credit and repaid over a long period of time. Therefore, this brand of pressure is one of the most effective in 'disciplining' striking textile workers into returning to work." Similarly, one of the central reasons that workers failed to respond to the intensive organizing efforts at the J. P. Stevens chain in the 1960s and 1970s was their fear of being fired and losing their material possessions. As one owner of a poolroom near a Stevens plant in Dublin, Georgia, explained, "A lot of these fellas buy everything on time payments. They figure they're gonna lose it all if the plant goes on strike even for a day." [25]

Similarly, companies have continued to match or exceed the pay scales and fringe benefits of unionized textile firms as an effective means of preventing unionization. The inability of the union to establish a clear differential between organized and unorganized plants remains its central problem into the 1990s. Thus, even when it won elections, as at the J. P. Stevens plant in Roanoke Rapids, North Carolina, in 1974, the union's inability to establish a differential robbed these victories of any impact. Indeed, J. P. Stevens deliberately held the wages of the Roanoke Rapids plant below those of its nonunion plants as a way of successfully preventing further unionization. In addition, Stevens and other southern companies continued to structure their effective preelection propaganda around the fact that unorganized workers already received the same pay and benefits as their union counterparts. [26]

In the years after 1955, indeed, the waning influence of the union reestablished the large nonunion companies' dominance in terms of wage levels. Between 1945 and 1955, southern textile workers had moved ever closer to the wages earned by northern, unionized industrial workers. After 1951, however, northern mass-production workers raced ahead of southern textile workers, who became entrenched in their position as low-paid manufacturing workers, the poor relations of the American industrial worker. Thus, the percentage of textile workers' wages to all private nonagricultural workers' wages declined from 89 percent in 1948 to 69 percent in 1978. [27] The low and static pay levels of the industry after 1951 make it easy to overlook the large-scale changes that occurred between 1941 and 1951. Because images of failed unionization, low pay, and lack of opportunity continue to prevail, it is easy to lose sight of the rapid increases in pay and social conditions that occurred in the 1940s. They become lost in a postwar continuum of low pay and continued exploitation. This problem is acute, as few historians have analyzed the postwar decades in detail; instead they have provided broad overviews from the late 1930s to the 1980s.[28] The TWUA itself, despite its bleak history in the region, deserves considerable credit for its role in lifting southern textile workers out of the depression and helping them "come into the real world." Nothing better illustrates the differing conceptions of this period for workers, on the one hand, and the union movement, on the other, than the southern textile story. For the TWUA, this period predated the decline of the American labor movement. For southern textile workers, it marked their emergence into the American mainstream, a period when, in the words of one, "everything was improving."[29] The mechanism that destroyed the TWUA in this period— the matching of union pay and conditions—also provides the union with a positive epitaph for these years. In 1947, one TWUA flyer summed up the wide variety of social changes generated by higher wages and the way that the TWUA could take justifiable pride in helping to bring southern textile workers into "the real world":

> Since 1937 the Textile Workers Union of America, CIO, has raised the earnings of southern textile workers from an average of 37 cents an hour to the present level of 94 cents an hour. . . . As a result of their higher earnings, southern textile workers *for the first time* [original emphasis] have begun to approach a standard of living which would permit full lives for themselves and their families. . . . The entire southern economy has benefited. Increased purchasing power for textile workers has brought new prosperity to the communities in which they live. Workers can now afford better food and clothing; they can buy homes and furnish them more attractively; they have funds for entertainment and for the services of doctors and dentists; they are able to contribute more liberally to community chests.

In sum, the flyer noted, "the entire character of the textile community has changed." This was a worthwhile achievement.[30]

notes

Tibbetts Papers	Norris Tibbetts Papers, unprocessed private collection on loan from Norris Tibbetts
TWUA	Textile Workers Union of America Papers, State Historical Society of Wisconsin, Madison, Wisconsin
UTW	United Textile Workers Papers, Southern Labor Archives, Georgia State University, Atlanta

Introduction

1. There was another, older, textile union, the AFL's United Textile Workers (UTW). This union was much smaller than the TWUA. In 1945, for example, the TWUA had 400,000 members and the UTW 60,000. This book concentrates on the TWUA, which was far more active in the South in these years. The UTW does come into the story after 1952, however, when many southern locals defected from the TWUA and joined the UTW as a consequence of the Rieve-Baldanzi split, discussed in Chapter 7.

2. The best overview of the recent scholarship is the chapter "Textile Workers and Historians" in Zieger, *Organized Labor in the Twentieth-Century South*, pp. 35–59. The quotation from Zieger is from p. 35. Studies concerned with worker culture include Newby, *Plain Folk in the New South*; Carlton, *Mill and Town*; Flamming, *Creating the Modern South*. Studies that engage the issues of worker culture in parts of their work include Griffith, *Crisis of American Labor*, and Hodges, *New Deal Labor Policy*. The view of an acquiescent worker culture is challenged by Hall et al., *Like a Family*. The quotations are drawn from Griffith, *Crisis of American Labor*, p. 59, and Hall et al., "Cotton Mill People," p. 250.

3. Hodges, *New Deal Labor Policy*, p. 192. Hodges emphasizes continuity in his epilogue, pp. 192–98. Other recent studies that have stressed continuity include Carlton, *Mill and Town*; Hodges, *New Deal Labor Policy*; Griffith, *Crisis of American Labor*. Carlton writes, "The hostilities of the period before 1920 produced an antipathy toward the town that is still discernible in southern mill centers, and the grievances of the operatives of that age against reformers live on in the operatives' present-day distrust of unions and liberals" (*Mill and Town*, p. 271). Studies by sociologists, both old and recent, have also stressed the static nature of southern mill towns. See, for example, Morland, *Millways of Kent*, and "Kent Revisited"; Gilman, *Human Relations in the Industrial Southeast*; Mc-Donald, "Textile Workers and Unionization." Douglas Flamming's recent work, *Creating the Modern South*, has pointed out that considerable social and economic changes were taking place in Dalton, Georgia. See especially pp. 262–81.

4. Griffith, *Crisis of American Labor*, p. xiv.

5. The importance of the industry's structure, and its omission from the existing historiography, was first brought to my attention by Tom Terrill in his review of Hall et al., *Like a Family*. See Terrill, "Southern Mill Workers," p. 594.

6. The hostility of "uptown" opinion to southern textile workers was first emphasized by Pope, *Millhands and Preachers*. On the mill owner's dominance over the community and its consequences for union activity in recent scholarship, see Hodges, *New Deal Labor Policy*, p. 38, and Griffith, *Crisis of American Labor*, pp. 45–61. Clark, "TWUA in a Southern Mill Town," pp. 296–330, illustrates

the role of state power and community opposition in breaking the strike at Harriet-Henderson Cotton Mills in Henderson, North Carolina, between 1958 and 1960. Clark shows that Governor Luther Hodges played a key role in breaking the strike and that many North Carolina governors before him had acted in a similar way.

Chapter 1

1. Solomon Barkin to author, November 27, 1993, copy in author's possession; Zieger, *American Workers, American Unions*, p. 137; *Textile Challenger*, June 1958. Education Director Larry Rogin shared Barkin's views; it was in this period that he realized the union would not be able to organize the South (Larry Rogin Interview, TWUA Oral History Project, TWUA).

2. Early studies emphasized the drive to create mills as a great community effort, asserting that mills were built for humanitarian purposes by entrepreneurs hoping to give steady employment to impoverished farmers. More recent studies have challenged this view and have stressed large profit margins rather than social motives. For the philanthropic interpretation, see Mitchell, *Rise of the Cotton Mills*, pp. 9–76, and Gilman, *Human Relations in the Industrial Southeast*, pp. 67–76. Studies challenging this view include Carlton, *Mill and Town*, pp. 72–81, and McLaurin, *Paternalism and Protest*.

3. Hodges, *New Deal Labor Policy*, pp. 9–16.

4. Katz, *Taft-Hartleyism in Southern Textiles*, p. 4.

5. Hodges, *New Deal Labor Policy*, p. 15.

6. "The Bolt in Cotton Textiles," *Fortune*, July 1947, pp. 61–62; Hodges, *New Deal Labor Policy*, pp. 18–19.

7. U.S. Congress, House, Committee on Labor, *Proposed Amendments to the Fair Labor Standards Act*, pp. 129–84; *Greensboro Daily News*, April 6, 1951; "Basic Wage and Cost Data: 1950 Negotiations with TWUA" folder, DRMC Papers; 1948 TWUA Executive Council Report, pp. 18–19.

8. "The Bolt in Cotton Textiles," *Fortune*, July 1947, p. 178; 1948 TWUA Executive Council Report, p. 22; Barkin interview. For the way that the union emphasized integration see Barkin, "Regional Significance," pp. 395–411.

9. Jewkes and Jewkes, "Hundred Years of Change," pp. 118, 130; Glass, *Textile Industry in North Carolina*, p. 84. Emphasizing the lack of structural change in the textile industry, Spencer Love, the founder of Burlington Industries, told a 1955 congressional hearing that large companies had few advantages in the textile industry because "the little man coming in can go and take the cream. He can enter when the going is good. . . . I believe that even a cursory survey of textile conditions should convince anyone that textiles are the last field in which any government really has to worry about a trend toward monopoly and the disappearance of competition" (U.S. Congress, Senate, Committee on the Judiciary, *Corporate Mergers and Anti-Trust Legislation*, 1st sess., pp. 732–62, 733, 741, 759).

10. *Southern Textile News*, January 26, 1952.

11. Dan River Mills executive Ray Gourley, for example, called the 1950s downturn "a depression as bad as the 1932 depression, as far as the textile

industry is concerned" (transcript of contract negotiations meeting of March 20, 1952, DRMC Papers).

12. *Wall Street Journal*, February 18, 1952, reported how "extremely adverse market conditions" were affecting textile companies in both the north and south.

13. Katz, *Taft-Hartleyism in Southern Textiles*, pp. 4–5.

14. Ibid.

15. Transcript of contract negotiations meeting of March 21, 1951, DRMC Papers; Hodges, *New Deal Labor Policy*, pp. 12–16.

16. Douglas Flamming writes, for example, that the 1934 strike failed to concern management at Crown Cotton Mill in Dalton, Georgia: "In an economic sense, the strike worked to the managers' advantage, for they already had warehouses full of goods they could not sell, and the strike provided a decrease in labor and production costs for which they bore no responsibility." See Flamming, *Creating the Modern South*, p. 200.

17. Fine, *Sit-Down*, pp. 66–68, 82, 89; Badger, *New Deal*, p. 129.

18. Brooks, "United Textile Workers," especially pp. 2–10, 293–320. On the weakness of organized labor before the New Deal, see, for example, Perlman, "Labor in Eclipse," pp. 105–45; Corbin, *Life, Work, and Rebellion*; Barrett, *Work and Community in the Jungle*. The most sustained period of labor protest before the New Deal occurred in the aftermath of World War I, but it was bitterly suppressed. Union membership rose to a peak of 5.1 million workers in 1920 but declined throughout the ensuing decade. As Robert H. Zieger has written, "The labor problem by the latter part of the decade seemed to have disappeared in most industries." See Zieger, *Republicans and Labor*, pp. 15–16; Taft, *Organized Labor*, pp. 319, 341–60.

19. According to one recent study of the strike, "No group responded with great reservoirs of hope to the opportunities offered by the New Deal than the Southern textile worker" (Irons, "Testing the New Deal," pp. xvii).

20. Irons, "Testing the New Deal," pp. 478–81; Hodges, *New Deal Labor Policy*, p. 126; *New York Times*, September 26, 1934

21. *Textile Bulletin*, August 30, September 13, 1934; Scott Hoyman interview E-10, SOHP; Marvin Masel to Paul Christopher, November 23, 1946, Box 241, ODA; *Greensboro Daily News*, June 26, 1950.

22. The strike's impact is discussed at length in the work of Bryant Simon. Simon shows that the strike caused thousands of South Carolina mill workers to permanently desert the house of labor. He concludes, "After 1934, a larger number of textile workers opted for the 'securities of job and home' over the 'air and promises' of trade unionism." Simon also argues, however, that "a committed remnant" did fight on, turning their attention to an unsuccessful political fight to win the right to strike. See Simon, "Fabric of Defeat," pp. 306, 307, 308–37.

23. Stabile, *Activist Unionism*, p. 18; Hodges, *New Deal Labor Policy*, p. 163.

24. Hodges, *New Deal Labor Policy*, pp. 176–77.

25. Fink, *Biographical Dictionary*, pp. 12–13, 306–7.

26. Stabile, *Activist Unionism*, p. 67; Tibbetts interview of March 9, 1994.

27. 1946 TWUA Executive Council Report, pp. 41–49; 1946 TWUA Convention Proceedings, p. 8; Hodges, *New Deal Labor Policy*, p. 193.

28. Hodges, *New Deal Labor Policy*, p. 128.

29. Contracts contained the automatic checkoff of union dues and maintenance-of-membership provisions, which prohibited workers from withdrawing from the union for the life of the contract. See Marshall, *Labor in the South*, pp. 226–30, for details of the NWLB's operations.

30. For the view that the war absorbed labor's militancy, see Lichtenstein, *Labor's War at Home*. The importance of the NWLB in the South, however, is made by Honey, *Southern Labor and Black Civil Rights*, p. 213.

31. *Gaffney Ledger*, August 28, 1945; McKee interview. As McKee recalled, the federal government did seize Gaffney Manufacturing Company in Gaffney, South Carolina, in 1945, and the army ran the textile plant for over three months. This incident is discussed in Chapter 4.

32. Julius Fry interview E-4, SOHP; Scott Hoyman interview E-10, SOHP.

33. Knight interview of October 26, 1993. Knight, a TWUA southern staffer who worked in most of the southern strikes that occurred after the war, felt that this time "was the worst possible time to be thinking of organizing." She added that management was trying to regain the ground it had lost during the war. Southern strikes will be discussed in Chapter 4.

34. George Taylor, the NWLB member who wrote the majority opinion in the "Big Cotton Case," claimed that "equitable wages are a prerequisite to securing more goods needed to fight the war. The country cannot afford to leave the cotton textile wage scales where they are now" (J. W. Kennedy, "History of the Textile Workers Union of America-CIO," p. 193).

35. *Textile Labor*, January, February 1945; 1946 TWUA Executive Council Report, p. 7.

36. "Fisher and Rudge Brief for Negotiations, Summer 1951" folder, DRMC Papers. Figures from Burlington Industries show that real weekly earnings rose 59.7 percent between August 1939 and July 1945. See Annette Wright, "Aftermath of the General Textile Strike," p. 92.

37. 1946 TWUA Convention Proceedings, pp. 2–7; 1946 TWUA Executive Council Report, p. 6; Richards, "History of the Textile Workers Union of America," p. 207.

38. *New-Bedford Standard-Times*, July 13, 1949; "Facts and Figures about the strike in Dan River Mills, Danville, Virginia and Strikes in the Southern Textile Mills" folder, DRMC Papers; Annette Wright, "Aftermath of the General Textile Strike," p. 92; *Textile Bulletin*, April 1951. At Cone Mills, another major southern textile company, the cost of living increased 40 percent between January 1946 and March 1951, while wages increased 84 percent. See also *Greensboro Daily News*, April 6, 1951.

39. The "family labor system" is explored by McHugh, *Mill Family*. It is clear that the company-owned mill village was also a means of controlling the labor force; see Hall et al., *Like a Family*, pp. 116–17.

40. Annette Wright, "Aftermath of the General Textile Strike," pp. 81–112, 106–8. In the sale of housing, as in many other areas of personnel management, Burlington led the way by selling its first houses in 1935, well before other major southern textile companies. Wright argues that Burlington sold its houses both

because the company wished to release capital for further expansion and modernization and because the advent of car ownership among workers meant they no longer had to live close to the plant.

41. *Daily News Record*, February 14, 1948; Herring, *Passing of the Mill Village*, pp. 16–17.

42. *Daily News Record*, February 14, 1948; Caesar Cone interview C-3, SOHP.

43. Historians have debated the extent to which mill workers drew on, or repudiated, their rural backgrounds. Thus, Hall et al., *Like a Family*, p. 114, stresses rural tradition and customs in mill villages, a view challenged by Flamming, *Creating the Modern South*, pp. xxvi–ii. Carlton, *Mill and Town*, pp. 271–72, argued that by 1920 workers had been weaned from rural independence and become a separate social class.

44. Survey conducted by Mildred Gwin Andrews, April 1946, Box 2, MGA. For the way that first-generation mill workers combined mill work with farming, see Hall et al., *Like a Family*, pp. 39–40, 153–54.

45. Survey conducted by Mildred Gwin Andrews, April 1946, Box 2, MGA. H. K. Hallett of Kendall Mills in Paw Creek, North Carolina, wrote Andrews that "from our experience to date in the sale of mill villages we find there is a great deal of pride in home ownership."

46. *Daily News Record*, February 14, 1948; survey conducted by Mildred Gwin Andrews, April 1946, Box 2, MGA.

47. For example, Herbert H. Taylor, an attorney in the textile town of Tarboro, North Carolina, recalled that "one of the things I noticed when I came back from service was how much living standards had improved here" (Taylor interview).

48. Scales interview.

49. May, *Homeward Bound*, p. 165.

50. *Rockingham Post-Dispatch*, June 11, 1952; Hall et al., "Cotton Mill People," pp. 250–54.

51. Cash, *Mind of the South*, p. 202. Other early works that made similar points include Blanshard, *Labor in Southern Cotton Mills*, and MacDonald, *Southern Mill Hills*.

52. Katz, *Taft-Hartleyism in Southern Textiles*, p. 11.

53. Harriet L. Herring interview with Mary Fredrickson and Nevin Brown, February 5, 1976, Southern Historical Collection, SOHP; Morland, *Millways of Kent*; Newman, "Textile Workers in a Tobacco County," p. 348.

54. Flamming, *Creating the Modern South*, p. 263; Hodges, *New Deal Labor Policy*, pp. 192–93; Griffith, *Crisis of American Labor*, pp. 46–61; Carlton, *Mill and Town*, p. 271.

55. Cole, Phifer, and Cross interviews.

Chapter 2

1. Van A. Bittner to "The Directors and Field Workers CIO Organizing Committee," June 3, 1946, Box 53, ODA; 1948 TWUA Convention Proceedings, p. 73; *Anderson Daily Mail*, May 29, 1952.

2. Marshall, *Labor in the South*, pp. 254–67; Griffith, *Crisis of American Labor*, pp. 49–61. Griffin quote is from p. 60. For Griffin's argument that Operation Dixie had ended by December 1966, see pp. 35–36. For differing reactions to Griffith's book, see Barkin and Honey, "Operation Dixie," pp. 373–85.

3. Zieger, *American Workers, American Unions*, p. 62; 1948 TWUA Executive Council Report, p. 5.

4. *Textile Labor*, April 1946; 1946 TWUA Convention Proceedings, p. 7. The *CIO News* claimed in its issue of May 13, 1946, that Operation Dixie would find "a vast, receptive audience among Southern workers." Rieve reasoned that the TWUA's wartime wage gains would help southern organizing. Citing an 86 percent increase in textile wages since January 1937, he claimed that "with that record of achievement, if we can't go out and organize half a million textile workers by our next convention, there's something wrong with us."

5. *Business Week*, December 18, 1948.

6. Griffith, *Crisis of American Labor*, pp. 23–24; Hodges, *New Deal Labor Policy*, pp. 128, 151. Lucy Randolph Mason rated both Daniel and Christopher highly, describing Christopher as "one of our best men . . . intelligent, honest, and energetic" (Lucy Randolph Mason to "Calvin," February 9, 1950, Box 166, ODA).

7. Van Bittner to "The Directors and Field Workers CIO Organizing Committee," June 3, 1946, Box 102; Franz Daniel to Van Bittner, June 25, 1946, and Van Bittner to Franz Daniel, July 2, 1946, Box 102, ODA; Van Bittner to Franz Daniel, July 3, 1946, Box 102, ODA; Van Bittner to Franz Daniel, August 21, 1946, Box 102, ODA. The PAC was launched by the CIO during World War II and concentrated on trying to bring about political change in the South by encouraging black and white workers to vote, a strategy that made it more controversial than an emphasis on the economic benefits of unionism would have been.

8. 1946 TWUA Convention Proceedings, pp. 95–97; *CIO News*, July 22, 1946; 1946 TWUA Convention Proceedings, p. 43.

9. Milton MacKaye, "The CIO Invades Dixie," *Saturday Evening Post*, July 20, 1946, p. 12.

10. Marshall, *Labor in the South*, pp. 254–55; *Business Week*, December 18, 1948. Anxious not to be portrayed as outside agitators, Van Bittner made sure that over 80 percent of organizers were native southerners and that a large proportion were also veterans. This attention to detail was seen by many as signifying a modern and sophisticated union strategy that would be difficult to discredit. The press detailed how "drawl-equipped" veterans stayed in respectable parts of town, drank chocolate sodas, and were careful not to visit women workers when their husbands were not at home (*Kannapolis Independent*, June 28, 1946).

11. George Baldanzi to Van Bittner, July 1, 1946, and to L. S. Buckmaster, June 21, 1946, both in Box 53, ODA.

12. Glass, *Textile Industry in North Carolina*, pp. 78–79; William Smith to Van A. Bittner, August 8, 1946, Box 53, ODA; *CIO News*, July 22, 1946; George Baldanzi to Van Bittner, July 1, 1946, Box 53, ODA. Tennessee lacked a comparable cotton textile giant, and most of the effort there was centered on the DuPont rayon plant in Old Hickory, described by Christopher as the most

important drive in his state. Considerable effort in Tennessee was also centered on the Standard-Coosa-Thatcher cotton chain based in Chattanooga. See correspondence between Paul Christopher and Helen Gregory, in Box 143, ODA.

13. Griffith, *Crisis of American Labor*, pp. 41–45. Griffith, for example, asks of the Avondale campaign: "How could they achieve with four people what they had failed to achieve with eight, and sometimes with fifteen?"

14. William Smith to Van Bittner, October 10, 1946, and George Baldanzi to L. S. Buckmaster, June 21, 1946, both in Box 53, ODA.

15. Thus, a 1949 internal report on the drive's progress concluded that the key to success in textiles lay in "intensive, concentrated, organizing work" rather than "being dissipated in too many small, relatively unimportant situations." William Smith to All Staff, September 12, 1946, Box 85, ODA; George Baldanzi to Van Bittner, July 1, 1946, Box 53, ODA; Report of CIO Organizing Committee, October 14, 1949, Box 101, ODA.

16. Ongoing drives included the Clark Thread Company chain in Albany and Acworth, Georgia, and the U.S. Rubber Company chain, which had plants in three southern states.

17. Simon, "Fabric of Defeat," pp. 240–45; *Anderson Daily Mail*, May 29, 1952; Lucy Randolph Mason to Mary Heaton Vorse, February 24, 1950, Folder 52, Box 1559, Ramsay Papers. Illustrating the shift in perspective, Emil Rieve declared in 1948 that "we are going to continue to organize the South . . . because we must go on, and we will win out in the end, whether it takes one year, or ten years" (1948 TWUA Convention Proceedings, p. 11). The Honea Path shooting, and its legacy in preventing subsequent unionization in Anderson County, is discussed in the recently released film on the 1934 strike by George Stoney and Vera Rony, "The Uprising of '34."

18. Stabile, *Activist Unionism*, p. 69; Katz, *Taft-Hartleyism in Southern Textiles*, p. 54.

19. Stabile, *Activist Unionism*, p. 69; Katz, *Taft-Hartleyism in Southern Textiles*, pp. 52–54; *Anderson Daily Mail*, May 29, 1952.

20. 1948 TWUA Convention Proceedings, p. 11. Larry Rogin, for example, thought that "while the CIO drive wasn't a success, we didn't come out of it weaker than before, we had organized some plants, we came out of it stronger" (Larry Rogin interview, TWUA Oral History Project, TWUA).

21. *Anderson Daily Mail*, May 29, 1952. Illustrating the way that the national CIO viewed the drive, one internal report grimly concluded, "Unless we organize the major plants in each industry, the winning of elections in relatively small units, no matter how numerous, will have little meaning in relation to the achievement of our goal, which is the total organization of the South" (Report of CIO Organizing Committee, October 14, 1949, Box 101, ODA).

22. Stabile, *Activist Unionism*, p. 69; Hodges, *New Deal Labor Policy*, pp. 141–79. Hodges stresses business resistance as central to the failure of the TWOC drive.

23. Harris, "Snares of Liberalism?," p. 179; Marshall, *Labor in the South*, p. 234.

24. Edmund Ryan to George Baldanzi, January 6, 1947, Box 53, ODA; *TWUA v. Bibb Manufacturing Company*, 1949, 82 NLRB, p. 338ff.

25. Leighton interview. Similar reports came in from a variety of areas. For example, Ryan wrote that a campaign at Danville Knitting Mills in Bon Air "blew up" when the company fired "two of our most active members" (Edmund J. Ryan to George Baldanzi, October 26, 1946, Box 53, ODA). The report of Jim Fullerton from a campaign in Pineville, North Carolina, was also typical: "one of the most active members of the committee on organization and his wife were discharged, as well as several others who were active for the union. These discharges have had the desired effect. . . . The others are afraid" (J. H. Fullerton Organizing Report, June 11, 1947, Box 83, ODA).

26. Zieger, *American Workers, American Unions*, pp. 109–11. The leading exponent of the argument that Taft-Hartley did not represent a significant shift in American labor relations policy is Tomlins, *State and the Unions*.

27. Marshall, *Labor in the South*, pp. 324–25.

28. *CIO News*, November 24, 1947, and March 15, 1948.

29. Harvey Mayo Organizing Report, May 27, 1950, Box 112, ODA.

30. William Smith to George Baldanzi, June 6, 1950, Box 53, ODA; Purnell Maloney Organizing Report, July 26, 1949, Box 144, ODA. From the DuPont campaign, for example, Maloney wrote, "People becoming anxious for an election, say they understand TWUA and are sold on our union so they do not see the need for more meetings unless we have some news of an election date." She complained that it was impossible to build strong support and add more signed cards with everyone "anxiously awaiting election."

31. Eastern North Carolina director R. C. Thomas, for example, wrote, "We should push for earlier election at the Weldon Knitting Mill. Here, too, the workers are wanting to know what is holding things up so long. That has been our trouble in not going in after workers have become organized" (R. C. Thomas to William Smith, December 5, 1946, Box 89, ODA).

32. At an American Enka plant in Lowlands, Tennessee, for example, Maxwell Lackey reported that the company was deliberately delaying the election "and seems to be getting away with it." Consequently, "our biggest problem is keeping our boys in line. They are disgusted over the delay in getting an election, and want to strike for recognition" (Maxwell Lackey Organizing Report, June 24, 1948, Box 162, ODA). Wade Lynch's report from Safie Mill in Rockingham, North Carolina, discussed the problem of despondency: he wrote that there was "low morale in the plant. Lots of the workers thought that the election would come off in a hurry so now they are waiting for the election to come off" (Wade Lynch Organizing Report, June 17, 1946, Box 76, ODA). The campaign at the Standard-Coosa-Thatcher Mill in Chattanooga, Tennessee, illustrated these problems well. On October 20, 1946, workers were "restless because of the delay in getting an election." A month later they were "getting rather disgusted because of the delay in getting an election." By December, organizers were desperately trying to avert a strike. Organizer John Neal reported a typical attitude: "the workers are ready to strike in order to make the NLRB board in Washington hand down a decision." An unsuccessful, unauthorized strike followed, with "many of the members . . . blaming the union for sending them back to work." Following the strike, the mistrust that had developed between the union and workers was evident when workers succeeded in abolishing weekly union meetings over the protest of the

organizers. As one organizer reported, "the people say they are not interested in meetings, they want an election." The company took advantage of the delay, foremen "running around in the mill telling the people that, well, the company has the union licked and that they are going to stall the election as long as possible, which is getting some of our members discouraged." By the time of losing the election, organizers reported that workers had lost confidence in the NLRB and the union: "the thing they tell me is that the Government don't protect them anymore" (John Neal Organizing Reports of October 20, 1946, November 20, 1946, February 22, 1947, and March 22, 1947, all in Box 182, ODA; Helen Gregory Organizing Reports, March 26, 1947, Box 143, and November 25, 1948, Box 144, ODA).

33. At an election at Davis Hosiery Mill in Fort Payne, Alabama, a vicious preelection campaign by the company resulted in the union's receiving only 125 votes after collecting 358 signed cards. Similar defeats occurred at Peerless Woolen Mills in Rossville, Georgia; Johnson Manufacturing Company in Charlotte, North Carolina, and Caroline Mills, Inc., in Carrollton, Georgia. In all of these cases, union majorities were destroyed by last-minute campaigns by the company (Katz, *Taft-Hartleyism in Southern Textiles*, p. 54). Paul Christopher wrote Helen Gregory that at Springfield Woolen Mills in Springfield, Tennessee, "twice before we have signed up majorities only to lose the elections when the heat was turned on in the last couple of days before election day" (Paul Christopher to Helen Gregory, March 25, 1948, Box 144, ODA).

34. William Smith to Van Bittner, Report from January 1, 1949 to July 22, 1949, Box 53, ODA; Katz, *Taft-Hartleyism in Southern Textiles*, p. 54; George Baldanzi to Paul Christopher, October 7, 1949, Box 127, ODA.

35. George Johnston, "Union Organizing for the CIO in the American South," paper written in 1987 and donated to the Southern Labor Archives. Highlighting the problem of controlling workers who had signed up and organized, Johnston recalled that these discharges occurred because "there was a feeling among my members that 'we are organized now and strong, and we're sick and tired of this shit and we're not going to take it anymore.'" As a result, workers "challenged the bosses, who were more than happy to get rid of the trouble-makers." Johnston felt that southern textile workers reacted to organizing campaigns in this way because "when you haven't had any power, even a little is an enticing thing."

36. George Baldanzi to Archie Joslin, February 22, 1950, and "Lucy Mason's visit to Anderson," March 1–3, 1950, both in Folder 155, Box 1568, Ramsay Papers. Unsuccessful attempts to unionize the U.S. Rubber Company's plant in Scottsville, Virginia, also failed largely because of the efforts of the Scottsville Lions Club, which conducted a vicious anti-union campaign. See Katz, *Taft-Hartleyism in Southern Textiles*, p. 43.

37. Helen Gregory Organizing Report, June 28, 1948, Box 166, ODA; Robert Freeman Organizing Report, December 10, 1955, File 17A, TWUA; Paul Christopher to Helen Gregory, October 11, 1948, Box 144, ODA; Dick Conn to Franz Daniel, May 27, 1951, Box 265, ODA.

38. An internal TWUA memo of 1949, for example, concluded simply that "since the enactment of the Taft-Hartley law we have been unable to organize many non-union plants" (January 1949, Box 89, ODA). Providing a summary of

the law's impact, William Billingsley, assistant North Carolina director for the CIO, wrote privately that "delay in securing an election date is often the cause of losing an election. Under the Taft-Hartley law, it is impossible to get a pre-hearing election, and during the long drawn-out process of going through a hearing, the workers frequently lose interest" (William Billingsley to John Ramsay, June 28, 1948, Folder 133, Box 1566, Ramsay Papers). Allan Swim, who worked for the drive's publicity department, wrote John Ramsay in the fall of 1948 that "I had lunch with Van [Bittner] the other day and he brought me up to date on the organizing drive. Together we did a lot of damning of the NLRB, which is understandable" (Allan Swim to John Ramsay, October 11, 1948, Folder 8, Box 1566, Ramsay Papers).

39. Lucy Randolph Mason to Paul Christopher, June 28, 1948, Box 166, ODA; Tennessee Meeting, August 16, 1951, Box 167, ODA. The literature examining the role of federal labor law in the decline of organized labor is reviewed in Goldfield, *Decline of Organized Labor*.

40. Hall et al., *Like a Family*, pp. 289–357, discusses workers' motives for joining a union during the New Deal.

41. Griffith, *Crisis of American Labor*, p. 64; *Charlotte Observer*, July 22, 1946.

42. Hall et al., *Like a Family*, pp. 66–67, and Rowan, "Negro in the Textile Industry," pp. 56–62. Rowan's figures show that in 1940 the textile industry in Alabama was 4.9 percent black; in Georgia, 5.6 percent; in North Carolina, 3.2 percent; in South Carolina, 4.4 percent, and in Virginia, 4.3 percent. By 1950, the figures had increased to 6.3 percent, 6.8 percent, 4.1 percent, 5.0 percent, and 5.4 percent respectively. The role of black workers in the textile industry and the effect of segregated local unions will be discussed further in Chapter 6.

43. McKee interview. David Burgess, an organizer who worked in South Carolina, also believed that "race was an issue, since in the late 1940s blacks were only employed as sweepers and workers doing other dirty jobs. Employers stated that if the union won, a certain percentage of employed workers would be black as required by the FEPC [the wartime Fair Employment Practices Commission]" (David Burgess, personal letter to author, September 3, 1994).

44. For the importance of race in the consciousness of American workers, see Saxton, *Indispensable Enemy*, and Roediger, *Wages of Whiteness*. Bruce Nelson has pointed out that the new labor history failed to deal with the autonomy of race from class, seeing class as a solvent for race (Nelson, "Organized Labor").

45. To the best of the author's knowledge, only South Carolina had a law prohibiting blacks from taking production jobs in the mills. Elsewhere, it was social custom that excluded blacks.

46. Frank Constangy to Frank deVyver, personnel manager of Erwin Mills in Durham, North Carolina, October 24, 1950, Box 1E, deVyver Papers.

47. Clark, a Charlotte native, was editor of the *Textile Bulletin*, previously named the *Southern Textile Bulletin*, for over forty years. The *Bulletin*'s racial editorials coincided with the beginning of Operation Dixie; see *Textile Bulletin*, June 15, July 1, October 15, and November 15, 1946.

48. Don McKee interview.

49. In a drive at Alco Textile Plant in Anderson, South Carolina, for example,

Christian Braen reported that a successful campaign could easily be based around African American workers: "the colored people represent our first problem. They are predominantly leftists and represent a problem of extreme importance. It would be comparatively easy to start a campaign in almost any factory here by working on the colored people through the PAC who also are mostly colored people." Such a campaign could then get help from the statewide PAC, which was also staffed by blacks. Braen concluded, however, that this approach was too controversial: "both Joe [Donovan] and myself feel that the other way, contacting the white employees first, while slower, is by far the safest and best way." Given the dismal failure of the Anderson drive, this was a fateful decision. See Christian Braen Organizing Report, June 17, 1947, Box 102, ODA.

50. Paul Christopher to Van Bittner, February 8, 1950, Box 203, ODA.

51. David Burgess to author, September 3, 1994; Stabile, *Activist Unionism*, p. 69.

52. Scales interview; *New Republic* clipping, n.d., in TWUA newspaper clipping file, Box 271, ODA.

53. Elijah Jackson to Paul E. Harding, October 12, 1950, Box 267, ODA; Paul Christopher to Franz Daniel, October 13, 1948, Box 104, ODA; R. C. Thomas to George Baldanzi, November 28, 1946, Box 89, ODA; Helen Gregory Organizing Report, October 1, 1947, Box 143, ODA.

54. *Textile Labor*, August 16, 1947. Kennedy's autobiography deals at length with his lifelong efforts to combat the Klan and other American hate groups (Stetson Kennedy, *Klan Unmasked*).

55. Klan Meeting, Knoxville, Tennessee, May 18, 1946; meeting of Klavern Atlanta Number 1, September 9, 1946, 1916–1950, Reel 1, SKC; Charles Auslander to C. Singleton Breedin, June 15, 1951, Box 101, ODA.

56. Newton and Newton, *Ku Klux Klan*, pp. 543–44; Dorothy Daniel Organizing Report, May 24, 1947, Box 139, ODA. Regarding the Klan revival in Lowlands, Carl Holt reported that "a KKK movement has been started. . . . And I personally know of one of our members at Enka that was in the parade last Thursday night" (Carl Holt Organizing Report, July 10, 1949, Box 148, ODA).

57. John Neal Organizing Report, October 28, 1946, Box 182, ODA; Paul Christopher to John Neal, October 29, 1946, Box 182, ODA; John Neal to H. S. Williams, January 13, 1947, Box 182, ODA; James Monroe Organizing Report, March 30, 1948, Box 178, ODA; James Monroe Organizing Report, October 25, 1948, Box 129, ODA.

58. Letter of March 2, 1950, in Tibbetts Papers; 1948 TWUA Convention Proceedings, p. 72.

59. George Baldanzi to Archie Joslin, February 22, 1950, Folder 155, Box 1568, Ramsay Papers; Robert Cahoon interview; and Ross Groshong interview.

60. *Textile Bulletin*, June 15, 1946; *Greenville News*, undated clipping in Box 101, ODA.

61. 1950 TWUA Convention Proceedings, pp. 104–5. The FEPC was the Federal Employment Practices Commission, set up during World War II to combat discrimination in employment.

62. 1956 TWUA Convention Proceedings, pp. 162–72; Rowan, "Negro in the Textile Industry," pp. 59–60, 64.

63. Lorell Weiss to Lucy Randolph Mason, November 14, 1950. Another church explained that African Americans who went to its general assembly "still stay in the little green shacks" that were servants' quarters. Although some attempts had been made to end this practice, the church admitted that "it has been slow" (Aubrey N. Brown to Lucy Randolph Mason, February 2, 1951, in Folder 57, Box 1559, Ramsay Papers).

64. Franz Daniel to Ping, April 3, 1947, Box 102, ODA.

65. Griffith, *Crisis of American Labor*, pp. 139–60; Scales interview.

66. Scales interview.

67. The only mention I found after reading the vast number of organizers' reports in the Operation Dixie collection was at DuPont in Old Hickory, Tennessee, where Purnell Maloney wrote, "They are discussing the CIO most all the time in the plant. They usually bring up the Communist element" (minutes of Tennessee staff meeting of September 29, 1949, Box 167, ODA).

68. Evans interview.

69. Scales interview.

70. Griffith, *Crisis of American Labor*, pp. 108–9; Reel 2, SKC.

71. *TWUA v. Bibb Manufacturing Company*, 1949, 82 NLRB, p. 357. The NLRB abandoned its usually reserved language in describing the role of the *Trumpet*, writing that the magazine fought the CIO "with every means at its command. . . . No propaganda, no matter how false, no lie no matter how easily disproved, was too base to be published if they were anti-union and anti-CIO. A more venal sheet is hard to imagine."

72. Salmond, *Miss Lucy of the CIO*, p. 136; Sherman Patterson to R. F. Keeling, May 3, 1949, Reel 2, SKC; Lucy Randolph Mason to Rowen J. McDavid, January 24, 1947, and to John Roy Carleson, April 15, 1946, Box 4, LRM; John Ramsay to Dudley Wood, August 13, 1952, Folder 198, Box 1572, Ramsay Papers.

73. *Anderson Independent*, December 1, 1951; Anderson Citizens' Committee Material, August 20, 1952, Folder 156, Box 1568, Ramsay Papers.

74. Lucy Randolph Mason to W. G. Watkins, November 5, 1946, Box 4, LRM; Lucy Randolph Mason to Cameron P. Hall, August 30, 1946, Box 4, LRM. Mason herself wrote with pride of the CIO: "in racial practices, in democracy, and in political as well as economic objectives it is, to my way of thinking, the most progressive organization in America" (Lucy Randolph Mason to Wiley A. Hall, Executive Secretary of Richmond [Va.] Urban League, July 5, 1945, Box 4, LRM).

75. For example, one Baptist minister in Union, South Carolina, declared that while he was not against unions, he could not support the CIO "because of the Communist label attached to it" (Ramsay report of November 1950 on Rev. George H. Johnson of Buffalo Baptist Church in Union, Folder 155, Box 1568, Ramsay Papers).

76. Ministers played a role in defeating the SOC in elections at Lyman and Easley, South Carolina; see David Burgess, "The Role of the Churches in Relation to the CIO Southern Organizing Drive," Folder 16, Box 1556, Ramsay Papers. Ramsay was delighted when he found a sympathetic minister in Anderson, but the cleric in question told him that he could not risk being "a contact man for

you in this community" (Ramsay report of January 17, 1950, Folder 52, Box 1559, Ramsay Papers).

77. Ramsay referred to the "development of religion in industry," explaining that "we have had to fight industry's use of religious hate papers." Describing the progress of right-wing forces, Ramsay explained that "once the ties between the church and labor were very close, but that relationship has deteriorated to a dangerous level." The NAM had made "great inroads" into religious institutions, especially Protestant churches, meaning that sympathetic ministers stayed quiet and that some workers were beginning to get "screwy ideas" about unions (John Ramsay to Philip Murray, July 20, 1950, Folder 8, Box 1445, Ramsay Papers).

78. Paul Christopher to Van Bittner, August 23, 1949, Box 187, ODA.

79. The problem with many textile elections that the SOC contested with the AFL was that neither union emerged victorious. The two unions battled each other to an election in at least fourteen plants, and of these fourteen, the company won six. Many campaigns against the AFL were also long and drawn-out, wasting a considerable amount of resources. As Christopher wrote, raiding did not produce the rich pickings that CIO leaders anticipated: "I know the temptation is hard to resist when workers under an AF of L contract are not getting any benefits and they want CIO, but we haven't had any spectacular success in taking over AFL locals. With some few exceptions, it just doesn't pan out and it costs a lot of money" (Paul Christopher to Franz Daniel, October 25, 1948, Box 104, ODA). Election figures come from *Anderson Daily Mail*, May 29, 1952. Operation Dixie also suffered from continual financial shortages. After the cutbacks decided on at Atlantic City in December 1946, all those who were involved in textile campaigns operated under constant shortages. Bittner acknowledged in September 1947 that "every state is crying for men." Several elections were lost after the SOC failed to commit the resources that organizers called for. By March 1949, Christopher admitted that "frankly, and not for public information, we don't have all the money we need or expected to have for the southern campaign." See Van Bittner to William Smith, September 17, 1947, Box 53, ODA; Howard Porter to Paul Christopher, March 28, 1949, Box 184, ODA; and Paul Christopher to Howard Porter, March 25, 1949, Box 184, ODA.

80. Paul Christopher report of September 1951, Box 1875, Christopher Papers.

Chapter 3

1. Griffith, *Crisis of American Labor*, pp. 46–61, makes no mention of rising wages; instead, Griffith emphasizes paternalism and the legacy of union defeat as crucial in textile failure. My account makes clear that rising wages could have had the effect of strengthening the paternalism that Griffith identifies. Older accounts, particularly Marshall, *Labor in the South*, pp. 254–65, stress the drive's financial limitations.

2. Leighton interview.

3. McKee interview; David Burgess to author, September 3, 1994.

4. John Neal Organizing Report, May 22, 1948, Box 182, ODA; Minutes of Tennessee Staff Meeting of May 28, 1948, Box 167, ODA.

5. Edmund Ryan Organizing Report, October 26, 1946, Box 53, ODA; *Pell City News*, January 27, 1949.

6. Paul Christopher to William Smith, October 10, 1946, Box 53, ODA; Jim Prestwood Organizing Report, July 8, 1946, Box 76, ODA. Prestwood wrote from Gambrill Mill in Bessemer City that "Plant has raised wages and committee cannot get started signing cards" (Jim Prestwood Organizing Report, July 21, 1946, Box 76, ODA).

7. Carl Holt Organizing Report, August 26, 1950, Box 148, ODA; Jim Fullerton Organizing Report, January 4, 1949, Box 83, ODA; William Billingsley to A. LeSourd, May 4, 1949, Box 300, Greensboro JBP; Paul Christopher to Van Bittner, March 16, 1948, Box 129, ODA. Fullerton also reported that attempts to unionize a Chadwick Hoskins mill in Charlotte had failed because workers in the nonunion Number 4 plant "get the same wage and other benefits that the three mills under contract get" (Jim Fullerton Organizing Report, January 6, 1947, Box 83, ODA).

8. *Textile Labor*, April 22, 1949; Edmund Ryan Organizing Report, October 25, 1946, Box 53, ODA; H. D. Lisk to Bruno Rantane, January 25, 1947, Box 300, Greensboro JBP.

9. H. V. Batchelor Organizing Reports, September 23, 30, 1950, Box 148, ODA.

10. Rains article, source unknown, dated March 6, 1952, in clipping file, Box 271, ODA.

11. *Charlotte News* clipping dated April 23, 1952, in Box 271, ODA.

12. *Greensboro Daily News*, June 26–30, 1950.

13. "Labor Drives South," *Fortune*, November 1946, pp. 139, 234.

14. Detailed primary sources indicating how specific companies reacted to Operation Dixie either do not exist or are not open to the public. On the whole, the records of management in this period are far less revealing than union records. Nevertheless, the mouthpieces of the southern textile industry were the *Textile Bulletin*, and, to a lesser extent, the *Southern Textile News*. The *Bulletin* published viciously anti-union editorials throughout Operation Dixie that made frequent use of the race issue. These editorials reflected the rabid anti-unionism of editor David Clark. However, articles by different mill owners and personnel managers written in the *Bulletin* do provide a good gauge of the changes taking place in the thinking of southern textile executives. However self-serving the editorials might have been, what is significant is that in the past the mill owners had no hesitation in justifying traditional union-busting tactics, whereas now they espoused a more enlightened approach.

15. Annette Wright, "Aftermath of the General Textile Strike," pp. 82–84, 91, 111–12.

16. *Textile Bulletin*, October 1, December 1, 1946, May 15, 1947.

17. Gregory interview of September 27, 1993.

18. Thomas D. Yutzy to Rush S. Dickson of the American Yarn and Processing Company, April 13, 1951, and Charles A. Cannon to Rush S. Dickson, April 10, 1951, Box 25, Cannon Mills Papers, Special Collections Department, Perkins Library, Duke University. For the national context of industrial-relations thinking in the 1940s, see Harris, *Right to Manage*.

19. George Baldanzi to Van Bittner, June 19, 1946, Box 53, ODA; Katz, *Taft-Hartleyism in Southern Textiles*, p. 5.

20. *Textile Labor*, July 10, 1954; Barkin interview.

21. *Kannapolis Independent*, August 11, 1946; Boyd Payton to Emil Rieve, October 5, 1954, TWUA correspondence on microfilm at the George Meany Center, Silver Spring, Maryland; Peckenham, "Out in the Cold at Cannon Mills."

22. Griffith, *Crisis of American Labor*, pp. 48–49.

23. *Kannapolis Independent*, September 13 and 22, 1946. The loss of radio time was particularly important in a community where, as Smith wrote, "our house to house contacts have proven that these people listen to the radio very carefully" (William Smith to Van Bittner, August 8, 1946, Box 53, ODA). Draper Wood wrote about the inability to secure an office in Kannapolis: "We are working out of the office in Concord and that somewhat handicaps the work . . . by being 7 or 8 miles from Kannapolis" (Draper Wood, Report of June 30, 1946, Box 76, ODA). Griffith's account of the Kannapolis campaign argues that the SOC was unable to overcome this corporate dominance; see Griffith, *Crisis of American Labor*, pp. 49–61.

24. Nancy Blaine Organizing Report, July 20, 1946, Box 81, ODA; Dean Culver Organizing Reports, July 9, 1946, and September 17, 1946, Box 85, ODA.

25. Nancy Blaine Organizing Report, July 26, 1946, Box 85, ODA.

26. Dean Culver Organizing Reports, July 9, 1946, and September 17, 1946, Box 85, ODA.

27. *Textile Labor*, July 10, 1954; Griffith, *Crisis of American Labor*, pp. 46–61.

28. Dean Culver Organizing Report, September 17, 1946, Box 85, ODA.

29. *Kannapolis Independent*, July 25, 1946; *Concord Tribune*, September 16, 1946.

30. Leighton interview.

31. For example, worker Henry Mabrey wrote, "He [Charles Cannon] has raised our wages several times in the past year and I can't see why anyone would be dissatisfied" (*Kannapolis Independent*, August 28, 1946).

32. *Kannapolis Independent*, October 2, 1946; Ruth Gettinger to Allan Swim, July 17, 1946, Box 85, ODA.

33. Dean Culver Organizing Reports, September 17, 1946, undated, Box 85, ODA; A. William Bell to Dean Culver, August 25, 1946, Box 81, ODA.

34. Dean Culver Organizing Reports, July 9 and September 17, 1946, Box 85, ODA.

35. Dean Culver to William Smith, August 28, 1946, Box 85, ODA. Some community members supported the SOC, and the amount of community opposition was far less than in many other textile campaigns. See Dean Culver Organizing Report of July 9, 1946, Box 85, ODA.

36. Dean Culver to William Smith, August 28, 1946, Box 85, ODA; Dean Culver Organizing Report, July 9, 1946, Box 85, ODA; *Kannapolis Independent*, July 25, 1947.

37. *Textile Bulletin*, December 27, 1946; *Kannapolis Independent*, September 29, 1946. Many veterans wrote to the *Independent* praising "GI Town."

38. Charles Gillman to Paul Christopher, July 3, 1947, Box 191, ODA; Bruno

Rantane to Solomon Barkin, March 13, 1948, Box 295, Greensboro JBP.

39. 1950 TWUA Convention Proceedings, p. 84; 1948 TWUA Executive Council Report, p. 39.

40. Lucy Randolph Mason, "Cotton Textile Industry and Its Workers," Box 166, ODA; McKee interview. The popularity of noneconomic benefits among organized workers is developed further in Chapters 4 and 8.

41. Paul Christopher to Lucy Randolph Mason, July 7, 1947, Box 166, ODA; John Ramsay to Rev. John S. Steele, April 13, 1950, Folder 155, Box 1568, Ramsay Papers; Joe Pedigo interview E-11, SOHP.

42. Knight interview of October 26, 1993. The attempt of Operation Dixie to impose a northern pattern on the drive has been explored well by Barbara Griffith; see Griffith, *Crisis of American Labor*, pp. 3–11, 167–76.

43. *Textile Labor*, June 20, 1953; Barkin interview; Van Bittner to William Smith, September 30, 1947, Box 53, ODA; 1946 TWUA Convention Proceedings, p. 86.

44. *CIO News*, December 2, 1946, and November 17, 1947.

45. 1946 TWUA Convention Proceedings, pp. 3–4; 1948 TWUA Convention Proceedings, p. 74; *Textile Labor*, July 3, 1948.

46. Campbell, *Women at War with America*, pp. 103–4; Howard, "Tennessee in War and Peace," pp. 56–65; Dorothy Daniel to Paul Christopher, November 19, 1949, and February 22, 1947, Box 139, ODA.

47. Gabin, "Women Workers and the UAW," pp. 5–31; Clive, "Women Workers in World War II," pp. 44–72.

48. These points are developed in Chapters 6 and 8.

49. Helen Gregory Organizing Report, April 5, 1947, and March 6, 1948, Box 139, ODA.

50. Purnell Maloney Organizing Report, January 22, 1951, Box 167, ODA; Purnell Maloney Organizing Reports, March 24, 1948, and May 16 and 19, 1949, Box 166, ODA.

51. The activism of women workers in other locations is discussed in Chapters 4 and 6.

52. The amount of lasting change the war produced has been the subject of considerable historical debate. See Blum, *V Was for Victory*, and Polenberg, *War and Society*, for a full discussion of these issues. Nash, *American West Transformed*, and Boyden, "Where Outsized Paychecks Grow on Trees," pp. 253–59, show the dramatic economic impact of the war on the southwestern states and California.

53. Paul Christopher to John Riffe, April 10, 1951, Box 1875, Christopher Papers.

Chapter 4

1. Griffith, *Crisis of American Labor*, p. 22; Lloyd Vaughn to Nicholas Fayad, July 19, 1951, Box 107, ODA; *Textile Labor*, May 3, 1947; 1950 TWUA Convention Proceedings, p. 7; 1948 TWUA Executive Council Report, p. 48.

2. As Robert Zieger has written of the postwar strike wave, "Unlike the great steel strike of 1919–20 or the sit-down strikes of 1937, the post-war strikes

posed little threat to the very existence of the unions" (Zieger, *American Workers, American Unions*, p. 104).

3. The best overview of the recent literature on southern textile workers and its concern with worker culture is "Textile Workers and Historians," in Zieger, *Organized Labor in the Twentieth-Century South*, pp. 35–59. Recent works that emphasize worker culture and paternalism include Griffith, *Crisis of American Labor*, and Flamming, *Creating the Modern South*. The image of an acquiescent worker culture is ably challenged by Hall et al., *Like a Family*.

4. 1946 TWUA Executive Council Report, pp. 53–54; Knight interview, October 26, 1993; Groshong and McKee interviews; Scott Hoyman interview E-10, SOHP, p. 30.

5. Hodges, *New Deal Labor Policy*, pp. 165–67; *Gaffney Ledger*, August 28, 1945; Charles Puckett to Roy Lawrence, July 28, 1946, File 2A, Box 4, TWUA. In the *Ledger*, the company took an intransigent stand on the checkoff issue, claiming that it was "unalterably opposed . . . on fundamental grounds of principle."

6. Charles Puckett to Emil Rieve, November 13, 1946, File 2A, Box 4, TWUA; Charles Puckett to Roy Lawrence, August 24, 1946, File 2A, Box 4, TWUA.

7. Charles Puckett to Emil Rieve, November 13, 1946, File 2A, Box 4, TWUA.

8. *Textile Labor*, October 1956.

9. On Gaffney's status as a test case, the *Spartanburg Journal*, for example, reported that "all textile management in the South" were intensely interested in the outcome of the Gaffney strike (*Spartanburg Journal*, May 29, 1946).

10. *Gaffney Ledger*, May 25, 1946, and July 17, 1947.

11. 1946 TWUA Executive Council Report, pp. 50–54; *Gaffney Ledger*, October 2, 1945.

12. 1948 TWUA Executive Council Report, pp. 49–51; *N&O*, April 29, 1951; *Thomasville News Times*, March 3, 1947 (quoting the general manager of the Amazon Mill in Thomasville, North Carolina). One of the most prominent checkoff strikes was the long and unsuccessful battle at Dallas Manufacturing Company in Huntsville, Alabama. This began in 1947 because the company refused the checkoff, claiming that it was fundamentally opposed "on the grounds of principle." *Huntsville Times*, December 2, 1947.

13. *Southern Textile News*, August 15, 1946.

14. Orrell interview; Knight interview, October 26, 1993.

15. As discussed in Chapter 8, it is clear that unionized workers in Rockingham, North Carolina, looked to the union for benefits such as seniority and a grievance procedure. They supported it as a means of breaking arbitrary company control. Workers across the South were very conscious that union and nonunion wages were the same, especially as this fact was emphasized in management propaganda.

16. 1948 TWUA Executive Council Report, p. 50; Knight interview, March 23, 1994.

17. NLRB Summary of Siler City strike in Box 300, Greensboro JBP; Charles Auslander to William Pollock, December 8, 1949, Box 277, Cherokee JBP; response of Nellie Frady on March 8, 1950, in Series 6, Box 9, Clifton Manufacturing Company Papers; Charles Auslander, report of January 30, 1950, in Box 277, Cherokee JBP.

18. Barkin, "Regional Significance," pp. 395–411; Charles Puckett to Emil Rieve, March 19, 1947, File 2A, Box 4, TWUA; Roy Lawrence to Emil Rieve, December 16, 1947, File 2A, Box 4, TWUA; notes of private meetings of textile executives held at Greensboro (N.C.) Country Club, taken by the Dan River Mills company representative in "Contract Negotiations 1956" folder, DRMC Papers.

19. Charles Auslander to Paul Christopher, September 14, 1950, Box 323, SCSDP; TWUA Press Release of August 17, 1950, Box 323, SCSDP.

20. Bruno Rantane to William Pollock, April 19, 1948, and May 12, 1948, Box 300, Greensboro JBP; report of August 5, 1948, case number 484-229, FMCS. Regarding the way that strikebreakers broke the Siler City strike, by August the strike had been broken so effectively by outside labor that a federal mediator concluded, "The company has replaced a great number of striking employees. . . . The plant is operating two full shifts, a sufficient number to produce as much material as management has sales for. . . . There is no inclination on the part of management to meet, the case has been kept open hoping the break would come but it seems further away than ever."

21. Nancy Blaine to "Folks," April 27, 1947, McKee Papers.

22. Larry Rogin interview, TWUA Oral History Project, TWUA; Cahoon interview; Raynor, "Unionism in the Southern Textile Industry," pp. 81–85.

23. 1950 TWUA Executive Council Report, pp. 26–36, 30.

24. CIO News, November 28, 1949. The arguments of the TWUA against Taft-Hartley were developed in Taft-Hartleyism in Southern Textiles, a lengthy document written by Katz that detailed how the act had encouraged refusal to bargain.

25. Cahoon and Conn interviews.

26. Textile Labor, May 3, 1947.

27. 1954 TWUA Convention Proceedings, pp. 62–63.

28. Charles Auslander Report, January 30, 1950, Box 277, Cherokee JBP; Charles Auslander to James J. Kelly, July 24, 1950, Box 319, SCSDP; minutes of the meetings of the Cherokee-Spartanburg Joint Board, April 1950, Box 274, Cherokee JBP.

29. For example, an organizer at Woodside Mills in Greenville, South Carolina, reported that the local agent of the company financing the sale of the mill-village houses "is using his position as mortgagee to strike fear into the hearts of the strikers that unless they returned to work they would lose their homes through foreclosure proceedings." From a strike at Safie Manufacturing Company in Rockingham, North Carolina, union representative R. C. Thomas wrote, "There are some things that I have not been able to provide for these people as we would like, meaning hospital bills, insurance, payments, clothes, and shoes." Illustrating the type of sacrifices that strikers had to make, Thomas, who continually overspent his relief budget, explained in one report that "I gave the strikers chickens as a morale builder, when morale seemed low, the only meat we had given them to speak of was fatback." See Isadore Katz to James J. Kelly, September 8, 1950, Box 323, SCSDP; R. C. Thomas to R. R. Lawrence, July 23, 1947, Box 83, ODA; R. C. Thomas to William Pollock, August 13, 1947, Box 83, ODA.

30. Nancy Blaine to Folks, April 27, 1947, McKee Papers.

31. Illustrating the chaotic situation that prevailed in many communities, the NLRB described a 1949 strike at Anchor Rome Mills in Rome, Georgia, where a hundred workers came from the mill "armed with sticks, hammers, wrenches, hatchets, blackjacks, and a variety of other weapons." Many scuffles took place between women workers: for example, nonstrikers Margaret Mills and Dollie Young assaulted striker Nettie Edwards, "Mills striking her in the face, Young pulling her hair and kicking her in the back" (*TWUA v. Anchor Rome Mills*, 1949, 86 NLRB, p. 1149).

32. *Thomasville News-Times*, October 9, 1947, and March 25, 1948.

33. Management reports of April 11 and April 7, 1950, Series 6, Box 9, Clifton Manufacturing Company Papers.

34. 1948 TWUA Executive Council Report, pp. 48–54; 1950 TWUA Executive Council Report, pp. 26–36.

35. 1948 TWUA Executive Council Report, pp. 99–100.

36. 1948 TWUA Executive Council Report, p. 100; 1950 TWUA Convention Proceedings, pp. 6–7.

37. One common company flyer, for example, declared, "Organizers for the CIO have told you about the wonderful life in the TWUA but, have they told you about CIO LOST STRIKES?" (flyer in Oversized Files, North Carolina Organizing Committee Papers, ODA).

38. Charles Auslander, Report of December 14, 1950, File 2A, Box 11, TWUA.

39. Larry Rogin interview, TWUA Oral History Project, TWUA.

40. TWUA 1948 Executive Council Report, p. 50.

41. Lewis Conn to All Staff Members, November 30, 1949, in Box 300, Greensboro JBP.

42. *Tarboro Daily Southerner*, June 6, 1949; Robert S. Cahoon to Reed S. Johnson of the NLRB, October 27, 1949, NLRB Case Number 34-CA-149, Box 150, NLRB.

43. Testimony of L. D. Lilley, NLRB Case Number 34-CA-149, Box 150, NLRB.

44. Statement of C. B. Stancil, Vol. 2, Box 180, TWUA. Stancil explained that the company's insistence that they would only meet international representatives also made life very difficult "because TWUA representatives are not able to get into Tarboro as often as needed."

45. Dawson and Worrell interviews; *TWUA v. Hart Cotton Mills*, 1950, NLRB 91, p. 747; NLRB Case Number 34-CA-149, Box 150, p. 100 of write-up, NLRB.

46. *N&O*, November 6, 1949 (includes reprint of November 1947 *Fortune* article on E. P. Cave). Cave, a sixty-seven-year-old executive, was described by *Fortune* as "the compass, quadrant, and sextant of Ely and Walker today." He had a long history of defeating unions. When the AFL had tried to organize one of Cave's mills in Philadelphia in the 1920s, he responded by liquidating the mill. Other attempts to unionize Ely and Walker plants met a similar fate. They reflected the personality of a man who "often indulges in private denunciations of 'outside' labor unions and the 'Communistic' tendencies of the Roosevelt and Truman administrations."

47. Testimony of Lewis Conn, NLRB Case Number 34-CA-149, Box 150, NLRB.

48. The maintenance-of-membership clause was common in contracts directed by the NWLB. It prohibited any member of the union from withdrawing from the union during the life of the contract.

49. Lewis Conn testimony, Box 150, NLRB; *TWUA v. Hart Cotton Mills*, 1950, NLRB 91, p. 744.

50. Lewis Conn testimony, Box 150, NLRB; *TWUA v. Hart Cotton Mills*, 1950, NLRB 91, pp. 733–50.

51. M. Weldon Rogers to Marcus Carter, February 17, 1949, Box 150, NLRB; Flamming, *Creating the Modern South*, p. 200; *TWUA v. Hart Cotton Mills*, 1950, NLRB 91, p. 739.

52. *TWUA v. Hart Cotton Mills*, 1950, NLRB 91, p. 738; Marcus Carter testimony, Box 150, NLRB. The fears of unionized companies of unorganized competition will be discussed further in Chapter 7.

53. Harris, *Right to Manage*, pp. 106–10; Marcus Carter testimony, Box 150, NLRB; *TWUA v. Hart Cotton Mills*, 1950, NLRB 91, pp. 747–48.

54. Carter himself explained, "We stated to the union that in principle, we didn't agree with checking off union dues for the reason that the checkoff system came into being during the war and was directed by the War Labor Board for the promise by labor that they would not strike during the war." Carter argued the standard line that union members should be willing to pay dues voluntarily (Marcus Carter testimony, Box 150, NLRB).

55. Large advertisements were placed in the local procompany local newspaper, the *Tarboro Daily Southerner*, stating that "we don't mind providing houses at a low rent . . . but when those persons are unwilling to go to work, we must protect ourselves" (*Tarboro Daily Southerner*, July 6 and September 13, 1949).

56. Supervisor Sine Robinson, for example, told striker Joe Lyon that "if you don't go back, you won't have a job and furthermore Mr Carter said he won't sign a contract, he said before he would sign he would move the mill." Similar threats were made to many others, while some were promised extra vacation pay if they returned (Joe Lyon testimony, Box 150, NLRB).

57. The hostility of "uptown" opinion to southern textile workers was first emphasized in Pope, *Millhands and Preachers*. On the mill owner's dominance of the community and its consequences for union activity in recent scholarship, see, for example, Hodges, *New Deal Labor Policy*, p. 38; Griffith, *Crisis of American Labor*, pp. 45–61. Clark, "TWUA in a Southern Mill Town," pp. 296–330 illustrates the role of state power and community opposition in breaking the strike at Harriet-Henderson Cotton Mills in Henderson, North Carolina, between 1958 and 1960. Clark shows that Governor Luther Hodges played a key role in breaking the strike and that many North Carolina governors before him had acted in a similar way.

58. Lewis Conn to All Local Unions, November 30, 1949, Box 300, Greensboro JBP; Dawson interview.

59. Lewis Conn to Emil Rieve, June 4, 1949, File 2A, Box 9, TWUA; Lewis Conn to Emil Rieve, September 2, 1949, File 2A, Box 9, TWUA; Lewis Conn

testimony before the House of Representatives Special Subcommittee of the Committee on Education and Labor, Atlanta, November 21, 1949, Box 150, NLRB; Lewis Conn to All Locals, July 6, 1949, Box 300, Greensboro JBP.

60. Responses of Gurney Mitchell, Walter Aldeman, Narcissus Porter, and Graham Griffin to supervisors' visits in Box 175, NLRB.

61. Dawson, Worrell, Wells, Gurkins, and Hoard interviews.

62. One, for example, explained that "before the union, on my job, I was taken off my set of speeders, because I complained about the lack of oiling being done to the steps of the speeders. Because I complained, someone else was given my set and I was given one of the worst ones." The worker continued, "When my set became vacant again I asked to have it back. The overseer walked away from me, refusing to speak to me, or discuss it. After the union, this set again was vacant and by seniority I was awarded the set, when I bid on it" (Charles Stancil testimony, Box 150, NLRB).

63. Lester Matthews testimony, Box 150, NLRB. Another striker wrote Governor Kerr Scott begging him to intervene in the dispute so that workers could have a union "and the chance to work and live like people" (Lottie Wade to Governor Kerr Scott, August 8, 1949, Box 21, Scott Papers).

64. Cahoon interview; testimony of Charlie Stancil, Henry Byrd, Melvin Hoard, J. C. Hughes, and Sylvester Sawyer, Box 255, TWUA; Dawson interview; *Textile Labor*, September 17, 1949. Among those who remembered how the community got closer during the strike was Gerald Worrell: "during the strike we got to know each other much better, the community got closer" (Worrell interview). Hall et al., *Like a Family*, highlights similar conclusions about how the closeness of southern textile communities sustained workers' resistance to company domination.

65. Knight interview of March 23, 1994. The strong support given to the strike by women reinforces other postwar contract strikes, as noted on pp. 109–10.

66. *Tarboro Daily Southerner*, May 21, 1949; Ray Holland interview. Another former striker, Floyd Morris, recalled a local grocer who also helped strikers a lot: "he knew that if anybody had a wife and children that were hungry, it's bad" (Morris interview).

67. Taylor interview; Knight interview, October 26, 1993. Mae Dawson felt that the plant's outside ownership also motivated strikers: "if it had been local, we would have got a better response . . . because people feel like it's something they own, but all this was foreign" (Dawson interview).

68. Tarboro Strike File, Box 21, Scott Papers; *TWUA v. Hart Cotton Mills*, 1950, NLRB 91, pp. 746, 757–58; Lewis Conn testimony, Box 150, NLRB.

69. *Textile Labor*, July 16, 1949, wrote that "newspaper opinion in North Carolina continued on the side of the strikers"; *N&O*, June 4, 1949; *Durham Sun*, June 20, 1949.

70. *Tarboro Daily Southerner*, June 29, 1949; *N&O*, October 2, 1949; testimony of Minnie Gunter and Donald McCracken, Box 175, NLRB; Dawson interview; Worrell interview. Striker Minnie Gunter, for example, rebuffed the visits of mill superintendent Fowler because "the union is feeding me good, paying my insurance, light bills, and taking care of the clinic."

71. Wier testimony, Box 150, NLRB.

72. Lewis Conn to All Local Unions, November 30, 1949, Box 300, Greensboro JBP. Conn claimed that "the fight still continues. . . . We may not have a contract, but we DO have a union which will fight."

73. Knight interview, March 23, 1994; Worrell and Hathaway interviews.

74. Morris interview; Lewis Conn to Miles E. Baker of TWUA Local 316, April 18, 1950, Volume 2, Box 255, TWUA; Lewis Conn to Emil Rieve, November 7, 1950, File 2A, Box 9, TWUA; Robert S. Cahoon to David Findling of the NLRB, January 8, 1951, Box 150, NLRB.

75. Robert Cahoon to Isadore Katz, August 27, 1951, Volume 2, Box 179, TWUA; Lewis Conn to George J. Bott, General Counsel of the NLRB, August 2, 1951, Volume 2, Box 179, TWUA; NLRB memorandum from Reed Johnston, November 6, 1949, Box 150, NLRB.

76. *Tarboro Daily Southerner*, December 10 and 20, 1952. Since Ely and Walker sold the mill, it has been owned by Burlington Industries and J. P. Stevens. It is currently run by Dixie Yarn.

77. Andrews, Worrell, and Morris interviews.

78. Andrews, Dawson, Gurkins, and Morris interviews.

79. Wells, Hoard, Dawson, Worrell, and Edmondson interviews.

80. Hathaway, Worrell, and Dawson interviews. In the absence of company records, it is difficult to prove that the company made these changes as a result of the strike. What is clear is that all those interviewed, including those who did not support the union, felt that conditions improved after the strike.

81. Hoard, Wells, and Dawson interviews.

82. Murray Kempton, "An Autopsy on a Strike," *New York Post*, December 6, 1949; *N&O*, May 19, 1950; Lewis Conn testimony, Box 150, NLRB.

Chapter 5

1. 1952 TWUA Executive Council Report, pp. 54–56; *Greensboro Daily News*, April 2, 1951. Contract Negotiating Meeting of March 23, 1951, DRMC Papers. The 1934 strike was conducted by the AFL's United Textile Workers (UTW).

2. This argument is put forward by Irons, "Testing the New Deal," pp. 271–74.

3. Solomon Barkin interview, TWUA Oral History Project, TWUA. Barkin's extensive publications were not restricted to textile unionism but covered a wide variety of labor and economic issues.

4. Sol Stetin and Ken Fiester interviews, TWUA Oral History Project, TWUA.

5. The 1934 strike has been the subject of some excellent recent scholarship. In addition to Irons's thesis, works that cover the strike in detail include Hall et al., *Like a Family*, pp. 289–357, and Hodges, *New Deal Labor Policy*, pp. 86–119. Hall's work makes use of a substantial body of letters written to federal authorities to provide a clear insight into the grievances of workers in the strike. Flamming, *Creating the Modern South*, covers the 1934 strike in Dalton, Georgia. An older study—Galambos, *Competition and Cooperation*—deals with the strike from the point of view of the industry. In contrast, the only work that deals with the 1951 strike in any detail is Williams, "Split in the Textile Workers Union of America." This work deals with the relationship of the 1951 strike to the Rieve-Baldanzi split. My account of the 1951 strike draws heavily on FMCS records

and records from the TWUA Papers in Madison, Wisconsin, including an oral history project conducted between 1978 and 1981 during which most of the TWUA's main officials from this period were interviewed. These interviews have also been used in other chapters. The Danville part of the story involves the private company papers of Dan River Mills and the private papers of Norris Tibbetts, a TWUA official in Danville. Tibbetts and another TWUA official, Boyd Payton, both wrote detailed diaries of the strike. Neither of these collections have been used before.

6. *Southern Textile News*, January 20, 1951.

7. The crucial cost-of-living formula was indeed copied direct from the contract between the electrical workers and General Electric. A similar formula had also been written into the pioneering auto industry contracts of the late 1940s— contracts that also included severance pay, another TWUA demand (Zieger, *American Workers, American Unions*, p. 148).

8. 1950 TWUA Convention Proceedings, pp. 4–6; 1948 TWUA Convention Proceedings, p. 11; *Durham Morning Herald*, April 2, 1951; *Textile Labor*, September 20, 1947.

9. Stabile, *Activist Unionism*, pp. 159–63; 1950 TWUA Executive Council Report, p. 22; *New Bedford Standard-Times*, July 13, 1949. Recent studies have shown that the decline of the industry in New England was not simply related to the wage differential. In many cases, mill owners preferred to liquidate mills and invest in other areas rather than to modernize their mills. See Hartford, "Unions, Labor Markets, and Deindustrialization."

10. 1948 TWUA Convention Proceedings, p. 7; Report on Southern Strike to Executive Council, June 26, 1951, Box 1, Section 5A, TWUA; Solomon Barkin interview. The interest of the UTW leadership in establishing uniform labor standards is emphasized by Janet Irons in her study of the 1934 strike. See Irons, "Testing the New Deal," especially pp. 3–27.

11. The *CIO News* reported triumphantly, "Textile Workers End [the] Dixie Differential" that "has long been a source of severe irritation to the CIO Textile Workers." This was an exaggeration, since New England workers still received more costly fringe benefits than southern workers, even though basic pay rates in some leading southern plants were on a par with the North (*CIO News*, November 10, 1947).

12. *Textile Labor*, February 22 and March 8, 1947; 1948 TWUA Executive Council Report, pp. 55–57; Solomon Barkin interview. Fall River and New Bedford were, at this time, major textile centers in Massachusetts.

13. *Textile Labor*, November 8, 1947, August 7, and July 3, 1948; 1948 TWUA Convention Proceedings, p. 74. The *Charlotte News*, for example, praised the union's effort to raise southern wages: "The Textile Workers Union of America deserves credit for the general 10 percent wage increase that now seems to be assured throughout the region" (*Charlotte News*, February 17, 1947).

14. 1952 TWUA Executive Council Report, p. 50; Stanback, "Short Run Instability," p. 7; Cross, *Dan River Runs Deep*, p. 15. The mill margin is the difference between the price mills paid for raw cotton and the price they received for their products.

15. *Charlotte Observer*, February 16, 1951; *Durham Morning Herald*, Febru-

ary 28, 1951; transcripts of meetings of southern strike leaders on April 16, 1951, and April 18, 1951, File 1A, Box 20, TWUA; *Danville Register*, April 1, 1951; Emil Rieve to Senator Burnet R. Maybank, April 16, 1951, Box 2588, FMCS.

16. *Greensboro Daily News*, March 16, 1951; 1952 TWUA Executive Council Report, p. 54; Tibbetts interview, March 9, 1994.

17. Solomon Barkin to author, January 10, 1994; Executive Council Meeting of April 8, 1951, File 1A, Box 20, TWUA. Seabury Stanton warned the union that "the increase we have proposed will place upon the mills a burden which will be unbearable in times of normal competition unless the TWUA fulfills its responsibility of increasing by at least a similar amount the wages of the textile mills of the South" (quoted in *Daily News Record*, March 15, 1951).

18. The full locations of the big five were: Dan River Mills, in Danville, Virginia; Cone Mills, in Greensboro, North Carolina; Erwin Mills, based in Durham, North Carolina; the Marshall Field chain, based in Leaksville, North Carolina; and the Lowenstein chain, with mills across the region, the main plant being Rock Hill Printing and Finishing Company, a giant bleachery in Rock Hill, South Carolina. See the *Huntsville Times*, April 1, 1951. The 2 percent offer was given by Dan River on March 31 and was the only offer the union secured from negotiations.

19. Williams, "Split in the Textile Workers Union of America," pp. 50–53; *Greensboro Daily News*, April 6, 1951; *Leaksville News*, March 15, 1951.

20. Erwin Mills File, Report of March 30, 1951, Box 2578, FMCS; Executive Council Meeting of April 8, 1951, File 1A, Box 20, TWUA; Julius Fry to James Bamford, February 21, 1951, Box 322, Greensboro JBP.

21. *Danville Bee*, May 5, 1951; letter to employees from Harold Whitcomb, general manager of Fieldcrest Mills, in "Fieldcrest Mills" folder, Eden Public Library, Eden, North Carolina; Report of March 30, 1951, Fieldcrest Mills File, Box 2578, FMCS; *Greensboro Daily News*, April 6, 1951; Executive Council Meeting of April 18, 1951, File 1A, Box 20, TWUA.

22. Emil Rieve to Senator Burnet R. Maybank, April 16, 1951, Box 2588, FMCS; 1952 TWUA Executive Council Report, pp. 51–53.

23. The *Daily News Record* gives solid coverage to the ACMI conference of March 29–31, 1951. Solomon Barkin regards this shift in management tactics in 1951 as crucial and adds that "nobody has up to now unfolded the reasons and meetings at which the policy of resistance was set." The Whitcomb quotation comes from the "Fieldcrest Mills" folder, Eden Public Library, Eden, North Carolina.

24. *Textile Bulletin*, April 1951; *Southern Textile News*, February 24, 1951.

25. Emanuel Boggs interview, TWUA Oral History Project, TWUA; 1952 Executive Council Meeting File, meeting of June 21, 1952, File 2A, Box 7, TWUA.

26. Sol Stetin interview, TWUA Oral History Project, TWUA. Council member Larry Rogin thought that "the influence of the political situation on the strike was that both sides were being too macho. There was an air of desperation, you had to find out could the union make a creative wage movement in the South. . . . If it hadn't been for the fight, it might have been that calmer heads would have prevailed." A TWUA vice president in the Midwest, Bill Gordon, expressed similar feelings: "they should never have pulled that strike. It was a political strike to

satisfy the needs of the time" (Larry Rogin and Bill Gordon interviews, TWUA Oral History Project, TWUA).

27. North Carolina director Lewis Conn, for example, claimed two days before the strike that "the strike will extend to some Cone mills that are not organized." The director of the union in Greensboro, North Carolina, Bill Billingsley, was also influential in pushing for a strike. He claimed that TWUA could complete the unionization of the Cone Mills chain if it struck for the 1951 demands, and he argued that the union had not been militant enough in the past (Williams, "Split in the Textile Workers Union of America," p. 60; Larry Rogin interview, TWUA Oral History Project, TWUA).

28. Larry Rogin interview, TWUA Oral History Project, TWUA.

29. The strike was mainly concentrated in Virginia and North Carolina. In North Carolina, the struck plants were Erwin Mills in Erwin, Neuse, Cooleemee, and Durham; Harriet-Henderson Cotton Mills in Henderson; Cone Manufacturing Company in Greensboro, Haw River, and Gibsonville; Marshall Field Company in Leaksville, Draper, and Spray; Lowenstein Manufacturing Company in Rockingham; Kendall Mills in Paw Creek; Wilkes-Barre Lace in Charlotte; Calvine Cotton Mills and the Spatex Corporation in Charlotte; Highland Cotton Mills in High Point; Pee Dee Manufacturing Company in Rockingham; Borden Manufacturing Company in Goldsboro; A. D. Julliard Company in Brookford; Royal Cotton Mills in Wake Forest; and Golden Belt Manufacturing Company in Durham. In South Carolina, the affected mills were Pacific Mills in Columbia; Kendall Mills in Newberry; and Industrial Cotton Mills and the Rock Hill Printing and Finishing Company in Rock Hill. In Tennessee the only mill affected was Holliston Mills in Kingsport. In Georgia, the affected plants were A. D. Julliard Company in Rome and Aragon and Cedartown Textiles in Cedartown. In Alabama, the strike affected Textron Southern Inc. in Cordova; Huntsville Manufacturing Company in Huntsville; and Lincoln Mills in Huntsville. In Louisiana the strike affected another Lowenstein mill, Lane Cotton Mills in New Orleans (report of May 17, 1951, Box 2578, FMCS).

30. *Textile Bulletin*, May 1951. The point about companies shutting down for the first few months of strikes is brought out in Chapter 5.

31. Danville business agent Norris Tibbetts wrote privately that "we would not be so impudent to suggest that there has been any collusion between Southern textile employers, but through some strange coincidence, all mills with the exceptions of Dan River closed their gates at the beginning of the strike and kept them closed until the latter part of last week. This turned loose some 40,000 prospective workers who were . . . available for strikebreaking in Dan River" (Norris Tibbetts to "Friends and Relations," May 11, 1951, in Tibbetts Papers).

32. The letters assumed a standard form for particular jobs, such as, "It has come to our attention that you are a qualified spinning frame doffer and that you are unemployed. We have openings for doffers and will be glad to have you come to our Employment Office . . . for an interview" (letter of April 7, 1951, from W. C. Daniel, Employment Manager of Dan River Mills, in folder labeled "Strike, April, 1951," DRMC Papers).

33. Southern textile management did act with a considerable degree of unity during this period. Nathaniel Gregory, who was vice president of Erwin Mills

at this time, recalled that the major southern companies acted together very closely in these years, especially when it came to deciding wages or dealing with the union. Every time the union petitioned for a wage increase, executives would meet and decide what course should be taken. Mill presidents such as Russell Newton of Dan River and Harold Whitcomb of Marshall Field were close friends and kept each other constantly informed, although "90% of it was on the golf-course or by telephone." The records of Dan River Mills also reveal that every contract change or union demand in other mills was transmitted to the personnel office. In May 1956, for example, Lowenstein wrote Dan River that they would increase wages "if five out of the nine companies below gave a wage increase." There were also frequent, confidential meetings of executives from the major union and nonunion southern companies. It is difficult, however, to firmly establish that management made a conscious decision to concentrate their efforts in the 1951 strike on Dan River, because most decisions were made orally, and those written records which do exist have often been discarded or are beyond the access of historians. Interestingly, Gregory recalled that there were tensions between union and nonunion executives, with relatively liberal companies such as Erwin regarding nonunion giants such as Elliott Springs and Charles Cannon as "dictators" (Nathaniel Gregory interview, February 28, 1994, in Durham, North Carolina; "Contract Negotiations 1956" folder, DRMC Papers).

34. Transcript of meeting of southern strike leaders on April 16, 1951, File 1A, Box 20, TWUA.

35. Thomas D. Yutzy to Rush S. Dickson of the American Yarn and Processing Company, April 13, 1951; C. A. Cannon to Rush S. Dickson, April 10, 1951, Box 25, Cannon Mills Papers, Special Collections Department, Perkins Library, Duke University.

36. Harold Whitcomb letter, "Fieldcrest Mills" folder, Eden Public Library; *Danville Register*, April 1, 1951; *Leaksville News*, April 19, 1951.

37. Heale, *American Anti-Communism*, p. 155; Fried, *Nightmare in Red*, pp. 113–19; Zieger, *American Workers, American Unions*, pp. 133–34.

38. *Lanett Valley Daily Times-News*, April 3, 1951; *Albany Herald*, April 4, 1951; *Leaksville News*, May 10, 1951.

39. *Brockton Enterprise and Times*, May 10, 1951. From the New England textile state of Maine, for example, the *Lewiston Sun* expressed its hope that the strike would be successful, because a further widening of the regional pay differential "has implications for the future of northern mills that are not good" (*Lewiston Sun*, April 4, 1951).

40. *Danville Bee*, May 5, 1951; *Anderson Daily Mail*, May 29, 1952.

41. For the Wake Forest incident, see the *Greensboro Daily News* and the *N&O* for April 28, 1951. Erwin Mills criticized Davie County sheriff Alex Tucker at their Cooleemee plant, for example, for failing to enforce law and order at the mill. The management of the Royal Cotton Mill also criticized local law enforcement officers. For coverage of the violence in Greensboro, see the *Greensboro Daily News*, April 1–May 5, 1951. For a discussion of the mill owners' close links to law enforcement officers before the war, and especially before the New Deal, see Hodges, *New Deal Labor Policy*, p. 39.

42. *Chattanooga News-Free Press*, April 18, 1951; *Fort Worth Press*, May 2, 1951.

43. The union had never managed to secure a strong position in any of the Cone plants, where overall union membership stood at around 55 percent. The company's large Proximity plant, where large numbers of workers had broken the picket lines, only had around 41 percent union membership and had narrowly survived two recent attempts to decertify the union. The union had gone ahead with the strike in the hope that it would help it to secure new members, but this had not happened. Rieve himself was philosophical about the Cone situation. He told the meeting that Cone was "lost" and concluded that this was because although the union had won elections, "we still didn't have the majority of people in the union." Transcripts of meeting of southern strike leaders on April 16, 1951, File 1A, Box 20, TWUA; Bruno Rantane report of December 1948 on membership in Cone Mills, Box 282, Greensboro JBP.

44. Boyd Payton's "Diary of the Danville Strike," pp. 20 and 42; transcript of meeting of southern strike leaders of April 16, 1951, File 1A, Box 20, TWUA; *Greensboro Daily News*, March 25, 1951.

45. 1952 TWUA Convention Proceedings, p. 10.

46. Transcripts of meetings of southern strike leaders on April 16 and 18, 1951, in File 1A, Box 20, TWUA.

47. Dan River president Russell Newton "stated frankly that his company had no desire to reach an accord with union officials, but preferred that the strike be permitted to run its course" (report of April 25, 1951, Box 2578, FMCS).

48. Transcript of meeting of southern strike leaders on April 18, 1951, File 1A, Box 20, TWUA Records.

49. This first objection referred to the precedent of World War II, when the FMCS had acted as a transmission agency for pay disputes. In 1951, however, no method of transmitting cases to the board had been established (report of May 5, 1951, Box 2578, FMCS).

50. Rieve's tactic gave ammunition to the charge heard across the South that the strike was forced on workers from above and did not reflect any real grievances. The manager of Gold-Tex Fabrics Corporation in Rock Hill, South Carolina, for example, declared that the strike was one of the national TWUA against the government. He typified the powerlessness that many smaller mills felt in the dispute: "this dispute is not one between Gold-Tex and its employees or a local matter and we know of no means to settle a National dispute" (*Rock Hill Evening Herald*, April 5, 1951).

51. For criticism of Gorman and the UTW, see particularly Irons, "Testing the New Deal." Irons argues that the UTW leaders failed to understand the grievances of southern textile workers and were seduced by the prospect that the federal government would help them win their demands.

52. Hall et al., *Like a Family*, p. 350; transcript of meeting of southern strike leaders on May 5, 1951, File 1A, Box 20, TWUA; *Textile Bulletin*, May 1951. Dan River president Russell Newton wrote that mediation "would serve no useful purpose so far as this company is concerned."

53. Transcript of meeting of southern strike leaders on May 5, 1951, File 1A, Box 20, TWUA.

54. *Textile Bulletin*, May 1951. Not surprisingly, the tripartite mediation panel set up as a means of settling the strike achieved little. Despite protests from William Pollock that the panel should have assumed "responsibility for the solution of this dispute," F. O. Clarkson, the public member of the panel, pointed out that the TWUA should be grateful for the panel because "the fact that it was appointed had a good effect in bringing about an end to a disastrous strike." The panel did not see its functions as extending any further; it argued that since the strike had failed to effectively halt defense production, the union could not present a valid case for certification of the dispute to the Wage Stabilization Board. Its main suggestion was merely to offer itself for mediation purposes in ongoing textile disputes (Cyrus Ching to William Pollock, December 13, 1951, and F. O. Clarkson to William Pollock, November 30, 1951, Box 2588, FMCS).

55. Larry Rogin interview, TWUA Oral History Project, TWUA; Norris Tibbetts to Friends and Relations, May 11, 1951, Tibbetts Papers; 1950 TWUA Convention Proceedings, p. 6.

56. Norris Tibbetts to Friends and Relations, May 11, 1951, Tibbetts Papers; *Textile Bulletin*, May 1951; *Greensboro Daily News*, May 7, 1951; George Baldanzi to Larry Rogin, March 24, 1952, Volume 2, Box 11, TWUA.

57. Transcript of meeting of southern strike leaders on May 5, 1951, File 1A, Box 20, TWUA.

Chapter 6

1. This account relies on a mixture of these company and union sources, together with press coverage and oral interviews.

2. The National Union of Textile Workers (NUTW), for example, selected Dan River as the base for the southern organizing drive that it conducted between 1898 and 1900. The AFL's United Textile Workers (UTW) also concentrated on Danville in their southern organizing drive launched in 1929 (Hall et al., *Like a Family*, pp. 101, 217–20).

3. For information on the 1930 strike in Danville, see Smith, *Mill on the Dan*, pp. 294–324. It is important to recognize that many of the union's wartime gains, as in Danville, were made on shaky wartime foundations and overextended the union beyond its natural power.

4. Smith, *Mill on the Dan*, p. 395. Labor journalist Mary Heaton Vorse called Danville the "gateway to the South" in a 1951 article titled " 'Tired of Being Pushed Around,' Say Danville Strikers," April 26, 1951, File 1A, Box 20, TWUA.

5. This description is based on the author's experiences in Danville. Details of Schoolfield's annexation by the city of Danville come from Cross, *Dan River Runs Deep*, p. 9. For information on Danville's tobacco past, see Smith, *Mill on the Dan*, pp. 7–9. Details of Dan River operations are drawn from "Fisher and Rudge Brief for Negotiations" folder, Summer 1951, DRMC Papers. The Dan River company records, a private collection held in the Personnel Building in Schoolfield, is not formally catalogued. It is arranged by titled folders, and this is how I will identify the information I cite.

6. As late as June 1947, for example, Dan River president G. S. Harris declared his opposition to the checkoff, claiming that it "enables a small minority

of militant bullies to dominate a situation in industry," taking away from the majority "the freedom of action to which they are entitled" (G. S. Harris to L. L. Moore, June 6, 1947, in Smith, *Mill on the Dan*, p. 501).

7. Danville also got what no other local union in the South had—a full-time industrial engineer, Bob Scherbak, who helped in overcoming workload problems. Danville also had four full-time business agents. Boggs remembered that the union and the company were able to settle grievances "rather effectively" (Emanuel Boggs interview, TWUA Oral History Project, TWUA).

8. There were, in fact, three Dan River locals—Dan River, Riverside, and a separate union for black workers, who made up around 15 percent of the workforce (Emanuel Boggs interview, TWUA Oral History Project, TWUA). The TWUA's project interviewed Boggs in 1981. My description is based on my own interview with Boggs in 1993. Boggs remembered that he was appointed in Danville because "this was such an important part of the textile union that there was a feeling on the part of the national union that anyone who was in charge there had to be someone with enough trade union background to handle the job."

9. Tibbetts interview of March 7, 1994; transcript of contract negotiations meeting of July 27, 1948, DRMC Papers; "Contract Negotiations, 1946" folder, DRMC Papers; transcript of contract negotiations meeting of March 23, 1951, DRMC Papers. Information on union membership comes from a report written by Lewis Conn to Emil Rieve on June 6, 1947, File 2A, Box 4, TWUA.

10. Indeed, in 1946 Dan River made a profit of $9.96 million, and profits rose to $15.10 million in 1948. After a short recession in 1949, high profits were restored in 1950, due mainly to the outbreak of the Korean War. To put these postwar profits in perspective, it is worth noting that even during World War II, a time of good business, Dan River never made more than $1.54 million of profit ("Basic Wage and Cost Data: 1950 Negotiations" folder, DRMC Papers).

11. Transcript of contract negotiations meeting of April 4, 1952, DRMC Papers.

12. The Frank Talbott comment comes from the transcript of a contract negotiations meeting of March 23, 1951, and Browder's comments come from transcript of contract negotiations meeting of November 20, 1951, both in DRMC Papers.

13. Norris Tibbetts to Joel Leighton, December 17, 1993, permission to cite given to author; transcript of contract negotiations meeting of April 4, 1952, DRMC Papers; Sol Stetin and Ken Fiester interviews, TWUA Oral History Project, TWUA.

14. The *Danville Bee*, for example, wrote after a wage increase in 1946 that "there can be no doubt that textile unionism has enriched the workers and provided the textile employee with a higher standard of living and a more attractive life." To put this praise into context, during Operation Dixie, Joel Leighton, looking for a way to revive the campaign, wrote Adelaide Fine of the southern drive's publicity department requesting copies of favorable commentary from the southern press. Fine wrote back that the Danville press was the only example she could find of favorable publicity. A disgruntled Leighton wrote, "I am most distressed to learn that, apparently, the *Danville Bee* has been the only newspaper in the U.S. that has ever had a good word to say about us. I am afraid it will be rather difficult to build an entire broadcast about this one editorial" (*Danville*

Bee, March 1, 1946; Joel Leighton to Adelaide Fine, November 15, 1946, Fine to Leighton, November 24, 1946, and Leighton to Fine, November 28, 1946, Box 85, ODA). The other local paper, the *Danville Register*, also praised the union, writing that "one cannot but compare what happens in Danville with the tragic losses and friction and confusion resulting from efforts to settle similar problems elsewhere" (*Danville Register*, March 1, 1946).

15. Mary Heaton Vorse, "The South Has Changed," *Harper's Magazine*, July 1949, pp. 28–30. Mason also cited many in Danville who praised the union's political action work among textile workers. Most felt that increased registration and voting had produced positive political change. Others felt that through higher wages and political responsibility, the union had brought workers "a new sense of their individual worth and social responsibility" (memo for A. L. Swim on visit to Danville by Lucy Randolph Mason, March 27–29, 1947, File 10A, Box 20, TWUA).

16. Vorse, "The South Has Changed," p. 28. Although the amount of time Rieve had spent in Danville was a politically contentious point, Rieve himself admitted at the start of negotiations that he had not been in Danville "for five or six years" (transcript of contract negotiations meeting of March 23, 1951, DRMC Papers).

17. Transcript of contract negotiations meetings of March 5, 1951, DRMC Papers; transcript of contract negotiations meeting of March 30, 1951, DRMC Papers.

18. Company figures indeed indicate that Dan River's hourly average in March 1951 was $1.32, about eleven cents higher than the average for the South as a whole, although major nonunion chains such as Cannon and Burlington, which the TWUA wanted to organize, paid roughly the same as Dan River. The company also had more fringe benefits than most of its southern competition, having initiated many benefits such as paid vacations and health insurance ("Negotiating Data 7-51 thru 4-52 Negotiations" folder, DRMC Papers).

19. "Basic Wage and Cost Data: 1950 Negotiations" folder, DRMC Papers.

20. Transcript of contract negotiations meeting of March 23, 1951, DRMC Papers; transcript of contract negotiation meeting of March 30, 1951, DRMC Papers; transcript of contract negotiation meeting of March 5, 1951, DRMC Papers.

21. Transcript of contract negotiations meeting of March 23, 1951, DRMC Papers; transcript of contract negotiations meeting of March 30, 1951, DRMC Papers.

22. Ibid.

23. Talbott and Browder both proposed that "we take a few weeks and give the situation a chance to clarify so that both of us will know more about what we are dealing with and what the effect is going to be when we try to make decisions." Browder also alluded to "our mutually satisfactory relationship" and added that the 1951 negotiations were the first to "bother my sleep" because "in this case we don't really know what we can do." Emanuel Boggs remembered that after negotiations had broken off and the union was about to take a strike vote, "management called in our committee and said 'Look, we've developed pretty good relations here, and we had hoped that we could continue to improve our relationship. In view of the fact that we have made so much improvement,

can't you exempt us from the strike?' Of course, I had to say no" (transcript of contract negotiations meeting of March 23, 1951, DRMC Papers; Emanuel Boggs interview, TWUA Oral History Project, TWUA).

24. Emanuel Boggs interview, TWUA Oral History Project, TWUA; Emanuel Boggs, interview by author.

25. Cross interview.

26. Transcript of contract negotiating session of March 23, 1951, DRMC Papers; Tibbetts interview, March 9, 1994.

27. Boyd Payton, "Diary of the Danville Strike," p. 2, File 1A, Box 20, TWUA; transcript of contract negotiating session of July 23, 1951, DRMC Papers.

28. Transcript of contract negotiations meeting of July 23, 1951, DRMC Papers.

29. Cross interview; transcript of contract negotiations meeting of March 30, 1951, DRMC Papers. Cross, who was centrally involved in the strike, claimed, "I never heard any conversation or anything" that would indicate that an agreement had been made with other companies. He added that "what Cone or Fieldcrest did was up to them."

30. Minutes of confidential meeting of March 13, 1951, "Strike, April, 1951" folder, DRMC Papers.

31. Gardiner interview; Cross, *Dan River Runs Deep*, p. 19; transcript of contract negotiations meeting of July 23, 1951, DRMC Papers.

32. Tibbett's strike diary was not intended for public consumption and was kept in his basement for over forty years. He gave it to me for use in this project.

33. Much of the company's effort was based on creating the impression of a broken strike rather than actually securing effective production. Norris Tibbetts wrote that the company picked people who had never worked before in a mill and "paid them $56 to ride through the gates." Inefficient workers who had been fired repeatedly for drinking or stealing were hired back (Norris Tibbetts Diary, April 4, 1951, Tibbetts Papers).

34. Like many of the companies that stayed shut down during the 1951 strike, Dan River recognized the importance of the "battle of words." The company began a sophisticated public relations campaign made up of newspaper advertisements, letters to workers and community leaders, and radio programs. Malcolm Cross considered this campaign successful: "our information carried the day against the union's propaganda." Indeed, on the eve of the strike, 88 percent of those polled were familiar with the company position. The union also complained about the effectiveness of the company's public relations campaign (Cross, *Dan River Runs Deep*, pp. 19–20; "Survey of Community Opinion for Dan River Mills March 1951 Negotiations with TWUA" folder, DRMC Papers; Mary Heaton Vorse, "Union-Busting Plans Get Try Out at Dan River," *CIO News*, April 30, 1951).

35. Payton, "Diary of the Danville Strike," April 4, 1951, File 1A, Box 20, TWUA; Gardiner interview; "Strike, April 1951" folder, DRMC Papers.

36. "Contract Negotiations July 1951–April 1952" folder, DRMC Papers; Cross interview; meeting of southern strike leaders on April 18, 1951, File 1A, Box 20, TWUA.

37. *Danville Register*, April 25 and 26, 1951; *Danville Bee*, April 18, 1951.

38. Several incidents in which nonstrikers' homes were dynamited, in particular, grabbed the headlines of newspapers across the South. On April 27, a local union official, John Crew, was arrested on charges of adultery and the possession of large quantities of dynamite after police raided his home. Although Crew took the blame, the dynamite had in fact been confiscated from strikers as the union struggled to steer its members away from violence. Norris Tibbetts recalled that a locked drawer of his desk in the union hall contained dynamite, pistols, and a variety of other weapons that he had confiscated from strikers. However, Tibbetts was unable to prevent one group of strikers from dynamiting the mill's power plant. They succeeded in depriving Schoolfield of electricity for nearly an hour. It is indicative of the mood of the strikers that when Crew was arrested on joint charges of adultery and the possession of dynamite, Payton noted, "Reaction of membership was strong on adultery charge but unconcerned about dynamite." Payton claimed at the end of the strike that "violence is endemic to the mill people of this area, whether it be industrial strife or any other kind of row." Meanwhile, Frank Talbott claimed that the company received "numerous and continuous reports of threats of violence and intimidation" against those who were working or nonunion members (Payton, "Diary of the Danville Strike," p. 36, File 1A, Box 20, TWUA; Tibbetts interview, March 9, 1994; *Textile Bulletin*, May 1951; "Arbitration Proceedings," July 16, 1951, DRMC Papers). The fact that the dynamite in Crew's possession had been confiscated from strikers was told to the author by Norris Tibbetts and was not made public. The dynamiting of the power plant was denied by the union at the time, and again, that this was committed by strikers comes from Norris Tibbetts. The name of the main person responsible has been withheld.

39. Historians of northern workers have highlighted the differing reactions of ethnic groups to unionization and strike situations. See, for example, Gerstle, *Working-Class Americanism*, for the importance of ethnicity in a northern textile center. Friedlander, *Emergence of a UAW Local*, also highlights the importance of ethnicity in the union-building process. In contrast, Flamming, *Creating the Modern South*, pp. 209–29, attempts to use quantitative analysis based on company records to identify particular characteristics of nonstrikers along the lines of gender, age, occupation, and so forth in a 1939 strike at Crown Cotton Mill in Dalton, Georgia. Flamming's conclusions are limited, however. He notes that workers from one mill were more supportive of the strike, but no clear pattern emerges to explain why this was the case.

40. Company Running Reports, "Strike, April, 1951" folder, DRMC Papers; *Danville Bee*, April 2, 1951.

41. It is difficult to make the assertion that women were more militant than men in the 1951 Danville strike. Unlike in the case of black workers, data is lacking to prove such a statement. What *is* clear is that they played a prominent role in the strike that deserves recognition. Women strikers helped to ensure that the union maintained a strong presence on the picket line for the duration of the strike. Concrete data shows that 97 percent of black workers remained on strike when the strike was called off, compared to 35 percent of white workers.

42. Norris Tibbetts to Friends and Relations, May 11, 1951, Tibbetts Papers. The role of women in the 1929 strikes is best examined by Hall, "Disorderly

Women," pp. 354–82. The 1934 extract comes from the *Textile Bulletin*, October 25, 1934. Janiewski, *Sisterhood Denied*, examines in detail the relationship between women and unionism in Durham, North Carolina, in the 1930s.

43. "Doris Nuchols Case" folder, November 2, 1951, Arbitration Hearings, DRMC Papers.

44. Ibid.

45. Ibid.

46. "Discharge: All Areas Affected" folder, Arbitration Hearings, DRMC Papers.

47. Cross wrote to a fellow manager that he had suspicions about the joint firings of Erna Bray and Fannie Mulkey for producing too many seconds (i.e., products of unacceptable quality) because "it did not seem to me possible that two women, with the experience of Mrs. Bray and Miss Mulkey, could do such a completely unsuitable job. At the time of the discharge and thereafter, I was concerned that there was a possibility that these two employees had been, to use an unpleasant term, framed. Yesterday, I asked Wally Beale to talk to Clarence Major about this and Clarence told him in the strictest confidence and with our agreement that we would not divulge his name in any way, that the sheets which were used as a basis for the discharge of these two women did not come from one case, taken from their table on a particular day, but represented sheets accumulated over a period of time" (Malcolm Cross to Harold D. Jefferson, November 18, 1952, "Erna Bray and Fannie Mulkey Discharge Number 5 Sewing," Case, Arbitration Proceedings, DRMC Papers).

48. TWUA radio program of April 18, 1951, "Union Publicity" folder, DRMC Papers; *Danville Register*, April 19, 1951; "The Laydown Case of the 16 Employees," July 17, 1951, DRMC Papers.

49. Payton, "Diary of the Danville Strike," pp. 4, 16, File 1A, Box 20, TWUA; "Survey of Community Opinions for Dan River Mills: March 1951 Negotiations with TWUA" folder, DRMC Papers. Personnel Manager Malcolm Cross also recalled that "it was much more difficult to get the black people to come in to work during the strike than the white people" (Cross interview).

50. This short treatment of black textile workers and the effects of segregated locals is part of a broader study on segregated locals I have published separately as part of the Odense American Studies International Series (OASIS): Timothy J. Minchin, " 'The Union Was Our Only Voice': African-American Textile Workers in Danville, Virginia, 1944–1957," Working Paper No. 17, U.S. Government Information Service, 1995. The Danville experience is compared in greater detail to other separate locals in my longer study.

51. The recent study of Douglas Flamming, *Creating the Modern South*, for example, is justified in omitting blacks, because the focus of the book, Crown Mill, hired no blacks at all (Flamming, pp. xxix–xxx). Hall et al., *Like a Family*, gives almost no attention to black textile workers or the wider race issue. Carlton, *Mill and Town*, and Newby, *Plain Folk in the New South*, both examine the resistance and determination of white textile workers to exclude blacks from the mills. Other recent studies, such as Hodges, *New Deal Labor Policy*, and Griffith, *Crisis of American Labor*, do not discuss black textile workers at all. The prewar

focus of most of these works makes it much easier to avoid any discussion of blacks.

52. Between 1940 and 1950, for example, the number of blacks employed in the southern textile industry increased from 24,764 to 44,640. The labor shortages of the war and immediate postwar years were largely responsible for this change. One manufacturer in Macon, Georgia, recalled that "about World War II, things started getting kind of rough. A lot of other industries came to this area, and your skilled people were the first ones they would hire away from you. They would move in here with the same wage scales they had up east, which was way above what we were paying down here." As whites began to leave textiles, the hiring of blacks increased. In one sample of 115 long-term African American textile workers in La Grange, Georgia, 48 percent began work between 1940 and 1944 (Frederickson, "Four Decades of Change," pp. 27–44).

53. Despite their low representation and exclusion, blacks were a vital part of the southern textile industry even before World War II. One 1950 study of seventy southern mills by Donald Dewey found that although no mill was more than 10 percent black, all mills made use of black labor for a variety of jobs, ranging from outside work to truck driving, sweeping, and machine cleaning. Indeed, the universal title of "mill laborer" given to black work hid a wide variety of tasks, including some that were semiskilled, such as mechanics or carpentry. As Mary Fredrickson has argued, despite their exclusion, "black men and women have always played a critical role in the growth and development of the industry in the South" (Rowan, "Negro in the Textile Industry," pp. 65–66; Frederickson, "Four Decades of Change," pp. 27–28).

54. Cross interview.

55. Marshall, *Negro and Organized Labor*, p. 190. Marshall points out how "at a multiplant local of the UAW in Atlanta, the greatest anti-Negro feeling was caused by the faction from a plant that had no Negroes. . . . Similarly, in Port Arthur, Texas, the greatest racial feeling was not in the Gulf Group within Oil, Chemical, and Atomic Workers Local 423, with many Negroes, but in the Texaco group of that local with very few."

56. Mayes Behrman visit with Ross Groshong, February 9, 1954, Mayes Behrman visit with Emanuel Boggs, September 12, 1955, both in "South-Eastern Regional Office 1947–1956" box, AFSC Records; Leighton interview; Knight interview, October 26, 1993. During the 1934 General Strike, black locals were formed in most major centers, such as Huntsville, Alabama; Macon, Georgia; Spartanburg, South Carolina; and the North Carolina towns of Durham, Hillsborough, and Erwin. Between 1945 and 1955, separate TWUA black locals existed in a variety of locations, including Fieldcrest Mills in Leaksville, North Carolina; Rock Hill Printing and Finishing Company in Rock Hill, South Carolina; Safie Manufacturing Company in Rockingham, North Carolina; Erwin Mills in Coolemee, North Carolina; and Dan River Mills in Danville, Virginia.

57. Further research is clearly needed to provide a full understanding of the effects of the segregated local. My longer study deals with the broader context of the Danville experience.

58. Other unions that at some time had segregated locals included the Tobacco

Workers International Union (TWUI); the International Association of Machinists (IAM); the International Longshoremen's Association (ILA); the International Ladies' Garment Workers Union (ILGWU); the International Union of Pulp, Sulphite, and Paper Mill Workers (PPS); the International Brotherhood of Teamsters, Chauffeurs and Warehousemen; the Brotherhood of Railway Carmen of America (BRC); the Amalgamated Clothing Workers (ACWA); the United Brotherhood of Carpenters and Joiners of America (UBCJ); and the American Federation of Teachers (AFT). This list is not exhaustive.

59. Knight interview, October 26, 1993; Marshall, *Negro and Organized Labor*, p. 190.

60. *Daily News Record*, July 10, 1944; G. S. Harris to K. W. Marriner, May 31, June 14, 1945, "War Production Board File," DRMC Papers; Smith, *Mill on the Dan*, pp. 508–11; Knight interview, October 26, 1993; Ken Fiester interview, TWUA Oral History Project, TWUA.

61. Ken Fiester interview, TWUA Oral History Project, TWUA. Slim Boggs also felt that the black local provided African American workers with more opportunity to participate in the union than would have been the case in an integrated union: "the reason for the black local was that prejudice was so deep among workers that it was impossible for the blacks to have anything approaching equality within the union unless they had their own structure" (Emanuel Boggs interview, TWUA Oral History Project, TWUA).

62. Norris Tibbetts to John D. Holmes, December 3, 1952, Tibbetts Papers.

63. Joe Pedigo interview E-11–1, SOHP; Tibbetts interview, March 14, 1994.

64. Norris Tibbetts to John D. Holmes, December 3, 1952, Tibbetts Papers; Emanuel Boggs interview, TWUA Oral History Project, TWUA; Mayes Behrman visit to Emanuel Boggs, September 12, 1955, "South-Eastern Regional Office 1947–1956" box, AFSC Records.

65. Coleman interview; Mayes Behrman visit with Emanuel Boggs, September 12, 1955, "South-Eastern Regional Office 1947–1956" box, AFSC Records; 1950 TWUA convention proceedings, p. 109. Norris Tibbetts, who recalled many examples of individuals whose prejudices were changed, believed what happened at these conventions was that "the blacks became a mascot for the Danville workers. The whites would support their own people who happened to be black" (Tibbetts interview, March 14, 1994).

66. Norris Tibbetts to John D. Holmes, December 3, 1952, Tibbetts Papers; Emanuel Boggs interview by author; Tibbetts interview, March 14, 1994.

67. "Survey of Community Opinions for Dan River Mills: March 1951 Negotiations with TWUA" folder, DRMC Papers.

68. Coleman interview.

69. Emanuel Boggs interview by author; Payton, "Diary of the Danville Strike," pp. 17, 26, File 1A, Box 20, TWUA; Norris Tibbetts to John D. Holmes, December 3, 1952, Tibbetts Papers.

70. Mayes Behrman visit with Ross Groshong, February 9, 1954, "South-Eastern Regional Office 1947–1956" box, AFSC Records; Larry Rogin interview, TWUA Oral History Project, TWUA; Leighton interview; Joseph Jacobs interview, July 5, 1991, by Cliff Kuhn and Millie Beik, Georgia Government Documentation project, Georgia State University, pp. 41–57.

71. Marshall, *Negro and Organized Labor*, p. 190. Marshall also found that many textile workers were members of the Klan and other segregationist organizations.

72. Norrell, "Caste in Steel," pp. 669–94. Many other studies highlight similar conclusions. Thus, a biracial union of packinghouse workers split apart in the early 1950s when black workers began to question racist social customs. White workers abandoned the union once blacks tried to use civil rights to alleviate longstanding racial grievances (Rick Halpern, "Interracial Unionism in the Southwest").

73. Bruce Nelson, "Organized Labor and Civil Rights," lecture delivered at Cambridge University on February 21, 1995. The events that took place in Danville in the 1960s highlighted the fact that the union had failed to change the basic discrimination facing blacks in Danville, especially those who worked in the mills, and illustrated the way that workers turned to civil rights organizations to tackle these problems (Cross, *Dan River Runs Deep*, pp. 93–95; "Affirmative Action" folder, DRMC Papers).

74. *Danville Bee*, April 2, 1951.

75. *Southern Textile News*, April 14, 1951.

76. Fisher and Rudge Brief for Negotiations, Summer 1951, DRMC Papers.

77. Melvin and Virgil Griffiths interview; Cross interview.

78. Payton, "Diary of the Danville Strike," pp. 12–13, File 1A, Box 20, TWUA; Norris Tibbetts diary, April 9, 1951, Tibbetts Papers; Tibbetts interview, March 9, 1994.

79. Tibbetts interview, March 9, 1994; Cross interview; U.S. Congress, Senate Committee on Labor and Public Welfare, *Fair Labor Standards Act Amendments of 1949*, pp. 929–30.

80. Norris Tibbetts to the Scherbaks, July 31, 1952, Tibbetts Papers; Payton, "Diary of the Danville Strike," pp. 13, 19, 35, File 1A, Box 20, TWUA.

81. Payton, "Diary of the Danville Strike," pp. 19–21, File 1A, Box 20, TWUA.

82. Ibid., p. 22; Norris Tibbetts's diary, April 8, 1951, Tibbetts Papers. Tibbetts argued that this was the way that "militant" groups like the miners held their strikes together.

83. Transcripts of meetings of southern strike leaders on April 16 and 18, 1951, File 1A, Box 20, TWUA.

84. Transcript of meeting of southern strike leaders, April 18, 1951, File 1A, Box 20, TWUA.

85. Transcript of meetings of southern strike leaders, May 5 and April 16, 1951, File 1A, Box 20, TWUA.

86. Transcripts of meetings of southern strike leaders, April 16, April 18, and May 5, 1951, File 1A, Box 20, TWUA; Payton, "Diary of the Danville Strike," p. 16, File 1A, Box 20, TWUA.

87. Baldanzi claimed that "when you talk about the strike in terms of union people folding up, it would be erroneous"(transcript of meeting of southern strike leaders, April 16, 1951, File 1A, Box 20, TWUA; Wright interview).

88. *Danville Bee*, March 1, 1946; *Danville Register*, April 1, 1951; *Danville Bee*, April 1, 1951; transcript of meeting of southern strike leaders, May 5, 1951, File 1A, Box 20, TWUA. Melvin Griffiths, an eighty-nine-year-old retired Dan

River worker who took part in the 1931 strike, went red in the face with anger when recalling the strike of 1931 in 1993. This was mainly because of the way that UTW leader Frank Gorman abandoned the Danville strike, supposedly "running off with the money."—"His name was Gorman and he went off with all that money, and they didn't have enough for those that were on strike, we got to where we didn't have a mouthful to eat in the house. . . . A lot of them learned a lot of things from that." The 1931 strike is known by many younger citizens of Danville, and is more easily recalled, on the whole, than the 1951 strike.

89. Sol Stetin, Ken Fiester, and Larry Rogin interviews, TWUA Oral History Project, TWUA; Norris Tibbetts to Friends and Relations, May 11, 1951, Tibbetts Papers.

90. Personal and Confidential Reports to Basil D. Browder, July 24 and 25, 1951, in "Contract Negotiations, July 1951–April 1952" folder, DRMC Papers.

91. "Outline of Economic Facts for Presentation at Contract Negotiations" folder, DRMC Papers; Malcolm Cross to Basil D. Browder, June 19, 1951, in "Proposals for Contract Changes" folder, DRMC Papers.

92. Transcript of contract negotiations meeting of July 23, 1951, DRMC Papers.

93. Emanuel Boggs interview by author; Tibbetts interview, March 9, 1994; *Textile Labor*, May 2, 1953; contract negotiations meeting of November 26, 1952, pp. 106–8, DRMC Papers; "Negotiations UTW-AFL 4/30/53-Contract" folder, DRMC Papers. Cross claimed that the 1953 contract brought twenty-three "substantive changes" to the company's advantage. The most significant were the weakening of the contract's model workload clause and the abolition of the wage reopening clause (Malcolm Cross to R. C. Gourley, April 23, 1953, "Negotiations UTW-AFL 4/30/53-Contract" folder, DRMC Papers).

94. Emanuel Boggs interview by author; Norris Tibbetts, "The Danville Story," Tibbetts Papers; Joe Jacobs to Lloyd Klenert, June 22, 1955, File 803, Box 413, UTW; Raynor, "Unionism in the Southern Textile Industry," pp. 80–81. Workers at the Proximity plant of Cone Mills also refused to pay dues to the union but defeated two attempts to decertify the union in 1948 and 1949.

95. Gardiner interview. The union's main effort to restore the checkoff was an unsuccessful strike in 1974. As in 1951, Gardiner felt that the company was victorious because it was determined to operate and "did everything it could to make it comfortable and convenient for employees to walk or ride through the picket lines." Malcolm Cross recalled that Dan River wanted a union: it actually gave them more freedom of action in changing workloads, because they were not frightened that if they annoyed workers, they might be organized (Cross interview).

96. Cross interview; Emanuel Boggs interview, TWUA Oral History Project, TWUA.

97. Cross interview; *Danville Bee*, April 10, 1951. The company's alienation from the union as a result of the strike violence was one of the reasons its officials refused the checkoff. Raymond Henderson wrote Browder that "until the union conducts their strikes on the basis of the full recognition of people's right to work and refrains from unlawful conduct, we can only assume that we are dealing with an immature and irresponsible organization" (Raymond Henderson to Basil

Browder, July 24, 1951, "Contract Negotiations, July 1951–April 1952" folder, DRMC Papers).

Chapter 7

1. Ken Fiester and Solomon Barkin interviews, TWUA Oral History Project, TWUA.

2. The union's figures showed that while domestic textile production declined steadily, from 786 million square yards in 1946 to 470 million in 1953, imports rose from 4 million to 25 million square yards. As early as 1954, the TWUA joined with management in calling for protection from "foreign low-wage competition." But the union also claimed that management was partly responsible for the depression because it had failed to modernize plants and to be aggressive enough in advertising and sales promotion (1954 TWUA Executive Council Report, pp. 25–40).

3. W. H. Tedford to Charles Auslander, May 30, 1951, Box 320, SCSDP. Similarly, at Rock Hill Printing and Finishing Company in Rock Hill, South Carolina, one of the TWUA's best southern locals, the contract was successfully renewed following the 1951 strike but only when, according to Personnel Director W. B. Byers, "the union agreed that it would cease in its attempts to use Rock Hill Printing and Finishing Company as a pattern-setter for any so-called 'southern wage pattern'" (W. B. Byers to Charles Auslander, January 21, 1952, Box 322, SCSDP).

4. *Daily News Record*, November 23, 1951.

5. *Textile Labor*, November 7, 1953, and September 1955; U.S. Congress, Senate, Committee on the Judiciary, *Corporate Mergers and Anti-Trust Legislation*, 2d sess., p. 781; Truchil, "Capital-Labor Relationships in the U.S. Textile Industry," p. 238.

6. *Textile Labor*, September 1955, November 1946; Charlie C. Hertwig to Charles Cannon, April 9, 1959, Charles Cannon Papers, unprocessed collection held at Wingate College in Wingate, North Carolina. Illustrating the way that Dan River had lost the wage initiative, in contract negotiations in 1963 the company told the union, "Just as soon as the pattern of adjustment is clear in the areas where our plants are located, we will go ahead with this wage increase." In 1969, another wage pattern was set simultaneously by nonunion Burlington and J. P. Stevens ("Contract Negotiations—Wage Re-Opening February, 1959" folder; "Contract Negotiations—Wage Re-Opening November, 1963" folder; "Wage Negotiations, 1963" folder, all in DRMC Papers).

7. Barkin interview; *Textile Labor*, May 19, 1951; Cross interview.

8. *Textile Labor*, January 26, 12, 1952; *New York Times*, June 19, 1955.

9. *Textile Labor*, April 18, 1953, May and August 1955.

10. Leading New England manufacturer Seabury Stanton said after the strike that half of all textile companies in the New Bedford–Fall River area were considering moving south because of the TWUA's failure to equalize wage costs. And in a private letter to Charles Cannon, another New England textile manufacturer blamed the wage differential that had opened up after the strike for the closure of mills (*Danville Register*, June 15, 1951; Kenneth B. Cook of Crown

Manufacturing Company in Pawtucket, Rhode Island, to Charles Cannon, October 3, 1951, Box 25, Cannon Papers, Wingate College, Wingate, North Carolina).

11. *Daily News Record*, March 5, 1952. Willard Shelton wrote in the *U.S. News and World Report* that "the collapse of a textile strike in eight states points up the weakness of unions in the South" and that this failure "is now being blamed for wage cuts, loss of jobs, and heavier workloads for some union workers in some cities of the north" (Shelton, "Operation Dixie: Union Setback," *U.S. News*, May 25, 1951, pp. 44–47, and "Textile Strike in Eight States Points up Weaknesses of Unions in the South," *U.S. News*, February 22, 1952, pp. 60–63).

12. Larry Rogin and Sol Stetin interviews, TWUA Oral History Project, TWUA.

13. TWUA Executive Council Meeting of October 27, 1952, File 2A, Box 7, TWUA; contract negotiations meeting of March 20, 1952, p. 40, DRMC Papers; *Textile Challenger*, June 1958; Stabile, *Activist Unionism*, pp. 159–63.

14. Members of TWUA Local Number 925 to Emil Rieve, March 25, 1952, Box 319, SCSDP; Robert Parker report of September 21, 1951, File 2A, Box 9, TWUA; Harold Griffiths report of August 2, 1951, File 2A, Box 9, TWUA. Howard Parker wrote from Durham in July 1951 that "since the strike 61 persons have written in requesting withdrawal of dues deduction authorization" (report of July 3, 1951, File 2A, Box 9, TWUA).

15. Cole and John Grant interviews.

16. Minutes of Executive Council Meeting of June 16, 1952, File 396, Box 7, TWUA.

17. Robert Parker report of January 14, 1954, File 17A, TWUA. Robert Parker, in charge of the Pickett strike, wrote that "some of them ask what goes with all the 50 cents they pay for union dues. . . . Some people soon forget what the union has done in the past, just what they are going to do now is what they want to know." Later in the strike he wrote emotionally, "Some things are said to us that hurt deep, we take it and try to get along." Parker also explained that the strike was causing a great deal of hardship because, as in Danville, workers had bought many items on credit that left them in a vulnerable position in a strike: "some of our people have been living high on the hog, buying everything they could on credit and now their bills are getting behind and they begin cussing everybody in general" (Robert Parker reports of May 11, May 15, and August 8, 1951, File 17A, TWUA).

18. Among other defeats of this nature was an election that the TWUA lost at Lynchburg Hosiery Mills in Lynchburg, Virginia, by a huge margin: of 889 eligible, 753 voted against the TWUA and 136 for. This defeat came as a big blow, especially as the union had been concentrating on organizing the mill for over two years. Virginia director Boyd Payton attributed the defeat to the Danville strike (*Textile Bulletin*, July 1951; Charles Auslander report, May 19, 1951, File 2A, Box 11, TWUA).

19. When the strike began, state director Charles Auslander noted that "within the last week or two things have slowed down a little bit due to the strike situation." Once the strike was abandoned, Auslander wrote despondently, "Following the unsuccessful strike at Industrial Cotton and the notoriety over the dyna-

miting cases, all of which has happened since we got almost all of the cards, things have remained at a standstill" (Charles Auslander reports, May 19 and June 17, 1951, File 2A, Box 11, TWUA).

20. *Southern Textile News*, June 2, 1951; Harold Griffiths report, May 24, 1951, File 2A, Box 9, TWUA. Another example occurred in May 1951, when an election was lost at Republic Cotton Mills in Great Falls, South Carolina, by a vote of 1,120 to 507. Auslander noted afterward that "the southern strike had its effect" (Charles Auslander report of May 19, 1951, File 2A, Box 11, TWUA).

21. In September 1951, an election was lost at Hudson Hosiery Company in Charlotte, North Carolina, by a bigger margin than in two previous attempts. A similar example occurred at Dyersburg Cotton Products in Dyersburg, Tennessee, another campaign in which the TWUA had spent an extended period of time trying to organize (*Textile Bulletin*, September 1951).

22. 1952 UTW Convention Proceedings, p. 8; James Bamford to Emil Rieve, August 29, 1951, File 2A, Box 11, TWUA.

23. Emanuel Boggs interview, TWUA Oral History Project, TWUA; Edwin E. Waller to Morris Pizer, August 26, 1951, Folder 573, UFWA Papers, Southern Labor Archives, Atlanta. I am indebted to George Waldrep for supplying me with this last quotation from his research on the UFWA.

24. Emanuel Boggs and Paul Swaity interviews, TWUA Oral History Project, TWUA.

25. The pre-1951 records of the Textile Committee on Public Relations, for example, continually emphasize that the CIO had resources greater than those available to southern textile management and that management would come off the worst if it tried a "confrontation with the CIO" (Thomas D. Yutzy to Rush S. Dickson, April 13, 1951, Box 25, Cannon Mills Papers, Special Collections Department, Perkins Library, Duke University).

26. Cross, *Dan River Runs Deep*, p. 22. Cross writes that "publicity about the abortive strike added to the difficulty of organizing the great majority of textile workers who were not unionized." In the unsuccessful campaign to organize Fieldcrest Mills workers in Fieldale, Virginia, for example, the company launched a campaign that made much of the fact that "in 1951 Fieldcrest workers at Leaksville, Draper, and Spray joined a five week nation-wide strike for an industry-wide hike. The North Carolina Fieldcrest workers lost about $1 million in wages during the strike. At Fieldale, workers stayed on their jobs." The *Textile Bulletin* gloated after it was over that the strike would provide management with an important weapon in the battle against unionization because "the Southern mill worker—both union and non-union—has a long memory" (*Leaksville News*, June 21, 1956; *Textile Bulletin*, June 1951).

27. Charles Auslander report of June 17, 1952, File 2A, Box 11, TWUA; James Bamford to Boyd Payton, October 26, 1951, File 2A, Box 12, TWUA; 1954 TWUA Executive Council Report, p. 61. It was also a telling sign that employers had raised the tempo when union veteran Franz Daniel wrote in May 1952 that he had never known a time when textile unions were under more pressure in the South (Franz Daniel to all CIO local unions in North Carolina, May 6, 1952, Box 75, ODA).

28. Purnell Maloney report of March 24, 1954, File 17A, TWUA; Garland

Brook report of March 17, 1953, File 17A, TWUA. Blaine Campbell reported from Utica-Mohawk mill in Seneca, South Carolina, that "the lay-off has put the fear of God in the workers and all reported that there is very little talk in the plant and their departments" (report of May 31, 1954, File 17A, TWUA). Similar problems were reported from a wide variety of other campaigns. Purnell Maloney wrote that in Rockmart, "most of our former very active people are now on lay-off. The company deliberately laid off these workers for two years so that they would lose their right to vote." Workers at Macon Textiles in Macon, Georgia, repelled an organizing campaign, telling Garland Brook that "the mill was on short time and they thought it would be useless at this time to attempt to organize, due to this" (Purnell Maloney report of June 10, 1954, File 17A, TWUA; Garland Brook report of July 6, 1954, File 17A, TWUA).

29. M. W. Lynch report of January 29, 1953, File 17A, TWUA. Payton's comments are drawn from Hodges, "J. P. Stevens and the Union," p. 4.

30. *Rock Hill Post*, June 25, 1951.

31. Rene Berthiaume, September 21, 1951, Box 318, SCSDP; Yates Heafner report, August 21, 1951, FMCS.

32. *Huntsville Times*, April 30 and May 6, 1951; report of May 10, 1951, Box 2588, FMCS; *Anderson Daily Mail*, May 11, 1951.

33. Julius Fry report of January 1952, File 2A, Box 13, TWUA; Herb Williams reports of December 9, 1953, and April 15, 1954, File 2A, Box 13, TWUA; C. D. Boartfield report of September 29, 1953, File 17A, TWUA.

34. Report of April 3, 1951–May 18, 1951, Box 2588, FMCS.

35. Julius Fry report of January 1952, File 2A, Box 13, TWUA; Herb Williams report of June and July 1954, File 2A, Box 13, TWUA; Herman Mullins reports of May 11, 1955, and August 1955, File 2A, Box 13, TWUA.

36. Bruno Rantane to George Baldanzi, February 7, 1948, Box 282, Greensboro JBP; Groshong interview.

37. Groshong interview.

38. Scott Hoyman interview, TWUA Oral History Project, TWUA; Garland Brook, reports of July 13 and July 7, 1955, File 17A, TWUA; report of Luther Carroll, March 28, 1952, File 2A, Box 16, TWUA; Raynor, "Unionism in the Southern Textile Industry," p. 93.

39. Reports on Lane Cotton Mills, Pacific Mills, A. D. Julliard, and Cedartown Textiles, May 1951, Box 2588, FMCS.

40. Baldanzi argued, for example, that the strike had failed because the negotiations had been conducted by Rieve and his supporters "even though they were unfamiliar with the problems of southern workers and management attitudes." This argument was repeated by Baldanzi's followers (Baldanzi quoted in Williams, "Split in the Textile Workers Union," p. 60).

41. *Textile Labor*, November 8, 1952.

42. In this respect, the split between Baldanzi and Rieve was a strange one. Unlike other contemporary battles in CIO unions, there was no clear political difference between the two, especially as both were acknowledged as social democrats and fervent anticommunists. This is in marked contrast, in particular, to the battle in the UAW. See Cormier and Eaton, *Reuther*, pp. 241–50, and Zieger, *American Workers, American Unions*, p. 129.

43. It was indeed the skills of Baldanzi as an organizer and orator that won him a following in the South. By working extensively in the South, Baldanzi developed a large following in the region, both among the rank and file and among union staff. He chose many of the TWUA staff that operated in the South and had a formative influence on their careers. From the beginning, Baldanzi attracted young, college-educated staff to the South. They were attracted by his enthusiasm for southern organizing and his tremendous speaking ability. Ross Groshong, a young Quaker who started working for the TWUA after World War II, remembered, "I liked Rieve but Baldanzi was the great orator, one of the best in the game, he could even put this character Ross Perot to shame, in a strike situation he could have people crying one minute and laughing the next." Pat Knight, an educated southerner who admitted to being "idealistic," felt that part of the reason the union had failed to organize the South was that "it stuck to the nuts and bolts of organizing. It did not try to dream of a glorious future. . . . This was why George Baldanzi appealed, because he could make these wonderful speeches. That was what the union lacked." Another strong Baldanzi supporter who worked in the South, Joel Leighton, felt that Baldanzi "commanded a great deal of loyalty and affection in the South" because he was "very warm, extrovert, outgoing, he was out on the picket lines or out on the gates giving out leaflets at six in the morning." Many Baldanzi supporters and, indeed, some Rieve followers regarded Baldanzi as one of the most promising labor leaders in the CIO at this time (Groshong interview; Knight interview, October 26, 1993; Leighton interview). In contrast, the support that Rieve received was largely from northern TWUA staff who felt that Baldanzi lacked the administrative skills needed to be president (William Gordon and Larry Rogin interviews, TWUA Oral History Project, TWUA).

44. 1952 TWUA Convention Proceedings, pp. 7–12, quote from p. 10; Paul Swaity interview, TWUA Oral History Project, TWUA; Emanuel Boggs interview by author; Leighton interview; Knight interview, October 26, 1993; Groshong interview.

45. "TWUA Mills Won By UTW in Secession Movement, 1952–1953," Volume 2, Box 11, TWUA; table titled "Results of NLRB Elections Arising out of the TWUA Split," in Williams, "Split in the Textile Workers Union," pp. 167–69. The only Erwin plant that stayed with the TWUA was the one in Erwin, North Carolina, where the TWUA defeated the UTW 725 to 717.

46. UTW pamphlets, Box 50, Erwin Mills Papers, Special Collections Department, Perkins Library, Duke University; *Fortune*, December 1952, pp. 84–86.

47. deVyver, "Union Fratricide," p. 380; "TWUA Mills Won by UTW in Secession Movement, 1952–1953," Volume 2, Box 11, TWUA; *Textile Labor*, July 11, 1953.

48. Groshong interview.

49. Katz, *Taft-Hartleyism in Southern Textiles*, p. 5; Emanuel Boggs to John Harkins, July 17, 1952, Volume 2, Box 11, TWUA.

50. Resolution by UTW Local 251 in Coolemee, North Carolina, n.d., File 805, UTW; John Grant interview; McCumbee interview; Elsie Hogan interview.

51. Scott Hoyman interview, TWUA Oral History Project, TWUA; organizers' reports of Garland Brook, L. A. Gossett, Robert A. Freeman, and Scott Hoyman

in File 17A, TWUA; deVyver, "Union Fratricide," p. 380; Ken Kramer to Emil Rieve, June 9 and August 21, 1952, Volume 2, Box 11, TWUA.

52. *Textile Labor*, November 8, 1952, and deVyver, "Union Fratricide," p. 383.

53. Sol Stetin interview, TWUA Oral History Project, TWUA. Bill Belanger, capturing the union's pessimistic poststrike mood, told the executive council in 1952 that "during the last two years we were concerned with personal survival and could not do much other work." Larry Rogin recalled how the internal battle stopped his education department from functioning: "you can't do education when there's a fight going on because you're pushed into taking sides. We really stopped education activity. . . . The union devoted two years to a political fight." In executive council meetings after the split, many members seemed exhausted and disillusioned, as the union struggled to regain its organizing zeal in the aftermath of a bruising political fight (Executive Council Meetings of June 21 and August 15, 1952, TWUA).

54. George Perkel interview, TWUA Oral History Project, TWUA.

55. Conn interview; Ken Fiester interview, TWUA Oral History Project, TWUA; Knight interview, October 26, 1993; Leighton interview.

56. Norris Tibbetts to Joe Hueter, May 26, 1952, Tibbetts Papers; McCumbee and Phifer interviews; John Grant interview; Tibbetts interview, March 9, 1994.

57. This argument is made by Griffith, *Crisis of American Labor*, p. 176, and Goldfield, *Decline of Organized Labor*, pp. 238–40.

58. Larry Rogin and Sol Stetin interviews, TWUA Oral History Project, TWUA; *Textile Labor*, June 20, 1953; Hodges, "J. P. Stevens and the Union," pp. 3–4; TWUA Convention Proceedings, p. 11.

59. See especially the impact of the "Roosevelt recession" of 1937–38 on the TWOC drive, as documented in Hodges, *New Deal Labor Policy*, pp. 154–56. For example, UTW secretary-treasurer James Starr admitted in the midst of the 1937–38 recession that "it is not an easy matter to organize workers, whether they are in textiles or any other kind, when they are walking the streets looking for jobs, many of them suffering the pangs of hunger."

60. 1952 TWUA Convention Proceedings, p. 11; Solomon Barkin interview, TWUA Oral History Project, TWUA.

Chapter 8

1. The works of Hall et al., *Like a Family*, and Griffith, *Crisis of American Labor*, in particular, rest heavily on extensive oral interviewing. Similarly, the main source for this chapter is twenty-seven interviews I conducted with retired workers from Aleo Manufacturing Company in Rockingham, North Carolina, between January and June 1994. I also interviewed retired workers from other mills in Rockingham.

2. Honeycutt and Honeycutt, *History of Richmond County*, pp. 351–74.

3. *Rockingham Post-Dispatch*, April 4, 1951.

4. Retired worker Addie Faye Wyatt, for example, explained that "the Entwistles was a family, they lived in Rockingham. They never had to deal with unions, people had always more or less said 'This is my lot.' . . . But when Lowenstein bought it, they were from the North and they had dealt with unions"

(Wyatt interview). Lowenstein operated union plants at Rock Hill, South Carolina; Huntsville, Alabama; and New Orleans, Louisiana.

5. Joel Leighton reports of December 7, 1950, and December 7, 1951, File 2A, Box 9, TWUA.

6. Ibid.; *Textile Labor*, February 20, 1954; McCumbee interview; Larry Rogin interview, TWUA Oral History Project, TWUA; John Grant interview; Phifer interview. Joel Leighton mentioned one wildcat strike, for example, in his report of July 24, 1950, File 2A, Box 9, TWUA.

7. On southern textile workers' history of unsuccessful protest, see especially Hall et al., *Like a Family*, pp. 328–54, and Zieger, "Textile Workers and Historians," pp. 42–43.

8. McCumbee and Crumbley interviews; Margaret Grant interview; *Rockingham Post-Dispatch*, August 15, 1945.

9. Kessler-Harris, *Out to Work*, pp. 40–41.

10. McCumbee and Conyers interviews.

11. Joel Leighton reports of June 14, 1949, and March 23 and October 17, 1950, File 2A, Box 9, TWUA.

12. Joel Leighton reports of June 7 and July 24, 1950, File 2A, Box 9, TWUA. Pleasants and Burns, *Frank Porter Graham*, pp. 203–72, 223, 227, 262, provides a detailed analysis of the 1950 Senate race between Frank Porter Graham and Willis Smith, the race to which Leighton refers. Smith's camp made considerable use of racial material on the eve of the election, including material widely circulated in mill villages that claimed that Graham's election would lead to the integration of the mills. Pleasants and Burns document that most textile workers reacted to this material in the way that was intended: most textile counties in the Piedmont switched from Graham to Smith. Richmond County, however, held for Graham.

13. Zieger, "Towards the History of the CIO," pp. 504–10, emphasizes that this type of "external" workers' control—as opposed to "internal" workers' control, which stressed "direct worker struggle to determine the content of jobs"—is at the heart of the CIO's history. The original definition of internal workers' control—a definition developed with regard to workers in the 1910s and 1920s—was propounded in Montgomery, *Workers' Control*.

14. Crumbley, McCumbee, Welch, and Ivey interviews. Another former worker, Linwood Starling, complained that "just about every mill had a ball [baseball] team, and a ball player came by and wanted a job, he got a job, they'd give them a job just to play ball, put somebody else out" (Starling interview).

15. Bateman and McCumbee interviews.

16. John Grant interview; Langley, Crumbley, Wyatt, and Bateman interviews. Former worker Howard Spivey also expressed the belief that "the poor people was kind of like slaves" (Spivey interview).

17. Identification with the company in the mill-village "family" has been stressed by a number of historians, particularly Flamming, *Creating the Modern South*, pp. xxvi–ii. By contrast, Hall et al., *Like a Family*, emphasizes alienation and community.

18. Cole, McCumbee, Crumbley, Conyers, Welch, and Shepherd interviews.

19. Phifer, Bateman, Barber, Crumbley, and Dennis interviews. The feelings of Elijah Conyers epitomized workers' appreciation of the grievance procedure: "I

couldn't go the lead man first. If I went to the head man first, they'd send me right down. And I liked that. . . . Nothing wrong with that, it's the way it should be" (Conyers interview).

20. Spivey, Cole, and Crumbley interviews; John Grant interview.

21. "The Bolt in Cotton Textiles," *Fortune*, July 1947, p. 178; Cole interview. Cole, like many others, emphasized that when local families owned the mills, "it was kind of a paternal thing, they kind of looked after for the people. They worked them to death as well, but they looked out for them. . . . People from New York and so forth came in here and bought these plants and they did away with the company store because they didn't want to mess with it."

22. Former worker Jesse Shepherd claimed that mill owner William Entwistle told him he would rather sell the mill than operate a union mill (Shepherd interview).

23. Barber interview; John Grant interview; Wyatt interview.

24. Langley and Barber interviews; Bill McDuffie interview; Bateman interview.

25. Margaret Grant interview; Barber and McCumbee interviews.

26. Blum, *V Was for Victory*, pp. 96–98; May, *Homeward Bound*, pp. 165–68.

27. May, *Homeward Bound*, p. 165.

28. Cole interview; Bill McDuffie interview.

29. Ivey, Conyers, Crumbley, and Barber interviews; Margaret Grant interview.

30. Phifer interview; John Grant interview; Crumbley interview.

31. Bateman interview; John Grant interview.

32. Langley interview.

33. Ibid.; John Grant interview; Cole interview.

34. *Richmond County Journal*, July 14, 1949.

35. Herring, *Passing of the Mill Village*, pp. 16–23; Flamming, *Creating the Modern South*, p. 267.

36. "Special Notice to Employees of Aleo Manufacturing Company," Box 21, Scott Papers, NCDAH; McAllister interview.

37. Robert Cahoon to Robert Denham, General Counsel of NLRB, November 2, 1949, Box 150, NLRB. Strikes over this issue occurred at, among other places, Mansfield Mills in Lumberton, North Carolina; Marshall Field Mills in Leaksville, North Carolina; and Berryton Mills in Berryton, Georgia.

38. *Richmond County Journal*, July 14, 1949; *N&O*, July 16, 1949.

39. Plant manager Sam Snoddy, reflecting the Aleo management's frustration with the strength of the union, made clear references to closing the mill to try and entice workers back: "we have had very little curtailment at Aleo entirely due to our consideration of our employees. Apparently our employees do not realize and do not appreciate this. Some day they will. That will be the day when we have one strike too many and by that time my company will be fed up with what's going on at Aleo and I will receive instructions to close the plant for all time" (*Richmond County Journal*, July 21, 1949).

40. These were the same reactions that Mildred Andrews, for example, received when she asked a range of southern mill owners about the effects of home ownership (survey conducted by Mildred Gwin Andrews, April 1946, Box 2, MGA).

41. Conyers, Baggett, Wyatt, Phifer, and Welch interviews; John Grant interview.

42. Langley, Wyatt, and Barber interviews. The work of Hall et al., *Like a Family*, has strongly brought out the closeness of mill-village communities and the positive benefits that this closeness had.

43. Barber interview.

44. Efforts were concentrated, however, at Safie Manufacturing Company, the biggest mill in the county.

45. The SOC's area director, Draper Wood, typified the early optimism. He wrote, "I find in Rockingham, so far, the best situation in the whole Southern area" (organizing report of June 19, 1946, Box 76, ODA). Organizer Wade Lynch, meanwhile, claimed, "I think that Safie is going to be easy compared to some of the other mills" (organizing report of July 21, 1946, Box 76, ODA). Early reports from Safie were also optimistic. As in many other campaigns, however, a vicious pre-election campaign eroded the union's support and led to a narrow union election victory of 494 to 445. Because the workforce was clearly divided, no contract resulted, and a long strike began in April 1947. Like other postwar textile strikes, the Safie strike was violent and bitter; it was finally broken by the company in October 1947. See, for example, *Richmond County Journal*, September 4 and October 13, 1947. Memories of the dispute's failure killed any hopes of future organizing activity for some time, both in Safie and in other plants. Comments by an organizer named R. C. Thomas illustrate how the strike killed organizing prospects in Rockingham: Thomas wrote that because of the strike, "it appears to me that so far as Rockingham is concerned at this time, that we are wasting both money and manpower so far as organizing is concerned" (R. C. Thomas Organizing Report of November 4, 1947, Box 83, ODA). Similarly, Joel Leighton, who came to Rockingham to be union director shortly after the Safie strike ended, remembered that he found the situation puzzling: "Safie I could never figure out. Presumably they had had an interest in the union to get the people out on strike, but by the time I got there it was cold, I mean intensely, we had no contacts there. It was as if they had never heard of a union, no one would be active" (Leighton interview). The strike also left bitter feelings between Safie workers that were still in evidence fifty years later. Safie worker Clayton Moree, for example, recalled that during the strike, "father and son was split, neighbors were split. . . . Today they still have bitter feelings toward each other" (Moree interview).

46. Langley and McCumbee interviews.

47. *Rockingham Post Dispatch*, February 26, 1947; Joel Leighton's reports, 1946–51, File 2A, Box 9, TWUA.

48. Phifer and Conyers interviews; Elsie Hogan interview; Crumbley interview.

49. Ivey and Bateman interviews.

50. Bill McDuffie interview; Bateman, Crumbley, Dennis, McCumbee, and Barber interviews. The closed shop was outlawed by the North Carolina "right to work" law of 1947.

51. Barber and McCumbee interviews.

52. Langley interview.

53. Joe Jacobs report, April 9, 1953, Folder 872, Box 416, UTW; John Grant interview; Cole interview.

54. *Textile Challenger*, February 1954; *Textile Labor*, February 6 and 20, 1954; Joe Jacobs to Bradford and Joe, March 20, 1955, Folder 872, Box 416, UTW.

55. *Rockingham Post-Dispatch*, November 18, 1954, February 10, 17, 23, and July 14–August 28, 1955. The failure of the national UTW to process grievances and "support" the Aleo local was the reason that a group of workers led by local union president Elsie Hogan switched back to the TWUA (Elsie Hogan to Anthony Valente, December 9, 1953, Folder 873, Box 416, UTW).

56. Rachel McDuffie interview; Elsie Hogan interview; Phifer interview.

57. John Grant and Margaret Grant interviews.

58. Cole interview.

59. Harris, "Snares of Liberalism," p. 185.

Conclusion

1. Chafe, *Unfinished Journey*, pp. viii, 80; May, *Homeward Bound*, p. 166.

2. Chafe, *Unfinished Journey*, p. viii, calls World War II "a turning point in our history." In contrast, the new labor history has overlooked the huge impact of both World War I and World War II on American society. Tentler, *Wage-Earning Women*, makes no mention of World War I and its impact on women workers. Similarly, Griffith, *Crisis of American Labor*, gives little attention to the impact of World War II, especially its economic role, in Operation Dixie's failure. Matthaei, *Economic History of Women in America*, makes no mention of World War I or World War II.

3. Fink, *Fulton Bag and Cotton Mills Strike*, pp. 144–46.

4. One organizer, for example, noted at a 1953 campaign in Dyersburg, Tennessee, that "these employees are very friendly to us organizers. They tell us 'the union is the only thing for the working people' and they realize the union has brought them over four hundred and sixty dollars a year increase since the 1951 campaign." They refused to sign cards, however, and the campaign collapsed. Another organizer reported this discussion among nonunion workers: "after an hour or more discussing the UNION the folks say 'well I know if it was not for the union we would not be making as much as we are today'" (Robert A. Freeman, Organizers' Report of July 11, 1953, File 17A, TWUA; Robert Parker, Organizers' Report of July 23, 1955, File 17A, TWUA).

5. Studies by economists have confirmed the disproportionate impact of national economic growth on the South during the 1940s and 1950s. The considerable economic impact of World War II on the South is explored in Schulman, *From Cotton Belt to Sun Belt*, pp. 63–87, and Wright, *Old South, New South*, pp. 239–57. Wright argues that the impact of national economic growth on the South caused the decline of the region as a distinct labor market.

6. Zieger, *American Workers, American Unions*, pp. 137–48.

7. Harris, "Snares of Liberalism," p. 185. In his examination of the decline of organized labor, Michael Goldfield reviews a wide range of reasons for the decline, but he gives the problem of free-riding very little attention (Goldfield, *Decline of Organized Labor*, pp. 94–112).

8. Flamming, *Creating the Modern South*, p. 263; Hodges, *New Deal Labor Policy*, pp. 192–93, Griffith, *Crisis of American Labor*, pp. 46–61; Carlton, *Mill and Town*, p. 271.

9. Chafe, *Unfinished Journey*, p. 118; Berger, *Working-Class Suburb*; Hodges,

New Deal Labor Policy, p. 192; Robert Parker, Organizers' Report of June 25, 1955, File 17A, TWUA; L. A. Gossett, Organizers' Report of May 21, 1954, File 17A, TWUA; John Grant interview; Loyd Ivey interview.

10. *Rockingham Post Dispatch*, September 24, 1953.

11. Ibid.

12. *Textile Neighbor*, August and September 1951, Box 25, Cannon Mills Papers, Special Collections Department, Perkins Library, Duke University.

13. This argument is made by Irons, "Testing the New Deal," and to some extent by an earlier dissertation, Brooks, "United Textile Workers."

14. Bell quoted in Zieger, *American Workers, American Unions*, p. 141. In addition to Bell, other studies included Berger, *Working-Class Suburb*; Komarovsky, *Blue-Collar Marriage*; Chinoy, *Automobile Workers*.

15. Griffith, *Crisis of American Labor*, pp. 59–60; Bill Evans interview.

16. Gerstle, review of Derber, *Labor in Illinois*, p. 396.

17. Stein, "Southern Workers in National Unions," p. 208; Korstad, "Daybreak of Freedom"; Honey, *Southern Labor and Black Civil Rights*.

18. Benefiting from the increasing time gap between the end of World War II and the present day, a number of recent studies have asserted that the attempt to organize the South in the decade after World War II was of critical importance with regard to the long-term decline of the labor movement. Michael Goldfield, for example, has claimed that "the central cause of the political weakness of U.S. labor unions, and the underlying reason for their generally defensive stance, is the failure to organize the South immediately after World War II." Similarly, Barbara Griffith has called Operation Dixie "a moment of high tragedy from which it [the U.S. labor movement] has yet to fully recover" (Goldfield, *Decline of Organized Labor*, p. 238; Griffith, *Crisis of American Labor*, p. 176). This argument is also used by Michael Honey in *Southern Labor and Black Civil Rights*. The argument is succinctly expressed by Michael Honey in "Operation Dixie," his review of Barbara Griffith's book.

19. As early as 1947, for example, Rieve had said of southern organizing, "I am not predicting that it will be done in a year or two, but I know it will be done no matter how long it will take" (Rieve quoted in Hodges, "J. P. Stevens and the Union," p. 3).

20. Honey, "Operation Dixie," pp. 379, 385.

21. Hodges, *New Deal Labor Policy*, p. 194.

22. Bernstein, "Growth of American Unions," pp. 131–57; Zieger, "Textile Workers and Historians," p. 35. Bernstein shows that by the late 1950s there was already a debate within the labor movement about whether the movement was beginning to decline. Those who argued that the movement was declining used the textile industry as one of their main examples; but the dominant view, stressed by Bernstein, stressed union growth. Sol Barkin remembered being "laughed at" in the early 1960s when he argued that the labor movement was declining (Barkin interview).

23. Paul Christopher to Purnell Maloney, October 11, 1948, Box 144, ODA.

24. Raynor, "Unionism in the Southern Textile Industry," pp. 81–85.

25. Ibid., p. 90; Don Freedman, "Labor on the Southern Front: New Tactics in the Textile War," *Nation*, December 10, 1977, p. 620. A 1974 strike at Dan

River Mills failed for the same reasons as the earlier 1951 strike: workers were forced back to work after falling behind with their "house, car, and utility payments" (*Washington Post*, September 2, 1974).

26. Bruce Raynor interview.

27. Truchil, "Capital-Labor Relationships," p. 238.

28. Hodges, *New Deal Labor Policy*, pp. 191–98, shows how easy it is to stress continuity when looking at the postwar period as a whole.

29. Emsley Phifer interview.

30. *Richmond County Journal*, September 29, 1947.

bibliography

Manuscripts

Atlanta, Georgia
  Southern Labor Archives, Georgia State University
    Paul Christopher Papers
    Stetson Kennedy Papers
    Don McKee Papers
    John Ramsay Papers
    United Textile Workers Papers
Chapel Hill, North Carolina
  North Carolina Collection, University of North Carolina
    Harriet L. Herring Clipping File
  Southern Historical Collection, University of North Carolina
    Mildred Gwin Andrews Papers
    Southern Oral History Project
Clemson, South Carolina
  Strom Thurmond Institute, Clemson University
    Clifton Manufacturing Company Papers
Danville, Virginia
  Dan River Mills, Inc.
    Dan River Mills Company Papers, Personnel Building, Dan River Mills
      (private collection)
Durham, North Carolina
  Special Collections, Perkins Library, Duke University
    Cannon Mills Papers
    Cherokee-Spartanburg Textile Workers Union of America Joint Board
      Papers
    Frank deVyver Papers
    Durham Bicentennial Commission Papers
    Erwin Mills Papers
    Greensboro-Burlington Textile Workers Union of America Joint Board
      Papers
    Lucy Randolph Mason Papers
    Operation Dixie Archives
    South Carolina Textile Workers Union of America State Director's Papers

Eden, North Carolina
  Eden Public Library
    Fieldcrest Mills Folders
Madison, Wisconsin
  State Historical Society of Wisconsin
    Textile Workers Union of America Papers
Philadelphia, Pennsylvania
  American Friends' Center
    American Friends Service Committee Papers
Raleigh, North Carolina
  Division of Archives and History
    Governor Kerr Scott Papers
Randolph, New Hampshire
  Norris Tibbetts Papers (private collection of Norris Tibbetts)
Silver Spring, Maryland
  George Meany Center
    Textile Workers Union of America correspondence
Washington, D.C.
  National Archives
    Federal Mediation and Conciliation Service Records
    National Labor Relations Board Records
Wingate, North Carolina
  Wingate College
    Charles Cannon Papers

Interviews

Alderman, Helen. Tarboro, N.C., July 21, 1994.
Andrews, Arky. Tarboro, N.C., March 1, 1994.
Ashley, Wilton. Mebane, N.C., September 14, 1993.
Baggett, Joan. Rockingham, N.C., March 21, 1994.
Barber, Minnie Lou. Rockingham, N.C., June 23, 1994.
Barkin, Solomon. Amherst, Mass., January 7, 1994.
Bateman, Leeander. Rockingham, N.C., February 3, 1994.
Boggs, Emanuel and Louise. Hendersonville, N.C., October 28, 1993.
Cahoon, Robert. Greensboro, N.C., December 20, 1993.
Cole, Ernest. Rockingham, N.C., March 4, 1994.
Coleman, Clyde. Danville, Va., January 14, 1994.
Conn, Richard. Washington, D.C., February 9, 1994.
Conyers, Elijah. Rockingham, N.C., May 26, 1994.
Cross, Malcolm. Georgetown, S.C., May 23, 1994.
Crumbley, Bernice. Rockingham, N.C., June 28, 1994.
Dawson, Mae. Tarboro, N.C., March 3, 1994.
Dennis, Mary. Rockingham, N.C., June 28, 1994.
Dunn, Carlton. Pee Dee, N.C., February 5, 1994.
Edmondson, Anna. Tarboro, N.C., June 27, 1994.

Evans, Bill. Orlando, Fla., November 11, 1993.

Gardiner, Robert. Danville, Va., April 1, 1994.

Grant, John. Rockingham, N.C., January 31, 1994.

Grant, Margaret. Rockingham, N.C., January 31, 1994.

Gregory, Nathaniel. Durham, N.C., September 21, 1993, and February 28, 1994.

Griffin, Graham. Tarboro, N.C., March 3, 1994.

Griffiths, Melvin and Virgil. Danville, Va., December 7, 1993.

Groshong, Ross. Greensboro, N.C., December 8, 1993.

Gurkins, Vivian. Tarboro, N.C., June 27, 1994.

Hathaway, Catherine. Tarboro, N.C., March 29, 1994.

Heath, Eugene. Spartanburg, S.C., November 23, 1993.

Hoard, Bill. Tarboro, N.C., June 27, 1994.

Hogan, Carl. Rockingham, N.C., April 7, 1994.

Hogan, Elsie. Rockingham, N.C., April 7, 1994.

Holland, Hayward. Tarboro, N.C., March 3, 1994.

Holland, Ray. Tarboro, N.C., June 27, 1994.

Ivey, Loyd. Rockingham, N.C., June 23, 1994.

Jeffries, Robert. Mebane, N.C., September 14, 1993.

Knight, Margaret [Pat]. Greensboro, N.C., October 26, 1993, and March 23, 1994.

Langley, John. Rockingham, N.C., February 1, 1994.

Leighton, Joel. Boston, Mass., January 6, 1994.

McAllister, Bill. Rockingham, N.C., March 4, 1994.

McCumbee, Beatrice. Rockingham, N.C., January 27, 1994.

McDuffie, Bill. Rockingham, N.C., March 24, 1994.

McDuffie, Rachel. Rockingham, N.C., March 4, 1994.

McKee, Don. Maplewood, N.J., November 26, 1993.

McKenzie, John. Rockingham, N.C., February 1, 1994.

Moree, Clayton. Rockingham, N.C., March 21, 1994.

Morris, Floyd. Tarboro, N.C., March 2, 1994.

Orrell, Walter. Linwood, N.C., November 19, 1993.

Overton, Amy. Tarboro, N.C., June 27, 1994.

Phifer, Emsley. Rockingham, N.C., April 7, 1994.

Raynor, Bruce. Greensboro, N.C., July 28, 1995.

Scales, Junius. Orlando, Fla., November 11, 1993.

Shepherd, Jesse. Roberdel, N.C., March 21, 1994.

Spivey, Howard. Rockingham, N.C., January 31, 1994.

Starling, Linwood. Rockingham, N.C., May 26, 1994.

Taylor, Herbert H. Tarboro, N.C., March 29, 1994.

Tibbetts, Norris. Madison, Wis., March 9, 1994, and March 14, 1994.

Welch, Eli. Rockingham, N.C., May 26, 1994.

Wells, Madelin. Tarboro, N.C., March 29, 1994.

Worrell, Gerald. Tarboro, N.C., March 29, 1994.

Wright, Elmer. Danville, Va., March 31, 1994.

Wyatt, Addie Faye. Rockingham, N.C., June 28, 1994.

Government Documents

U.S. Congress. House. Committee on Labor. *Proposed Amendments to the Fair Labor Standards Act.* 81st Cong., 1st sess., Washington, D.C., 1949.

U.S. Congress. Senate. Senate Committee on Labor and Public Welfare. *Fair Labor Standards Act Amendments of 1949.* 81st Cong., 1st sess., Washington, D.C., 1949.

————. Senate Committee on the Judiciary. *Corporate Mergers and Anti-Trust Legislation.* 84th Cong., Washington, D.C., 1955.

Newspapers

Albany Herald
Anderson Daily Mail
Anderson Independent
Brockton Enterprise and Times
Charlotte News
Charlotte Observer
Chattanooga News-Free Press
Concord Tribune
Daily Worker
Danville Bee
Danville Register
Durham Morning Herald
Durham Sun
Fort Worth Press
Gaffney Ledger
Greensboro Daily News
Greensboro Free Press
Greenville News
Huntsville Times
Kannapolis Independent
Lanett Valley Daily Times-News
Leaksville News
Lewiston Sun
New Bedford Standard-Times
New York Journal of Commerce
New York Post
New York Times
Pell City News
Raleigh News and Observer
Richmond County Journal
Richmond Times-Dispatch
Rock Hill Evening Herald
Rock Hill Post
Rockingham Post-Dispatch
Saturday Evening Post

Spartanburg Journal
Tarboro Daily Southerner
Thomasville News-Times
Wall Street Journal
Washington Post

Trade, Popular, and Union Journals

Business Week
CIO News
Daily News Record
Danville Textile Worker
Fortune
Harper's Magazine
Nation
New York Post
Southern Textile Bulletin
Southern Textile News
Textile Bulletin
Textile Challenger
Textile Labor
Textile Neighbor
U.S. News

Books and Articles

Arthur, Bill. "The Darlington Mills Case: Or 17 Years before the Courts." *New South* 28 (Summer 1973): 40–47.

Badger, Anthony J. *The New Deal: The Depression Years, 1933–40.* New York: Noonday Press, 1989.

Barkin, Solomon. "The Regional Significance of the Integration Movement in the Southern Textile Industry." *Southern Economic Journal* 15 (April 1949): 395–411.

Barkin, Solomon, and Michael K. Honey. "Operation Dixie: Two Points of View." *Labor History* 31 (Summer 1990): 373–85.

Barrett, James R. *Work and Community in the Jungle: Chicago's Packinghouse Workers, 1894–1922.* Urbana: University of Illinois Press, 1987.

Bell, Daniel. *The End of Ideology: On the Exhaustion of Political Ideas in the Fifties.* Glencoe, Ill.: Free Press, 1960.

Berger, Bennett M. *Working-Class Suburb: A Study of Auto Workers in Suburbia.* Berkeley: University of California Press, 1960.

Bernstein, Irving. "The Growth of American Unions, 1945–1960." *Labor History* 2 (Spring 1961): 131–57.

Blanshard, Paul. *Labor in Southern Cotton Mills.* New York: New Republic, 1927.

Blum, John Morton. *V Was for Victory: Politics and American Culture during World War II.* New York: Harcourt Brace Jovanovich, 1976.

Boyden, Richard. "Where Outsized Paychecks Grow on Trees: War Workers in the San Francisco Shipyards." *Prologue* 23 (1991): 253–59.

Braeman, John, ed. *Change and Continuity in Twentieth-Century America: The 1920s.* Columbus: Ohio State University Press, 1968.

Campbell, D'Ann. *Women at War with America: Private Lives in a Patriotic Era.* Cambridge: Harvard University Press, 1984.

Carlton, David L. *Mill and Town in South Carolina, 1880–1920.* Baton Rouge: Louisiana State University Press, 1982.

Cash, W. J. *The Mind of the South.* New York: Alfred A. Knopf, 1941.

Chafe, William H. *The Unfinished Journey: America since World War II.* New York: Oxford University Press, 1986.

Chinoy, Ely. *Automobile Workers and the American Dream.* Garden City, N.Y.: Doubleday, 1955.

Clive, Alan. "Women Workers in World War II: Michigan as a Test Case." *Labor History* 20 (Spring 1979): 44–72.

Corbin, D. A. *Life, Work, and Rebellion in the Coalfields: The Southern West Virginia Miners, 1880–1922.* Urbana: University of Illinois Press, 1981.

Cormier, Frank, and William J. Eaton. *Reuther.* Englewood Cliffs, N.J.: Prentice-Hall, 1970.

Cross, Malcolm A. *Dan River Runs Deep: An Informal History of a Major Textile Company, 1950–1981.* New York: The Total Book, 1982.

Derber, Milton, et al. *Labor in Illinois: The Affluent Years, 1945–1980.* Urbana: University of Illinois Press, 1988.

de Vyver, Frank T. "Union Fratricide: The Textile Workers Split." *South Atlantic Quarterly* 63 (Summer 1964): 363–84.

Fine, Sidney. *Sit-Down: The General Motors Strike of 1936–1937.* Ann Arbor: University of Michigan Press, 1969.

Fink, Gary M., ed. *Biographical Dictionary of American Labor Leaders.* Westport, Conn.: Greenwood Press, 1974.

———. *The Fulton Bag and Cotton Mills Strike of 1914–1915: Espionage, Labor Conflict, and New South Industrial Relations.* Ithaca, N.Y.: ILR Press, 1993.

Fink, Gary M., and Merl E. Reed. *Essays in Southern Labor History: Selected Papers, Southern Labor History Conference, 1976.* Westport, Conn.: Greenwood Press, 1977.

Flamming, Douglas. *Creating the Modern South: Millhands and Managers in Dalton, Georgia, 1884–1984.* Chapel Hill: University of North Carolina Press, 1992.

Frederickson, Mary. "Four Decades of Change: Black Workers in Southern Textiles, 1941–1981." *Radical America* 16 (November–December 1982): 27–44.

Fried, Richard M. *Nightmare in Red: The McCarthy Era in Perspective.* New York: Oxford University Press, 1990.

Friedlander, Peter. *The Emergence of a UAW Local, 1936–1939: A Study in Class and Culture.* Pittsburgh: University of Pittsburgh Press, 1975.

Gabin, Nancy. "Women Workers and the UAW in the Post World War II Period, 1945–54." *Labor History* 21 (Winter 1979): 5–30.

Galambos, Louis. *Competition and Cooperation: The Emergence of a National*

Trade Association. Baltimore: Johns Hopkins University Press, 1966.

Gerstle, Gary. Review of *Labor in Illinois: The Affluent Years, 1945–80*, by Milton Derber. *Labor History* 33 (Summer 1992): 396–97.

———. *Working-Class Americanism: The Politics of Labor in a Textile City, 1914–1960.* Cambridge: Cambridge University Press, 1989.

Gilman, Glen. *Human Relations in Industrial Southeast: A Study of the Textile Industry.* Chapel Hill: University of North Carolina Press, 1956.

Glass, Brent D. *The Textile Industry in North Carolina: A History.* Raleigh: Division of Archives and History, North Carolina Department of Cultural Resources, 1992.

Goldfield, Michael. *The Decline of Organized Labor in the United States.* Chicago: University of Chicago Press, 1987.

Griffith, Barbara S. *The Crisis of American Labor: Operation Dixie and the Defeat of the CIO.* Philadelphia: Temple University Press, 1988.

Hall, Jacquelyn Dowd. "Disorderly Women: Gender and Labor Militancy in the Appalachian South." *Journal of American History* 73 (September 1986): 354–82.

Hall, Jacquelyn Dowd, James Leloudis, Robert Korstad, Mary Murphy, Lu Ann Jones, and Christopher B. Daly. "Cotton Mill People: Work, Community, and Protest in the Textile South, 1880–1940." *American Historical Review* 91 (April 1986): 245–86.

———. *Like a Family: The Making of a Southern Cotton Mill World.* Chapel Hill: University of North Carolina Press, 1987.

Halpern, Rick, "Interracial Unionism in the Southwest: Fort Worth's Packinghouse Workers, 1937–1954." In *Organized Labor in the Twentieth-Century South*, ed. Robert H. Zieger. Knoxville: University of Tennessee Press, 1991.

Harris, Howell J. *The Right to Manage: Industrial Relations Policies of American Business in the 1940s.* Madison: University of Wisconsin Press, 1982.

———. "The Snares of Liberalism?: Politicians, Bureaucrats, and the Shaping of Federal Labour Relations Policy in the United States, ca. 1915–47." In *Shop Floor Bargaining and the State: Historical and Comparative Perspectives*, edited by Steven Tolliday and Jonathon Zeitlin, pp. 148–91. Cambridge: Cambridge University Press, 1985.

Hartford, William F. "Unions, Labor Markets, and Deindustrialization: The Holyoke Textile Industry." In *Labor in Massachusetts: Selected Essays*, edited by Kenneth Fones-Wolf and Martin Kaufman, pp. 207–32. Westfield, Mass.: Institute for Massachusetts Studies, 1990.

Heale, Michael. *American Anti-Communism: Combating the Enemy Within, 1830–1970.* Baltimore: Johns Hopkins University Press, 1990.

Herring, Harriet L. *Passing of the Mill Village: Revolution in a Southern Institution.* Westport, Conn.: Greenwood Press, 1949.

Hodges, James A. *New Deal Labor Policy and the Southern Cotton Textile Industry, 1933–1941.* Knoxville: University of Tennessee Press, 1986.

Honey, Michael K. "Operation Dixie: Two Points of View." Review of Barbara S. Griffith, *The Crisis of American Labor: Operation Dixie and the Defeat of the CIO* (Philadelphia: Temple University Press, 1988). *Labor History* 31 (Summer 1990): 373–85.

————. *Southern Labor and Black Civil Rights: Organizing Memphis Workers.* Chicago: University of Illinois Press, 1993.

Honeycutt, Ida C., and Janes E. Honeycutt. *A History of Richmond County.* Raleigh: Edwards and Broughton Company, 1976.

Howard, Patricia Brook. "Tennessee in War and Peace: The Impact of World War II on State Economic Trends." *Tennessee Historical Quarterly* 51 (Spring 1992): 51–65.

Janiewski, Dolores E. *Sisterhood Denied: Race, Gender, and Class in a New South Community.* Philadelphia: Temple University Press, 1985.

Jewkes, John and Sylvia. "A Hundred Years of Change in the Structure of the Cotton Industry." *Journal of Law and Economics* 9 (1966): 115–34.

Katz, Isadore. *Taft-Hartleyism in Southern Textiles: Feudalism with a New Face.* New York: TWUA Publications, 1950.

Kennedy, Stetson. *The Klan Unmasked: I Rode with the KKK.* Boca Raton: University Presses of Florida, 1990.

Kessler-Harris, Alice. *Out to Work: A History of Wage-Earning Women in the United States.* New York: Oxford University Press, 1982.

Komarovsky, Mirra. *Blue-Collar Marriage.* New York: Vintage Books, 1967.

Lahne, Herbert. *The Cotton Mill Worker.* New York: Farrah and Rinehart, 1944.

Lemert, Ben F. *The Cotton Textile Industry of the Southern Appalachian Piedmont.* Chapel Hill: University of North Carolina Press, 1933.

Lichtenstein, Nelson. *Labor's War at Home: The CIO in World War II.* Cambridge: Cambridge University Press, 1982.

MacDonald, Lois. *Southern Mill Hills: A Study of Social and Economic Forces in Certain Textile Mill Villages.* New York: Alex L. Hillman, 1928.

McHugh, Cathy L. *Mill Family: The Labor System in the Southern Cotton Textile Industry, 1880–1915.* New York: Oxford University Press, 1988.

McLaurin, Melton Alonza. *Paternalism and Protest: Southern Cotton Mill Workers and Organized Labor, 1875–1905.* Westport, Conn.: Greenwood Publishing Corporation, 1971.

Magdol, Edward, and Jon L. Wakelyn, eds. *The Southern Common People: Studies in Nineteenth-Century Social History.* Westport, Conn.: Greenwood Press, 1980.

Marshall, F. Ray. *Labor in the South.* Cambridge: Harvard University Press, 1967.

————. *The Negro and Organized Labor.* New York: John Wiley and Sons, 1965.

Matthaei, Julie A. *An Economic History of Women in America: Women's Work, the Sexual Division of Labour, and the Development of Capitalism.* New York: Schocken Books, 1982.

May, Elaine Tyler. *Homeward Bound: American Families in the Cold War Era.* New York: Basic Books, 1988.

Mitchell, Broadus. *The Rise of the Cotton Mills in the South.* Baltimore: Johns Hopkins University Press, 1921.

Montgomery, David. *Workers' Control in America: Studies in the History of Work, Technology, and Labor Struggles.* New York: Cambridge University Press, 1979.

Morland, John Kenneth. "Kent Revisited: Blue-Collar Aspirations and Achievements." In *Blue-Collar World: Studies of the American Worker*, edited by Arthur B. Shostak and William Gomberg, pp. 134–43. Englewood Cliffs, N.J.: Prentice-Hall, 1964.

———. *Millways of Kent*. Chapel Hill: University of North Carolina Press, 1958.

Nash, Gerald D. *The American West Transformed: The Impact of the Second World War*. Bloomington: Indiana University Press, 1985.

Nelson, Bruce. "Organized Labor and the Struggle for Black Equality in Mobile." *Journal of American History* 80, no. 3 (December 1993): 952–88.

Newby, I. A. *Plain Folk in the New South: Social Change and Cultural Persistence, 1880–1915*. Baton Rouge: Louisiana State University Press, 1989.

Newman, Dale. "Textile Workers in a Tobacco County." In *The Southern Common People*, ed. Magdol and Wakelyn, pp. 345–68.

Newman, Dale. "Work and Community in a Southern Textile Town." *Labor History* 19 (Spring 1978): 204–25.

Newton, Michael, and Judy Ann Newton. *The Ku Klux Klan: An Encyclopedia*. New York: Garland Publishers, 1991.

Norrell, Robert J. "Caste in Steel: Jim Crow Careers in Birmingham, Alabama." *Journal of American History* 73 (December 1986): 669–94.

Peckenham, Nancy. "Out in the Cold at Cannon Mills." *Nation*, September 16, 1991, 298–302.

Perlman, Mark "Labor in Eclipse." In *Change and Continuity in Twentieth-Century America: The Twenties*, ed. John Braeman, pp. 103–45. Columbus: Ohio State University Press, 1968.

Pleasants, Julian M., and Augustus M. Burns. *Frank Porter Graham and the 1950 Senate Race in North Carolina*. Chapel Hill: University of North Carolina Press, 1990.

Polenberg, Richard. *War and Society: The United States, 1941–1945*. Philadelphia: J. B. Lippincott, 1972.

Pope, Liston. *Millhands and Preachers: A Study of Gastonia*. New Haven: Yale University Press, 1942.

Raynor, Bruce. "Unionism in the Southern Textile Industry: An Overview." In *Essays in Southern Labor History: Selected Papers, Southern Labor History Conference, 1976*, edited by Gary Fink and Merl E. Reed, pp. 80–99. Westport, Conn.: Greenwood Press, 1977.

Rhyne, Jennings J. *Some Southern Cotton Mill Workers and Their Villages*. Chapel Hill: University of North Carolina Press, 1930.

Roediger, David R. *The Wages of Whiteness: Race and the Making of the American Working-Class*. New York: Verso, 1991.

Rowan, Richard L. "The Negro in the Textile Industry." In *Negro Employment in Southern Industry: A Study of Racial Policies in Five Industries*, edited by Herbert R. Northrup and Richard L. Rowen. Philadelphia: University of Pennsylvania Press, 1970.

Salmond, John A. *Miss Lucy of the CIO: The Life and Times of Lucy Randolph Mason, 1882–1959*. Athens: University of Georgia Press, 1988.

Saxton, Alexander. *The Indispensable Enemy: Labor and the Anti-Chinese Movement in California*. Berkeley: University of California Press, 1971.

Schulman, Bruce J. *From Cotton Belt to Sun Belt: Federal Policy, Economic Development, and the Transformation of the South, 1938–1980.* New York: Oxford University Press, 1991.

Smith, Robert Sidney. *Mill on the Dan: A History of Dan River Mills, 1882–1950.* Durham, N.C.: Duke University Press, 1960.

Stabile, Donald R. *Activist Unionism: The Institutional Economics of Solomon Barkin.* New York: M. E. Sharpe, 1993.

Taft, Philip. *Organized Labor in American History.* New York: Harper and Row, 1964.

Tannenbaum, Frank. *Darker Phases of the South.* New York: Putnam, 1924.

Tentler, Leslie Woodcock. *Wage-Earning Women: Industrial Work and Family Life in the United States, 1900–1930.* New York: Oxford University Press, 1979.

Terrill, Thomas E. "Southern Mill Workers." *Reviews in American History* 16 (December 1988): 591–98.

Tomlins, Christopher L. *The State and the Unions: Labor Relations, Law, and the Organized Labor Movement in America, 1880–1960.* Cambridge: Cambridge University Press, 1985.

Wright, Annette C. "The Aftermath of the General Textile Strike: Managers and the Workplace at Burlington Mills." *Journal of Southern History* 60 (February 1994): 81–112.

Wright, Gavin. *Old South, New South: Revolutions in the Southern Economy since the Civil War.* New York: Basic Books, 1986.

Wynn, Neil A. *The Afro-American and the Second World War.* Rev. ed. New York and London: Holmes and Meier, 1993.

Zieger, Robert H. *American Workers, American Unions, 1920–1985.* Baltimore: Johns Hopkins University Press, 1986.

———. *Republicans and Labor, 1919–1929.* Lexington: University of Kentucky Press, 1969.

———. "Toward the History of the CIO: A Bibliographical Report." *Labor History* 26 (Winter 1985): 485–516.

———, ed. *Organized Labor in the Twentieth-Century South.* Knoxville: University of Tennessee Press, 1991.

Unpublished Dissertations and Conference Papers

Brooks, Robert R. R. "The United Textile Workers of America." Ph.D. diss., Yale University, 1935.

Clark, Daniel. "The TWUA in a Southern Mill Town: What Unionization Meant in Henderson, North Carolina, 1943–1958." Ph.D. diss., Duke University, 1990.

Hodges, James A. "J. P. Stevens and the Union: Struggle for the South." Unpublished paper given to me by Hodges, with permission to cite.

Irons, Janet. "Testing the New Deal: The General Textile Strike of 1934." Ph.D. diss., Duke University, 1988.

Kennedy, J. W. "A History of the Textile Workers Union of America-CIO." Ph.D. diss., University of North Carolina, 1950.

Korstad, Robert. "Daybreak of Freedom: Tobacco Workers and the CIO, Winston-Salem, North Carolina, 1943–1950." Ph.D. diss., University of North Carolina, 1987.

McDonald, Joseph A. "Textile Workers and Unionization: A Community Study." Ph.D. diss., University of Tennessee, 1981.

McHugh, Cathy L. "The Family Labor System in the Southern Cotton Textile Industry, 1880–1915." Ph.D. diss., Stanford University, 1981.

Richards, Paul David. "The History of the Textile Workers Union of America, CIO, in the South, 1937 to 1945." Ph.D. diss., University of Wisconsin, 1978.

Simon, Bryant. "A Fabric of Defeat: The Politics of South Carolina Textile Workers in State and Nation, 1920–1938." Ph.D. diss., University of North Carolina at Chapel Hill, 1993.

Stanback, Thomas Melville. "Short Run Instability in the Cotton Broad Woven Goods Industry." M.A. thesis, Duke University, 1954.

Truchil, Barry Elliot. "Capital-Labor Relationships in the U.S. Textile Industry." Ph.D. diss., State University of New York–Binghamton, 1982.

Williams, T. Webster. "The Split in the Textile Workers Union of America, CIO." M.A. thesis, Duke University, 1956.

Zieger, Robert H. "From Primordial Folk to Redundant Workers: Southern Textile Workers and Social Observers, 1920–1990." Unpublished paper in author's possession.

index